CORE READY LESSON SETS

A Staircase to Standards Success
for English Language Arts

The Shape of Story
Yesterday and Today

Pam Allyn
Executive Director of LitLife and LitWorld

PEARSON

Boston • Columbus • Indianapolis • New York • San Francisco • Upper Saddle River
Amsterdam • Cape Town • Dubai • London • Madrid • Milan • Munich • Paris • Montreal • Toronto
Delhi • Mexico City • São Paulo • Sydney • Hong Kong • Seoul • Singapore • Taipei • Tokyo

Vice President, Editor in Chief: Aurora Martínez Ramos
Acquisitions Editor: Kathryn Boice
Associate Sponsoring Editor: Barbara Strickland
Editorial Assistant: Katherine Wiley
Senior Marketing Manager: Christine Gatchell
Production Editor: Karen Mason
Project Coordination, Art Rendering, and Electronic Page Makeup: Jouve
Cover Designer: Diane Lorenzo and Jenny Hart
Grade Band Opening and Lesson Set Illustrations: Steve Morrison

Text Credits: The Common Core State Standards for the English Language Arts are © Copyright 2012. National Governors Association Center for Best Practices and Council of Chief State School Officers. All rights reserved. Page xx, "5 Principles for Teaching Content to English Language Learners." by Jim Cummins, Retrieved from www.PearsonELL.com. Reprinted with permission.

Photo Credits: All photos not credited are courtesy of the author.

Library of Congress Control Number
2013948380

10 9 8 7 6 5 4 3 2 1

ISBN 10: 0-13-290744-5
ISBN 13: 978-0-13-290744-6

About the Author

Pam Allyn is an authority in the field of literacy education and a world-renowned expert in home and school literacy connections. As a motivational speaker, expert consultant, author, teacher, and humanitarian advocating for children, she is transforming the way we think about literacy as a tool for communication and knowledge building.

Pam currently serves as the executive director of LitLife, a national literacy development organization providing research-based professional development for K–12 educators. She founded and leads LitWorld, a groundbreaking global literacy initiative that reaches children across the United States and in more than 60 countries. Her methods for helping all students achieve success as readers and writers have brought her acclaim both in the United States and internationally. Pam is also recognized for founding the highly acclaimed initiative Books for Boys for the nation's most struggling readers.

Pam is the author of 19 books for educators and parents, including the award-winning *What to Read When: The Books and Stories to Read with Your Child—And All the Best Times to Read Them* (Penguin Avery), *Pam Allyn's Best Books for Boys* (Scholastic), and *Your Child's Writing Life: How to Inspire Confidence, Creativity, and Skill at Every Age* (Penguin Avery). Her work has been featured on "Good Morning America," "The Today Show," "Oprah Radio," *The Huffington Post*, and *The New York Times* and across the blogosphere.

About the Core Ready Series

Core Ready is a dynamic series of books providing educators with critical tools for navigating the Common Core State Standards. The foundational text, *Be Core Ready: Powerful, Effective Steps to Implementing and Achieving the Common Core State Standards*, provides practical strategies for how to implement core ideas to make all students college- and career-ready scholars. The Core Ready Lesson Sets, including three grade bands with four books per grade band, provide an easy-to-use way to access and organize all of the content within the standards. Readers see how to take complex concepts related to the standards and turn them into practical, specific, everyday instruction.

Acknowledgments

I thank the team at Pearson for believing in the Core Ready vision. Aurora Martínez is a passionate and radiant leader who makes all things possible. Thanks to Karen Mason for her superb dedication to this work, to Christine Gatchell, Kathryn Boice, and Krista Clark for their great energy, and to Kevin Bradley, Katrina Ostler, and Steve Rizzo and their amazing team at Jouve for their wonderful care for this project.

Thanks to my colleagues at LitLife, most especially to the dream team on this project: Carolyn Greenberg, Jen Scoggin, Katie Cunningham, and Debbie Lera. They are teachers, leaders, and big thinkers who never forget it is about children first. I am blessed to work with them. Many, many thanks to Flynn Berry, Megan Karges, David Wilcox, Shannon Bishop, Rebekah Coleman, Marie Miller, Erin Harding, Danny Miller, Ingrid O'Brien, and Jim Allyn for glorious input at every step.

I would like to thank our reviewers who provided valuable feedback: Christine H. Davis, Hillcrest Elementary (Logan, Utah); Wendy Fiore, Chester Elementary School in Connecticut; Keli Garas-York, Buffalo State College in New York; Karen Gibson, Springfield Public Schools in Illinois; Timothy M. Haag, Greater Albany Public Schools, New York; Katie Klaus Salika Lawrence, William Paterson University of New Jersey; Edward Karl Schultz, Midwestern State University (Wichita Falls, TX); Elizabeth Smith, Saint Joseph's College in New York; and Rhonda M. Sutton, East Stroudsburg University in Pennsylvania. Finally, I thank Steve Morrison for his extraordinary illustrations, which were, like everything else about everyone who has participated in the creation of this series, so perfect all together.

Contents

Grade K *Tell Me a Story:*
Elements of Fiction 2

Grade 1 Could It Really Happen?: An Introduction to Fantasy 80

Writing Lessons 125

Grade 2 *Once Upon a Time: A New Look at Fairy Tales* 156

Appendixes

Welcome

Welcome to the Core Ready Lesson Sets for Grades K to 2: A Staircase
to Standards Success for English Language Arts—The Shape of Story:
Yesterday and Today. Here you will find rich and detailed lesson
plans, and the specifics and daily activities within them, that you can
use to make your Core Ready instruction come to life.

The Four Doors to the Common Core State Standards

We have synthesized the expanse of the Common Core State Standards document into four essential doors to the English Language Arts. These Four Doors organize the CCSS into curriculum, identifying the most critical capacities our students need for the 21st century—skills, understandings and strategies for reading, writing, speaking and listening across subject areas. "The Four Doors to the Core" group the CCSS into lesson sets that match the outcomes every college and career-ready student must have. The magic of the Four Doors is that they bring together reading, writing, speaking, and listening skills together into **integrated lesson sets.** Rather than face an overwhelming array of individual standards, teachers, students, parents and administrators together can use the Four Doors to create the kind of curriculum that simplifies the schedule and changes lives. Here are the Four Doors to the Core:

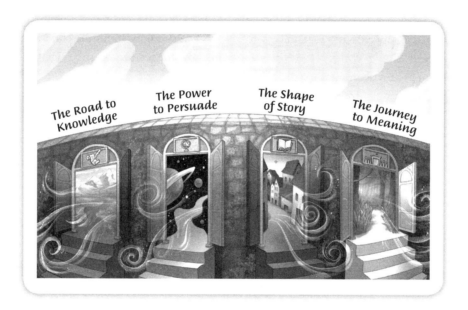

▶ The Road to Knowledge: Information and Research

This Door to the Core—The Road to Knowledge—encompasses research and information and the skills and strategies students need to **build strong content knowledge and compose informational text** as suggested by the Common Core State Standards.

▶ The Power to Persuade: Opinion and Argument

This Door to the Core—The Power to Persuade—encompasses instruction that explores the purposes, techniques, and strategies to **become effective readers and writers of various types of opinion text** as delineated in the Common Core State Standards.

▶ The Shape of Story: Yesterday and Today

This Door to the Core—The Shape of Story—encompasses exploration of a variety of genres with the corresponding craft, structures, and strategies one needs to be a **successful consumer and producer of literary text** as required by the Common Core State Standards.

▶ The Journey to Meaning: Comprehension and Critique

This Door to the Core—The Journey to Meaning—encompasses the strategies and skills our students need to **comprehend, critique, and compose literary text** as outlined in the Common Core State Standards.

Get Ready to Enter the Shape of Story: Yesterday and Today

We seek to develop students who approach reading with the experience that will allow them to know what to expect in a variety of genres and apply appropriate strategies to each with purpose and flexibility. In these lesson sets, students will read closely to explore the elements of various types of stories, contemporary and classical. They will discover new characters and settings, follow how plots develop, and consider how it all comes together to suggest a theme or message for the reader. They will have opportunities to read closely, retell, draw and dramatize the stories they read.

They will use literature from a variety of genres as models for their own writing. They will compose original stories through drawing and writing incorporating story elements and the techniques of strong writers. They will learn what it means to revise and edit and make critical choices about how to publish their work for others. They will share their writing and thinking with others both orally and in writing with appropriate tools and technologies. The child who recognizes, appreciates, and writes in a variety of genres is truly entering a lifelong journey of deep literacy. The understanding of genres of many types and origins gives the child an anchor and a field guide for understanding how to "read the world." That's what this strand is all about.

Walk Through a Lesson Set

This section is meant to take the reader through the major features of the lesson set with snapshots of design elements/icons, etc. to illustrate.

Why This Lesson Set?

This section establishes the rationale for the lesson set and provides helpful background information about the lesson set focus.

Common Core State Standards Alignment

All of the Common Core State Standards addressed in the lesson set are listed here, including the individual grade-level standards.

Essential Skill Lenses
(PARCC Framework)

This table provides specific examples of how in this lesson set, Core Ready students will build the essential skills required by the Partnership for Assessment of Readiness for College and Careers (PARCC), a multi-state coalition that is currently developing Core Standards–aligned assessments that are slated to replace many statewide assessments across the United States. This alignment helps to ensure that Core Ready students will be prepared when states begin to use these assessments.

Core Questions

Core Questions are thought-provoking, open-ended questions students will explore across the lesson set.

We expect students' responses to the Core Questions to evolve as their experience and understanding become richer with each lesson. For best results, post these questions somewhere in your classroom and use them to focus your instruction.

Lesson Set Goals

Here you will find a list of goals for student learning summarized in clear language in three to five observable behaviors for each reading and writing lesson set, listed with corresponding Common Core State Standards that the goals address.

Choosing Core Texts

For best practice to occur and for all our students to achieve success, all teaching of reading and writing should be grounded in the study of quality literature. Here you will find lists of books, poems, articles, and other texts for you and your students to use for modeling and close reading to achieve the instructional goals of the lesson set. We also explain the types of texts that will focus and enrich your students' reading and writing during this lesson set. Any text that is used specifically as an exemplar in a lesson appears here in the first list. We also recommend additional texts with similar features and qualities to supplement your work in this lesson set.

Teacher's Notes

This section relays a personal message from us to you, the teacher, meant to give the big picture of what the lesson set is all about, the impact we hope it will have on students, and tips or reminders to facilitate your teaching.

Core Message to Students

This segment speaks directly to students, providing background knowledge and rationale about the lesson set to come. We encourage you to share this message with your students to set the stage for their learning.

Building Academic Language

This section provides a list of key terms and phrases chosen to help your students read, write, listen, and speak during the course of the lesson set. Introduce these terms to your students in context gradually; scaffold their use by making them visible to everyone, with bulletin boards and manipulatives; and encourage students to use the new words as they communicate during your study together. See the glossary at the end of each grade's lesson set for more information about important lesson vocabulary.

Recognition

The successful conclusion of each grade's lesson set is a time for recognition. Find specific suggestions for how to plan meaningful recognition opportunities for your students here.

Assessment

In this section you will find information about where to find assessment tools in every lesson set, along with suggestions specific to that grade.

Also see the Reading Lessons and Writing Lessons sections to find Milestone Performance Assessments for monitoring progress and for standards-aligned reading and writing rubrics.

Core Support for Diverse Learners

Here we provide guidance for how to pace and plan instruction and provide materials that will help all students in your class be successful during the lessons.

Complementary Core Methods

This segment offers specific ideas for how to use key instructional structures (read-aloud, shared reading, shared writing, etc.) to reach the goals of the lessons.

Core Connections at Home

This section suggests ways to keep caregivers at home informed and involved.

The Reading and Writing Lessons

Each set of reading and writing lessons is separated into two sections with the following contents for either reading or writing:

- The Core I.D.E.A. / Daily Instruction at a Glance table

- Reading and writing rubrics aligned to unit goals and Common Core State Standards

- Detailed lesson plans (10 for reading, 10 for writing, and 1 Language Companion Lesson)

What to Look for in the Core I.D.E.A. / Daily Instruction at a Glance Table

Specifies the I.D.E.A. framework stage for each lesson

Lists any extra teacher support found in the lesson:
- Milestone Performance assessment
- Speaking and listening opportunities
- Suggestions for English language learner (ELL) support
- Technology suggestions
- Close reading opportunity

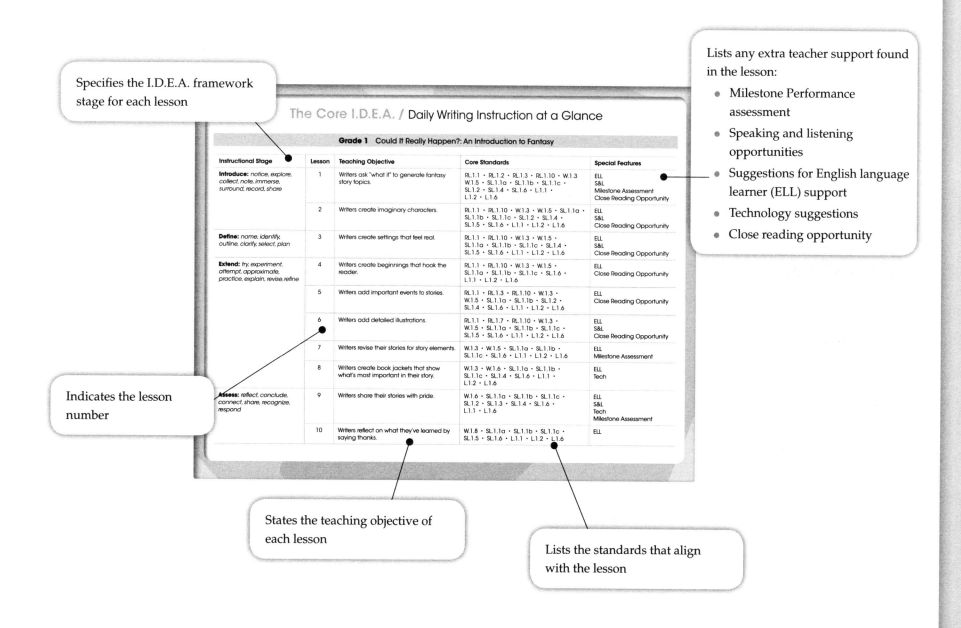

The Core I.D.E.A. / Daily Writing Instruction at a Glance

Grade 1 Could It Really Happen?: An Introduction to Fantasy

Instructional Stage	Lesson	Teaching Objective	Core Standards	Special Features
Introduce: notice, explore, collect, note, immerse, surround, record, share	1	Writers ask "what if" to generate fantasy story topics.	RL.1.1 · RL.1.2 · RL.1.3 · RL.1.10 · W.1.3 W.1.5 · SL.1.1a · SL.1.1b · SL.1.1c · SL.1.2 · SL.1.4 · SL.1.6 · L.1.1 · L.1.2 · L.1.6	ELL S&L Milestone Assessment Close Reading Opportunity
	2	Writers create imaginary characters.	RL.1.1 · RL.1.10 · W.1.3 · W.1.5 · SL.1.1a · SL.1.1b · SL.1.1c · SL.1.2 · SL.1.4 · SL.1.5 · SL.1.6 · L.1.1 · L.1.2 · L.1.6	ELL S&L Close Reading Opportunity
Define: name, identify, outline, clarify, select, plan	3	Writers create settings that feel real.	RL.1.1 · RL.1.10 · W.1.3 · W.1.5 · SL.1.1a · SL.1.1b · SL.1.1c · SL.1.4 · SL.1.5 · SL.1.6 · L.1.1 · L.1.2 · L.1.6	ELL S&L Close Reading Opportunity
Extend: try, experiment, attempt, approximate, practice, explain, revise, refine	4	Writers create beginnings that hook the reader.	RL.1.1 · RL.1.10 · W.1.3 · W.1.5 · SL.1.1a · SL.1.1b · SL.1.1c · SL.1.6 · L.1.1 · L.1.2 · L.1.6	ELL Close Reading Opportunity
	5	Writers add important events to stories.	RL.1.1 · RL.1.3 · RL.1.10 · W.1.3 · W.1.5 · SL.1.1a · SL.1.1b · SL.1.2 · SL.1.4 · SL.1.6 · L.1.1 · L.1.2 · L.1.6	ELL Close Reading Opportunity
	6	Writers add detailed illustrations.	RL.1.1 · RL.1.7 · RL.1.10 · W.1.3 · W.1.5 · SL.1.1a · SL.1.1b · SL.1.1c · SL.1.5 · SL.1.6 · L.1.1 · L.1.2 · L.1.6	ELL S&L Close Reading Opportunity
	7	Writers revise their stories for story elements.	W.1.3 · W.1.5 · SL.1.1a · SL.1.1b · SL.1.1c · SL.1.6 · L.1.1 · L.1.2 · L.1.6	ELL Milestone Assessment
	8	Writers create book jackets that show what's most important in their story.	W.1.3 · W.1.6 · SL.1.1a · SL.1.1b · SL.1.1c · SL.1.4 · SL.1.6 · L.1.1 · L.1.2 · L.1.6	ELL Tech
Assess: reflect, conclude, connect, share, recognize, respond	9	Writers share their stories with pride.	W.1.6 · SL.1.1a · SL.1.1b · SL.1.1c · SL.1.2 · SL.1.3 · SL.1.4 · SL.1.6 · L.1.1 · L.1.6	ELL S&L Tech Milestone Assessment
	10	Writers reflect on what they've learned by saying thanks.	W.1.8 · SL.1.1a · SL.1.1b · SL.1.1c · SL.1.5 · SL.1.6 · L.1.1 · L.1.2 · L.1.6	ELL

Indicates the lesson number

States the teaching objective of each lesson

Lists the standards that align with the lesson

What to Look for in the Reading and Writing Rubrics

In both the reading and writing lesson sets, we provide a discipline-specific performance rubric, including performance descriptors for four levels of proficiency. A score of 3 ("Achieving") indicates that by the end of the lesson set, a student has demonstrated solid evidence of success with the elements of the task or concept and can perform independently when required by the standards.

Lesson set goals

Standards alignment—the Core standards that match each goal

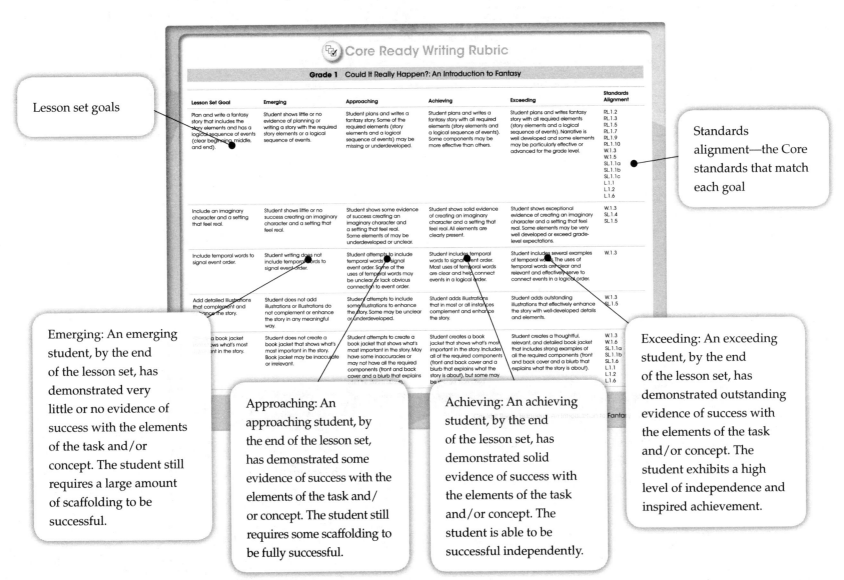

Emerging: An emerging student, by the end of the lesson set, has demonstrated very little or no evidence of success with the elements of the task and/or concept. The student still requires a large amount of scaffolding to be successful.

Approaching: An approaching student, by the end of the lesson set, has demonstrated some evidence of success with the elements of the task and/or concept. The student still requires some scaffolding to be fully successful.

Achieving: An achieving student, by the end of the lesson set, has demonstrated solid evidence of success with the elements of the task and/or concept. The student is able to be successful independently.

Exceeding: An exceeding student, by the end of the lesson set, has demonstrated outstanding evidence of success with the elements of the task and/or concept. The student exhibits a high level of independence and inspired achievement.

What to Look for in the Detailed Lesson Plans

Teaching Objective: A succinct statement that captures the primary focus of the lesson.

Standards Alignment: A list of the standards that the students will practice and apply during the lesson.

Materials: List of the texts, resources, equipment, and so on that you should gather in preparation for the lesson.

Indented text indicates scripted suggestions for what you might say to students.

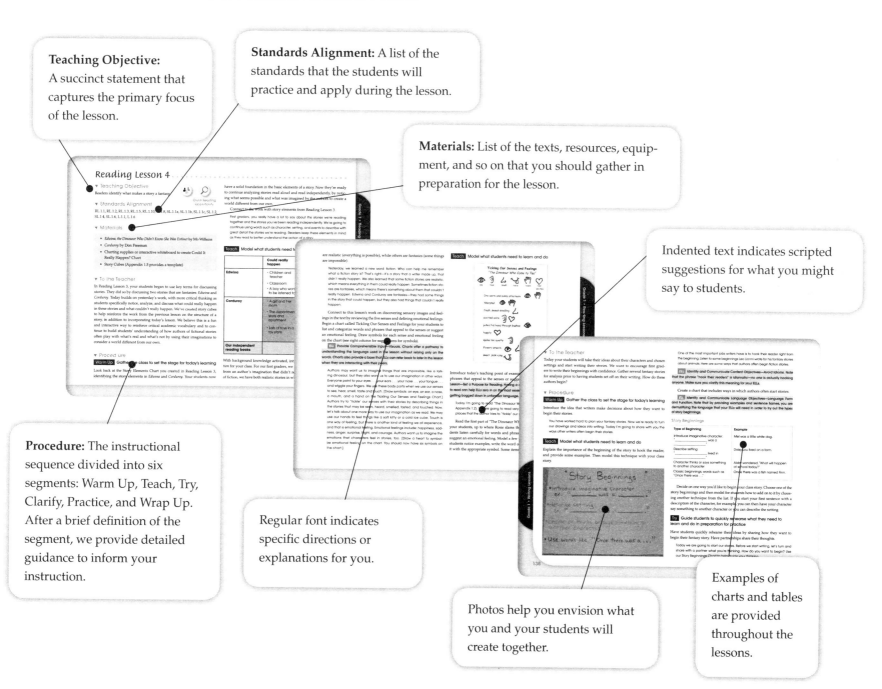

Procedure: The instructional sequence divided into six segments: Warm Up, Teach, Try, Clarify, Practice, and Wrap Up. After a brief definition of the segment, we provide detailed guidance to inform your instruction.

Regular font indicates specific directions or explanations for you.

Photos help you envision what you and your students will create together.

Examples of charts and tables are provided throughout the lessons.

Special Features Marked with an Icon

Look for these icons to help you find the following important elements within each lesson set.

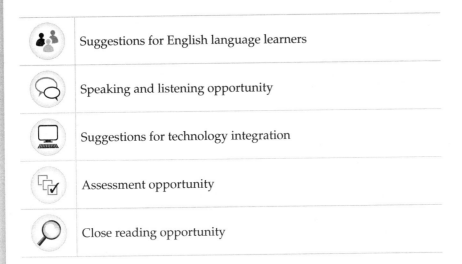

Suggestions for English language learners

Speaking and listening opportunity

Suggestions for technology integration

Assessment opportunity

Close reading opportunity

ELL Support

Across the lesson set, we highlight specific strategies embedded in the lesson to shelter instruction for ELL students. Based on Jim Cummins's *Five Principles for Teaching Content to English Language Learners* (www .pearsonschool.com), these strategies will help ELL students participate successfully in the whole-group lesson and will support the development of their language skills. Wherever you see this icon, you can expect to find which of the 5 Principles is being employed alongside helpful advice and information to support your English language learners in any lesson you teach. (See Figure 1 for a complete list with descriptions of the Five Principles for Teaching Content to English Language Learners).

Speaking and Listening Opportunities

Speaking and listening skills are essential for career- and college-ready students, yet these two capacities are frequently underrepresented in classrooms. We have embedded frequent opportunities for students to grow in these areas. Look for the speaking and listening icon to see where. Also, see the appendix of any Core Ready lesson set book for a standards-aligned checklist to help you assess student performance in these areas.

Technology Options

The Common Core State Standards require that students use technology strategically and capably, and for today's student, this is essential work across the disciplines. Each lesson set provides several suggestions, marked with the Technology icon, for how to build student technology skills and enhance the lessons with various technological tools. Beside each English Language Arts Goal we list for students, we present both high- and low-tech options for your classroom. Although we strongly advocate using a high-tech approach, we recognize that circumstances of funding, training, or even those annoying times when equipment just refuses to function may make it difficult to rely completely on technology. Therefore, we also suggest a low-tech method to achieve the goal—tools that are easily available and inexpensive or free.

Milestone Assessments

Every lesson set includes several suggested Milestone Performance Assessments to assess students' progress toward the lesson set goals. Each of these performance-based assessments aligns directly with one or more Common Core State Standards for reading or writing. With each milestone assessment, we include a checklist of indicators for you to observe with specific guidelines for where to gather the evidence. See each grade's appendix for "copy and clip" masters of these checklists.

Close Reading Opportunities

Every lesson set includes several lessons that require focused, text-based reading where teachers model and students practice reading closely to determine what the text says explicitly, making logical inferences from it, and citing specific textual evidence when writing or speaking to support conclusions drawn from the text. This icon marks a close reading opportunity.

Figure 1 Five Principles for Teaching Content to English Language Learners

1. Identify and Communicate Content and Language Objectives

When presenting content objectives.

- Simplify language (active voice, use same terms consistently)
- Paraphrase
- Repeat
- Avoid idioms and slang
- Be aware of homophones and multiple-meaning words
- Clarify (with simplified language, gestures, visuals)
- Check for understanding

When working with language objectives focus on

- Key content vocabulary
- Academic vocabulary found across the curriculum
- Language form and function essential for the lesson

2. Frontload the Lesson

Provide opportunities to frontload or preteach lesson elements.

- Activate prior knowledge by connecting to students' academic, cultural, or personal experiences
- Build background by explaining new vocabulary or unfamiliar facts and concepts
- Preview text by reviewing visuals, headings, and/or highlighted text
- Set a purpose for reading by clarifying comprehension questions at the end of the lesson
- Make connections by helping students see relationships between the lesson and other aspects of their lives

3. Provide Comprehensible Input

Make oral and written content accessible by providing support.

- Visuals: photos, illustrations, cartoons, multimedia
- Graphics: graphs, charts, tables
- Organizers: graphic organizers, outlines
- Summaries: text, audio, native language
- Audio: recordings, read-alouds
- Audiovisual aids: videos, dramatizations, props, gestures
- Models: demonstrations and modeling
- Experiences: hands-on learning opportunities, field trips

4. Enable Language Production

Structure opportunities for oral practice with language and content.

Listening and speaking

- Make listening input understandable with a variety of support
- Model language
- Allow wait time for students to plan what they say

Reading and writing

- Tailor the task to each student's proficiency level
- Provide support and scaffolding
- Expect different products from students with different levels of proficiency

Increasing interaction

- Provide collaborative tasks so students can work together
- Encourage the development of relationships with peers
- Lower anxiety levels to enable learning, as indicated by brain research

5. Assess for Content and Language Understanding

Monitor progress and provide reteaching and intervention when necessary.

Diagnostic Assessment

- Determine appropriate placement
- Identify strengths and challenges

Formative Assessment

- Check comprehension in ongoing manner
- Use appropriate instruction and pacing

Summative Assessments

- Provide alternative types of assessment when possible, such as projects and portfolios
- Provide practice before administering formal tests

Accommodations

- Provide extra time
- Use bilingual dictionaries
- Offer oral presentation of written material

Source: Jim Cummins, "Five Principles for Teaching Content to English Language Learners." Retrieved from www.pearsonell.com. Reprinted with permission.

FAQs about the Core Ready Lesson Sets

Q **How does Core Ready ensure alignment with the Common Core State Standards?**

A We have carefully examined, analyzed, and synthesized the standards to create for all students rich, engaging learning experiences—many of which touch on multiple standards—with the goal that within a single grade level, Core Ready students will experience the full breadth of Core Standards in reading, writing, speaking, and listening. Every grade-level standard in these three areas is listed in one or more of the lessons for that grade level, and most appear in multiple lessons.

As the Common Core document on "Focus and coherence in instruction and assessment" states, not every standard appears as a stand-alone instruction and assessment objective:

> While the Standards delineate specific expectations in reading, writing, speaking, listening, and language, each standard need not be a separate focus for instruction and assessment. Often, several standards can be addressed by a single rich task. (CCSS, p. 5)

We consider every standard we list in the Common Core State Standards Alignment section to be an integral part of what students must do in order to achieve one or more instructional objective of the multifaceted tasks that make up each lesson set.

Q **How do you address Foundational Standards for Reading and Language Standards?**

A The Core Ready Lesson Sets provide an optimal, authentic context to help students meet the Foundational Standards for Reading and Language Standards; however, the full range of Foundational Standards for Reading and Language Standards is outside the scope of these lesson sets.

We recommend that teachers plan opportunities for students to build Reading Foundations Skills by exploring grade-level-appropriate skills in the context of the Core Texts from each lesson set and applying this knowledge to their independent reading and writing. Schools might also want to acquire developmentally appropriate curricular materials specific to this area. *Words Their Way* by Donald Bear et al. is an excellent example of a program that addresses this need.

Regarding the teaching and application of language standards, we endorse the position statement of the National Council of Teachers of English:

> [T]he use of isolated grammar and usage exercises not supported by theory and research is a deterrent to the improvement of students' speaking and writing and that, in order to improve both of these, class time at all levels must be devoted to opportunities for meaningful listening, speaking, reading, and writing. (NCTE Position Statement on the Teaching of Grammar, 1998–2009)

The primary goal of grammar study is to improve writing and speaking skills. Students acquire such skills best not from isolated drill and practice of grammar rules, but from engagement in authentic language experiences requiring active participation in reading, writing, listening, and speaking.

> The inclusion of Language standards in their own strand should not be taken as an indication that skills related to conventions, effective language use, and vocabulary are unimportant to reading, writing, speaking, and listening; indeed, they are inseparable from such contexts. (CCSS, 2012, p. 25)

Q **What are the Language Companion Lessons?**

A The Core Ready Lesson Sets provide the type of authentic integrated experiences that will help all students expand their language skills. Explicit instruction in selected language concepts benefits students as they try to navigate the complex rules and requirements of conventional English. To this end, we have provided Language Companion Lessons, one per grade, as resources and models for the explicit teaching of language standards within the context of each lesson set topic.

When choosing teaching objectives for the Language Companion Lessons, we considered a few factors. First, we made sure to include a lesson for each of the standards listed in the Language Progressive Skills, which are specially marked in the standards as being particularly likely to require extended attention over time. The inclusion of these growth-targeted standards will help Core Ready teachers start addressing these important topics.

Second, we made sure that the lesson set and Language Companion Lessons were compatible in focus so that students could immediately connect and apply the language learning to their reading and writing experiences. For example, a lesson on punctuating dialogue would not be a very good match for a lesson set on writing editorials—while dialogue might be included in editorials, it is not very common. A lesson on using domain-specific words would be a better language match for that lesson set. Teaching this lesson will enhance your students' language use during the lesson set. The Language Companion Lessons can also be used as models for teaching other language standards that couple well with the content of the lesson set.

Q How do you address the Common Core State Standard requirements for text complexity (Standard 10)?

A We have reflected the Core requirements by suggesting texts that meet the standards' call for appropriate text complexity for the lesson set grade level. In addition to our own suggestions for grade-level appropriate text, we have used many exemplars from Appendix B of the Common Core State Standards across each lesson set book.

We support the Common Core State Standards' assertion that the ability to read complex text independently and proficiently is essential for high achievement in college and the workplace and important in numerous life tasks. To this end, we also agree with the Core Standards tenet that all students deserve opportunities to read and engage with high-quality literature. We stand firmly, however, by years of research that suggests that students who are learning to read need extended practice (Allington, 2009; Kuhn et al., 2006) with texts that they can read with accuracy and comprehension (Allington, 2012; Ehri, Dreyer, Flugman, & Gross, 2007) in order to improve their abilities. This means time spent reading appropriately leveled text, which may be above, within, or below grade level depending on an individual's needs and skills. This type of differentiation typically takes place in small-group and independent settings. It should also be noted that at times students can and should most certainly engage with complex texts above their levels when reading independently if they have been taught skills to grapple with texts and if they are confident in working with them.

Q Do I have to use the core texts recommended in the lesson set? What if I can't get a text or I have a different one in mind?

A Although we always provide specific suggestions for texts that we feel will serve you and your students well for each lesson, there is always room to make thoughtful substitutions. Can't find the text cited in the lesson? Already have a great piece in your classroom collection? No problem. Use the description of what to look for in the introduction to guide you to substitute texts you already own or already love.

Q Are teachers required to use the text exemplars listed by the Common Core State Standards in Appendix B?

A The writers of the Core Standards intended the text exemplars as models of appropriate texts for each grade band, not a required list, as stated below:

> The choices should serve as useful guideposts in helping educators select texts of similar complexity, quality, and range for their own classrooms. They expressly do not represent a partial or complete reading list. (Common Core, 2011, p. 2)

We have included some of the Appendix B texts in the lesson sets alongside our own choices of texts that meet the parameters suggested by the exemplars.

Q You include a special feature for speaking and listening opportunities and strategies to support ELLs in only some lessons, yet there seem to be lots of speaking and listening and similar ELL strategies in practically every lesson. Why don't you mark every instance with a special feature?

A Special features are added where we felt teachers should purposefully focus their instruction and attention on a particular element. Core Ready Lessons are rich with practices that strengthen speaking, listening, and language skills, such as conversing with a classmate, but we do not include a feature in every instance. We hope that by highlighting effective practices in selected lessons, we will increase teachers' awareness of how to build speaking, listening, and language skills in any lesson they teach.

Q Must the lesson sets be taught in any particular order?

A Each set of 10 reading and writing lessons has been designed to be modular; that is, the sequence in which you teach the lesson sets may vary in response to local curricular needs, testing schedules, or other factors that influence a school calendar.

Q Should the individual lessons be taught in the order they appear in the book?

A Yes. The lessons within the Core Ready lesson sets are arranged in a purposeful sequence that reflects respected models of how students learn, such as the "gradual release of responsibility" model (Pearson and Gallagher, 1993) and "cognitive apprenticeship theory" (Collins, Brown, & Newman, 1989). Across the lessons, the teacher guides the students toward increasing levels of independence with the lesson set goals. The teaching objectives of each lesson generally build on the knowledge gained in the previous lesson and many student products are developed in a series of steps across multiple lessons. Therefore, the lessons are designed to be taught as a set and are best delivered in the sequence we provide.

There are four stages in a Core Ready lesson set: Introduce, Define, Extend, and Assess. We use the acronym I.D.E.A. to refer to this structure. Each stage is described below. For a much more detailed description of these stages, please see the foundational book of this series, *Be Core Ready: Powerful, Effective Steps to Implementing and Achieving the Common Core State Standards*.

▶ **Introduce** The Introduce stage activates students' background knowledge and builds a big-picture understanding of the topic of study.

▶ **Define** The Define stage provides students with essential knowledge, terms, and structures that will guide their learning about the topic across the unit.

▶ **Extend** If you compare the types of lessons found in the Define stage of the unit to a road map to learning, the Extend stage might be likened to a series of guided day trips designed to help students become increasingly independent travelers. This is the phase in which students apply and refine the skills and strategies they need to achieve the goals of the unit.

▶ **Assess** The Assess stage serves to wrap up each lesson set in a meaningful way intended to encourage students to recognize and commit to how they have grown as readers, writers, listeners, and speakers.

Q Is it important to teach both the reading and the writing lessons?

A The reading and writing lesson sets are strategically connected, and we have long advocated teaching reading and writing in an integrated manner. That is, what we study with our classes in reading is directly related to what we study in writing. For example, a reading lesson set on successful reading of folktales is taught alongside writing lessons on how to write folktales. Or a set of reading lessons on determining theme in traditional text is accompanied by lessons on theme-related written response to literature.

We have found that the confluence of reading and writing benefits both students and teachers. Each area, reading or writing, helps students be more successful in the other via the natural connections that students make between the two disciplines. A reading experience helps students gain knowledge that helps them develop and enhance the content and structure of connected writing tasks. As students read folktales, for example, they gain a sense of the literary elements, author's purpose, and craft techniques that they will need to consider and include as they write folktales. Likewise, a close study of how to write folktales raises student awareness of what to expect in this genre, leading them be more confident and perceptive readers.

Teachers intuitively understand that such connections help students, but often, curricular materials do not align reading and writing together. Core Ready's dynamically integrated reading and writing lesson sets make it easy for teachers to help students see important connections clearly and immediately. "In reading yesterday, we talked about how folktales usually include magic and fantasy. Today in writing, you begin to imagine how magic and fantasy can be an important part of your original tale."

Because of the close relationship between our reading and writing lesson sets, we strongly recommend that they be taught side by side. Is it possible to teach just the reading lessons or just the writing lessons? In most cases, with some adjustments, this could be done, but again, we recommend that reading and writing be presented simultaneously to maximize the benefits for students and teachers.

Q You provide a lot of specific guidelines for what teachers should say aloud and do during the lessons. Should I follow those specifications exactly?

A It depends. There are all kinds of cooks out there. Some like to follow the recipe to the letter. Some like to refer to a recipe and immediately improvise with the ingredients and procedure. Others like to follow a recipe exactly the first time, and figure out places they want to modify next time to suit their tastes and needs. It is much the same with teachers and lesson plans. We expect that some teachers will adopt these plans as written and others will adapt them to suit their teaching style, needs, and resources. The quotes and directions are there to model how the teaching might go. The most nonnegotiable elements by far are the teaching objectives and standards alignment. If you keep your eye on those as your ultimate destinations, there are many roads that will get you there. These lessons are designed to guide you along the way.

Q Are the lessons meant to be taught in one class period?

A **Allow ample time for independent practice.** Courtside instruction and pep talks from the coach are helpful to a budding basketball player, but nothing builds a player's skills like playing the game. Likewise, while young readers and writers certainly need your teaching and guidance, but what they really need most is to *read* and *write*—eyes on the text or screen, pencils on paper or hands on keyboard, actively thinking and engaging in the reading and writing process *themselves*. This is where the students get to apply the teaching objective of the lesson on their own using their own texts or writing. This is where they work through the hard stuff of reading and writing, which builds capacity, confidence, and stamina. Students need focused practice, collaboration with other learners, making and revising mistakes, making choices, and revising their thinking and understanding of how language works. It is perfectly okay, even necessary, for you to coach from the sidelines, but if students are to become independent readers and writers, they must have extended time working independently and semi-independently in teacher-led groups. Younger students and students who are unaccustomed to working independently will need to build up to longer periods of independent work. Start with shorter sessions and grow from there. By the end of the school year, you can expect kindergarten students to read independently for 10 to 15 minutes, first graders to read independently for 15 to 20 minutes, and second graders 25 to 30 minutes. While your students are working independently, you may be holding teaching conferences with individual students, working with small groups to differentiate instruction, or making assessment notes to inform your planning.

A variety of options for allocating lesson plan time are in the table on the next page. All are based on a 50-minute class period. If you have more or less time, scale up or scale down the number of minutes accordingly, keeping proportions similar. If you choose the options with lengthier practice times, planning a mixture of small groups, centers, and independent practice of the teaching objective will maximize young students' levels of engagement.

Timing Guidelines for a Lesson

	Days (Minutes)	Lesson Segment (Minutes)
A lesson that includes all six segments in one 50-minute session	Day 1 (50)	Warm Up (3), Teach (10), Try (5), Clarify (2), Practice (25), Wrap Up (5)
A lesson that spans 2 days	Day 1 (50)	Warm Up (10), Teach (20), Try (15), Clarify (5)
	Day 2 (50)	Practice (45), Wrap Up (5)
A lesson that spans 3 days with extended time for the independent practice	Day 1 (50)	Warm Up (10), Teach (20), Try (15), Clarify (5)
	Day 2 (50)	Practice (50)
	Day 3 (50)	Additional Practice (40), Wrap Up (10)
A lesson that spans 2 days, plus a reteach based on Milestone Performance Assessment data to allow students more time to achieve the teaching objective	Day 1 (50)	Warm Up (10), Teach (20), Try (15), Clarify (5)
	Day 2 (50)	Practice (45), Wrap Up (5)
	Day 3 (50)	Reteach Based on Milestone Data Warm Up (3), Teach (10), Try (5), Clarify (2), Practice (25), Wrap Up (5)

PD TOOLKIT ™

Accompanying *Core Ready for Grades K–2*, there is an online resource site with media tools that, together with the text, provides you with the tools you need to implement the lesson sets.

The PDToolkit for Pam Allyn's *Core Ready* Series is available free for 12 months after you use the password that comes with the box set for each grade band. After that, you can purchase access for an additional 12 months. If you did not purchase the box set, you can purchase a 12-month subscription at **http://pdtoolkit.pearson.com.** Be sure to explore and download the resources available at the website. Currently the following resources are available:

- Pearson Children's and Young Adult Literature Database
- Videos
- PowerPoint Presentations
- Student Artifacts
- Photos and Visual Media
- Handouts, Forms, and Posters to supplement your Core-aligned lesson plans
- Lessons and Homework Assignments
- Close Reading Guides and Samples
- Children's Core Literature Recommendations

In the future, we will continue to add additional resources. To learn more, please visit **http://pdtoolkit.pearson.com.**

Common Core State Standards Alignment

Available in the PDToolkit is a matrix that details the Common Core State Standards alignment for each Core Ready lesson set in all of the Core Ready books. See sample shown below.

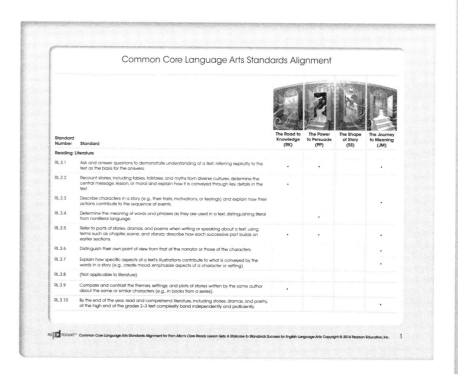

Grade K

Tell Me a Story: Elements of Fiction

Introduction

Each of our lives is a collection of stories—stories from the past, present, and our imaginations. As human beings we connect to one another through these stories of our lives, whether we have had a similar experience or not. Everyone loves a story. Some stories are timeless and can be enjoyed across generations, while other stories speak to a specific audience.

Kindergartners love a good story. At this age, most can recognize and tell a good story. They come to school with an inherent desire to hear and share stories. Most kindergartners learn quickly to recognize and anticipate the characters, setting, events, and conclusion of a story and with guidance will see that when we put these story elements together, they form a story. This lesson set is about helping to build students' academic knowledge and understanding of what a story is. As readers, students will notice and utilize the

Why This Lesson Set?

In this lesson set, students will:

- Identify and use story elements strategically to make meaning

- Be engaged in their reading as they ask and answer questions about a story to make meaning

- Use story elements to retell a story, including character, setting, events, and conclusion

- Compare and contrast characters across texts

- Dramatically retell stories, focusing on the oral storytelling

- Use story elements to plan and write several forms of narrative, both personal and imaginative

- Orally share stories in small groups using pictures to provide detail

story elements to better enjoy and understand stories read. As writers, students will learn to utilize the story elements to craft their own stories, both real and imagined. This lesson set is designed for students of all abilities, honoring students who are reading pictures and those who are reading both pictures and words. It also allows students to explore writing stories using pictures and words at their developmental level.

In support of reading, writing, listening, and speaking standards, students are taught to think, listen, collaborate, and create stories that convey ideas and mood around an event. Each day, students will have the opportunity to discuss and share their ideas in both small-group and whole-class settings. This unit is engaging, playful, and rich with information and activities to help students better understand and enjoy the stories they read and write.

Common Core State Standards Alignment

Reading Standards

RL.K.1 With prompting and support, ask and answer questions about key details in a text.

RL.K.2 With prompting and support, retell familiar stories, including key details.

RL.K.3 With prompting and support, identify characters, settings, and major events in a story.

RL.K.4 Ask and answer questions about unknown words in a text.

RL.K.5 Recognize common types of texts (e.g., storybooks, poems).

RL.K.6 With prompting and support, name the author and illustrator of a story and define the role of each in telling the story.

RL.K.7 With prompting and support, describe the relationship between illustrations and the story in which they appear (e.g., what moment in a story an illustration depicts).

RL.K.9 With prompting and support, compare and contrast the adventures and experiences of characters in familiar stories.

RL.K.10 Actively engage in group reading activities with purpose and understanding.

Writing Standards

Range of Writing

W.K.1 Use a combination of drawing, dictating, and writing to compose opinion pieces in which they tell a reader the topic or the name of the book they are writing about and state an opinion or preference about the topic or book (e.g., *My favorite book is . . .*).

W.K.3 Use a combination of drawing, dictating, and writing to narrate a single event or several loosely linked events, tell about the events in the order in which they occurred, and provide a reaction to what happened.

W.K.5 With guidance and support from adults, respond to questions and suggestions from peers and add details to strengthen writing as needed.

W.K.6 With guidance and support from adults, explore a variety of digital tools to produce and publish writing, including in collaboration with peers.

W.K.7 Participate in shared research and writing projects (e.g., explore a number of books by a favorite author and express opinions about them).

W.K.8 With guidance and support from adults, recall information from experiences or gather information from provided sources to answer a question.

Speaking and Listening Standards

SL.K.1 Participate in collaborative conversations with diverse partners about kindergarten topics and texts with peers and adults in small or larger groups.

a. Follow agreed-upon rules for discussions (e.g., listening to others and taking turns speaking about the topics and texts under discussion).

b. Continue a conversation through multiple exchanges.

SL.K.2 Confirm understanding of a text read aloud or information presented orally or through other media by asking and answering questions about key details and requesting clarification if something is not understood.

SL.K.3 Ask and answer questions in order to seek help, get information, or clarify something that is not understood.

SL.K.4 Describe familiar people, places, things, and events and, with prompting and support, provide additional detail.

SL.K.5 Add drawings or other visual displays to descriptions as desired to provide additional detail.

SL.K.6 Speak audibly and express thoughts, feelings, and ideas clearly.

Language Standards

L.K.1 Demonstrate command of the conventions of standard English grammar and usage when writing or speaking.

L.K.2 Demonstrate command of the conventions of standard English capitalization, punctuation, and spelling when writing.

L.K.4 Determine or clarify the meaning of unknown and multiple-meaning words and phrases based on kindergarten reading and content.

L.K.6 Use words and phrases acquired through conversations, reading and being read to, and responding to texts.

Essential Skill Lenses (PARCC Framework)

The Partnership for Assessment of Readiness for College and Careers (PARCC) is a coalition of over twenty states that has come together with "a shared commitment to develop an assessment system aligned to the Common Core State Standards that is anchored in college and career readiness" (http://www.parcconline.org). As part of its proposal to the U.S. Department of Education, PARCC has developed model content frameworks for English language arts to serve as a bridge between the Common Core State Standards and the PARCC assessments in development. PARCC has provided guidelines for grades 3 to 11. At the K to 2 grade levels, however, we expect students to engage in reading and writing through eight PARCC-specified skill lenses in order to build a foundation for future grades. The table below details how each skill lens is addressed across the lesson set (PARCC, 2012).

	Reading	Writing
Cite Evidence	Students use text as evidence to identify story elements.	Students cite story elements from reading to help them create original, real, or imagined stories.
Analyze Content	Students analyze story elements across texts.	Students analyze story elements to utilize them as they craft stories.
Study and Apply Grammar	Students notice sentence structure.	When orally sharing and writing stories, students apply grammar lessons from reading, in particular how to form a sentence.
Study and Apply Vocabulary	Specific academic language is included in this lesson set. Students encounter this language during reading experiences and use it in conversations.	Students use academic language when speaking and writing.
Conduct Discussions	Students follow rules that encourage and maintain productive conversations about reading. Students engage in conversation about the story elements, building off of others' thoughts.	Students follow rules that encourage and maintain productive conversations about writing. Students engage in conversation about the story elements, building off of others' thoughts.
Report Findings	Students identify and share story elements daily with partners and in class discussions.	Students write and share stories orally, identifying the story elements they include.
Phonics and Word Recognition	Plan opportunities for students to build Reading Foundational Skills by exploring grade-level appropriate skills in the context of the Core Texts from each lesson set and applying this knowledge to their independent reading and writing. Schools may also wish to acquire developmentally appropriate curricular materials specific to this area. *Words Their Way: Word Study in Action* by Donald Bear et al. is an excellent example of a program that addresses this need.	
Fluency	Students build fluency through shared reading and reader's theater experiences. Encourage students to work on building reading stamina across the lesson set.	Students engage in shared writing experiences and experience many opportunities for quick-writes. Toward the end of the lesson set, students add details to a story for the purpose of sharing.

Core Questions

- Why do we read, retell, create, and share stories?
- What do all stories have in common?
- How does the understanding of story elements help us read stories?
- How do story elements help us to create stories?

Ready to Get Started?

As you work through this lesson set, you will feel the gentle, gradual release from modeling to shared experiences, inside of whole and small groups, to finally releasing the students to independently comprehend and create stories. This is a student-centered, engaging lesson set that is intended to be playful and purposeful. Students will have fun, while gaining a solid understanding of how the components of a story help us to become lifelong readers and writers of stories.

Lesson Set Goals

There are many goals we as teachers want to help our students reach in this lesson set. Those goals are as follows:

Lesson Set Goals Reading

- Identify and describe the story elements (character, setting, major events, and conclusion). (RL.K.1, RL.K.3, RL.K.7, RL.K.10, SL.K.1a, SL.K.1b, SL.K.2, SL.K.3, SL.K.6, L.K.1, L.K.6)
- Use the story elements, pictures, and words to make meaning as he or she reads classic and contemporary stories. (RL.K.1, RL.K.2, RL.K.3, RL.K.5, RL.K.7, RL.K.10, W.K.8, SL.K.1a, SL.K.1b, SL.K.6, L.K.1, L.K.6)
- Use the story elements to plan and perform a play based on a story. (RL.K.1, RL.K.3, RL.K.10, SL.K.1a, SL.K.1b, SL.K.2, SL.K.3, SL.K.6, L.K.1, L.K.6)

- Compare and contrast characters across stories. (RL.K.1, RL.K.2, RL.K.3, RL.K.9, RL.K.10, SL.K.1a, SL.K.1b, SL.K.6, L.K.1, L.K.6)
- Ask and answer questions about unknown words in a text. (RL.K.4, L.K.4)
- With prompting and support, ask and answer questions about key details in a text. (RL.K.1)
- Actively engage in group reading activities with purpose and understanding. (RL.K.10)
- Use a combination of drawing, dictating, and writing to compose opinion pieces in which he or she tells a reader the topic or the name of the book he/she is writing about and states an opinion or preference about the topic or book (e.g., My favorite book is . . .). (W.K.1)
- In collaborative discussions, exhibit responsibility in regard to the rules and roles of conversation. (SL.K.1 a, SL.K.1b)
- Speak audibly and express thoughts, feelings, and ideas clearly. (SL.K.6)
- Demonstrate knowledge of standard English and its conventions. (L.K.1, L.K.2)
- Use words and phrases acquired through conversations, reading and being read to, and responding to texts. (L.K.6)

Lesson Set Goals Writing

- Use story elements to create stories. (RL.K.1, RL.K.3, RL.K.7, RL.K.10, W.K.3, W.K.5, W.K.7, W.K.8)
- Use his/her experiences and imagination to inspire stories. (W.K.7, SL.K.1a, SL.K.1b, SL.K.4, SL.K.5, SL.K.6, L.K.1, L.K.2, L.K.6)
- Orally share original stories, real or imagined. (SL.K.1a, SL.K.1b, SL.K.4, SL.K.5, SL.K.6, L.K.1, L.K.6)
- With guidance and support from adults and peers, share writing with others in meaningful ways. (W.K.6)
- With prompting and support, ask and answer questions about key details in a text. (RL.K.1)
- Actively engage in group reading activities with purpose and understanding. (RL.K.10)

- With guidance and support from adults, respond to questions and suggestions from peers and add details to strengthen writing as needed. (W.K.5)

- In collaborative discussions, exhibit responsibility in regard to the rules and roles of conversation. (SL.K.1 a, SL.K.1b)

- Speak audibly and express thoughts, feelings, and ideas clearly. (SL.K.6)

- Demonstrate knowledge of standard English and its conventions. (L.K.1, L.K.2)

- Use words and phrases acquired through conversations, reading and being read to, and responding to texts. (L.K.6)

Choosing Core Texts

To prepare for the teaching in this lesson set, you'll need to gather enough texts for your students to read during independent practice.

- *And the Dish Ran Away with the Spoon* by Janet Stevens and Susan Steven Crummel
- *Bear Snores On* by Karma Wilson
- *Bigmama's* by Donald Crews
- *The Carrot Seed* by Ruth Krauss
- *Cinder-Elly* by Frances Minters
- *Corduroy* by Don Freeman
- *Duke on Bike* by David Shannon
- *Franklin Rides a Bike* by Paulette Bourgeois and Brenda Clark
- *Koala Lou* by Mem Fox
- *The Little Red Hen* by Paul Galdone
- *Night at the Fair* by Donald Crews
- *No, David* by David Shannon
- *Olivia Acts Out* by Ian Falconer
- *Penny and Her Song* by Kevin Henkes
- *Peter's Chair* by Ezra Jack Keats
- *The Rabbit and the Turtle* by Eric Carle

- *Rocket Writes a Story* by Tad Hills
- *"Slowly, Slowly, Slowly," Said the Sloth* by Eric Carle
- *Tacky the Penguin* by Helen Lester
- *Thunder Cake* by Patricia Polacco
- *Wemberly Worried* by Kevin Henkes

Additional text suggestions:

- *Frog and Toad Are Friends* by Arnold Lobel
- *Little Bear* by Elsa Holmelund Minarik and Maurice Sendak
- *Owl at Home* by Arnold Lobel
- *Read-Aloud Rhymes for the Very Young* by Jack Prelutsky and Marc Brown
- *When I Am Old with You* by Angela Johnson

A Note about Addressing Reading Standard 10: Range of Reading and Level of Text Complexity

This lesson set provides all students with opportunities to work with texts deemed appropriate for their grade level as well as texts at their specific reading level. Through shared experiences and focused instruction, all students engage with and comprehend a wide range of texts within their grade-level complexity band. We suggest a variety of high-quality, complex texts to use within the whole-group lessons and recommend a variety of additional titles under Choosing Core Texts to extend and enrich instruction. During independent practice and in small-group collaborations, however, research strongly suggests that all students need to work with texts they can read with a high level of accuracy and comprehension (i.e., at their developmentally appropriate reading level), in order to significantly improve their reading (Allington, 2012; Ehri, Dreyer, Flugman, & Gross, 2007). Depending on individual needs and skills, a student's reading level may be above, within, or below his or her grade level band.

It should also be noted that at times students can and should most certainly engage with complex texts above their levels when reading independently if they have been taught skills to grapple with texts and if they are confident in working with them.

Teacher's Notes

Kindergartners love a story, whether real or imagined. They love hearing new stories yet also want their favorites read over and over again. In the kindergarten classroom we enjoy time thinking and talking about favorite characters and their adventures. Children at this age begin to think about different characters and how they are alike or different, helping them to form preferences. Kindergartners come to school eager for our read-alouds and to find an ear to listen to all the happenings and stories of their lives, some real and some not. As human beings, we all want to feel connected to others. We love hearing stories that resonate with us, and we yearn to share stories that help us leave a print on the world. Kindergarten is the year for students to be given the tools to help them understand the components of a story and how these components help us make meaning and create meaningful stories.

As you work through this lesson set, we understand that some children are mostly reading pictures, while others are reading the pictures and words. This lesson set has something to offer all children.

Some materials that you will find helpful throughout this lesson set are the story elements chart, the bookmark, and the graphic organizer, which all mirror each other. Additionally, having baskets of story books prepared (or computer folders, if reading electronic text) will help ensure that students have stories at their fingertips.

Core Message to Students

Before the first lesson, gather your students to talk about story and how you are about to dig deeply into stories, old and new.

Do you have a favorite storybook? Maybe you have a favorite author or illustrator? How about a favorite character whose adventures and experiences you love to

hear? Do you like stories that feel real, maybe something similar to what you have experienced? Or do you prefer stories that feature talking animals and people flying in the sky? During this lesson set, we are going to read, reread, retell, and create stories together. All stories, whether new or old, real or imagined, are made up of story elements. Throughout this lesson set, identifying the various story elements will help us make meaning of a story and help us create stories to share with our friends. I look forward to enjoying and sharing stories together.

See Appendix K.1 for an enlarged version to reproduce and share with students.

Questions for Close Reading

The Core Ready lessons include many rich opportunities to engage students in close reading of text that require them to ask and answer questions, draw conclusions, and use specific text evidence to support their thinking (Reading Anchor Standard 1). These opportunities are marked with a close reading icon. You may wish to extend these experiences using our recommended Core Texts or with texts of your choosing. Use the following questions as a resource to guide students through close-reading experiences while reading stories.

- Is this a story? How do you know?
- What emotions does the story make you feel?
- Who wrote the story?
- Why do you think the author wrote this story?
- Who illustrated the story?
- How did you find and learn the meaning of unfamiliar words?
- Who is in the story? Where do we see this character? What words can we use to describe this character?
- Where and when is the story taking place? How do we know?
- What is happening in the story? What words and illustrations tell us this?
- How does the story end? What words and illustrations show how the story ends?
- What do you learn from this story? How does the author teach you this?

Building Academic Language

To the right is a list of academic language to build your students' comprehension of the focus of this lesson set and facilitate their ability to talk and write about what they learn. There are words and phrases listed to the right. Rather than introduce all the words at once, slowly add them to a learning wall as your teaching unfolds. See the glossary at the end of this chapter for definitions of the words. Also listed are sentence frames that may be included on a sentence wall (Carrier & Tatum, 2006), a research-proven strategy for English language learners (Lewis, 1993; Nattinger, 1980), or as a handout to scaffold student use of the content words. Some students, especially English language learners, may need explicit practice in using the sentence frames. Encourage all students to use these words and phrases regularly in their conversations and writing.

Recognition

At the end of the each lesson and lesson set, it is critical that we recognize what our students have learned and the efforts they have put forth to learn and grow. At the end of the reading lessons, students will perform a reader's theater. This is an excellent tool to help them bring a story to life, dramatizing the story elements: character, setting, events, and conclusion. At the end of the writing lessons, students will share a story they have created, using the story elements as their structure to follow. Your students will know the important components of a story and see themselves as capable and interesting storytellers.

Assessment

Assessment in this lesson set is both ongoing and culminating, meaning that as teachers we are constantly kid-watching and observing how students are making meaning and interpreting new material. Throughout this lesson set, look for performance-based assessments, called Milestone Performance Assessments, each marked with an assessment icon. Milestone Performance

Core Words

adventures	imagined
character	narrative
compare	plot
conclusion	real
contrast	retell
differences	sentence
ending	setting
events	similarities
experiences	story

story elements
storytellers

Core Phrases

- The main character of this story is _____.

- The setting of this story is _____. I know this because _____ (textual evidence to support your thinking).

- Some important events of the story are _____.

- At the end of the story, _____.

- I think this is a _____ story because _____ (textual evidence to support your thinking).

- I think the character in this story is _____ because _____ (textual evidence to support your thinking).

    Which part of the illustration shows the character?

    Which line names the character?

- I learned _____ from this story (textual evidence to support your thinking).

Assessments are opportunities to notice and record data on standards-aligned indicators during the course of the lesson set. Use the results of these assessments to determine how well students are progressing toward the goals of the lesson set. Adjust the pace of your teaching and plan instructional support as needed.

Also, we encourage you to use the Core Ready Reading and Writing Rubrics, also marked with an assessment icon, with each lesson set to evaluate overall student performance on the standards-aligned lesson set goals. In this lesson set, the original stories students write will be an essential piece of evidence when you assess student performance that can be analyzed and placed in a portfolio of student work.

In addition, we have provided a Speaking and Listening Checklist (see PDToolKit) that provides observable Common Core State Standards–aligned indicators to assess student performance as speakers and listeners. There are multiple opportunities in every Core Ready lesson set to make such observations. Use the checklist in its entirety to gather performance data over time, or choose appropriate indicators to create a customized checklist to match a specific learning experience.

Core Support for Diverse Learners

This lesson set was created with the needs of a wide variety of learners in mind. Throughout the day-by-day lessons, you'll find examples of visual supports, graphic organizers, highlighted speaking and listening opportunities, and research-driven English language learner supports aimed at scaffolding instruction for all learners. However, we urge you to consider the following more specific challenges for which your students may need guided support.

Reading

The selection of storybooks is limitless. When choosing stories to read, carefully consider content and aim to find plots that are appropriate and accessible for kindergarten students. Additionally, some books have stronger story elements than others. Using stories with strong story elements is essential for kindergartners' success in this lesson set. When finding texts, make sure you have various levels represented in your classroom library. Also make sure to have books with print that is accessible to students who can read text as well as rich illustrations for students who are mostly reading pictures.

Your students may benefit from repeated exposure to a lesson's teaching point over several days. This can be accomplished with the whole class or in small-group settings.

Closely monitor students who have a limited vocabulary or who struggle to express themselves clearly, and determine whether they are in need of additional support with any of the Common Core Reading Standards for Foundational Skills listed for kindergarten.

As students dig into increasingly more complex stories, they will encounter characters, settings, and plots that are new to them. Be aware of simple stories and complex stories, and support students inside of whole-class lessons as well as individualized and small-group lessons.

As you continue your work with students, use observational notes and reading assessment data to create two to three specific short-term goals for your students with diverse needs. For example, these goals may be related to various foundational reading skills, building vocabulary, or enhancing comprehension. Throughout this lesson set, tailor your individualized and small-group instruction so that it addresses and evaluates student progress toward these goals.

Writing

When teaching children how to write a story, it is important to point out that all stories are created using story elements. When creating shared writing experiences, make sure to include all students in this whole-class process. Have students in preplanned partnerships in which they can talk through their ideas. Well-matched partnerships occur when students are around the same level and help one another have meaningful conversations. Make sure to have enough shared writing opportunities so that all children are contributing and experiencing the story writing process and have the tools to create stories independently.

Our goal is for students to share their ideas and lives through real and imagined stories via text and orally. Providing ample time for students to orally rehearse their ideas with partners will help them process and structure their ideas so they are able to create clear and interesting stories.

As with the reading lessons, your students may benefit from several days on a single lesson's teaching point. This can be done with the whole class or in small-group settings.

English Language Learners

While it is always our goal as teachers to get to know all of our students deeply, both in and out of the classroom setting, this work is perhaps more critical when considering our English language learners. Honoring families' cultural traditions and experiences is important to getting to know, understand, and work with your students in meaningful ways.

We also encourage you to use your ELLs' home languages as a resource. Researchers on second language acquisition are nearly unanimous on this point: using the home language enhances learning—both content development *and* English language and literacy acquisition. Even if you don't speak your students' home languages, look for every opportunity to have them leverage what they already know as you teach new information. Multilingual practices, like asking students how to say something in their home language, or encouraging students to discuss texts bilingually, also send welcoming messages that school is a place for people of all linguistic backgrounds.

English language learners are learning about stories and being asked to comprehend, retell, and create stories alongside native English speakers in your classroom, but they are also simultaneously learning English. It is essential for our English language learners to develop their ability to easily hold conversations about their reading and writing and to build their academic language base. Goldenberg (2008) defines "academic English" as the more abstract, complex, and challenging language that permits us to participate successfully in mainstream classroom instruction. English language learners will over time be responsible for understanding and producing academic English, both orally and in writing. However, language acquisition is a process, and our English language learners range in their development of English language acquisition. We urge you to consider your students along a spectrum of acquisition: from students new to this country, to those who are proficient conversationally, to those who have native-like proficiency.

Refer to the English language learner icons ELL throughout this lesson set for ways to shelter instruction for English language learners. These elements will help English language learners participate successfully in the whole-group lesson and will support the development of their language skills. Although these moments during instruction are designed to support English language learners, many schools are adding a separate English language development (ELD) block targeted at oral English language development, to further support their students in language acquisition.

Students with growing English proficiency will benefit from reading and writing word walls to build vocabulary (see Core Words and Phrases). Story Elements Bookmarks, introduced in Reading Lesson 2, will give students help with conversations and offer all students a layer of support, especially your language learners. Visual aids will further support students and give them a reference to what words are important to this study and what they mean.

Some students will benefit from several days on the same teaching point. You may consider gathering small groups of readers or writers for repeated instruction or using one-on-one conferences as an opportunity to revisit teaching points.

Complementary Core Methods

Read-Aloud

Take this opportunity to share a wide variety of stories. Consider multiple reads of the same text. In your first read, you are providing a foundation for the story as a whole as well as the benefits of a read-aloud without repeated interruption. In your second read-aloud of the text, pausing to think aloud or asking for students' thoughts as you spot the story elements may help their understanding of how to utilize story elements to help comprehend a story. Use your knowledge of students' interests to select texts that will inspire and excite your class. When appropriate, use your read-aloud as another chance for students to practice one or two of the following skills:

- Identifying and describing the character(s)
- Identifying and describing the setting
- Describing or naming the mood of a story
- Determining if the story is real or imagined
- Answering questions, using details from the story as textual evidence to support their thinking

Shared Reading

Shared reading provides a wonderful opportunity to use excerpts from read-alouds for close reading. Use shared reading to reinforce the idea of reading to learn (versus learning to read). In this lesson set in particular, consider focusing on one story element at a time. Below are some prompts you may want to use in your conversations about these visual texts:

- Who are the characters?
- Do we know these characters? From where?
- Does a character remind you of another character? Explain.
- What are the characters doing?
- Are you like one of the characters? How?
- What is the setting of the story? How do you know?
- How does the setting relate to the story?
- What are the important events of the story?
- How does the story end?
- Does this plot remind you of another story? Explain.
- What is the mood of this story? How can you tell?
- Is there a lesson to be learned? What is it?

Shared Writing

Shared writing is a tool needed for a gradual release to take place from teacher to students in learning how to navigate the writing process. This lesson set begins with modeling and then moves to shared experiences. Offering shared experiences allows students to be a part of writing a story in a positive, non-threatening manner. Students will benefit from working together as a group to craft stories, providing them the knowledge and inspiration to create their own stories, real and imagined.

Core Connections at Home

Ask students to bring a favorite book from home. Have them share their books in small groups, identifying story elements and examining the illustrations. For homework, have students take home a favorite book they discovered in school and share it with a family member, pointing out story elements and illustrations as practiced in class. The family member can share with the student his or her reactions to the story.

Invite family members to come to class to share favorite family stories. Ask guests to share when they first heard their story, who told it, and why the story is a favorite. Ask students to recount who the story was about, its setting, and major events.

Have students share their reader's theater and final writing stories with their families. Have a Storybook Day in which family members can come in to enjoy and learn about all the stories the children have read, retold, and created as a group and independently. Ask family members to leave notes sharing their reactions to the stories, or have a place set up for parents to leave video recordings for students to view later.

Reading Lessons

The Core I.D.E.A. / Daily Reading Instruction at a Glance table highlights the teaching objectives and standards alignment for all 10 lessons across the four stages of the lesson set (Introduce, Define, Extend, and Assess). It also indicates which lessons contain special features to support English language learners, technology, speaking and listening, close reading opportunities, and formative ("Milestone") assessments.

The following CORE READY READING RUBRIC is designed to help you record each student's overall understanding across four levels of achievement as it relates to the lesson set goals. We recommend that you use this rubric at the end of the lesson set as a performance-based assessment tool. Use the Milestone Performance Assessments as tools to help you gauge student progress toward these goals. Reteach and differentiate instruction as needed. See the foundational book, *Be Core Ready: Powerful, Effective Steps to Implementing and Achieving the Common Core State Standards,* for more information about the Core Ready Reading and Writing Rubrics.

The Core I.D.E.A. / Daily Reading Instruction at a Glance

Grade K   Tell Me a Story: Elements of Fiction

Instructional Stage	Lesson	Teaching Objective	Core Standards	Special Features
Introduce: *notice, explore, collect, note, immerse, surround, record, share*	1	Readers have favorite stories.	RL.K.1 • RL.K.5 • RL.K.7 • RL.K.10 • SL.K.1a • SL.K.1b • SL.K.2 • SL.K.3 • SL.K.6 • L.K.1 • L.K.6	ELL S&L Tech Close Reading Opportunity
Define: *name, identify, outline, clarify, select, plan*	2	Readers notice story elements.	RL.K.1 • RL.K.3 • RL.K.4 • RL.K.7 • RL.K.10 • SL.K.1a • SL.K.1b • SL.K.2 • SL.K.3 • SL.K.6 • L.K.1 • L.K.4 • L.K.6	ELL S&L Close Reading Opportunity
	3	Readers notice story elements throughout a story.	RL.K.1 • RL.K.3 • RL.K.7 • RL.K.10 • SL.K.1a • SL.K.1b • SL.K.2 • SL.K.3 • SL.K.6 • L.K.1	ELL S&L Milestone Assessment Close Reading Opportunity
Extend: *try, experiment, attempt, approximate, practice, explain, revise, refine*	4	Readers read and reread classics that have been enjoyed for many years.	RL.K.1 • RL.K.3 • RL.K.5 • RL.K.10 • SL.K.1a • SL.K.1b • SL.K.2 • SL.K.3 • SL.K.6 • L.K.1 • L.K.6	ELL S&L Tech Close Reading Opportunity
	5	Readers notice what they like about story elements and why.	RL.K.1 • RL.K.3 • RL.K.5 • RL.K.7 • RL.K.10 • W.K.1 • SL.K.1a • SL.K.1b • SL.K.2 • SL.K.3 • SL.K.6 • L.K.1 • L.K.6	ELL S&L Close Reading Opportunity
	6	Readers revisit stories through retelling.	RL.K.1 • RL.K.2 • RL.K.3 • RL.K.7 • RL.K.10 • SL.K.1a • SL.K.1b • SL.K.2 • SL.K.3 • SL.K.6 • L.K.1 • L.K.6	ELL S&L Milestone Assessment Close Reading Opportunity
	7	Readers compare the experiences of characters across books.	RL.K.1 • RL.K.3 • RL.K.9 • RL.K.10 • SL.K.1a • SL.K.1b • SL.K.2 • SL.K.3 • SL.K.6 • L.K.1 • L.K.6	ELL S&L Close Reading Opportunity
	8	Readers think about story elements as they act out stories in reader's theater.	RL.K.1 • RL.K.3 • RL.K.10 • SL.K.1a • SL.K.1b • SL.K.2 • SL.K.3 • SL.K.6 • L.K.1 • L.K.6	ELL S&L Close Reading Opportunity
	9	Readers use story elements to dramatize favorite stories.	RL.K.1 • RL.K.3 • RL.K.7 • RL.K.10 • SL.K.1a • SL.K.1b • SL.K.6 • L.K.1 • L.K.6	ELL S&L Milestone Assessment Close Reading Opportunity

Instructional Stage	Lesson	Teaching Objective	Core Standards	Special Features
Assess: *reflect, conclude, connect, share, recognize, respond*	10	Readers reflect on how story elements help them.	RL.K.3 • RL.K.10 • W.K.8 • SL.K.1a • SL.K.1b • SL.K.3 • SL.K.6 • L.K.1 • L.K.6	ELL S&L Close Reading Opportunity

Core Ready Reading Rubric

Grade K   Tell Me a Story: Elements of Fiction

Lesson Set Goal	Emerging	Approaching	Achieving	Exceeding	Standards Alignment
Identify and describe the story elements (character, setting, major events, and conclusion).	Student is unable to effectively use clues from text and/or illustrations to identify the story elements (character, setting, events, and conclusion). Little or no textual evidence to support thinking.	Student attempts to use clues from text and/or illustrations to identify the story elements (character, setting, events, and conclusion). Inaccuracies may be present. May provide insufficient textual evidence to support thinking.	Student uses clues from text and/or illustrations to identify the story elements (character, setting, events, and conclusion). Provides sufficient textual evidence to support thinking. Some components may be more developed than others.	Student uses clues from text and/or illustrations to identify the story elements (character, setting, events, and conclusion). May also notice subtle details or make inferences. Provides detailed and thoughtful textual evidence to support thinking.	RL.K.1 RL.K.3 RL.K.7 RL.K.10 W.K.8 SL.K.1a SL.K.1b SL.K.2 SL.K.3 SL.K.6 L.K.1 L.K.6
Use the story elements, pictures, and words to make meaning as they read classic and contemporary stories.	Student is unable to use the story elements, pictures, and or/words to make meaning as he/she reads classic and contemporary stories.	Student attempts to use the story elements, pictures, and/or words to make meaning as he/she reads. May not be able to demonstrate his/her understanding of story elements accurately (e.g., by speaking, writing, or dictating).	Student uses the story elements, pictures, and words to make meaning as he/she reads. Demonstrates his/her understanding in a variety of ways (e.g., speaking, drawing, writing, dictating).	Student uses the story elements, pictures, and words to make deep meaning as he/she reads. Thoughtfully and accurately demonstrates a deep understanding in a variety of ways (e.g., speaking, drawing, writing, dictating), providing textual evidence to support thinking. May demonstrate independence reading text above grade-level expectations.	RL.K.1 RL.K.2 RL.K.3 RL.K.5 RL.K.7 RL.K.10 SL.K.1a SL.K.1b SL.K.6 L.K.1 L.K.6

Core Ready Reading Rubric, Grade K, *continued*

Lesson Set Goal	Emerging	Approaching	Achieving	Exceeding	Standards Alignment
Use the story elements to plan and perform a play based on a story.	Student does not use the story elements to plan and perform a play based on a story.	Student attempts to use the story elements to plan and perform a play based on a story. May not include all the story elements and/or play may contain several inaccuracies.	Student uses the story elements to plan and perform a play based on a story. Includes all the story elements but some may be better developed than others.	Student uses the story elements to plan and perform a play based on a story. Accurately and thoughtfully includes all the story elements.	RL.K.1 RL.K.3 RL.K.10 SL.K.1a SL.K.1b SL.K.2 SL.K.3 SL.K.6 L.K.1 L.K.6
Compare and contrast characters across stories.	Student shows little or no evidence of being able to compare and contrast characters across stories.	Student attempts to compare and contrast characters across stories. Some inaccuracies or lack of textual evidence may be present.	Student is able to compare and contrast characters across stories and provide textual evidence to support thinking.	Student is able to clearly and articulately compare and contrast characters across stories. Provides detailed and thoughtful textual evidence to support thinking.	RL.K.1 RL.K.2 RL.K.3 RL.K.9 RL.K.10, SL.K.1a SL.K.1b SL.K.6 L.K.1 L.K.6
Ask and answer questions about unknown words in a text.	Student makes little or no attempt to ask and answer questions about unknown words in a text.	Student attempts to ask and answer questions about unknown words in a text.	Student asks and answers questions about unknown words in a text.	Student ask and answers effective questions about unknown words in a text. At times, is able to make meaning of unfamiliar words.	RL.K.4 L.K.4
With prompting and support, ask and answer questions about key details in a text.	Student demonstrates little or no evidence of asking and/or answering questions about the text even with extensive prompting and support.	Student shows some evidence of asking and/or answering questions about key details in a text with prompting and support. Student may at times lack focus and accuracy.	Student shows solid evidence of asking and/or answering questions about key details in a text with focus and accuracy. Student may require some prompting and support.	Student demonstrates exceptional evidence of asking and/or answering questions about key details of a text with focus and accuracy. Student requires little prompting and support.	RL.K.1
Actively engage in group reading activities with purpose and understanding.	Student shows little or no evidence of engaging in group reading activities.	Student shows some evidence of effectively engaging in group reading activities with purpose and understanding.	Student shows solid evidence of actively engaging in group reading activities with purpose and understanding.	Student shows exceptional evidence of actively engaging in group reading activities with a sharp focus, sense of purpose, and thorough understanding.	RL.K.10

Lesson Set Goal	Emerging	Approaching	Achieving	Exceeding	Standards Alignment
Use a combination of drawing, dictating, and writing to compose opinion pieces in which they tell a reader the topic or the name of the book they are writing about and state an opinion or preference about the topic or book (e.g., My favorite book is . . .).	Student shows little or no evidence of successfully composing an opinion piece. Opinion piece lacks a topic or opinion statement or both. Drawing may be irrelevant.	Student shows some evidence of successfully composing an opinion piece. Student attempts a topic and opinion statement but writing and/ or drawing may lack clarity or focus. Drawing, if included, loosely connects to opinion.	Student shows solid evidence of successfully composing an opinion piece. Student includes a clear topic and states a relevant opinion or preference about the topic. Drawing, if included, connects to opinion.	Student shows outstanding evidence of composing a successful opinion piece. Student includes a clear topic and states a relevant opinion or preference. Ideas may be particularly thoughtful or sophisticated. Student may include relevant reasoning for the opinion. Drawing, if included, is relevant and detailed.	W.K.1
In collaborative discussions, exhibit responsibility to the rules and roles of conversation.	Student makes little or no attempt to participate in collaborative discussions and often disregards the rules and roles of conversation even with prompting.	Student inconsistently participates in collaborative discussions. Student observes the rules and roles of conversation but needs frequent prompting.	Student usually participates in collaborative discussions. Student observes the rules and roles of conversation. May need some prompting.	Student consistently participates in collaborative discussions. Student observes the rules and roles of conversation with little or no prompting.	SL.K.1a SL.K.1b
Speak audibly and express thoughts, feelings, and ideas clearly.	Student usually lacks clarity when expressing thoughts, feelings, and ideas and/or speaks inaudibly to others.	Student sometimes lacks clarity when expressing thoughts, feelings, and ideas and/or sometimes struggles to speak audibly to others.	Student usually expresses thoughts, feelings, and ideas clearly and speaks audibly.	Student consistently expresses thoughts, feelings, and ideas clearly. May be exceptionally thoughtful or detailed when communicating ideas. Speaks audibly with energy and expression.	SL.K.6
Demonstrate knowledge of standard English and its conventions.	Student demonstrates little or no knowledge of standard English and its conventions.	Student demonstrates some evidence of knowledge of standard English and its conventions.	Student consistently demonstrates knowledge of standard English and its conventions.	Student demonstrates an exceptional understanding of standard English and its conventions. Use of conventions is sophisticated for grade level and accurate.	L.K.1 L.K.2
Use words and phrases acquired through conversations, reading and being read to, and responding to texts.	Student shows little or no evidence of the acquisition and/or use of grade-appropriate words and phrases.	Student shows some evidence of acquiring and using grade-appropriate words and phrases.	Student shows solid evidence of acquiring and using grade-appropriate words and phrases.	Student shows a high level of sophistication and precision when using grade-appropriate words and phrases.	L.K.6

Reading Lesson 1

▼ Teaching Objective

Readers have favorite stories.

Close Reading
Opportunity

▼ Standards Alignment

RL.K.1, RL.K.5, RL.K.7, RL.K.10, SL.K.1a, SL.K.1b, SL.K.2, SL.K.3, SL.K.6, L.K.1, L.K.6

▼ Materials

- Charting supplies or interactive whiteboard to create Stories We Love Chart
- *Corduroy* by Don Freeman
- Favorite class read-aloud stories in baskets (on tablets if available)
- Favorite class storybooks

▼ To the Teacher

Most kindergartners love a good story, whether it be a favorite read to them, a story told by a friend, or one of their own. Today you will be launching your reading lesson set focused on story, both classic and contemporary. Over the next few weeks, your students and you will retell the stories you love. A story is an account of events across time. Throughout this lesson set, your students will be learning about the narrative elements of character, setting, and the events, including the conclusion, that make up the plot. Knowing and understanding the genre of narrative will help your students for years to come. Before beginning today's lesson, have on tabletops baskets of books you have read aloud, for your students to look through and remind themselves of stories they love. Partnerships can look through the books baskets together. Students will come back to these stories across the weeks as you immerse yourselves in the world of story.

▼ Procedure

Warm Up **Gather the class to set the stage for today's learning**

Gather your students and announce that for the next few weeks you are going to be listening to, reading, and rereading stories and that today is all about enjoying the sound of stories and thinking about our favorites.

> Kindergartners, today we will begin to talk about what makes a story a story. We are going to enjoy rereading and talking about some of our favorite stories. As we enjoy a story today, we are going to think and talk about what makes a story so enjoyable.

Teach **Model what students need to learn and do**

Display the front covers of favorite stories read together this year. **ELL** Frontload the Lesson—Make Connections. Connecting the new lesson and content to familiar stories helps ELLs anticipate what they will learn and see its

Annie Pickert Fuller/Pearson Education

relevance to things they have already learned. If you are not able to have the original texts, use pictures; include hand-drawn pictures or clip art or illustrations.

Also have a basket of favorite books to refer to during the lesson. If your class uses digital books on computers, tablets, and so on, please realize that for you, baskets may be electronic folders or menus. Begin a chart titled Stories We Love. Model for students how to think back on books we have read, and conduct a think-aloud where you share your thinking about books, using the story elements to refer to why you loved the story. Make sure to focus on the illustrations and how the pictures help tell the story. (The language below is an example of how one teacher related her love of the *Corduroy* story). Define a story for your class. Use several examples of familiar read-alouds to support this conversation.

> When a writer tells us about something that happened, we call it a story. We listen to and reread books to discover and enjoy stories we love. Each of us here has stories that we want to hear over and over again. Each time we listen to or reread our favorite stories, we imagine what the characters are doing, how it might feel to be where the story is taking place, and what the characters are experiencing. Stories become our favorites when we feel as though we are right there with the characters, experiencing the place of the story and the things that happen. Let me share what I think about a very well-written story, *Corduroy* by Don Freeman.

> One of my favorite stories is *Corduroy*. I can remember my father reading this book to me over and over again when I was a little girl. Each time I read this book, I pretend that I am Corduroy, the main character in the story, living in that big department store, wishing for the little girl to return to bring me home and trying to make myself better by fixing my overalls so that the little girl will want me. I love the part where the little girl takes Corduroy home and fixes his button. Each time I read the words and look at the illustrations and see how she carefully sews the button for him, I smile. I always have a good feeling at the end of this story when Corduroy is safe in his new home.

Try Guide students to quickly rehearse what they need to learn and do in preparation for practice

Referring to the images of front covers of favorite books and the basket of favorite books, have students turn and talk about another class favorite book of your choosing or theirs. **ELL** Enable Language Production—Increasing Interaction. Having ELLs turn and talk with their peers gives them a chance to rehears what they want to say, and to hear model responses from more-proficient peers.

> Now I want you to think about this book and why it is one of our favorites. Think back to how I shared my thoughts about why I love *Corduroy*.

Focus student discussion on the following questions. The questions in bold refer to the basic story elements and are repeated across the lesson set. The questions that follow each bold question prompt the reader to provide text evidence for his or her thinking:

- **Who is in the story?** Where do we see this character? What words can we use to describe this character?
- **Where and when is the story taking place?** How do we know?
- **What is happening in the story?** What words and illustrations tell us this?
- **How does the story end?** What words and illustrations show how the story ends?

Clarify Briefly restate today's teaching objective and explain the practice task(s)

Discuss with students how you want them to work in partnerships to find favorite books or new books that capture their attention. Have them share their thoughts about the characters, where and when the story is taking place, what is happening in the story, and how the story ends.

> Today, your partner and you are going to look through the baskets of books on the tabletops to think and talk about your favorite stories. Take turns talking about the different characters in the stories, where and when the stories take place, what is happening in the stories, and how they end. After you and your partner have talked about a favorite story, we will come back together as a group to remind each other of our favorites.

As your students work in partnerships, take the opportunity to promote and encourage several key speaking and listening behaviors such as facing one another; taking turns speaking; listening with care and speaking audibly; and expressing thoughts, feelings, and ideas clearly.

(SL.K.1a, SL.K.6) **ELL** Enable Language Production—Increasing Interaction. When partnering ELLs with other students, think of how partners can support language and content acquisition through sharing in the home language, translating, and modeling.

Practice Students work independently and/or in small groups to apply today's teaching objective

Students will explore books in baskets with partners to choose favorite stories. Emphasize how talking about the characters, where and when the story is taking place, what is happening in the story, and how it ends helps in our understanding and enjoyment of the story.

Wrap Up Check understanding as you guide students to share briefly what they have learned and produced today

Bring the class back to the gathering area and draw their attention to the Stories We Love Chart. Have them share the story they revisited with their partners and one part of the story that makes it a favorite. Instruct the students to refer directly to the pictures in their books as they share their story. Chart responses.

Today we have put ourselves inside of stories and thought about reasons why we love certain stories.

We thought to ourselves:

- Who is in the story?
- Where and when does the story take place?
- What happens in the story?
- How does the story end?

Thinking through these questions can help us understand a story and focus on what makes us enjoy a story. What story did you think and talk about today? Share one part of the story you loved.

Move around the room and watch how students use the illustrations of their books to share and talk about their story. Assess if students are identifying the story elements as they talk about their stories. **ELL** Identify and Communicate Content and Language Objectives—Check for Understanding. This is a time for ELLs to practice their thinking out loud in English and an opportunity for you to clarify any misunderstandings you see. Be sure to notice whether they are struggling with content (what does it mean to have a favorite story?) or with finding the language to express their opinions.

Goal	Low-Tech	High-Tech
Students revisit favorite stories.	Students look at books in tabletop baskets.	Students view and listen to stories on a tablet or on computers, visiting websites such as Starfall, Bookflix, or Tumblebooks.

Reading Lesson 2 . . . .

▼ Teaching Objective

Readers notice story elements.

Close Reading
Opportunity

▼ Standards Alignment

RL.K.1, RL.K.3, RL.K.4, RL.K.7, RL.K.10, SL.K.1a, SL.K.1b, SL.K.2, SL.K.3, SL.K.6, L.K.1, L.K.4, L.K.6

▼ Materials

- Stories We Love Chart from Reading Lesson 1
- Story Elements Chart prepared in advance (see next page)
- Story Elements Bookmarks (Appendix K.2) for each student
- Story Elements Icons (Appendix K.3)

- Baskets of storybooks, including books from the Stories We Love Chart, if possible

- *Peter's Chair* by Ezra Jack Keats (or another book of your choice with strong story elements)

- *Bigmama's* by Donald Crews (or another book of your choice with strong story elements)

▼ To the Teacher

It will be helpful if before today's lesson you have read aloud to the students the books used today for finding story elements. Exploring these elements will offer the children a chance to look closely at these familiar stories through a new, critical lens. It can be a challenge to get students to slow down as they read; however, if this lesson is approached with care, it can feel more like a game. You may hear children shouting out, "I found the setting!" Encourage this excitement and let it propel you into the upcoming lessons in this set. Use the Story Elements Icons (Appendix K.3) to create your own Story Elements Chart. Copy matching Story Elements Bookmarks (Appendix K.2) for each of your students to use today and throughout the lesson set to help them identify the elements as they are introduced in their stories. The Common Core State Standards require that kindergartners retell character, setting, and events. In this lesson set, we use these terms as well as the term *conclusion* to ensure that students remember the ever-important and often-forgotten ending when retelling and discussing stories together. For the sake of consistency, we suggest students practice naming three key events when retelling and writing stories, but this number is flexible and may be adjusted as needed. Additionally, as students come across unknown words, remind them to use the important strategy of asking questions about the words and carefully listening to the suggestions their classmates provide.

▼ Procedure

Warm Up Gather the class to set the stage for today's learning

Gather your students. Before today's lesson, it may be a good idea to have a few of the storybooks students identified on the Stories We Love Chart visible or to add images or drawings of familiar favorite characters to the chart. This will help children recognize their favorite stories immediately and support the use of illustrations as a means for reading. Also, have Story Elements Bookmarks (Appendix K.2) ready for students to use as they spot the story elements in their books.

> In Reading Lesson 1, we had a great time looking at books and talking about them. We created a chart called Stories We Love, listing different books that we enjoy. Let's talk about some of the books we put on this chart.

Have students turn and talk and share a book title they love. Then bring the group back together and let one partnership share a book title to the group. **ELL** Enable Language Production—Increasing Interaction. Both increasing interaction and offering opportunities to talk give ELLs time to practice their learning in English or their home language.

Teach Model what students need to learn and do

> Friends, today we are going to look closely at what makes a story. Story elements are the parts that make up a story. Let's look at our Story Elements Chart to see the different elements that make up a story.

ELL Identify and Communicate Content and Language Objectives—Key Content Vocabulary. Knowing and using these terms will be an important part of mastering the content of this lesson set. By introducing them explicitly here, you are giving your ELLs a base from which they will build a rich understanding of story elements in the coming days.

> Here is an example chart. Make sure to add icons to the words so all children can access this chart throughout the lesson set. **ELL** Provide Comprehensible Input—Graphics. Charts can make your teaching points clearer to ELLs. When you continue to display them, they also offer visual support for ELLs to refer back to when they are working independently. If you are not able to take pictures, include hand-drawn pictures or clip art to illustrate the chart.

Story Elements Chart

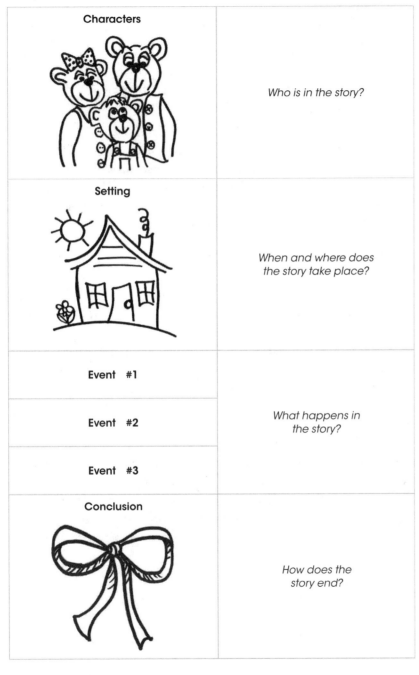

Characters	Who is in the story?
Setting	When and where does the story take place?
Event #1	
Event #2	What happens in the story?
Event #3	
Conclusion	How does the story end?

Today I am going to read another favorite book of mine, *Peter's Chair*. As I am reading, I am going to use the illustrations and words to look closely for the story elements. As you listen, see if you can identify them.

Read to your class *Peter's Chair* or any favorite book with strong story elements. Mark story elements with sticky notes as you read. After you have read the story, think aloud, asking yourself the questions from the Story Elements Chart you created earlier. Clearly identify the story elements, referring back to the pages in the book and using the illustrations to answer the questions as you think aloud. Direct students to find unknown words in their stories and to ask questions to try and determine their meanings. **ELL** Identify and Communicate Content and Language Objectives—Models. Modeling lets your ELLs hear you demonstrate your thought process as you analyze text evidence. By referring back to the Story Elements Chart, you are also deepening their understanding of key vocabulary.

When I read a story, I am always asking myself these questions:

- Who is in the story?
- Where and when does the story take place?
- What happens in the story?
- How does the story end?

Define *character* for students.

Who is in the story? These are the *characters*. In *Peter's Chair*, Peter, Willie, his mother, father, and baby sister are the characters.

Define *setting* for students.

Where and when does the story take place? This is called the *setting*. The story is taking place in and outside of Peter's apartment during the day.

Define *events* and *conclusion* for students. You might want to mention that the events of a story, including the conclusion, are called the *plot* of a story.

What happens in the story? The things that happen in a story are called *events*. In the beginning, Peter is playing and his mother asks him to be quiet because his baby sister is sleeping. Then Peter's dad asks him to help paint Peter's old high chair pink. Instead, Peter takes his little chair and runs away with Willie.

How does the story end? We call the ending of a story the *conclusion*. In the end, Peter realizes that he cannot fit into his baby things and he helps his dad paint his little chair pink for his sister. We use a bow on the chart to remind us that the conclusion ties up the story.

Friends, today we are learning that all stories have similar parts called story elements: character, setting, events, and conclusion. Noticing these elements help us slow down and think about the important parts of the story. Readers think about these parts of the story and connect them from beginning to end to understand the story. When we read we always try to understand and make meaning of the words and illustrations. You also may come across words that you don't know as you read through the stories. Make a note about any unknown words and when you work with your partners, ask and answer questions about the words to try and find out what they mean.

ELL Identify and Communicate Content and Language Objectives—Key Content Vocabulary. Repetition of the core words of this lesson, accompanied by examples, illustrations, and explanations, will help ELLs develop a deeper understanding of their meaning.

Try Guide students to quickly rehearse what they need to learn and do in preparation for practice

Every time we read a story we can identify the various story elements. Let's read another story right now. As you are listening, look for the story elements. Put your thumbs up each time you hear one of the story elements.

ELL Frontload the Lesson—Set a Purpose for Reading. Clearly stating *why you and the students are reading* helps your ELLs focus their thoughts during the story and increases their comprehension of key elements. Read *Bigmama's* by Donald Crews, or another story of your choice with strong story elements. Monitor the children's reactions to the story as you read. Give them a chance to turn and talk halfway through so you can listen to their thoughts. Reinforce that they are listening and noticing story elements as they view the illustrations. Be aware of your pacing because you are reading two stories today and you want to keep the children engaged. Use the chart as a reference to build students' familiarity with the terms and icons. **ELL** Identify and Communicate Content and Language Objectives— Check for Understanding. Repetition of core concepts is an effective tool in ELL

language and content acquisition. ELLs are able to clarify and learn from their peers during this time in an informal forum. This is an opportunity to notice which of your students, especially ELLs, might be confused about the lesson goal and to "whisper in" support when needed.

As your students work in partnerships, take the opportunity to promote and encourage key speaking and listening behaviors such as facing one another; taking turns speaking; listening with care; developing the conversation through multiple exchanges; and expressing thoughts, feelings, and ideas clearly. (SL.K.1a, SL.K.1b, SL.K.6)

Clarify Briefly restate today's teaching objective and explain the practice task(s)

Today we are noticing story elements as we read. Pay close attention to the illustrations, as they may help us answer the following questions:

- Who is in the story?
- Where and when is the story taking place?
- What is happening in the story?
- How does the story end?

Direct the students to read books from their baskets during Practice. Offer students a Story Elements Bookmark to remind them of the elements so they can spot them as they read. Additionally, the Story Elements Bookmark will help students keep track of the story elements for sharing their findings at the end. The bookmark helps students be on the lookout for the elements as they read. Encourage students to stop and point to an element on the bookmark as they come across it while reading.

Practice Students work independently and/or in small groups to apply today's teaching objective

Characters

Setting

Event #1

Event #2

Event #3

Conculsion

Have students read independently, using the illustrations to notice the story elements and keeping track of their findings with their Story Elements Bookmarks. Some students may begin to reread and/or retell their stories, using the bookmark as a guide.

Wrap Up Check understanding as you guide students to share briefly what they have learned and produced today

Gather students back together, asking them to bring one book in which they found story elements. Then ask students to share these story elements with partners, using the Story Elements Bookmarks and referring to the illustrations in their books. Partners should:

- Name the title
- Use Story Elements Bookmarks as they refer to illustrations and text in their books to explicitly share the story elements with peers
- Take turns listening and speaking

Circulate and assess students' understanding as they talk with partners. Stress that today's purpose was to notice that stories are made up of story elements. Have one student share with the group where he or she found story elements, using the Story Elements Bookmark and referring to illustrations.

Friends, today we had fun looking closely at our stories to notice the story elements. As readers, we know that stories are made up of these different elements.

Reading Lesson 3 ·

▼ Teaching Objective

Readers notice story elements throughout a story.

Close Reading
Opportunity

▼ Standards Alignment

RL.K.1, RL.K.3, RL.K.7, RL.K.10, SL.K.1a, SL.K.1b, SL.K.2, SL.K.3, SL.K.6, L.K.1.

▼ Materials

- *Bear Snores On* by Karma Wilson or any fictional narrative with basic story elements
- *Franklin Rides a Bike* by Paulette Bourgeois and Brenda Clark or any fictional narrative with basic story elements
- Story Elements Bookmark for each student
- Story Elements Chart

▼ To the Teacher

Today's lesson builds off of the success of Reading Lesson 2. Learning how to recognize and think deeply about story elements lays the groundwork for helping students to become lifelong readers. Young readers sometimes mistakenly think that story elements are to be noticed only at the beginning or end of a story, but we want them to understand that a reader can and should pay attention to story elements all across a story, noticing new developments and changes. Simple questions can help guide your discussion: Who are the characters? Have we met any new characters? What is the setting? What is the setting *now*? What is happening? What is happening *now*?

Make sure to have included *Bear Snores On* and *Franklin Rides a Bike* (or other books you may be using for this lesson) in your read-alouds before today's lesson so the focus can be on story elements inside familiar stories.

▼ Procedure

Warm Up Gather the class to set the stage for today's learning

Gather the class. Remind the students that in the previous lesson we noticed and defined story elements as we read our books. Allow a few students to share the title of a book in which they found story elements.

Teach Model what students need to learn and do

Today's lesson asks students to listen for and discuss key details related to story elements. Therefore, this portion of the lesson provides you with an excellent opportunity to take note of students' ability to listen to and comprehend a story told aloud. (SL.K.2) **ELL** Identify and Communicate Content and Language Objectives—Language Form and Function. Offering opportunities to listen and speak lets ELLs practice their learning in English. You will be able to hear the vocabulary and language levels of your ELLs and determine the support needed to ensure they both comprehend the lesson content and can perform the lesson goals.

Today, we are going read closely to see how we can think about story elements throughout the stories we read.

Introduce the notion that readers think about story elements throughout a story.

As a reader of a story, I know that the characters and setting will usually be introduced early in the story. I also pay careful attention to what is happening—the events—in the story right from the beginning. But I don't stop thinking about these things there. I keep paying attention to the characters, setting, and events all through the story because as a story continues, these things change. Noticing how the characters, setting, and events change is part of what makes a story interesting to a reader. Finally, I will also pay attention to the conclusion at the end. The conclusion is what happens at the end of the story.

As you read *Bear Snores On* by Karma Wilson, use the Story Elements Bookmarks to guide a close reading of the story using the following questions. Ask the character, setting, and events questions several times across the story, making special note of when any element changes, such as the addition of new characters, a change of setting, or new events. Use both the illustrations and words as sources for your thinking. Emphasize that there are story elements to notice all throughout a story. As the story comes to an end, focus on the conclusion also. **ELL** Enable Language Production—Listening and Speaking. Repetition of the key questions of this lesson set will make your language increasingly comprehensible to your ELLs. Be sure to allow ample wait time as you ask these questions to give ELLs a chance to organize their thoughts and respond.

CHARACTERS: Who are the characters? What are they saying and doing? What words and pictures describe this?

SETTING: What is the setting? Where are they? Is it day or night? How can you tell?

EVENTS: What is happening? What important events are we reading about? What are the characters experiencing? How do we know?

At the end of the story, focus on the conclusion:

CONCLUSION: What happens at the end? What do the characters do at the end of the story? What words and pictures tell us this? How does the conclusion make the reader feel? Why?

Try Guide students to quickly rehearse what they need to learn and do in preparation for practice

> Friends, it is your turn to try now. As I read *Franklin Rides a Bike*, remember to look closely at the illustrations and words. Let's use the words and pictures to answer these questions.

As you read, pause at appropriate places and ask the story elements questions provided in the Teach section, scaffolding the experience with your students. Model using the story elements chart icons to help remind you what story elements to think about. **ELL** Provide Comprehensible Input—Graphics, Models. When you refer back to icons that consistently represent the same concepts, you help your ELLs surmount language barriers that might limit their access to content. Furthermore, explicitly modeling your thought process makes academic thinking visible to your ELLs.

Remind students how to engage effectively in collaborative discussions by following agreed-upon rules for discussions: listening with care, one voice speaking at a time, and building on the thoughts of others. Help students notice how we can build upon others' ideas and express thoughts, feelings, and ideas clearly. (SL.K.1a, SL.K.1b, SL.K.6)

Clarify Briefly restate today's teaching objective and explain the practice task(s)

> Today, as you read your stories, looking at the illustrations, stop and think about each of the story elements we've discussed. Use your Story Elements Bookmark to help keep track of what to think about so you can share with your partner during our Wrap Up. Remember that you should think about characters, setting, and events anytime in the story, but the conclusion only happens at the end. **ELL** Identify and Communicate Content and Language Objectives—Repeat. By restating your directions one more time, you are reinforcing your core teaching points for your ELLs.

Consider having students place sticky notes toward the beginning, middle, and end of the story to remind them to stop and think about story elements.

Practice Students work independently and/or in small groups to apply today's teaching objective

Students read independently, using the illustrations and words to stop and think about the story elements as they read. Circulate the room and encourage

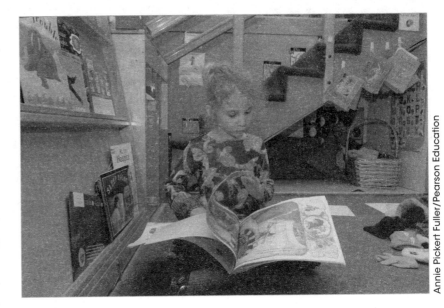

students to use the Story Elements Bookmark to help them keep track of their reading and thinking. Ask students to share with you what they are noticing. Do any story elements change across the book? **ELL** Identify and Communicate Content and Language Objecives—Check for Understanding. As you conference with your ELLs, be sure to distinguish gaps in their *content* understanding from gaps in their *language* proficiency. Students may need help with one, both, or neither, but notice the good thinking that is going on behind the "imperfect" language.

Wrap Up Check understanding as you guide students to share briefly what they have learned and produced today

Gather students back together, asking them to bring one book in which they identified story elements. To gather data, ask students to turn and talk, sharing their thinking about story elements with partners, using their Story Elements Bookmark, and referring to the illustrations in their books. **ELL** Enable Language Production—Increasing Interaction. This is an opportunity for ELLs hear how their more-proficient peers express learning that is similar to their own. Partners should:

- Name the title
- Use Story Elements Bookmark, referring to illustrations in book to share their thinking about the story elements
- Take turns listening and speaking

As students are sharing, assess students' understanding. Note exemplary ideas and share one or two with the class. If you seek to gather individual data on each student, hold conferences to do so.

Analyze students' understand of the story elements as a performance-based assessment to determine if students need additional instruction or support as a whole class, in small groups, or one on one. **ELL** Assess for Content and Language Understandings—Formative Assessment. You can also use this time to assess your ELLs' language and/or content needs and then use this information to inform upcoming work and to determine how you may need to scaffold access to upcoming lessons.

Standards Alignment: RL.K.1, RL.K.3, RL.K.7, SL.K.1a, SL.K.1b, SL.K.2, SL.K.6

Task	Achieved	Notes
Name story elements (character, setting, events, conclusion).		
Refer to illustrations and/or words in book to share thinking about the story elements.		
Speak audibly when sharing ideas.		

Milestone Performance Assessment

Identifying and Using Story Elements.

 Use this checklist to assess students' identification and use of story elements.

Reading Lesson 4

▼ Teaching Objective

Readers read and reread classics that have been enjoyed for many years.

Close Reading Opportunity

▼ Standards Alignment

RL.K.1, RL.K.3, RL.K.5, RL.K.10, SL.K.1a, SL.K.1b, SL.K.2, SL.K.3, SL.K.6, L.K.1, L.K.6

▼ Materials

- Familiar nursery rhymes enlarged on charts. Here are a few of our favorites: Itsy-Bitsy Spider, Pat-a-Cake, Row, Row, Row Your Boat, Who Tool the Cookie from the Cookie Jar? (see Nursery Rhymes in the PDToolKit)
- Story Elements Chart
- Story Elements Bookmarks

▼ To the Teacher

Prior to teaching this lesson, you will want to have read many nursery rhymes inside of your read-aloud and your shared reading experiences. In this lesson, you want the children to recognize the nursery rhymes and have fun with them. **ELL** Frontload the Lesson—Activate Prior Knowledge, Build Background. ELLs may not be familiar with the rhymes you plan to use, and so you will need to do some pre-teaching to give them access to the main lesson. Read the rhymes with them in advance, and connect the new rhymes to those they might have learned at home, in their home language, drawing attention to common elements like rhythm. You may need to enlist a parent or a bilingual staff member to help you find appropriate home-language rhymes.

The goal is to help students understand that story elements are used to create all kinds of stories. Today's stories are classics and look different than stories they read in books. We want to help students understand that there are many forms of stories. The children will love the singing and acting out of these familiar rhymes.

▼ Procedure

Warm Up Gather the class to set the stage for today's learning

Friends, we have been reading and using story elements to help us better understand and enjoy the stories we read.

When I was a child, there were certain stories that I loved to have read to me over and over again. Even today as an adult, I love to read and reread these stories. It is especially fun because many of them can also be sung.

Now, sing "Itsy-Bitsy Spider." Please remember, this lesson must be front-loaded with the reading of nursery rhymes during read-aloud and shared reading times. **ELL** Frontload the Lesson—Make Connections. Making connections with work already covered provides ELLs with something familiar in which to ground their comprehension of new material. This allows the ELLs to feel comfortable taking part in the conversation.

When I sang "Itsy-Bitsy Spider," did you hear the rhythm or sound of this story? This type of story is called a nursery rhyme. Nursery rhymes are also made up of the story elements we've discussed. Nursery rhymes are usually short and have a nice rhythm and rhyme. Many nursery rhymes have been put to music, just like "Itsy-Bitsy Spider." Children usually enjoy them because they are fun to sing and chant.

Teach Model what students need to learn and do

Friends, in this lesson, we are going to read, reread, sing, and act out some well-known nursery rhymes that have been around for a long time; they are classics.

Have your Story Elements Bookmark or chart available to refer to as you notice the story elements in the nursery rhymes.

Take note that these nursery rhymes are stories. They have the same story elements. Listen for the characters, setting, events, and conclusion. Nursery rhymes may be shorter and simpler than other stories, but they are considered stories because of the use of story elements. Nursery rhymes are special because they have been around for so long.

Listen as I read "Pat-a-Cake."

Read "Pat-a-Cake." Emphasize the pattern of language and rhythm when reading this nursery rhyme. Use hand motions to accompany the words of the story. Encourage children to join in with you. Help them connect the meaning of the words with the hand motions: pat a cake, roll it, pat it, mark it, put it in the oven, and so on. Reread it a second time to make sure all the children are able to participate with the hand motions. Discuss the story elements with the students. **ELL** Enable Language Production—Increasing Interaction. Modeling the actions while reciting the nursery rhyme will help ELLs acquire new words and language structures.

As I read "Pat-a-Cake," did you hear the rhythm? Did you enjoy doing the hand motions? Nursery rhymes are fun. I love to read, sing, and act out nursery rhymes. Let's read another nursery rhyme together. This one is called "Row, Row, Row Your Boat." This has a nice tune to it. Listen as I sing it the first time, then join in with me and add hand motions to match the words.

As I said, nursery rhymes are often stories with story elements. In "Pat-a-Cake" there are story elements. There is a baker in a kitchen making the cake that he finally shares with others. Do you see how this is a story? Today, you and your partners will have a chance to reread, sing, and act out nursery rhymes.

You may choose to add hand motions or actually move your whole body to go along with the words.

Try Guide students to quickly rehearse what they need to learn and do in preparation for practice

> Let's try it together. Sing "Row, Row, Row Your Boat."

Guide students to listen and read closely to examine the words needed to create hand motions that match the words. Discuss the very simple story elements in this rhyme. See if the students can figure out that the character is the reader or listener (referred to as *you* in the rhyme)! The setting is the stream. The event is rowing down the stream. It concludes by comparing life on the stream to a dream.

> Now, I will read "Who Took the Cookies"? As I read it, think of hand and body movements that may go along with the words. Remember how we added movements to "Itsy-Bitsy Spider," "Pat-a-Cake," and "Row, Row, Row Your Boat."

Give students some space, and offer ideas for hand and body movements for the students to copy. Students should be encouraged to join in, even if their movements are different than yours. Make sure to use your eyes and facial expressions as well as your arms and bodies. As you act out the nursery rhymes, make sure to help the students notice the story elements and think of actions for each of them. **ELL** Enable Language Production—Increasing Interaction. When ELLs are allowed to freely interpret the nursery rhymes through facial expressions and body language, they are able to practice their understanding of new stories in a low-anxiety way and express comprehension non-verbally. At this moment, you are only requiring them to work on one part of language at a time: listening.

Clarify Briefly restate today's teaching objective and explain the practice task(s)

> Friends, today you are going to have fun reading, singing, and acting out nursery rhymes. Remember to think about the story elements: characters, setting, events, and conclusion as you imagine the actions to match the words. This will be helpful. You may imagine movements for more than one rhyme if time allows.

Practice Students work independently and/or in small groups to apply today's teaching objective

Allow students to act out additional nursery rhymes that have been read aloud previously, or they may play with those modeled in the lesson. Students may work in small groups. **ELL** Enable Language Production—Increasing Interaction. Providing collaborative tasks lets ELLs check their understanding of the assignment as they interact with more-proficient peers and gives them a chance to hear models of fluent language. As you move around the room, help children with identifying the story elements of the nursery rhymes. Model using the Story Elements Bookmark or chart to help keep track of the story elements. This will help them remember or imagine hand and body motions. For example, if a group is acting out "Five Little Monkeys," they would know the monkeys are the characters; the setting is in their bed; and the events are jumping on the bed, bumping their heads, and mama calling the doctor. Finally, the conclusion is the doctor saying that the monkeys are not allowed on the bed anymore.

While students work in small groups, it is a great opportunity to circulate and encourage students to engage effectively in collaborative discussions by following agreed-upon rules for discussions: listening with care, one voice speaking at a time, and building on the thoughts of others. Help students notice how we can build upon others' ideas and express thoughts, feelings, and ideas clearly. (SL.K.1a, SL.K.1b, SL.K.6)

Wrap Up Check understanding as you guide students to share briefly what they have learned and produced today

Gather students back together as a group. Have the groups share their rhyme with their hand and body motions, making sure they share the title first. Help the children to see that each story element has an action to accompany it. **ELL** Enable Language Production—Listening and Speaking. Allowing plenty of wait time gives ELLs the chance to put their ideas into words. When you are forming groups, consider members who may speak an ELL's home language so that, if needed, the group discussion could be in English and the home language.

Goal	Low-Tech	High-Tech
Students revisit and creatively share favorite classic stories.	Students take turns sharing their nursery rhymes to small groups of children from your class or another class.	Students share their nursery rhymes, creating YouTube videos to share with children in your own class, other classes, and friends and family.

Reading Lesson 5 . . . .

▼ Teaching Objective

Readers notice what they like about story elements and why.

Close Reading Opportunity

▼ Standards Alignment

RL.K.1, RL.K.3, RL.K5, RL.K.7, RL.K.10, W.K.1, SL.K.1a, SL.K.1b, SL.K.2, SL.K.3, SL.K.6, L.K.1, L.K.6

▼ Materials

- *No, David!* by David Shannon (or another book with strong story elements)
- *Duck on a Bike* by David Shannon (or another book written by the same author as your first book, with strong story elements)
- Storybooks in baskets that match interests of students in class, connecting to favorite authors, illustrators, and themes
- Story Elements Bookmarks
- Story Elements Chart
- I Like/I Also Like Graphic Organizers for students (see page 32)

▼ To the Teacher

The goal of Reading Lesson 5 is for students to deepen their understanding of story elements through exploration of new stories. Before this lesson, it is important to know what stories your students like and why these stories resonate with them. Having this knowledge will help you fill the book baskets (or tablets, if your school has them) with books that match your students' interests and needs. As a reader, it helps me tremendously to know what I like about a story. I hunt for books written by authors I love and topics that interest me. Learning about personal likes and dislikes will help your students for the rest of their lives. This is what we do as readers! Help your students get to know themselves as readers and capture the joy that the children experience as they find new stories to love. Before today's lesson, make sure to read *No, David!* by David Shannon (or another book of your choice with strong story elements) with the class and list it on the Stories We Love Chart.

▼ Procedure

Warm Up Gather the class to set the stage for today's learning

Friends, yesterday we had fun reading, singing, and acting out classic nursery rhymes.

Today we are going to continue our study of story. Remember how we listed the stories we love earlier in this lesson set? Well, today we are going to find new stories to love.

Teach Model what students need to learn and do

Have a copy of *No, David!* and *Duck on a Bike* by David Shannon (or your two selections authored by the same person), and show the covers, pointing out the author's name. **ELL** Provide Comprehensible Input—Visuals. Original texts and visuals offer ELLs a pathway to understanding without relying only on the words. If you do not have original texts, use pictures; include hand-drawn pictures or clip art to illustrate the lesson.

> As a reader, I have my favorite stories. However, I like to continually find new stories to enjoy. The other day I reread one of our favorite books, *No, David!* After reading this book, I thought . . . hmm . . . I really like how this book makes me laugh. Then I thought . . . I wonder if I can find more stories just like this one. So, I searched for similar books online and found this book, *Duck on a Bike*. David Shannon is the author of this story AND *No, David!*

> Listen as I read *Duck on a Bike*. As I read, listen for the story elements: characters, setting, events, and conclusion.

Read *Duck on a Bike*. Point out story elements as you encounter them.
Ask: *What did you like about this story?*

🗨 Guide students to incorporate story elements as part of their response; for example, "The *characters* in both these stories are silly," or "The *setting* of the book was beautiful." Encourage more conversations about the various story elements students identify. For example, some students may refer to the humorous *events* in the book. Help them notice that they may like the funny events in one story, so they may look for other books with funny events. (SL.K.1b)

> Readers often think about the characters and if they like them or not. Readers think about the settings of stories and either feel connected to familiar places or enjoy learning about new places. Readers like to read about plots similar to their lives and plots that are hard to imagine. As a reader, I like books with happy endings or conclusions. Some readers like endings that seem just like life. As readers, we think about the story elements in stories and try to find stories similar to the ones we already like.

Try Guide students to quickly rehearse what they need to learn and do in preparation for practice

Have available for students baskets of books that contain books from your read-alouds and new books that are similar in author, illustrator, or character. For example, if you know students like Froggy, include new Froggy books in the baskets.

> OK, now it is your turn to browse these book baskets and find a new story that may interest you. Remember, sometimes we look for stories that are similar to stories we already like. As you look through the baskets, think about our list of the Stories We Love and talk with your friends about some of your old favorites and why you like these books.

Some questions to help students connect what they enjoy to story elements:

- Do you like the characters? What about them?
- Do you like the setting? What do you like about it?
- Are the events interesting? Why do you find them interesting?
- How does the conclusion make you feel? What makes you feel this way?

Circulate the room and listen to students in their partnerships as they look through the basket of books. Take note of students who use the story elements in their conversations. Allow students 5 to 10 minutes to talk together. **ELL** Enable Language Production—Increasing Interaction. Your ELLs likely already have strong opinions about the books they know! However, they may not have the words to express what they feel. Peer interaction will help ELLs find the language they need.

🗨 As you listen in to various partnerships, take the opportunity to reinforce respectful speaking and listening behaviors such as listening to others and taking turns speaking about the topics and texts under discussion. (SL.K.1b)

Clarify Briefly restate today's teaching objective and explain the practice task(s)

I like . . .	I also like . . .

After students have had time to browse book baskets and talk with partners, refocus the class.

I love to reread old favorite stories and to find new stories to add to my list of favorites. Did you find new books that you think you may like? Why do you think you would like these new books?

Guide students to share, with a focus on story elements.

Today during Practice, I want you to continue to browse through these baskets of stories. Think about books you already like; then try to find a book that is similar in some way. You can track your thinking on this I Like/I Also Like Graphic Organizer. Notice that on the left side it says, "I like . . ." and on the right side it says, " I also like . . ." and on the bottom it says, "because . . ." Jot down a book you currently like on the left side, and once you find a similar book you like, jot it down on the right side. Finally, be prepared to tell your partner a reason you like both books, using the word *because*. When we come back together, I would like you to bring your graphic organizer to share with your partner. Happy reading!

I Like/I Also Like Graphic Organizer

I like . . .	I also like . . .
Because . . .	

ELL Provide Comprehensible Input—Organizers. Putting the work to be done in the form of a table can help visually clarify the task for ELLs.

Practice Students work independently and/or in small groups to apply today's teaching objective

Students will read from the baskets of storybooks. As students are reading, check in with individual students to monitor student understanding. **ELL** Identify and Communicate Content and Language Objectives—Language Form and Function. This organizer provides sentence stems and connecting words that ELLs will need in their peer conversations. Draw their attention to these scaffolds, and model how to use them.

Do students look for books based on interest? As the students read the books, do they use their understanding of story elements to better understand and enjoy the story? Look over their graphic organizers to see if students are able to form and share opinions about books they like through pictures and words. Do their opinions center around story elements? Help them make these connections. This is a nice opportunity for an oral rehearsal of the thinking needed to meet writing standard W.K.1.

Wrap Up Check understanding as you guide students to share briefly what they have learned and produced today

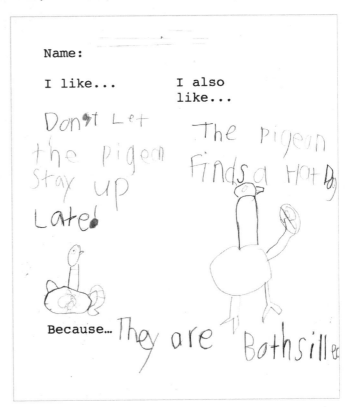

Gather the class back at your meeting area. Ask students to share their graphic organizer with their partners, making sure they share why they like both books and refer to specific story elements. Circulate and join in supporting students to use their past interests in books and story

elements as they share a new favorite story. Encourage students to speak audibly and express thoughts, feelings, and ideas clearly. (SL.K.6)

> Did you find new stories to add to our Stories We Love Chart? Patrick, I noticed you brought *The Pigeon Wants a Puppy* by Mo Willems. Why did you like this story?

Guide conversation to connect student preferences with story elements as you have a few students share with the whole group.

Jot book titles down for future read-alouds. Guide the conversation around making connections between past favorites and new favorites, referring to the story elements in the discussion.

Reading Lesson 6

▼ Teaching Objective

Readers revisit stories through retelling.

Close Reading Opportunity

▼ Standards Alignment

RL.K.1, RL.K.2, RL.K.3, RL.K.7, RL.K.10, SL.K.1a, SL.K.1b, SL.K.2, SL.K.3, SL.K.6, L.K.1, L.K.6

▼ Materials

- *The Carrot Seed* by Ruth Krauss (or a book of your choice with strong story elements)
- *The Little Red Hen* by Paul Galdone (or a book of your choice with strong story elements)
- Baskets of books the students have read throughout the lesson set, including books from class read-alouds
- Charting materials to create *Little Red Hen* Story Elements Chart

▼ To the Teacher

Today you will introduce the students to retelling. Share with your students that retelling is to tell something again, focusing on the important parts. Retelling helps students think about and better understand the stories they read. Retelling helps us decide what is most important in a story, and that helps us know the main idea. Make sure to refer to what happens in both the pictures and the words as you retell the story. Include the words *problem* and *solution* in your conversations when appropriate. Also, help students

remember the author's name when appropriate. Be sure to read *The Carrot Seed* by Ruth Kraus or another story with strong story elements to the class in advance, and chart it on the Stories We Love Chart.

▼ Procedure

Warm Up Gather the class to set the stage for today's learning

Revisit of the class list of new favorite stories created in Reading Lesson 5.

> Friends, yesterday we thought about our favorite stories and looked for new stories to love. When browsing new storybooks, we looked closely at the authors, illustrators, and story elements.

Teach Model what students need to learn and do

Today's lesson asks students to listen for and note when they hear story elements. This portion of the lesson provides you with an excellent opportunity to take note of students' ability to listen and comprehend a story told aloud. (SL.K.2)

> Today we are going to learn about retelling. Retelling means "to tell something again." Readers read stories and then retell the stories to others. To retell well, one must retell mostly the important parts. The important parts are the story elements we've discussed: character, setting, events, and conclusion. Listen as I retell one of our Stories We Love, *The Carrot Seed* by Ruth Krauss. I will use my fingers and hand to make sure I only retell the important parts and keep them in order.

As you retell the story, use your first finger (thumb) for the characters; second (index finger) for the setting; third, fourth, and fifth fingers for major events; and your closed hand to share the conclusion. Use transition

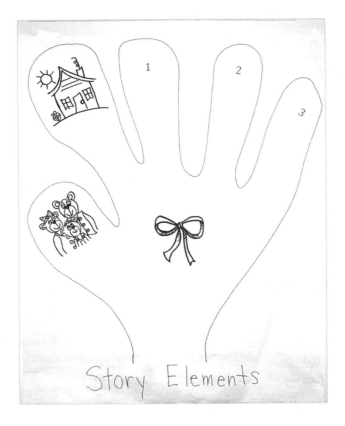

Story Elements

words such as *first, next, then,* and *finally.* **ELL** Identify and Communicate Content and Language Objectives—Academic Vocabulary. Here you are teaching your ELLs about a set of high-utility words that authors use across the curriculum to help readers understand the flow of a text. Using your fingers as a simple visualization will assist ELLs with retaining newly acquired vocabulary.

Telling a Story Across Your Hand

Characters (thumb)
Setting (index finger)
Three major events in the plot (across next three fingers)
Conclusion (close hand when sharing conclusion)

The title of this book is *The Carrot Seed,* and the author is Ruth Krauss. The little boy is the main character, and his mother, father, and brother are also characters. The setting of the book is in his yard. First, the boy plants a carrot seed. Next, his mother, father, and brother all tell him that the carrot seed will not grow. Then the boy ignores them and weeds and waters the seed. Finally, the boy's hard work pays off and his carrots grow.

This is retelling. Did you notice how I retold all the important parts using the story elements? Retelling helps me slow down and really think about the stories I read. To retell well, I must use the story elements to decide the most important parts. Retelling helps me better understand the stories I love and gives me a chance to share these stories with others.

ELL Provide Comprehensible Input—Modeling, Visuals. This retelling strategy, accompanied by the mnemonic of ticking off on one's fingers and by the poster explaining the finger strategy, will help make the task at hand very clear to your ELLs and help them keep their thinking organized as they search for the right language.

Try Guide students to quickly rehearse what they need to learn and do in preparation for practice

Now let students have a try at retelling, using the story elements. First read *The Little Red Hen,* using the illustrations as you read.

OK, now it is your turn to retell. Let's retell *The Little Red Hen* by Paul Galdone. Remember that in order to retell well, we must think about the story elements. This will help us decide what is important in the story. Let's use our fingers and hand to keep track of the story elements and the order of events.

Guide students to first state the title. When appropriate, help students with the author's name.

Then retell across your hand as above.

Clarify Briefly restate today's teaching objective and explain the practice task(s)

Friends, when we retell stories, we use the story elements to slow down and think about the most important parts of the story to share. That's what we just did together retelling the most important parts of *The Little Red Hen.*

Recap the retelling on a chart. **ELL** Provide Comprehensible Input—Graphic Organizers. This chart will help your ELLs understand your lesson and will be an anchor they can refer back to later. Use words and illustrations to show thinking.

Little Red Hen Story Elements

Characters	Little Red Hen, Cat, Dog, and Mouse
Setting	Cozy house, a farm field
Event #1	Little Red Hen asks for help, but no one helps her to do the housework or plant the wheat.
Event #2	Little Red Hen cuts the wheat, carries the wheat, and turns it into flour.
Event #3	Little Red Hen makes a cake and the others ask to eat the cake, but she does not share because they did not help.
Conclusion	Finally, Cat, Dog, and Mouse learn that they must help Little Red Hen.

Practice Students work independently and/or in small groups to apply today's teaching objective

Students will choose books from baskets to retell, using their hand to keep track of the story elements.

Wrap Up Check understanding as you guide students to share briefly what they have learned and produced today

Annie Pickert Fuller/Pearson Education

Call students back to the meeting area, reminding them to bring one book to retell to their partner. Gather data as students share with partners, assessing their use and understanding of the story elements as they retell. Do students know the characters and setting? Do they choose important events to retell? Do students share the ending? It is important to listen in on all students. **ELL** Assess for Content and Language Understanding—Formative Assessment. This is an opportunity for you to assess your ELLs' language needs, especially listening skills, and use this information to inform upcoming lessons. You can also check for any confusion about the lesson's content that might be based on language barriers.

Analyze student's retelling of stories as a performance-based assessment to determine if students need additional instruction or support as a whole class, in small groups, or one on one.

Milestone Performance Assessment

Retelling Stories Using the Story Elements

 Use this checklist to assess the use of story elements to retell stories.

Standards Alignment: RL.K.1, RL.K.2, RL.K.3, RL.K.7, SL.K.1a, SL.K.1b, SL.K.2, SL.K.6

Task	Achieved	Notes
Identify important characters in retelling.		
Identify setting in retelling.		
Retell major events.		
Include conclusion in retelling.		
Speak audibly when retelling.		

Reading Lesson 7

▼ Teaching Objective

Readers compare the experiences of characters across books.

Close Reading Opportunity

▼ Standards Alignment

RL.K.1, RL.K.3, RL.K.9, RL.K.10, SL.K.1 a, SL.K.1b, SL.K.2, SL.K.3, SL.K.6, L.K.1, L.K.6

▼ Materials

- *Koala Lou* by Mem Fox
- *Olivia Acts Out* by Ian Falconer
- *Tacky the Penguin* by Helen Lester
- *Wemberly Worried* by Kevin Henkes

- Optionally, any books of your choice with characters who have similar but not identical experiences
- Charting supplies or interactive whiteboard to create Character Experiences Chart
- Pairs of texts with strong characters for students to compare in practice

▼ To the Teacher

This lesson needs to be frontloaded by having read stories with strong characters to your students during past whole-class read-alouds. You can refer back to the Stories We Love Chart and identify the stories with strong characters and plots. In our Teach and Try, we compare the main characters of *Wemberly Worried* to *Koala Lou* and *Tacky the Penguin* to *Olivia Acts Out*. Reading these books in advance will allow you to use your lesson time addressing the teaching point. The goal of this lesson is to compare and contrast the adventures and experiences of characters across books. If you don't have the suggested books, any two books that have characters with similar but not identical experiences would be very suitable.

▼ Procedure

Warm Up Gather the class to set the stage for today's learning

> Friends, today we are going to continue talking and thinking about stories. As I look at our list of favorite stories, I notice there are some characters we all love. I think we love these characters for different reasons. We may love them because they are fun, adventurous, courageous, or silly or because they seem like good friends. Some characters are just like us and others are quite different. All of these different reasons are what make us want to read these characters' stories.
>
> As we look back at our Stories We Love Chart, who can name a character we enjoy reading about in books?

Teach Model what students need to learn and do

For this lesson, *Tacky the Penguin* and *Olivia Acts Out* are good selections to compare and contrast. The authors provide detailed descriptions of these characters, which will support the children's ability to compare and contrast their experiences.

> We have read, reread, sung, acted out, and retold many stories together. Today, we are going to look closely at the plots of stories we have read. We will discuss and chart how two characters are similar and different. Let's think about how some books remind us of other books because of what the characters experience in the story.
>
> When I think about these two books, *Tacky the Penguin* and *Olivia Acts Out*, I notice that some of their experiences are similar, or alike, and some are different, or not alike.

ELL Frontload the Lesson—Set a Purpose for Reading. Narrowing students' listening goals will allow ELLs to focus on processing the most important information and help them filter out extraneous details.

Create a chart here to jot down thoughts as you think aloud about these characters and their experiences in the stories.

Character Experiences Chart

Just Tacky	Both Characters	Just Olivia
Swims with friends in cold weather	Spend time with friends	Acts in a play with friends at school
Plays a loud instrument instead of singing sweetly like friends	Sometimes cause problems with friends	Calls out during play instead of following the script
Scares hunters so they leave friends alone	Help friends in need	Whispers lines to friend to save the play

Review the story elements—character, setting, events, and conclusion—as you think aloud.

> Tacky and Olivia have some similar and different experiences. When I read about Tacky, his experiences make me think of Olivia. This is what we do as readers. When we read and reread, we think about characters from other books and how their experiences are similar, or alike, and different, or not alike, across stories.

Try Guide students to quickly rehearse what they need to learn and do in preparation for practice

> Let's think about *Wemberly Worried* and *Koala Lou*.

Create a chart to record students' thinking, using both pictures and words. **ELL** Provide Comprehensible Input—Graphic Organizers. Tables and charts help ELLs to understand the sense behind what others are saying and to express their own thoughts in an orderly way. Make sure to guide students to use the story elements to think about the similarities and differences of the experiences of the characters. Use *alike* and *not alike* to help students understand similarities and differences.

> OK, hmmm . . . let's think about the characters and the setting of these books. What experiences are similar, or alike, for Wemberly and Koala?

Jot down similar experiences in the center of the chart.

> What experiences are different, or not alike, for these characters?

Guide students to be specific when sharing their thoughts about similarities and differences. For example, both Wemberly and Koala have worries. Wemberly is worried about attending school. Koala is worried that her mother does not love her anymore.

Continue adding items to the chart as per the discussion with the class.

Clarify Briefly restate today's teaching objective and explain the practice task(s)

Today we are paying close attention to the similarities and differences between two characters and their experiences in the stories. We are thinking deeply about how characters and their experiences are alike and different across two books. Remember to use the story elements as you think about the two characters and their experiences.

Practice Students work independently and/or in small groups to apply today's teaching objective

Have baggies for each partnership, containing two books for them to read, think about, and discuss the characters' similar and different experiences. Providing familiar books will scaffold students' ability to work independently. **ELL** Enable Language Production—Reading and Writing. Using previously read books is a way to scaffold ELLs' work in this lesson—they will already

be familiar with both the content of the stories and the language needed to discuss them. You can also use books of varying complexity to accommodate different students' proficiency levels. Circulate the room and guide students to use the story elements as they think about characters and their experiences across stories.

Wrap Up Check understanding as you guide students to share briefly what they have learned and produced today

Gather students in your meeting area. **ELL** Enable Language Production—Increasing Interaction. ELLs will have the opportunity to share what they have been working on in a low-pressure environment and hear models of proficient English from their peers. Have students share with a partner their thinking about characters from two different books. Move around as students are sharing, and assess if they are using story elements to think about characters and their experiences across books. When we think closely about characters in this way, it helps us better understand and enjoy what we are reading.

As you circulate around the room, encourage students to listen closely to each other and build upon others' thoughts. (SL.K.1b)

Reading Lesson 8 ·

▼ Teaching Objective

Readers think about story elements as they act out stories in reader's theater.

Close Reading
Opportunity

▼ Standards Alignment

RL.K.1, RL.K.3, RL.K.10, SL.K.1a, SL.K.1b, SL.K.2, SL.K.3, SL.K.6,. L.K.1, L.K.6

▼ Materials

- *"Slowly, Slowly, Slowly," Said the Sloth* by Eric Carle (or alternate play "Animal Friends" provided in Appendix K.4)
- Charting paper for *"Slowly, Slowly, Slowly," Said the Sloth* to be displayed

▼ To the Teacher

This lesson must be frontloaded by having read the book *"Slowly, Slowly, Slowly," Said the Sloth* as a shared reading experience so that children are familiar with the story, words, and sounds of the book. Have a chart prepared, with the words from the book clearly displayed, using color to identify each group's speaking parts. **ELL** Provide Comprehensible Input—Graphic Organizers. A chart makes your instruction easier to understand and provides ELLs with a model to refer back to when working independently. The last page does not need to be on the chart paper, as the teacher should read this page. The vocabulary is wonderful; however, it is too difficult for most kindergartners to read.

Also have each group's lines on sentence strips, ideally written in the same color as on the class chart, for them to take away and practice. This will help students know when it is their turn to speak.

Today is a chance to have fun while strengthening your students' speaking and listening skills. Take note how we emphasize the importance of students reading slowly, clearly, and with expression to entertain the audience. Additionally, we teach students to be good listeners by reminding them that their body should face the speakers, with their eyes and ears open and mouth closed. Finally, notice how we guide students to think about beginning, middle, and ending by having them identify when their lines will come up. This is a concrete way to help students to think about the structure of story.

If *"Slowly, Slowly, Slowly," Said the Sloth* is not available to you, we have provided the alternate script "Animal Friends" in Appendix K.4 that may be used for this lesson.

▼ Procedure

Warm Up Gather the class to set the stage for today's learning

Present the plan for today's reading together.

> We have been studying some excellent stories. Today we are going to continue our study by performing a reader's theater together.

Teach Model what students need to learn and do

Explain to the class that reader's theater is a form of drama in which people read a book together, taking turns reading the lines. In reader's theater, the readers read slowly, clearly, and with expression to entertain the audience. **ELL** Identify and Communicate Content and Language Objectives—Language Form and Function. Reader's theater will help ELLs rehearse language structures as they are used in texts, while reinforcing their understanding of story elements.

> We have enjoyed sharing the reading of Eric Carle's book "*Slowly, Slowly, Slowly," Said the Sloth*. Who remembers the main character? Who are the other characters? Where and when is the setting? Would someone remind us of the major events of this story? Don't forget the ending!

Congratulate the children for remembering the story elements. Let them know that we use books/texts that we have read and reread many times for

reader's theater so we can focus on reading slowly, clearly, and with expression. Remind the students that reader's theater is meant to entertain the listening audience. Good listeners have their body facing the speakers, with their eyes and ears open and mouth closed.

> Students, as I read, please remember to listen with your body facing me, the speaker, with your eyes and ears open and mouth closed.

After you have modeled reading the story and students have practiced listening well, give students their lines on sentence strips. Match the color of the writing on the sentence strips to the chart to help children know when it is their turn to speak. **ELL** Provide Comprehensible Input—Visuals. Matching colors in this part of the lesson will make it clear to ELLs when it is their turn to speak, in case they find oral directions more difficult to follow. Put children in groups of two to four to read their lines.

Pass out the sentence strips and explain that the color of the writing on the chart matches the color of the writing on the sentence strips. Explain that they will read their sentence strips at the appropriate time and listen to their classmates read their sentence strips. Remind them that they know the sequence of the story, and ask students to silently read along on the chart until it is their turn to read. Ask the students to notice if their lines are in the beginning, middle, or end of the story.

Try Guide students to quickly rehearse what they need to learn and do in preparation for practice

> Did you notice how I read slowly, clearly, and with expression? Did you enjoy listening to me read the story? Now it is your turn. Whisper read your lines quietly to yourself. Think about how the character might sound.

Circulate and help students as they practice whisper reading individually. **ELL** Enable Language Production—Listening and Speaking, Reading and Writing. Like all your students, ELLs will benefit from this rehearsal time, so they can feel confident when it is their turn to share before the group. In addition, this is an opportunity for you to tailor this task to your students' individual proficiency levels: More advanced ELLs can get sentences with more complex structures.

Clarify Briefly restate today's teaching objective and explain the practice task(s)

OK, today you are going to practice your line(s) with your partners. Remember to read slowly, clearly, and with expression. Think about the meaning of your line to help you with how to say it.

Also, think about if your lines are in the beginning, middle, or ending of the story. Who speaks right before you? This will help you to be ready to read when it is your turn.

Practice Students work independently and/or in small groups to apply today's teaching objective

Students will practice reading their lines with their partners. **ELL** Enable Language Production—Increasing Interaction. ELLs can work with English-proficient peers to learn how to pronounce their lines correctly and to hear reinforcement of correct sentence structure.

Today's independent practice will only last 5 to 10 minutes, as you will need time to perform the reader's theater during Wrap Up.

Circulate around the room and help students read slowly, clearly, and with expression. Remind students to think about the story and to remember if their lines are in the beginning, middle, or ending of the story and who speaks right before them. This will help their preparedness. Also, as you circulate and listen in on students, take this opportunity to reinforce essential speaking and listening skills such as following agreed-upon rules and speaking audibly and clearly. (SL.K.1b, SL.K.6)

Wrap Up Check understanding as you guide students to share briefly what they have learned and produced today

Friends, it is time for us to come back together and perform our reader's theater of Eric Carle's *"Slowly, Slowly, Slowly," Said the Sloth.* Let's make sure

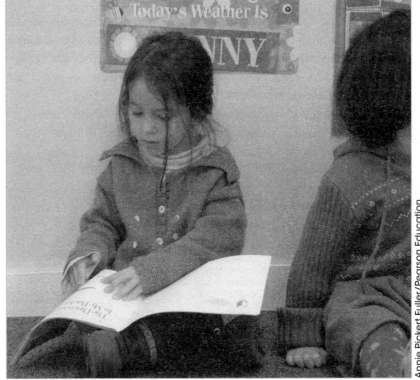

Annie Pickert Fuller/Pearson Education

to sit with our partners and think about if our lines take place in the beginning, middle, or ending of the story. I will be the final reader, reading the last page of the story. Remember to read slowly, clearly, and with expression. Also, remember to listen with your body facing the speakers and your eyes and ears open, but your mouth closed. Let's have fun!

Celebrate with your students following the reader's theater. Congratulate them on working together to perform this wonderful story in a reader's theater format.

Reading Lesson 9 ·

▼ Teaching Objective

Readers use story elements to dramatize favorite stories.

Close Reading
Opportunity

▼ Standards Alignment

RL.K.1, RL.K.3, RL.K.7, RL.K.10, SL.K.1a, SL.K.1b, SL.K.6, L.K.1, L.K.6

▼ Materials

- *The Rabbit and the Turtle* by Eric Carle
- Charting supplies or interactive whiteboard
- Story Elements Bookmark and Story Elements Chart

▼ To the Teacher

Include some classic fables in your read-alouds before today's lesson so you can refer back to them. "The Lion and the Mouse," "The Rabbit and the Turtle," "The Grasshopper and the Ants," and "The Cat and the Mouse" are four wonderful fables that can be found in Eric Carle's book *The Rabbit and the Turtle*. If you don't have this book, short fables are easy to find on the Internet. We suggest fables because of their succinct, clear story elements and to expose young children to this classic form of literature. Students could use practically any short story or picture book with strong story elements to dramatize in small groups.

Consider having a drama center filled with dress-up clothes, small toys, paper and other materials for creating props, cubes with the story elements on each side to prompt storytelling, and picture books from your read-alouds. Playacting comes naturally to most children, and they will love the opportunity to act out their favorite stories from books or their imaginations throughout the year.

▼ Procedure

Warm Up Gather the class to set the stage for today's learning

Gather students to the meeting area. Congratulate them on a job well done with reader's theater. Explain today's plan.

> Reader's theater is a form of drama. A drama is a kind of writing that people act out—like a play or a TV show. Today we are going to act out some of our favorite stories. Acting out a story through words and actions is another form of drama. Acting out a story is fun and helps us to work on our speaking and listening skills, while entertaining our audience.

Teach Model what students need to learn and do

As you teach this lesson, make sure to refer to the illustrations as the children recall the story. **ELL** Provide Comprehensible Input—Visuals. Visuals offer ELLs a pathway to understanding without relying only on the words. The goal of today's lesson is for the children to use the story elements to help them imagine a play that represents a familiar story. Model using the Story Elements Bookmark to track your thinking. The lines do not need to be written down and can change from Practice to Wrap Up. Divide students in small groups before the lesson.

> Friends, do you remember the story *The Rabbit and the Turtle*? This story is called a *fable*. A fable is another type of classic story. Fables use story elements to tell us a story and teach us a lesson
>
> Let's talk about this story:
>
> - Who are the characters in this story?
> - What is the setting (where and when)?
> - What are the major events?
> - How does the story end?
> - What did we learn from this story?

Let students answer the questions as you think aloud.

> These are the questions that come to my mind as I read a fable. Notice that we added "What did we learn from this story?" to our usual list of story elements. A lesson is another kind of story element that fables are known for. The characters, setting, events, and conclusion of a fable come together to teach a lesson.

Fill in a blank story elements chart as you talk through the elements for this fable.

> Now we know the story. Let's imagine how we can act this out in a small group. Let's use the story elements to make plans for our play.

Here is what your chart may look like:

Rabbit and Turtle Story Elements

Characters	Rabbit, Turtle, Fox, and other animals
Setting	Outside, day, and into the night
Event #1	Rabbit wants to race Turtle
Event #2	When Rabbit and Turtle are racing, Rabbit takes a nap because he is so far ahead of Turtle. Turtle passes Rabbit sleeping.
Event #3	Rabbit wakes up and tries to catch up to Turtle.
Conclusion	Turtle wins the race by working hard and not sleeping.
Lesson	Hard work and persistence pay off!

Try Guide students to quickly rehearse what they need to learn and do in preparation for practice

This is an opportunity to reinforce the importance of speaking audibly and expressing ideas clearly. (SL.K.6) Refer back to Reading Lesson 8 and remind students that we must speak slowly, clearly, and with expression for the audience to understand and enjoy the story. **ELL** Enable Language Production—Listening and Speaking. Modeling the kind of language you expect lets ELLs hear how such language sounds, rather than leaving them trying to interpret an abstract description of such language. This is also a great opportunity to show students what active listening as an audience member looks like and sounds like:

• body faces the speaker(s)

• eyes and ears open

• mouth closed

OK, now that we know all the story elements, let's act out this story. There is no one correct way to act it out, but we do need to use the story elements so the audience can follow along. Work with your small groups to imagine how you might act out "The Rabbit and the Turtle." This is a quick production. We are having fun using our imaginations to tell our friends these stories through plays.

Circulate and help children use the story elements as they are using their imaginations. Remind students to refer to their Story Elements Bookmarks and class chart to track the story.

Clarify Briefly restate today's teaching objective and explain the practice task(s)

Refocus students' attention. Let them stay in their groups around the room. Provide another story, or let them choose one, for them to act out.

OK, nice job working together in your groups. I noticed how you thought about the story elements and used these to help you imagine a play. Now, let's try this again with some other fables. Once I give you another story to act out, remember to work together and use the story elements as you imagine your play of the story.

Have the chart used earlier in the lesson clearly displayed for reference. **ELL** Provide Comprehensible Input—Graphic Organizers. ELLs can refer back to this resource to help them order their thinking as they act out the fables. You might let students review illustrations from the story to help them recall the story elements for imagining their plays.

Practice Students work independently and/or in small groups to apply today's teaching objective

Nailia Schwarz/Fotolia

Students work in small groups, using the story elements to help them imagine and act out their stories. Offer construction paper and markers in case they would like to make props to accompany the story. Some may make masks, puppets, or background scenes. Let the children be creative, and provide choices through art supplies for how they might dramatize the fables. Give them enough time to have fun, but emphasize that there is no expectation for a formal play production. **ELL** Enable Language Production—Increasing Interaction. Consider forming multi-lingual groups that include ELLs and bilingual peers, so they can act out their story in both the home language and English. Home-language support can help ELLs deepen their understanding of the content *and* learn English more quickly.

Again, the goal of today is for students to play inside of a story, using story elements as their framework.

Circulate and help students to use the story elements to jump into imagining the story as a play.

Wrap Up Check understanding as you guide students to share briefly what they have learned and produced today

Refocus students.

> As I moved around the room, I noticed how well you were using the story elements to create your plays. Many of you used your Story Elements Bookmark to keep your play focused. Now, let's celebrate by sharing our plays with each other.

As the groups take turns presenting their fables, ask them to share the title of their fable and the story elements for the group to listen and watch for as they perform. **ELL** Enable Language Production—Listening and Speaking. Having students clarify what their classmates are to look for will help ELLs focus their attention on story elements during the play. At the end, let the students share the specific lesson learned from the fable.

Note that extended time will be needed in this lesson segment for students to present their fables.

ELL Assess for Content and Language Understandings—Formative Assessment. This is an opportunity for you to assess your ELLs' language and content needs and then use this information to inform upcoming lessons.

Analyze students' performances as a performance-based assessment to determine if students need additional instruction or support as a whole class, in small groups, or one on one.

Milestone Performance Assessment

Using Story Elements to Dramatize Stories

 Use this checklist to assess student dramatization of their favorite stories.

Standards Alignment: RL.K.1, RL.8.3, SL.K.1a, SL.K.1b, SL.K.6

Task	Achieved	Notes
Speak slowly, clearly, and with expression.		
Include story elements in dramatization of fable.		
Practice good listening by facing the speaker with eyes and ears open and mouth closed when in the audience.		

Reading Lesson 10

▼ **Teaching Objective**

Readers reflect on how story elements help them.

Close Reading Opportunity

▼ **Standards Alignment**

RL.K.1, RL.K.3, RL.K.7, RL.K.10, W.K.8, SL.K.1a, SL.K.1b, SL.K.3, SL.K.6, L.K.1, L.K.6

▼ Materials

- Charting supplies or interactive whiteboard
- Stories We Love Chart (from Reading Lesson 1)
- Story Elements Chart
- Core Question displayed
- Writing paper (space for drawing and a few lines of writing)

▼ To the Teacher

Encourage students to reflect on the stories you have shared together. The goal is for your students to understand that story elements are the building blocks for many different forms of narrative.

▼ Procedure

Warm Up Gather the class to set the stage for today's learning

Refer back to your Stories We Love Chart.

Kindergartners, we have read, reread, sang, shared aloud, and acted out many old and new stories. As we look back on our list of Stories We Love, who can think of any other stories they'd like to add to the list?

ELL Enable Language Production—Listening and Speaking. Give your students, especially your ELLs, plenty of time to think about their answer to this question. ELLs may need a little more time to turn their memory of a story into the words of the title.

Let students offer any new stories they'd like to add.

What do all these stories have in common? Yes! All of these stories have story elements.

Look back on the Story Elements Chart.

You have worked very hard during this lesson set to know and use story elements to understand and enjoy stories.

Teach Model what students need to learn and do

Lead the class in a shared writing response of the Core Question: How does the understanding of story elements help us read stories?

Now that we've worked together to better understand and discuss the story elements in our reading, let's think about how we can share all that we've learned. Let's look at a Core Question for this study and see how we can answer this question as a way of learning.

💬 As the discussion unfolds, begin to craft a shared response to the question. **ELL** Provide Comprehensible Input— Summaries. You can paraphrase and condense your students' responses so that the set of things learned is organized for ELLs. Ideally, your class response should include the lessons that have been taught. Take this opportunity to connect back to past conversations from the lesson set. (SL.K.1b) However, this is truly a moment for you to assess the understanding of your class as a whole group. As students are sharing their ideas, document their thinking in a list. Then model for students how to transfer that list into complete sentences. The phrase "Studying story elements helped me to . . ." will keep the students focused in conversations. **ELL** Identify and Communicate Content and Language Objectives—Language Form and Function. Sentence stems help ELLs craft the language to express their ideas.

Try Guide students to quickly rehearse what they need to learn and do in preparation for practice

Ask students to think about the discussion around what we have learned as a group. Then ask them to turn and talk with a partner to discuss what has most helped them as individuals. **ELL** Enable Language Production— Increasing Interaction. ELLs can consolidate their learning by hearing their peers' answers and by practicing articulating their own thoughts.

Guide students to think, "Studying story elements helped me to . . ." Students may respond:

- ". . . learn that all stories have a character, a setting, events, and a conclusion."
- ". . . know if the character is mean or nice, which helps me understand the story."
- ". . . know the setting, and that helps me know where the story is happening."
- ". . . watch for events, which helps me know what the character does. Also, it helps me decide if I like the character or want to be the character."

- "...enjoy the story because I like reading about what happens."
- "...discover that when we like a character we can try to find more books about him or her."
- "...know there will be an ending. The ending helps me see what happens to the character and his or her friends at the end."

Clarify Briefly restate today's teaching objective and explain the practice task(s)

Today, you are going to answer the Core Question as an individual. Think back to our group discussion and what you just shared with your partner.

Practice Students work independently and/or in small groups to apply today's teaching objective

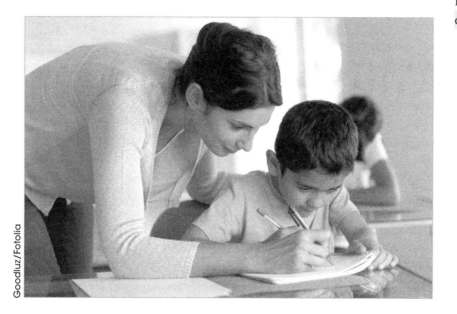

Goodluz/Fotolia

For this task, provide writing paper with room to draw and write a few lines. Students will work to write or dictate to share their thoughts on the Core Question. Encourage students to include a drawing that represents their learning about story elements. These drawings will further show how students understand that story elements make up story and help us understand our reading. **ELL** Assess for Content and Language Understandings—Summative Assessment. Allow ELLs to express their understanding of story elements using whatever skills for communication they have, including through pictures and through the home language. At the same time, listen for progress in these students' language development.

Wrap Up Check understanding as you guide students to share briefly what they have learned and produced today

Have volunteers share their writing with the class. **ELL** Assess for Content and Language Understandings—Summative Assessment.

Grade K

Writing Lessons

The Core I.D.E.A. / Daily Writing Instruction at a Glance table highlights the teaching objectives and standards alignment for all 10 lessons across the four stages of the lesson set (Introduce, Define, Extend, and Assess). It also indicates which lessons contain special features to support English language learners, technology, speaking and listening, and formative ("Milestone") assessments.

The following Core Ready Writing Rubric is designed to help you record each student's overall understanding across four levels of achievement as it relates to the lesson set goals. We recommend that you use this rubric at the end of the lesson set as a performance-based assessment tool. Use the Milestone Performance Assessments as tools to help you gauge student progress toward these goals. Reteach and differentiate instruction as needed. See the foundational book, *Be Core Ready: Powerful, Effective Steps to Implementing and Achieving the Common Core State Standards,* for more information about the Core Ready Reading and Writing Rubrics.

Grade K   Tell Me a Story: Elements of Fiction

Instructional Stage	Lesson	Teaching Objective	Core Standards	Special Features
Introduce: *notice, explore, collect, note, immerse, surround, record, share*	1	Writers tell stories.	RL.K.1 • RL.K.3 • RL.K.6 • RL.K.10 • SL.K.1a, • SL.K.1b • SL.K.2 • SL.K.3 • SL.K.6 • L.K.1 • L.K.6	ELL Close Reading Opportunity
	2	Writers get ideas from their experiences.	RL.K.1 • RL.K.3 • RL.K.10 • W.K.7 • SL.K.1a • SL.K.1b • SL.K.2 • SL.K.3 • SL.K.4 • SL.K.6 • L.K.1 • L.K.6	ELL S&L Close Reading Opportunity
Define: *name, identify, outline, clarify, select, plan*	3	Writers use story elements to create stories.	RL.K.1 • RL.K.3 • RL.K.10 • W.K.3 • W.K.7 • W.K.8 • SL.K.1a • SL.K.1b • SL.K.2 • SL.K.3 • SL.K.4 • SL.K.6 • L.K.1 • L.K.2 • L.K.6	ELL S&L Close Reading Opportunity
Extend: *try, experiment, attempt, approximate, practice, explain, revise, refine*	4	Writers write stories about their lives using story elements.	RL.K.1 • RL.K.3 • RL.K.10 • W.K.3 • W.K.5 • W.K.8 • SL.K.1a • SL.K.1b • SL.K.2 • SL.K.3 • SL.K.4 • SL.K.6 • L.K.1 • L.K.2 • L.K.6	ELL S&L Milestone Assessment Close Reading Opportunity
	5	Writers write imaginative stories using story elements.	RL.K.1 • RL.K.10 • W.K.3 • W.K.5 • SL.K.1a • SL.K.1b • SL.K.2 • SL.K.3 • SL.K.4 • SL.K.6 • L.K.1 • L.K.2 • L.K.6	ELL Tech Close Reading Opportunity
	6	Writers use their imaginations to write new versions of classic nursery rhymes.	RL.K.1 • RL.K.2 • RL.K.3 • RL.K.10 • W.K.3 • W.K.5 • SL.K.1a • SL.K.1b • SL.K.2 • SL.K.3 • SL.K.5 • SL.K.6 • L.K.1 • L.K.2 • L.K.6	ELL S&L Milestone Assessment Close Reading Opportunity
	7	Writers use their imaginations to write new versions of classic fairy tales.	RL.K.1 • RL.K.3 • RL.K.10 • W.K.3 • W.K.5 • SL.K.1a • SL.K.1b • SL.K.2 • SL.K.3 • SL.K.5 • SL.K.6 • L.K.1 • L.K.2 • L.K.6	ELL S&L Close Reading Opportunity
	8	Writers choose a favorite form of narrative writing from this lesson set to explore further.	W.K.3 • W.K.5 • W.K.8 • SL.K.1a • SL.K.1b • SL.K.3 • SL.K.5 • SL.K.6 • L.K.1 • L.K.2 • L.K.6	ELL
	9	Writers publish stories.	W.K.3 • W.K.5 • W.K.6 • SL.K.1a • SL.K.1b • SL.K.3 • SL.K.5 • SL.K.6 • L.K.1 • L.K.2 • L.K.6	ELL S&L Milestone Assessment
Assess: *reflect, conclude, connect, share, recognize, respond*	10	Writers share stories with others.	W.K.3 • SL.K.1a • SL.K.1b • SL.K.3 • SL.K.4 • SL.K.5 • SL.K.6 • L.K.1 • L.K.6	ELL S&L Tech

Core Ready Writing Rubric

Grade K Tell Me a Story: Elements of Fiction

Lesson Set Goal	Emerging	Approaching	Achieving	Exceeding	Standards Alignment
Use story elements to create stories.	Student does not use the story elements to create stories.	Student attempts to use the story elements to create stories. May only include some story elements or story may contain some inaccuracies.	Student uses the story elements to create stories. Includes all the story elements.	Student demonstrates a thorough understanding of how to use the story elements to create stories. Accurately includes all of the story elements.	RL.K.1 RL.K.3 RL.K.7 RL.K.10 W.K.3 W.K.5 W.K.7 W.K.8
Use their experiences and imagination to inspire stories.	Student shows little or no evidence of using his/her experiences and imagination to inspire stories	Student shows some evidence of using his/her experiences and imagination to inspire stories. May not include all story elements or may mix up what is imaginary and what is from his/her experience.	Student shows solid evidence of using his/her experiences and imagination to inspire stories. Includes all story elements and draws from both imaginary and real experiences.	Student shows solid evidence of using his/her experiences and imagination to inspire stories. Includes all of the elements and draws from both imaginary and real experiences with cohesiveness and a logical and thoughtful flow.	W.K.7 SL.K.1a SL.K.1b SL.K.4 SL.K.5 SL.K.6 L.K.1 L.K.2 L.K.6
Orally share original stories, real or imagined.	Student shows little or no evidence of attempting to orally share original stories, real or imagined.	Student attempts to orally share original stories, real or imagined.	Student successfully orally shares original stories, real or imagined.	Student clearly, thoroughly, and effectively orally shares original stories, real or imagined.	SL.K.1a SL.K.1b SL.K.4 SL.K.5 SL.K.6 L.K.1 L.K.6
With prompting and support, ask and answer questions about key details in a text.	Student demonstrates little or no evidence of asking and/or answering questions about the text even with extensive prompting and support.	Student shows some evidence of asking and/or answering questions about key details in a text with prompting and support. Student may at times lack focus and accuracy.	Student shows solid evidence of asking and/or answering questions about key details in a text with focus and accuracy. Student may require some prompting and support.	Student demonstrates exceptional evidence of asking and/or answering questions about key details of a text with focus and accuracy. Student requires little prompting and support.	RL.K.1
Actively engage in group reading activities with purpose and understanding.	Student shows little or no evidence of engaging in group reading activities.	Student shows some evidence of effectively engaging in group reading activities with purpose and understanding.	Student shows solid evidence of actively engaging in group reading activities with purpose and understanding.	Student shows exceptional evidence of actively engaging in group reading activities with a sharp focus, sense of purpose, and thorough understanding.	RL.K.10

Lesson Set Goal	Emerging	Approaching	Achieving	Exceeding	Standards Alignment
With guidance and support from adults, respond to questions and suggestions from peers and add details to strengthen writing as needed.	Student makes little or no attempt to strengthen writing as needed by responding to feedback or adding details, even with adult prompting and support.	Student attempts to strengthen writing as needed by responding to feedback and adding details. Revisions may not connect to suggestions or strengthen piece effectively.	Student strengthens writing as needed by responding to feedback and adding details. Revisions usually connect to feedback and enhance the piece.	Student effectively strengthens writing as needed by responding to feedback and adding details. Revisions are relevant and thoughtful and consistently serve to enhance piece. May proactively seek feedback to improve writing.	W.K.5
With guidance and support from adults and peers, share writing with others in meaningful ways.	Student shows little or no evidence of attempting to share writing with others in meaningful ways.	Student attempts to share writing with others in meaningful ways.	Student successfully shares writing with others in meaningful ways. In most or all instances, student uses a variety of tools and effective collaboration to prepare the piece for presentation.	Student clearly, thoroughly, and effectively shares writing with others in a meaningful way. Student accurately uses a variety of tools and proactively seeks collaboration, when necessary, in order to prepare the piece for presentation.	W.K.6
In collaborative discussions, exhibit responsibility to the rules and roles of conversation.	Student makes little or no attempt to participate in collaborative discussions with multiple exchanges and often disregards the rules and roles of conversation even with prompting.	Student inconsistently participates in collaborative discussions with multiple exchanges. Student observes the rules and roles of conversation but needs frequent prompting.	Student usually participates in collaborative discussions with multiple exchanges. Student observes the rules and roles of conversation. May need some prompting.	Student consistently participates in collaborative discussions with multiple exchanges. Student observes the rules and roles of conversation with little or no prompting.	SL.K.1a SL.K.1b
Speak audibly and express thoughts, feelings, and ideas clearly.	Student usually lacks clarity when expressing thoughts, feelings, and ideas and/or speaks inaudibly to others.	Student sometimes lacks clarity when expressing thoughts, feelings, and ideas and/or sometimes struggles to speak audibly to others.	Student usually expresses thoughts, feelings, and ideas clearly and speaks audibly.	Student consistently expresses thoughts, feelings, and ideas clearly. May be exceptionally thoughtful or detailed when communicating ideas. Speaks audibly with energy and expression.	SL.K.6
Demonstrate knowledge of standard English and its conventions.	Student demonstrates little or no knowledge of standard English and its conventions.	Student demonstrates some evidence of knowledge of standard English and its conventions.	Student consistently demonstrates knowledge of standard English and its conventions.	Student demonstrates an exceptional understanding of standard English and its conventions. Use of conventions is sophisticated for grade level and accurate.	L.K.1 L.K.2
Use words and phrases acquired through conversations, reading and being read to, and responding to texts.	Student shows little or no evidence of the acquisition and/or use of grade-appropriate words and phrases.	Student shows some evidence of acquiring and using grade-appropriate words and phrases.	Student shows solid evidence of acquiring and using grade-appropriate words and phrases.	Student shows a high level of sophistication and precision when using grade-appropriate words and phrases.	L.K.6

Writing Lesson 1

▼ **Teaching Objective**

Writers tell stories.

▼ **Standards Alignment**

RL.K.1, RL.K.3, RL.K.6, RL.K.10, SL.K.1a, SL.K.1b, SL.K.2, SL.K.3, SL.K.6, L.K.1, L.K.6

Close Reading
Opportunity

▼ **Materials**

- Charting supplies or interactive whiteboard to create Learning about Characters chart
- Books by favorite authors
- Stories We Love Chart (created in Reading Lesson 1)
- Video clips from Readingrockets.org of David Shannon, Eric Carle, and Patricia Polacco. (David Shannon's and Eric Carle's clips are within the Video and Podcast section, under Meet the Author. Patricia Polacco can be found in the Video Interviews.)

▼ **To the Teacher**

Kindergartners are natural storytellers. They come to school eager to share the tales of their lives and imaginations. We know that kindergartners can create a story in which they are flying through the sky—and that as they tell their make-believe story, they almost believe it is true! This lesson set is about capturing your students' love for story and offering them the tools to tell a story, across many forms of narrative.

Today, you and your students will view video clips of children's authors. You can use any videos you have of authors your children love, but the ones listed here are terrific and easily accessible. Make sure to view clips before you show them to the children. Today's goal is to help students think about the writer behind the story and see themselves as writers, just like David Shannon or the other authors you learn about today.

Please note that if you do not have Internet access, "Author's Note" pages in printed books include a lot of wonderful and helpful information about writers and their stories.

▼ **Procedure**

Warm Up Gather the class to set the stage for today's learning

Begin by holding up some favorite books. Have a few books from several different authors. Any authors familiar to at least some of the children will do.

> Friends, these are some books that we love. Remember *David Gets in Trouble* and *David Goes to School*? *The Very Hungry Caterpillar* and *The Artist Who Painted a Blue Horse*? *Thunder Cake* and *The Keeping Quilt*?

Allow students to share a favorite part of these stories. Celebrate their thoughts, and focus on the fact that all of these stories are made up of story elements: character, setting, events, and a conclusion. **ELL** Assess for Content and Language Understanding—Diagnostic Assessment. This is a perfect time to listen to how your ELLs talk about their favorite stories and consider what language support they may need in coming lessons.

Teach Model what students need to learn and do

> Yes, we love these stories. David Shannon, Eric Carle, and Patricia Polacco are three authors. *Author* is another name for writer. Authors are writers. Writers tell stories. Today, we are going to meet these writers and learn about who they are, where they get their ideas from, and how they create their stories.

> Let's listen and learn about these authors.

View the video clips of the three authors on Readingrockets.org. **ELL** Provide Comprehensible Input—Audiovisual Aids. ELLs benefit from nonlinguistic representations of material. Offer audio, visuals, and graphics whenever possible to increase students' understanding of the lesson. David Shannon's and Eric Carle's clips are within the Video and Podcasts section, under Meet the Author. Patricia Polacco can be found in the Video Interviews.

David Shannon shares how he wrote the first draft of *No, David!* when he was a child. Eric Carle shares how he wants to bring beauty to the world. Patricia

Polacco's clips—called "Fire-Talk," "Family Stories," and "Thunder Is Just Noise"—share insights into how to tell stories and where our ideas come from.

Isn't it fun to meet these writers and learn about them? What do these writers all have in common? Yes, they are storytellers.

Create a Learning about Writers chart listing what the children noticed. **ELL** Provide Comprehensible Input—Graphic Organizers. Tables and charts help ELLs understand what you are teaching and organize their own thinking. Your chart may begin: Writers . . . And you may include such things as:

- Tell stories
- Get their ideas from their lives and families
- Match words to pictures
- Make changes as they read and reread their writing

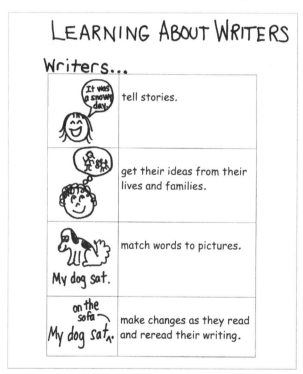

Make sure to use words and icons so children can follow along.

Class, writers create the books we love. When I think about *No, David!* I like the way this writer, David Shannon, tells a silly story. This story always makes me laugh. Writers are storytellers. Today, we are going to look at the stories we love (refer to chart from Reading Lesson 1) and think about which writers we really love and why.

Try Guide students to quickly rehearse what they need to learn and do in preparation for practice

Let's think about the writers we met in the videos today. What do you enjoy about their stories? As I think about these three writers—David Shannon, Eric Carle, and Patricia Polacco—I think they are all wonderful and different. Their styles are unique. I like the way David Shannon tends to write silly stories. I like the way Eric Carle writes fun stories, and I also like the way Patricia Polacco writes serious stories. Spend a few moments thinking about these writers. Then turn to your partner and share: "I like the way . . ." **ELL** Enable Language Production—Listening and Speaking. Wait time and sentence stems help ELLs get ready to talk.

Circulate the room and listen in to students' conversations. Guide students to think about the writers. David Shannon tends to tell stories in which his characters do outrageously silly things. Eric Carle uses beautiful illustrations to tell fun stories with great patterns. And Patricia Polacco tells serious stories, encouraging us to think about the importance of our families and the things we do together. Help students think about these writers and how they are storytellers. **ELL** Enable Language Production—Increasing Interaction. ELLs can hear how their more-proficient peers express their opinions of authors, and rehearse their own answers in a low-anxiety context.

Clarify Briefly restate today's teaching objective and explain the practice task(s)

Our job today is to look through books and think about why we like these authors' stories. Remember, think to yourself, "I like the way _____ (author's name) _____ . . ." Then share your thoughts with your partner.

Practice Students work independently and/or in small groups to apply today's teaching objective

Students will look through books with their partners, thinking about the authors and what they like about their stories. Students who may not be familiar with many authors should still explore books with a partner to begin to discover the books you have in your class. If you have favorite class read-alouds, be sure to include them.

If you feel students are ready to extend their thinking about the authors in the collection, prompt them to examine the texts with additional questions such as:

- What do you think the author is writing about in that book? How do you know?
- Have you ever seen this author before? Do you enjoy his/her books? Why?
- How would you describe the pictures in that book?
- Where do you think that author gets his/her ideas?

Wrap Up Check understanding as you guide students to share briefly what they have learned and produced today

Gather the class. Once students have shared with a partner, have a few students share their thinking about why they liked a story from a certain writer. Encourage the children to share something text-specific they liked either in words, drawing, or both. **ELL** Enable Language Production—Increasing Interaction. This offers ELLs time to clarify their thinking and vocabulary, as well as expand language and learning through the peer conversation and references to the text. Stress that writers tell all kinds of stories.

I like the way

Eric Carl mes his Books

Writing Lesson 2

▼ **Teaching Objective**

Writers get ideas from their experiences.

Close Reading Opportunity

▼ **Standards Alignment**

RL.K.1, RL.K.3, RL.K.10, W.K.7, SL.K.1a, SL.K.1b, SL.K.2, SL.K.3, SL.K.4, SL.K.6, L.K.1, L.K.6

▼ **Materials**

- Charting supplies or interactive whiteboard
- *Thunder Cake* by Patricia Polacco
- Writing paper with large space to draw plus a few lines to write

▼ To the Teacher

Have you ever had a blank piece of paper in front of you and you had no idea what to write? Today's focus is to help students realize that our lives are filled with stories to write across those blank pages. Stories can be as simple as going to the park with a friend or as monumental as learning to ride a bike. Every moment we experience is a story to be told. Today you will focus on group experiences in kindergarten. Having a shared writing experience will offer the scaffolding needed for upcoming lessons of sharing personal stories. Shared writing is when the teacher walks the students through a writing experience, guiding the students and using their ideas to craft a piece of writing as a group. Help your students recognize that their lives are worthy of sharing with others. While you may mention story elements as part of your modeling, students are not yet expected to address these specifically when they share their stories today. This becomes the focus of Writing Lesson 3.

▼ Procedure

Warm Up Gather the class to set the stage for today's learning

Begin today's discussion by helping students understand that authors write about their experiences. Authors get their ideas from the things they do in their lives.

In Writing Lesson 1, we had a great time getting to know the writers behind some of the stories we love. Today, I want us to think back to these authors and where they said they got ideas for their stories. They said they shared stories about their experiences in life. Do you remember where Patricia Polacco got her idea for her story called *Thunder Cake*? She said that she experienced lots of thunderstorms when she was a little girl and her grandmother decided they should make "thundercakes" during the storm. Patricia Polacco wrote about an experience she had as a child. She turned this experience into a story to share with other people.

Teach Model what students need to learn and do

Guide the students to decide on an experience they have all had together to use as a topic for writing. Sketch and write as students are sharing this class experience. Model for students how to think through the experience and create a picture to go along with their story. **ELL** Enable Language

Production—Reading and Writing. Your model of how to connect stories and drawings will help your ELLs work independently later on.

Friends, writers get ideas from their experiences and then turn their ideas into stories to share. Each of us has had many experiences in our own lives. When we share these experiences, we are sharing our stories. This makes us writers, just like the writers in the books we love. How about we write a story together? Hmm . . . what are some experiences we have shared together as a kindergarten class?

Let students share their experiences. Most likely they will share ones such as reading books together, learning math together, caring for a class pet, playing outside, parents visiting for a special occasion at school, and so on.

Look at all the experiences we have shared together. These are our stories. We have lots of stories. What do you think if we use one of these experiences to write a story together? What do you think if we write about when [insert an experience your class shared together]? [We will model with a parent/caregiver visit to the class library.]

OK, what do we want to share first in our story?

[Begin with characters.] Who is the story about? "Mrs. Miller's kindergarten class."

[Describe the setting.] Where are we? "We are in our classroom." When? "At the beginning of the school year, and in the morning time."

[Describe the events.] What happened? "Our parents and caregivers came to visit our classroom so we could show them our new class library." What happened first? "We showed them the new baskets and new books we just got." What happened next? "We each shared one of our favorite books." Then what happened? "We listened to you read a book, Mrs. Miller."

[Describe the conclusion.] What happened at the end? "We said goodbye to our parents and caregivers."

Any experience will work. The goal of today's lesson is to get the students talking about their group experiences. This will help them support each other as storytellers and experience the writing process with support. Take this opportunity to support students in describing people, places, and events while providing details. (SL.K.4) **ELL** Provide

Comprehensible Input—Models. Modeling how to compose a text will set ELLs up for success later on when they write their own stories. Hearing peer contributions will help them understand how to express story elements.

Try Guide students to quickly rehearse what they need to learn and do in preparation for practice

Refocus students and make a connection between class experiences and individual experiences.

> OK, now let's try this on our own. Think about an experience you have had here at school that you would like to turn into a story. Now, turn and talk and share your experience with your partner.

Circulate and encourage students to have fun talking about experiences they have had in kindergarten. **ELL** Enable Language Production—Reading and Writing. Having students discuss their ideas before releasing them to work independently is a great scaffold for your ELLs. Encourage your ELLs to use their home language to get their ideas out before they attempt to write in English.

> Great job turning your experiences into stories!

Clarify Briefly restate today's teaching objective and explain the practice task(s)

Refocus students and help them to understand that stories come from our life experiences.

> Think about how we turned into a story our experience of having our parents and caregivers visit our classroom to see our new library. Think about the experience you shared with your partner. Our job today is to share our experiences in kindergarten. We are sharing our stories.

Practice Students work independently and/or in small groups to apply today's teaching objective

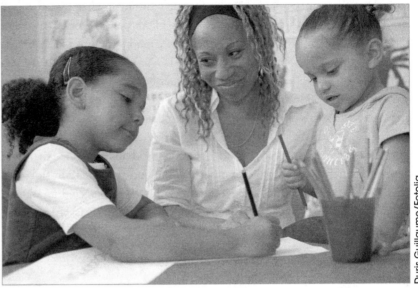

Duris Guillaume/Fotolia

Students will sketch and write about an experience in kindergarten. Refer back to the class story as a model. **ELL** Provide Comprehensible Input—Models. Models offer a strong support for your ELLs to anchor the composition of their own texts. You can use models as a base from which to practice prompts before or after a lesson.

Wrap Up Check understanding as you guide students to share briefly what they have learned and produced today

Gather the class in your meeting area. Have partners tell their stories to each other. Note exemplary work and share a few with the whole group.

Writing Lesson 3 ●

▼ **Teaching Objective**

Writers use story elements to create stories.

Close Reading
Opportunity

▼ **Standards Alignment**

RL.K.1, RL.K.3, RL.K.10, W.K.3, W.K.7, W.K.8, SL.K.1a, SL.K.1b, SL.K.2, SL.K.3, SL.K.4, SL.K.6, L.K.1, L.K.2, L.K.6

▼ Materials

- *Rocket Writes a Story* by Tad Hills or any book of your choice with strong story elements
- Charting supplies or interactive whiteboard for shared writing to create What Rocket Does as a Writer chart
- Writing paper with large space to draw plus a few lines to write

▼ To the Teacher

Today's lesson will build off of Writing Lesson 2 and also connects with Reading Lesson 2. Again, you will offer your students a shared writing experience, scaffolding the process. The goal is to help students recognize the importance of story elements as a necessary tool for sharing rich and interesting stories.

▼ Procedure

Warm Up Gather the class to set the stage for today's learning

Gather class and read *Rocket Writes a Story* by Tad Hills. If you don't have this text available, choose any familiar story and point out for your teaching objective today how the author includes story elements as a foundation.

> Friends, yesterday we had fun writing about our kindergarten experiences together. Last night, I read this amazing book, *Rocket Writes a Story*. As I was reading it, I realized that we did the same things that Rocket did when writing. Today I want you to listen to Rocket's story and think about how we are all writers, just like Rocket.

When you finish reading, go back to the page at the end where Rocket reads his story to Owl. Emphasize the character, setting, events, and conclusion. **ELL** Identify and Communicate Content and Language Objectives—Key Content Vocabulary. Knowing and using these terms will be an important part of mastering the content of this lesson set. By introducing them explicitly here, you are giving your ELLs a base from which they will build a rich understanding of story elements in the coming days.

> This is an excellent story. Rocket is a writer just like you and me. He thinks about things in his life to write about and then uses the story elements to create stories to share with the world. Let's think about what Rocket does well as a writer. Let's closely reread the page where he reads his story to Owl.

ELL Frontload the Lesson—Set a Purpose for Reading. Giving ELLs a focus as they listen to the story will help them identify the most important information and filter out extraneous details.

Begin a chart titled What Rocket Does as a Writer, listing what Rocket does as a writer. Guide conversation around the story elements.

- Who is in the story?
- Where and when is the story taking place?
- What is happening in the story?
- How does the story end?

Your chart may look like this:

What Rocket Does as a Writer

Rocket is a story writer because he has . . .
• Characters: Rocket, Little Yellow Bird, and Baby Owl • Setting: Outside and probably during spring because Little Yellow Bird is around and Rocket is still in "school" • Events: Little Yellow Bird encourages Rocket to use words from the tree to create a story • Conclusion: Rocket meets Baby Owl and writes a story about his new friend

Now guide students in a shared writing experience to create a class story with story elements. **ELL** Enable Language Production—Listening and Speaking. Hearing their teacher and peers use the language of story will help form a base from which ELLs can work independently.

Teach Model what students need to learn and do

> Rocket has all the story elements in his story. Let's learn from Rocket and use story elements to create our own stories. Let's write another story together about kindergarten, making sure to use the story elements. Yesterday, we wrote about our parents and caregivers visiting the classroom. What should we write about today?

Any story will do for this shared writing experience. In this model, we guide students to write an imaginary story about a class pet or school mascot. We use hand motions to help students track the elements in the story. Sketch and write the story as you and the children create it together, building off of each other's ideas. **ELL** Enable Language Production—Reading and Writing. Shared writing gives ELLs a model of both content (story elements) and language (how we express them) from which they will work later when they write their own compositions.

 Encourage students to speak clearly when expressing thoughts and ideas. (SL.K.6) Guide students with the story element questions:

- Who is in the story?
- Where and when is the story taking place?
- What is happening in the story?
- How does the story end?

Here is how a story may unfold with your guidance:

What a great idea to write a story about Tiger, our school mascot. Let's use our hands to keep track of the story elements as we think about our story.

Hold up a thumb as you choose a character.

We know from Rocket that our story must have a character. So, Tiger is our character.

Sketch Tiger.
Write: *"Our school has a mascot named Tiger."*
Hold up first finger as you include a setting. *Where and when does the story take place? In the playground? Good idea.*
Sketch a playground around Tiger.
Write: *"Tiger was on the playground during recess."*
Hold up next three fingers as you describe the events. *What is happening?* Have children suggest events. Sketch and write each event.

"At first, the students were surprised to see him come alive."

"The kindergartners ask him to play with them."

"They had fun playing kickball together."

Close fist as you compose a conclusion. *How does the story end?* Decide on a conclusion to the story. Sketch and write the conclusion.

"When the bell rang, Tiger thanked the kindergartners for playing nicely, and he went back to standing still in the front hallway. But he is different because his face has a smile now."

We are story writers, just like Rocket. We used the story elements, and our story will be fun for anyone to read.

Try Guide students to quickly rehearse what they need to learn and do in preparation for practice

Now take a moment and think of your own story. Use your hand to keep track of the story elements as you share your story with your partner. Make sure to take turns listening and speaking.

Circulate, guiding students to use the story elements as they imagine and share their stories. Think aloud your story, tracking the story elements across your hand: Character (first finger), setting (next finger), events (1, 2, 3 events across three fingers), and conclusion (close hand to show the ending of the story).

 Take this opportunity to encourage students to speak audibly and express ideas clearly. (SL.K.6)

Clarify Briefly restate today's teaching objective and explain the practice task(s)

Our job today is to be like Rocket. Let's write our stories down, making sure to use the story elements. Remember how we sketched our story and added words to match our picture.

Practice Students work independently and/or in small groups to apply today's teaching objective

Students work independently to draw and write their stories, using the story elements. It is important to circulate and conference with students, guiding individual students at their current development stage of writing. Some students will need assistance with matching pictures to their thoughts, while others will need help with crafting descriptive sentences. **ELL** Enable Language Production—Reading and Writing. Use this time to confer with your

Wrap Up Check understanding as you guide students to share briefly what they have learned and produced today

Gather the class. Have partners turn and talk, sharing their stories. Point out ways in which students were successful with their stories, and choose a few to share with the whole group. What story elements are present in the drawings and writing?

Writing Lesson 4

▼ Teaching Objective

Writers write stories about their lives using story elements.

Close Reading
Opportunity

▼ Standards Alignment

RL.K.1, RL.K.3, RL.K.10, W.K.3, W.K.5, W.K.8, SL.K.1a, SL.K.1b, SL.K.2, SL.K.3, SL.K.4, SL.K.6, L.K.1, L.K.2, L.K.6

▼ To the Teacher

In this lesson, students further explore writing using story elements as they write new stories based on their experiences.

▼ Materials

- *Night at the Fair* by Donald Crews or another book of your choice that could be based on the author's own personal experience
- Charting supplies or interactive whiteboard to create a story
- Story Elements Graphic Organizer, enlarged for modeling and copies for students (Appendix K.5)

▼ To the Teacher

Today's lesson builds off earlier lessons; it expands the creation of experience stories in Writing Lesson 2 by adding the structure of story elements from Writing Lesson 3. It will also reinforce student understanding of the

simplicity of where many writers gather ideas for their stories. We can learn so much about this from Donald Crews's books. *Bigmama's* by Donald Crews is an example of authors writing from what they know and do. Donald Crews is an excellent model for the children to learn where writers get their ideas for stories. Other well-known writers that draw from personal experience include Tomie DePaola, Cynthia Rylant, Patricia Polacco, and Lester Laminack.

▼ Procedure

Warm Up Gather the class to set the stage for today's learning

Gather students together in your meeting area. Hold up some of the children's stories from Writing Lesson 3 to celebrate their writing. Have their shared writing from the past few days displayed.

> Let's look back at our stories from yesterday where we used story elements to create stories.

Teach Model what students need to learn and do

> As we study story and learn about writers, let's think some more about where writers get their ideas for stories. Do you remember where David Shannon got his idea for *No, David*? Where did Rocket get his idea for his story? (Allow time for answers.) Yes, both these writers got their ideas from their real lives. Listen closely as I read *Night at the Fair* by Donald Crews. As I read, think about where Donald Crews may have gotten his idea for this story.

Read *Night at the Fair*.

So, where do you think Donald Crews got his idea to write this story? [Allow time for partnerships to discuss briefly.] Donald Crews probably went to the fair and had this real-life experience. He got his idea from his own life. Then he used the story elements to write a story about visiting the fair.

Briefly review the story elements of this story: character, setting, events, conclusion. **ELL** Identify and Communicate Content and Language Objectives—Repeat. Repetition is another strategy that will help ELLs remember new language or content vocabulary.

As writers, we think about our real lives, the people we know, the places we visit, the things we like to do, and we say to ourselves, "I remember when I . . ."

Conduct a think-aloud about a story from your own life. Think aloud, "I remember when I . . ." Include life experiences that can help the children generate their own ideas. For example, you may share when you and your family went out for pizza, visited the park, played with a pet, or learned how to ride a bike. Share simple experiences from recently or long ago that will help the children reflect upon their own life experiences. Model thinking through a few experiences and then choose one to write about, using the story elements.

Use the finger modeling from the previous lesson to help track the elements in your story while you are sketching and writing in the spaces on the Story Elements Graphic Organizer. **ELL** Provide Comprehensible Input—Graphic Organizers. The Story Elements chart will help ELLs understand what is asked of them and will assist them to clearly express their thoughts as they compose.

Try Guide students to quickly rehearse what they need to learn and do in preparation for practice

Now it is your turn. We are all writers, just like Donald Crews. Each of us has many life experiences that we can turn into stories for the world to hear. Let me think. What do I want to write a story about today? What is something in my life that I would like to share with the world? "I remember when I . . ." Turn and share the story you are thinking of with your partner. Make sure to use your fingers to help you include all of the story elements (model using your hand to track the story). Character (first finger), setting (next finger), events (1, 2, 3 events across three fingers), and conclusion (close hand to show the ending of the story).

Story Elements

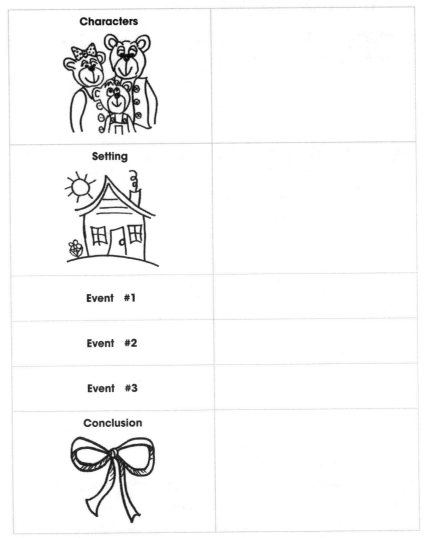

Allow partnerships to share their ideas and stories. Move around the room. Listen to students and take note of exemplary ideas to share with the class. **ELL** Enable Language Production—Increasing Interaction. ELLs can learn a lot about both language and content by talking to their peers. Circulate and whisper in when needed, or just listen to gather information about how to support their individual needs.

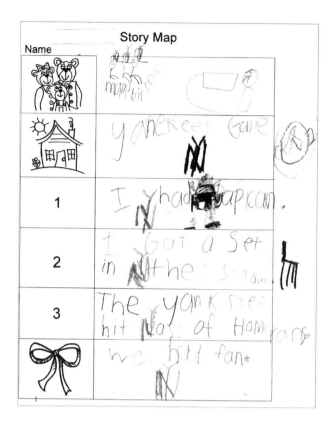

Remind students of how to engage effectively in collaborative discussions by following agreed-upon rules for discussions: listening with care, one voice speaking at a time, and building on the thoughts of others. Help students notice how we can build upon others' ideas and express thoughts, feelings, and ideas clearly. (SL.K.1a, SL.K.1b, SL.K.6)

Clarify Briefly restate today's teaching objective and explain the practice task(s)

Refocus the children and help the students understand how authors such as Donald Crews can help us learn how to share our own life stories.

> Our job today is to share a life experience, using the story elements to guide our stories. Think about how Donald Crews shared the characters, setting, events, and conclusion in *Night at the Fair*. By using the story elements, he not only told a great story; he made us feel like we were with him at the fair.

Practice Students work independently and/or in small groups to apply today's teaching objective

Students will sketch and write a story about their own real-life experience, using the story elements on a blank Story Elements Graphic Organizer.

Wrap Up Check understanding as you guide students to share briefly what they have learned and produced today

Gather students back in your meeting area. Have partnerships share their stories. Note exemplary stories, and have a few students share with the group. Celebrate their writing and the importance of turning life experiences into stories. To gather data, listen in as students share stories in partnerships and collect stories to assess understanding. **ELL** Assess for Content and Language Understandings—Formative Assessment. This is an opportunity for you to assess your ELLs' language and content needs and then use this information to inform upcoming lessons. Remember that they may need additional support to grasp the content due to language barriers

Collect and analyze the Story Elements Graphic Organizer and student stories as a performance-based assessment to determine if students need additional instruction or support as a whole class, in small groups, or one on one.

Milestone Performance Assessment

Sharing I Remember Stories with Story Elements

 Use student stories to assess understanding of how to use life experiences and story elements to create stories.

Standards Alignment: W.K.3, W.K.5, W.K.8, SL.K.1a, SL.K.1b, SL.K.4, SL.K.6, L.K.1, L.K.6

Task	Achieved	Notes
Choose one idea from life experience to share.		
Utilize story elements to share life experience.		

Task	Achieved	Notes
Speak audibly and express thoughts, feelings, and ideas clearly.		

Writing Lesson 5

▼ Teaching Objective

Writers write imaginative stories using story elements.

Close Reading
Opportunity

▼ Standards Alignment

RL.K.1, RL.K.10, W.K.3, W.K.5, SL.K.1a, SL.K.1b, SL.K.2, SL.K.3, SL.K.4, SL.K.6, L.K.1, L.K.2, L.K.6

▼ Materials

- *Penny and Her Song* by Kevin Henkes or another imaginary story of your choice
- Charting supplies or interactive whiteboard
- Story Elements Graphic Organizer (Appendix K.5)

▼ To the Teacher

Today's lesson is about connecting real-life experiences to our imaginations. Some of our best ideas can start with our real life and be turned into fantastic stories once we use our imaginations to add things. Today, help students by referring to favorite stories such as *Don't Let the Pigeon Drive the Bus! Koala Lou, The Mitten, The Three Little Pigs, Froggy,* and *Olivia.* The goal of today's lesson is for students to see the connection between real life and their imaginations in story making by including fantastic elements such as talking animals or magic. How fun is it to be a writer and imagine a world how you would like it to be?

▼ Procedure

Warm Up Gather the class to set the stage for today's learning

> We have been enjoying ourselves as we share our stories. Yesterday, we shared stories from our real-life experiences.

Share a story from Writing Lesson 4 and remind students that it came from a real-life experience. **ELL** Frontload the Lesson—Make Connections. ELLs have an easier time understanding instruction when they can tie what is being said to something familiar.

> Writers get ideas from their real lives. Today, we are going to learn how to connect real life to our imaginations. Listen closely as I read *Penny and Her Song* by Kevin Henkes. As I read, think about where Kevin Henkes got his idea to write this story.

Teach Model what students need to learn and do

> Where do you think Kevin Henkes got his idea for this story about Penny?

Students may say from his real life. Help the students see that writers get ideas from their real lives AND their imaginations. Writers use ideas from their real life and ideas from their imaginations to make up stories.

Kevin Henkes first thought about his real life and then thought, "I imagine . . ." He got ideas from his real life and then used his imagination to make up this lovely story about Penny having trouble as she tried to share her song with her parents.

- What parts of the story do you think are from his real life?
- What parts of the story do you think came from his imagination (things that could not really happen)?

Allow students to share their thoughts about these questions in partnerships before having a few students share with the whole group. Listen in as students talk in their partnerships. **ELL** Enable Language Production— Increasing Interaction. Here ELLs are able to practice language and content and learn from their peers in an informal forum. This is an opportunity to listen in and gather information about how best to support their language and content needs.

> Kevin Henkes may have thought about how he felt when a new baby came into the house. This part of the story was from his real life. Then he used his imagination to bring the mice to life to be the characters of the story. Mice cannot talk like humans. He used his real life and his imagination together to make a story. Writers use some ideas from their real lives and some ideas from their imaginations in their stories. We can learn from Kevin Henkes.

Share your story. As you do, track the character, setting, events, and ending on your hand and complete a Story Elements Graphic Organizer. **ELL** Provide Comprehensible Input—Graphic Organizers. Graphic organizers offer a strong visual support for your ELLs to refer back to when they are working independently.

> Let me try to make up a story. First, let me think about my real life. *(Share some ideas.)* I love my dog, Jake. I spend a lot of time with Jake. I can think of many real-life experiences with Jake. I take Jake to the park all the time, and there are always other dogs there. I think I want to create a story about Jake. The real part of the story is that Jake is my dog who likes to go to the park to play with other dogs. I can use my imagination now to make up a story about Jake going to the park.

> I imagine . . . Jake meeting the neighborhood dogs down at the park on his own. At the park, the dogs sit in the sun, sharing stories about their families, swimming in the lake, and sharing peanut butter sandwiches before happily going home to take a nap.

> The imaginary part of my story is that Jake can go to the park by himself and talk with other dogs.

Who can think of stories we have read in which the writer used real-life experiences and his or her imagination to make up a story?

Allow students to share familiar titles as examples. For example:

Good Dog, Carl by Alexandra Day

Miss Spider's Tea Party by David Kirk

Poppleton by Cynthia Rylant

The Very Hungry Caterpillar by Eric Carle

Writers use their real-life experiences and imaginations to create stories. Just like Kevin Henkes, we can say to ourselves, "I imagine . . ." to make up stories.

Try Guide students to quickly rehearse what they need to learn and do in preparation for practice

> Now it's your turn. Think about your real life and then think, "I imagine . . ." Turn to your partner and share your story. Use your hand to keep track of the story elements as you share with your partner.

As you circulate and listen, you may hear a story like this one:

> "I imagine that when I play in my yard, the animals talk to me. Some days we play baseball. Other days we play tag. My favorite game to play with the animals is hide and seek. It is fun! When my mommy comes outside to tell me it is dinner, all the animals stop talking."

Clarify Briefly restate today's teaching objective and explain the practice task(s)

> OK, today we are going to think about our real lives and then think, "I imagine . . ." to make up stories.

Practice Students work independently and/or in small groups to apply today's teaching objective

Students will work independently to draw and write stories, thinking, "I imagine . . ." Use the blank Story Map Graphic Organizer.

Circulate to help students as they connect real-life experiences and imaginations.

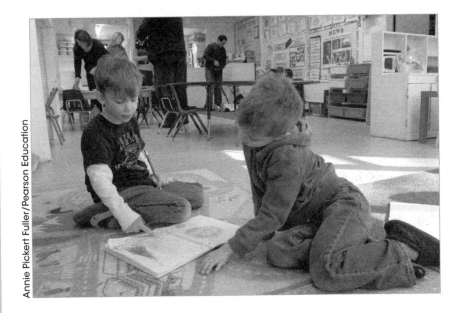

Annie Pickert Fuller/Pearson Education

Story Map

Name:

	A little boy went for a walk.
	He wacked threw the park.
1	He stept on a leet.
2	The leet picked him up and he flew
3	He flew over town and saw his frends.
	When he was tired he flew home and took a nap.

Wrap Up Check understanding as you guide students to share briefly what they have learned and produced today

Gather the class in your meeting area. Ask partners to share what is real and what comes from their imagination in their new stories. Have a few students share the real and imagined parts of their stories. **ELL** Enable Language Production—Increasing Interaction. It is important to create an atmosphere of supportive sharing in your classroom, so that your ELLs in particular feel comfortable sharing their stories with their peers, and can benefit from collective support.

Goal	Low-Tech	High-Tech
Students will write stories from their imaginations.	Students will write stories from their imaginations on paper.	Students will type their stories from their imaginations using Word or Pixie. Another option is Voicethread.com, which allows students to present their stories orally with pictures and receive comments from viewers.

Writing Lesson 6

▼ Teaching Objective

Writers use their imaginations to write new versions of classic nursery rhymes.

Close Reading Opportunity

▼ Standards Alignment

RL.K.1, RL.K.2, RL.K.3, RL.K.10, W.K.3, W.K.5, SL.K.1a, SL.K.1b, SL.K.2, SL.K.3, SL.K.5, SL.K.6, L.K.1, L.K.2, L.K.6

▼ Materials

- *And the Dish Ran Away with the Spoon* by Janet Stevens and Susan Steven Crummel (or another adapted version of a classic rhyme or story)
- "The Three Little Kittens Who Lost Their Mittens" (in Nursery Rhymes—PDToolKit)
- Charting supplies or interactive whiteboard

▼ To the Teacher

And the Fish Ran Away with a Spoon is a fantastically fun contemporary nursery rhyme. Today's goal is to have fun, while pushing your students to think critically as they compare and contrast classic and contemporary versions of nursery rhymes. You will offer your students the opportunity of writing a contemporary nursery rhyme through a shared writing experience. Today's lesson is a perfect opportunity for children to strengthen their speaking and listening skills as they build off of each other's ideas to create nursery rhymes and then present them to each other at the end of class.

▼ Procedure

Warm Up Gather the class to set the stage for today's learning

Gather students in your meeting area and remind them about how they created original, imaginative stories in Writing Lesson 5.

> Yesterday we had a great time connecting our life experiences to our imaginations for creating stories.
>
> Today, I am going to read another story. The writers, Janet Stevens and Susan Stevens Crummel, have taken the classic nursery rhyme "Hey Diddle Diddle" and used their imaginations to change some of the original story elements to write a new version of the nursery rhyme. Listen closely to see if you recognize the nursery rhyme, and then hear how these writers turned this classic nursery rhyme into a full story by adding the story elements.

> **ELL** Frontload the Lesson—Build Background. ELLs may not be familiar with the original version of this nursery rhyme. If they are to understand today's lesson, you may need to pull a small group for a brief study of "Hey Diddle Diddle" beforehand.

Teach Model what students need to learn and do

Refocus students and help them see how these authors took a story and changed it, using their imaginations and story elements to come up with another version.

> Today we are going to play with nursery rhymes. We are going to take a classic nursery rhyme and use our imaginations to change some of the story elements to make up another story. What nursery rhyme should we play with today? Yes; let's do "The Three Little Kittens." We know the story of the three little kittens and how they lost their mittens. Let's think.

- Who is in the story?
- Where and when is the story taking place?
- What is happening in the story?
- How does the story end?

Let students identify the story elements.

> Now, let's have some fun with this nursery rhyme. Let's use the story elements and change the story.

Here is what the experience might sound like with your students. Notice how you guide the students and then help them form their ideas into sentences, using the story elements to create a story that makes sense. **ELL** Enable Language Production—Reading and Writing. Through modeling and thinking aloud, you are scaffolding both ELLs' understanding of the lesson content and their ability to put their ideas into words. They will be more successful during independent practice as a result.

> Who is in our story? OK, Let's keep the three kittens **characters** but replace their mother with a teacher.
>
> Where and when is the story taking place? What a great idea! Let's have the **setting** of the story take place at school during centers.
>
> What is happening in the story? For the first **event**, we will have the kittens playing in the drama center. Then another **event** will be when they begin to fight over who plays the king in their play. Now, let's plan one more **event**. The teacher comes over and says they must leave the center if they cannot get along.
>
> How does the story end? Our **conclusion** will be that they decide to do their play a few times and each of them will get to play the king.
>
> What would be a good title for our nursery rhyme? "The Three Kittens Who Want to Be King!"
>
> Great. You have taken this nursery rhyme and used story elements and your imagination to make up a story. Now we are going to work in groups, using illustrations and words to put our story, "The Three Kittens Who Want to Be King," on paper. You will work in a group and be given one of the story elements to display on paper.

Have children in groups for each of the story elements:

Character

Setting

Events (three groups, one for each event)

Conclusion

Try Guide students to quickly rehearse what they need to learn and do in preparation for practice

Now, turn to your group partners and discuss your story element. Retell the story to each other, and share ideas for how your section of the story might look on paper, using illustrations and words.

Circulate the room and help students share time speaking and listening as they imagine their element of the story for their paper.

Clarify Briefly restate today's teaching objective and explain the practice task(s)

Today we are having fun with nursery rhymes! Your job is to work with your group to put your story element of "The Three Kittens Who Want to Be King" on paper, using illustrations and words. When we come back together, we will connect all the story elements together to retell our story as a class.

Practice Students work independently and/or in small groups to apply today's teaching objective

Students will work together in their groups to display their story element on a big piece of paper, using illustrations and words to retell their story element. Circulate and listen in on conversations as partners talk. **ELL** Enable Language Production—Increasing Interaction. Group work allows ELLs to use their peers as resources for their own learning of both language and content. When you are forming groups, consider members who may speak an ELL's home language so that, if needed, the group discussion could be in English and the home language.

Support children as they create drawings to depict their story elements. (SL.K.5)

Wrap Up Check understanding as you guide students to share briefly what they have learned and produced today

Gather the students back together. Refer to your Story Elements Chart. Have students retell their contemporary nursery rhyme, "The Three Kittens Who Want to Be King," with groups sharing their illustrations and words,

following the story elements sequentially. Remind students to speak slowly, clearly, and with expression. Celebrate their work!

ELL Assess for Content and Language Understandings—Formative Assessment. This is an opportunity for you to assess your ELLs' language and content needs and then use this to inform upcoming lessons. Remember to look past language errors when assessing content understanding, but note also what types of language students need practice with.

Collect and analyze student work as a performance-based assessment to determine if students need additional instruction or support as a whole class, in small groups, or one on one.

Milestone Performance Assessment
Creating and Retelling Contemporary Nursery Rhyme

Use the shared writing experience to assess understanding of how to listen and build upon one another's ideas and story elements to create stories.

Standards Alignment: RL.K.1, RL.K.3, W.K.3, W.K.5, SL.K.1a, SL.K.1b, SL.K.2, SL.K.5 SL.K.6

Task	Achieved	Notes
Participate in group conversation to plan story elements of contemporary nursery rhyme.		
Demonstrate understanding of story element through contribution to the story element drawing.		
Retell contemporary nursery rhyme.		
Speak audibly and express thoughts, feelings, and ideas clearly.		

Writing Lesson 7

▼ Teaching Objective

Writers use their imaginations to write new versions of classic fairy tales.

Close Reading Opportunity

▼ Standards Alignment

RL.K.1, RL.K.3, RL.K.10, W.K.3, W.K.5, SL.K.1a, SL.K.1b, SL.K.2, SL.K.3, SL.K.5, SL.K.6, L.K.1, L.K.2, L.K.6

▼ Materials

- *Cinder-Elly* by Frances Minters
- Story Elements Chart
- Large pieces of blank paper
- Charting supplies or interactive whiteboard

▼ To the Teacher

Today is another shared writing experience for your students. Shared writing is a necessary instructional tool in these early years, as it scaffolds the learning process to meet the developmental needs of your students as they progress toward being independent writers.

Today you will write a contemporary fairy tale. We are using *Cinder-Elly* to help students imagine a new twist on the story. To help students recognize this contemporary fairy tale, make sure to read the classic version of Cinderella before today's lesson. **ELL Frontload the Lesson—Activate Prior Knowledge and Build Background. Many cultures have their own versions of the Cinderella story, so be sure to find out whether your ELLs are already familiar with its plot and themes. At the same time, reading the classic English tale will make sure all your students are on the same page before listening to *Cinder-Elly*.** While each class, of course, will have their own original ideas about how to change the story, we provide this model of how you and your students might develop a new version of a fairy tale. Guide your students by prompting them with questions about the story elements. Help students

build off of each others' ideas. Use this shared experience as a chance to help students see the process of writing a story. Explain how the story elements help a story flow and make sense. Enjoy as your students step inside the fanciful world of fairy tales, where everything is almost always happily ever after.

▼ Procedure

Warm Up Gather the class to set the stage for today's learning

Gather students in your meeting area. Refer to Writing Lesson 6 and celebrate their creativity in using "The Three Little Kittens" to help them imagine a new version of the story, "The Three Kittens Who Want to Be King." Make a connection between Writing Lessons 6 and 7.

> Kindergartners, we have been having lots of fun with our study of story. Yesterday, you used the story elements to create a contemporary nursery rhyme.
>
> Today, we are going to use our imaginations and story elements again. This writer, Frances Minters, has taken the classic fairy tale "Cinderella" and used her imagination to change the story elements to write this new, modern-day version of the story, called Cinder-Elly. These are both fairy tales. Fairy tales are created with story elements. Something unique to fairy tales is that they often begin with "Once upon a time . . ." and end with "happily ever after . . ."
>
> Listen closely to see if you recognize the fairy tale.

Teach Model what students need to learn and do

> What did you think? Did you recognize this as a modern version of Cinderella?

If needed, help students to see the connection of this story to Cinderella. **ELL Identify and Communicate Content and Language Objectives—Check for Understanding.** This is a good time to check in with ELLs to evaluate their understanding and to help them put their ideas into words.

> Frances Minters used her imagination and story elements to make up this story. She kept the necessary story elements but changed the traditional story we all know.

Today we are going to play with this fairy tale, just like we played with a nursery rhyme yesterday. We are going to use our imaginations and story elements to make up a new version of a familiar tale. Ready? Let's think about *Cinder-Elly* . . .

- Who is in the story? "Elly, sisters, stepmother, Godmother, Prince Charming"
- Where and when is the story taking place? "Manhattan, fall/winter"
- What is happening in the story? "Elly's sisters went to basketball game all dressed up to meet Prince Charming. Elly stayed at home, but her god-mother visited and put a cool outfit on her. Then she sent Elly to the basket-ball game in a cool car. In the real Cinderella, she wore a ball gown and rode to the party in a fancy carriage with horses. At the game, Elly caught a ball and Prince Charming noticed her. Elly had to leave because she was supposed to be home by 10:00. She lost her glass sneaker."
- How does the story end? "The prince found the sneaker, found Elly, and took her for pizza!"

Let students identify the story elements of *Cinder-Elly*. Some may answer by comparing and contrasting *Cinder-Elly* to "Cinderella." Encourage this process of comparing and contrasting, but stay focused on story elements.

Now let's have some fun! Let's take *Cinder-Elly* and use the story elements to change and make up a new fairy tale.

Here is an example of how a story may come together. The goal is for the children to have another shared writing experience using the story elements. **ELL** Enable Language Production—Reading and Writing. By offer-ing opportunities to speak and listen, you are helping ELLs get ready to write in English.

- Who is in our story?

  Cinder-Puppy? OK, we can make our main character a puppy. And the neighbor dog has three puppies that are mean to him.

- Where and when is the story taking place?

  In a neighborhood with lots of houses and dogs, during the school day so all the children are away at school.

- What is happening in the story?

  First, Cinder-Puppy wants to play at the park with all the neighborhood dogs. But the next-door neighbor puppies growl at him and will not let

Cinder-Puppy past their house to get to the park. The three puppies next door take turns staying home and growling, so Cinder-Puppy is scared to go to the park.

Next, a fox sees Cinder-Puppy crying and asks him what is wrong. Cinder-Puppy tells the fox his story. The fox is magical and he gives Cinder-Puppy a special treat for him to eat. Then Cinder-Puppy eats the treat and turns into a big dog so the mean neighbor puppies do not recognize him when he passes the puppies to get to the park to play.

Then Cinder-Puppy makes lots of friends at the park.

- How does the story end?

  Finally, the mean neighbor puppies realize that Cinder-Puppy is getting past them as a big dog. When they try to scare Cinder-Puppy at the park, all the other puppies stand up for Cinder-Puppy and tell the mean neighbor puppy brothers to leave him alone. Cinder-Puppy lives happily ever after, playing at the park everyday.

- What would be a good title for our fairy tale?

  Cinder-Puppy.

  Good work taking this fairy tale and using story elements and your imagi-nation to make up a story. Now, just like yesterday, we are going to work in groups to write out our story, "Cinder-Puppy," using illustrations and words. You will work in a group, using this large piece of paper to share one story element through illustrations and words.

Have students work in the same groups as in Writing Lesson 6.
Assign each group one of the following story elements:

  Character

  Setting

  Events (three groups, one for each event)

  Conclusion

Try Guide students to quickly rehearse what they need to learn and do in preparation for practice

Now, turn to your group partners and discuss your story element. Retell the story to each other and share ideas for how your section might look on paper, using illustrations and words.

Move around the room and facilitate conversations as students imagine and talk about their element of the story for their paper.

Clarify Briefly restate today's teaching objective and explain the practice task(s)

> Friends, today we are having fun with fairy tales. Your job is to work with your group to put your story element of "Cinder-Puppy" on paper, using illustrations and words. When we come back together, we will connect all the story elements to retell our story together as a class, just like yesterday.

ELL Identify and Communicate Language and Content Objectives—Repeat. Clarifying the directions for work one more time will help ELLs feel confident about what is expected of them.

Practice Students work independently and/or in small groups to apply today's teaching objective

Students will work together in their groups to show their section of the story on a big piece of paper, using illustrations and words to retell their story element.

Writing Lesson 7 follows the same structure as Writing Lesson 6. Support children as they create drawings to depict their story element. (SL.K.5)

Circulate the room and guide students as they retell their story element in small groups. In a conversational manner, ask students about other parts of the story and how their part fits in the whole story. **ELL** Enable Language Production—Increasing Interaction. This is a perfect time to listen in and support conversations. Take care to model the words and phrases used to talk about stories as an additional language support for your ELLs.

This is a great opportunity to help them really think through how they are depicting their section of the story.

Wrap Up Check understanding as you guide students to share briefly what they have learned and produced today

Gather students back together. Refer to your Story Elements Chart. Have students retell their fairy tale, "Cinder-Puppy," with groups sharing their illustrations and words sequentially. Remind students to speak slowly, clearly, and with expression. **ELL** Enable Language Production—Listening and Speaking. Be sure to tailor your expectations for ELLs' presentations to their individual levels of proficiency; all students can and should speak before the class, but some may only be able to express a few words at this stage. Celebrate their writing!

Writing Lesson 8

▼ Teaching Objective

Writers choose a favorite form of narrative writing from this lesson set to explore further.

Close Reading Opportunity

▼ Standards Alignment

W.K.3, W.K.5, W.K.8, SL.K.1a, SL.K.1b, SL.K.3, SL.K.5, SL.K.6, L.K.1, L.K.2, L.K.6

▼ Materials

- Story Elements Graphic Organizer, enlarged for modeling and copies for students (Appendix K.5)
- Story Elements Chart
- Charting supplies or interactive whiteboard

▼ To the Teacher

Today you will encourage your students to imagine their own stories. You have spent the whole lesson set helping your students identify and learn how to use the story elements to create a story. By now, your students probably have many stories that will come to mind, and they will probably feel eager to create their own independently. Your job today is to circulate through the room and confer with students, addressing their specific needs as they choose their idea and plan out their own stories on the Story Elements Graphic Organizer. Today is important, as you will see how well students move from a shared, guided experience to an independent one. Assess if students are able to imagine their own stories and if they understand how the story elements help them create a complete story that makes sense.

▼ Procedure

Warm Up Gather the class to set the stage for today's learning

Gather students in your meeting area.

> Friends, you have written many stories. You have written stories about your real-life experiences, stories you've imagined, a nursery rhyme, and a fairy tale. You have created stories on your own and as a class. The one thing all of these stories have in common is that you used the story elements.

Teach Model what students need to learn and do

> Today, you are going to write a new story. You can write any kind of story you like: real, imaginary, or a little bit of both. You can even write a new version of a nursery rhyme or fairy tale.

> Let's think about what we have learned about story.

Have your Story Elements Graphic Organizer displayed as you think aloud and model creating a story. **ELL** Provide Comprehensible Input—Graphic Organizers. This familiar chart will help ELLs understand what they are to do today and give them a tool for expressing their own stories in a comprehensible manner.

> First, I need to decide what I want to write about today. I think I want to write a story that is a little bit real AND imaginary. Let me think . . . I remember when my family and I went to the beach . . . AND I imagine that we . . . In

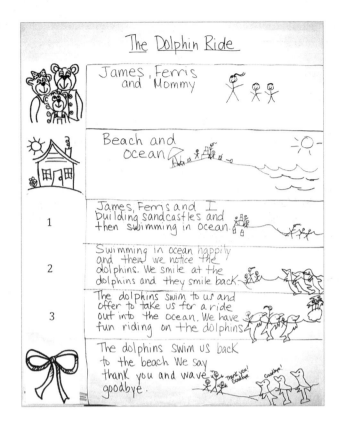

my story, I want the real part to be playing on the beach with my family, and the imaginary part to be something about swimming with dolphins. I have always wanted to swim with dolphins! OK, so let me use the story elements to think through and make up my story.

Jot down ideas on your Story Elements Graphic Organizer, using pictures and key words as you think through your story. Use words such as *first, next, after that,* and *finally* as your share your story. **ELL** Identify and Communicate Content and Language Objectives—Academic Vocabulary. Transition words are used in academic writing throughout the curriculum. Explicitly teaching these high-utility words will help induct ELLs into the world of authors and readers.

> Today I used my real life and my imagination to make up a story. Thinking through the story elements helped me create a story that is interesting and makes sense.

Try Guide students to quickly rehearse what they need to learn and do in preparation for practice

Take a moment and think about a story that you want to create today.

Students may choose any type of story from the lesson set.

a story about real life

a story that is real AND imaginary

an adapted nursery rhyme or a fairy tale

Allow partnerships to share ideas. Circulate around the room as partners are talking. Listen and take note of ideas you would like to share with the class. Refocus students and share some of the ideas you overheard. **ELL** Enable Language Production—Increasing Interaction. This is a perfect time to listen in and support conversation. Model language for your ELLs if you notice they need such support, and clarify any misunderstandings they may still have about the content.

Clarify Briefly restate today's teaching objective and explain the practice task(s)

Our job today is to write stories. Now that you have your idea for your story, think it through using pictures and words.

Practice Students work independently and/or in small groups to apply today's teaching objective

Students work independently using pictures and words to fill out their Story Elements Graphic Organizer to create a new story.

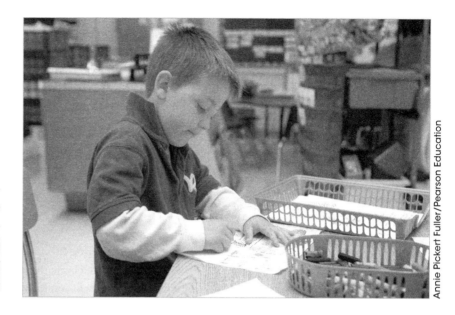

Wrap Up Check understanding as you guide students to share briefly what they have learned and produced today

Gather students back at the meeting area. Allow partnerships to share stories, encouraging them to ask and answer each other's questions about their stories. Ask two or three students to share their graphic organizers, orally telling their stories. **ELL** Enable Language Production—Increasing Interaction. Asking students to share their work provides additional fluent models to ELLs; additionally, this is a great chance for ELLs to shine by showing off a product that they have had ample time to prepare.

Writing Lesson 9

▼ Teaching Objective

Writers publish stories.

▼ Standards Alignment

W.K.3, W.K.5, W.K.6, SL.K.1a, SL.K.1b, SL.K.3, SL.K.5, SL.K.6, L.K.1, L.K.2 L.K.6

▼ Materials

- Story Elements graphic organizers from Writing Lesson 8
- Charting supplies or interactive whiteboard
- Writing paper with space to draw and a few lines to write

▼ To the Teacher

Our goal is to help students understand narrative stories. Using the story elements helps them create a story around one topic with character, setting, and linked events. Today, the students will produce the story across several pages, transferring the story elements on their graphic organizers to paper. They will have the opportunity to create detailed illustrations and match words to their pictures.

▼ Procedure

Warm Up Gather the class to set the stage for today's learning

Gather students in your meeting area. Begin the lesson by referring to one of the student's graphic organizers from Writing Lesson 8, and celebrate their use of story elements to plan a story. Congratulate all the students on their hard work as writers.

> Each of you used the story elements to plan your own story. Today, we are going to use our graphic organizers to put our stories on paper, using illustrations and words.

Teach Model what students need to learn and do

Model turning your notes from your graphic organizer into a story, adding details to the pictures and words as you draw and write. Think aloud as you reread your story and draw the pictures. Model matching words and illustrations, one page at a time. **ELL** Provide Comprehensible Input—Graphic Organizers. This graphic organizer will be a strong anchor that your ELLs refer to when writing. The organizer also helps make your thinking more visual, so ELLs can follow your process more easily.

Your modeling could unfold like this:

> First I will draw and write about the characters and setting. OK, the story I planned out has me and my two boys as the characters. I am going to draw us all on the beach on a sunny day. I want to add that we are building a sand castle right on the shoreline. Here are our buckets and shovels. Now, I will write, "James, Ferris, and I were on the beach building sand castles."

Keep referring back to your graphic organizer as you think aloud, draw, and write your story.

> Now this is where I will create pages for my key events. I am going to start a new page for the next part of my story. First, we were swimming in the ocean and the dolphins were swimming a little farther out in the sea. Let me draw that on this page. [Model creating a drawing with details that show this event. Then compose a sentence to match.] "We were swimming far from the dolphins."

> On the next page, I will draw us swimming with the dolphins. I will write, "We swam to the dolphins." [Model accordingly.]

> Then, I will draw another event on a new page. [Draw the dolphins carrying the characters on their backs.] I will write, "The dolphins put us on their backs and swam us way out into the ocean!"

> Let me get one final page to show the conclusion for my story. I am drawing the boys and me waving good-bye to the dolphins. The dolphins waved too. Everyone had big smiles, thinking about what a fantastic adventure we just took together. I will write, "Finally, we returned to shore and waved good-bye to our new dolphin friends. James and Ferris both said, 'I hope we see our dolphin friends again!'"

Explain to students how you used your graphic organizer to remind you of your story. Then you included story elements as you drew and wrote your story. **ELL** Provide Comprehensible Input—Models. Explicitly modeling the task at hand demystifies the work to come—a good strategy for all your students, but it especially supports your ELLs.

Try Guide students to quickly rehearse what they need to learn and do in preparation for practice

Have students turn and talk with their partners, reminding themselves of their stories and thinking through the story elements. **ELL** Identify and Communicate Content and Language Objectives—Check for Understanding. Listen to how your ELLs express their understanding of story elements. They may understand the concepts, but need linguistic support in order to express their knowledge.

Circulate and help students say more about their stories as they talk with their partners.

Clarify Briefly restate today's teaching objective and explain the practice task(s)

When writing today, make sure to use your graphic organizer as you draw and write your story, remembering to use the story elements.

Practice Students work independently and/or in small groups to apply today's teaching objective

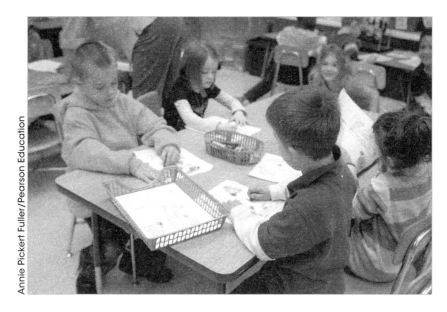

Annie Pickert Fuller/Pearson Education

Provide students with paper. Allow students to use several pieces of paper so they can write their stories across multiple pages. Guide students to refer to their organizers and include all the story elements across their pages, matching words and illustrations. Please note that this may take more than one sitting, and each student may use a different amount of pages to write his or her story.

How students break up the elements of their stories across pages is flexible, but a tried-and-true structure is:

Page 1: character and setting

Page 2: event #1

Page 3: event #2

Page 4: event #3

Page 5: conclusion

You may choose to differentiate the experience by allowing emergent writers to label their drawings or dictate their sentences. More advanced writers can compose sentences to match each drawing. **ELL** Enable Language Production—Reading and Writing. ELLs may differ in their ability to express their thoughts in English and will likely find that task even more challenging when they're writing. Allow them to use whatever linguistic resources they have to make their meaning clear. It is all right to expect different products from different students, as long as the rigor of the *content* in question (story elements) remains high.

Provide time to color and add additional details to illustrations. Option: Have students title their stories, create a cover, and attach the pages together to form storybooks.

Wrap Up Check understanding as you guide students to share briefly what they have learned and produced today

Gather students in your meeting area. Have students orally share their story with their partners. **ELL** Enable Language Production—Increasing Interaction. This gives ELLs a chance to hear language models from a variety of English speakers, not just the teacher.

Celebrate their use of story elements to create stories. Support children as they use drawings when sharing their story. (SL.K.5) This sharing experience is good practice for Writing Lesson 10, which pays close attention to building presentation skills.

ELL Assess for Content and Language Understandings—Summative Assessment. This is an opportunity for you to assess your ELLs' language and content needs and then use this to inform upcoming lessons.

Collect, listen in on, and analyze student stories as a performance-based assessment to determine if students need additional instruction or support as a whole class, in small groups, or one on one.

Milestone Performance Assessment

Publishing Stories

Use student stories to assess understanding of how to use story elements to create real or imagined stories.

Standards Alignment: W.K.3, W.K.5, W.K.6, SL.K.1a, SL.K.1b, SL.K.5, SL.K.6

Task	Achieved	Notes
Choose one idea, real or imagined, to develop into a story.		
Use story elements to create story.		
Match words and illustrations.		
Include details in drawings and/or words to describe story elements.		
Publish a story with all required components.		
Speak audibly when sharing with partner.		

Writing Lesson 10 . . . .

▼ Teaching Objective

Writers share stories with others.

▼ Standards Alignment

W.K.3, SL.K.1a, SL.K.1b, SL.K.3, SL.K.4, SL.K.5, SL.K.6, L.K.1, L.K.6

▼ Materials

- Writing from Writing Lesson 9
- Charting supplies or interactive whiteboard

▼ To the Teacher

Connect today's lesson explicitly to the speaking and listening standards. Today is about students celebrating and telling their stories. They have been completely immersed in all types of stories. Now students can display what they have learned, while feeling satisfaction in knowing how to craft a story that is their unique creation and interesting to others.

Before today's lesson, create small groups of five to six children. Small groups for sharing are developmentally appropriate and exciting for kindergartners. Remind students to speak slowly, clearly, and with expression. Model what a good listener looks like and sounds like. Listeners have their body facing the speaker, eyes and ears open, and mouth closed.

▼ Procedure

Warm Up Gather the class to set the stage for today's learning

Gather students. Congratulate your class on a job well done.

> Friends, you have created and written beautiful stories, using the story elements as a guide. Today we are going to celebrate and share our stories. After we read our stories, we are going to make a "story quilt" by connecting the stories together to hang on the wall. Our unique stories put together will create a beautiful "story quilt."

Teach Model what students need to learn and do

> You thought about your real lives, used your imaginations, and took what you learned about different forms of story and story elements to create magnificent stories. Nice work.

Model reading one of the stories your students created together. Emphasize that you are speaking slowly, clearly, and with expression. Assess student listening. **ELL** Provide Comprehensible Input—Models. By actually showing your students what clear oral presentation looks like, rather than just telling them what to do, you are making your expectations clearer, especially for your ELLs.

Take this opportunity to reinforce the importance of speaking audibly and expressing ideas clearly. (SL.K.6)

Try Guide students to quickly rehearse what they need to learn and do in preparation for practice

Have students practice speaking and listening, using stories you have created together as a group. Circulate and support children.

Clarify Briefly restate today's teaching objective and explain the practice task(s)

Today students will orally share their stories. Remind students what good speakers and listeners look like and sound like.

Practice Students work independently and/or in small groups to apply today's teaching objective

Students will read their own stories to their small groups. Emphasize to students that they should practice speaking slowly, clearly, and with expression.

Wrap Up Check understanding as you guide students to share briefly what they have learned and produced today

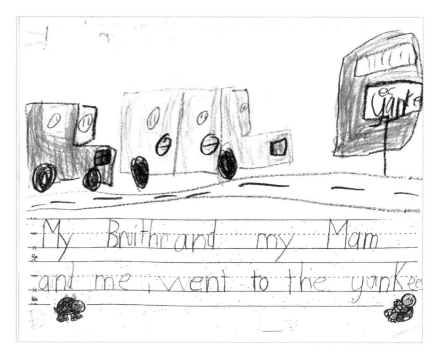

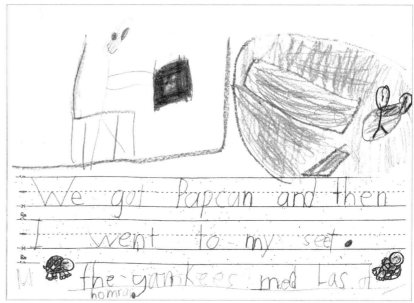

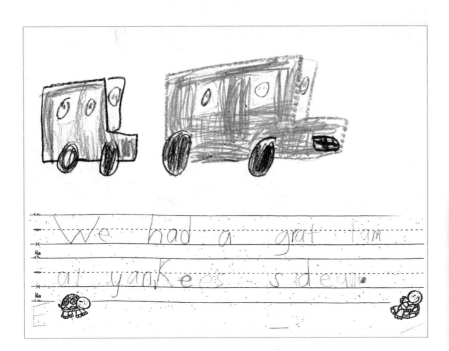

We had a grat tam at yankees stadeum

Have students share what they have learned about writing stories. Guide the conversation to focus on the story elements. The goal of this lesson set is for students to understand that story elements help us be storytellers who tell many different types of story. **ELL** Assess for Content and Language Understandings—Summative. This is an opportunity for you to assess your ELLs' language and content needs and then use this information to plan upcoming lessons. Remember to listen not just for language errors—what kind of literary understanding are your ELLs showing behind the errors?

Goal	Low-Tech	High-Tech
Students will orally share original stories.	Students will orally share stories to classmates in small groups.	Students will take videos of each other sharing stories and then have a storytelling party, viewing the video clips of their stories.
	Students will post illustrations of stories on a class bulletin board for all to view.	Students will record themselves sharing their illustrations and stories to upload to Voicethread or a similar site so classmates and family members can enjoy.

Language Companion Lesson

Teach this lesson early in the lesson set and encourage students to apply their learning to their reading and writing.

▼ Teaching Objective

Readers and writers are able to recognize and name different types of end punctuation.

▼ Standards Alignment

L.K.2b

▼ Materials

- Charting supplies of interactive whiteboard for sharing examples.

▼ To the Teacher

The following lesson introduces three ending punctuation marks: periods, question marks, and exclamation points. Depending on the needs of your class, you may either discuss all three symbols in one day as suggested here or split the teaching into three separate lessons. Regardless of your choice, many students will need lots of review and practice in reading and writing before they will consistently recognize and begin to use these symbols. We have intentionally exposed students to standard terminology and definitions in this lesson so that they may gradually begin to recognize, name, and use them. Mastery will come in time.

▼ Procedure

Warm Up Gather the class to set the stage for today's learning

Display a large question mark, period, and exclamation point to the students.

> These three things are a very important part of writing. You may have seen them while reading or used them in your own writing. When writers use them

correctly, they help readers better understand what the writers mean. Who thinks they know the names of these symbols? Turn and talk to the person next to you and see if they agree.

Have students share what they think the names of the symbols are. If students correctly identify a symbol, write its name under it. Help them name and label all three. **ELL** Identify and Communicate Content and Language Objectives—Academic Vocabulary. Knowing end punctuation—both the names and their meanings—is a key part of being a member of a literate, academic community. By explicitly teaching both, you are inducting your ELLs into this community.

Teach Model what students need to learn and do

Explain the purpose of each type of punctuation mark with example sentences.

> Congratulations, class! We've named all three of these very important symbols. We have a period, a question mark, and an exclamation point. Now let's talk a little bit about how we use each of these symbols in our writing.

> Periods:

> First we have a period. This is the symbol that we use the most. We put a period at the end of a sentence that is a statement. A statement is a sentence that tells us something or describes something.

> Here are some examples of statements:

>> The girl is named Sally.

>> My brother likes to play basketball.

>> The apple is red.

> Notice how at the end of each of these sentences I put a period [circle, highlight, or underline the periods]. The period tells us when the sentence is over and that it is a statement. This is really important when we read two sentences in a row. Like this:

>> [Display]

The girl is named Sally. She likes to read.

See that period in the middle of the page? [Circle, highlight, or underline] That's telling us that the first sentence is done and we should pause before reading the next sentence. Let's read our sentences again, stopping at each period.

Question Marks:

Now let's look at the question mark. This symbol is used at the end of sentences that ask questions. When we see a question mark on the page, we know that what we're reading is a question and not a statement. It lets us know that we may need to come up with an answer.

Here are some sentences that are questions: [Display]

What is the girl's name?

Does your brother play a sport?

What color is the apple?

Notice how there is a question mark at the end of every one of these sentences. [Highlight] This helps me know how to read the sentence. If there were periods at the end of these sentences, I would read them like this: [Read each sentence very flatly.]

But, because the question marks are there, I know they should be read like this: [Read with exaggerated inflection.]

ELL Identify and Communicate Content and Language Objectives—Language Form and Function. Keep in mind that ELLs might have difficulty identifying questions in English. They may not recognize interrogative words, and they may speak languages that use a different intonation pattern for questions. This would be a good place to check for student understanding by asking them to give examples of questions.

Exclamation Points:

Last, we have the exclamation point! We use this in our writing when we are very excited or when something is very important. An exclamation point helps a sentence stand out and gives it more meaning. Let's look at our sentences from earlier: [display original three sentences]. When I read these with periods, they're pretty normal, boring sentences [read out loud again]. But when they have exclamation points on the end, I know to read them very differently. [Display sentences with exclamation points; read them aloud with exaggerated excitement.]

Try Guide students to quickly rehearse what they need to learn and do in preparation for practice

Engage students in a game that asks them to identify which type of punctuation mark is used in a sentence read aloud.

We have learned so much today about how to write and read sentences! Now we're going to play a little game. I'm going to read some sentences out loud, and I need you all to tell me if they have a period, a question mark, or an exclamation point at the end. Instead of yelling out, though, I want you to show me what kind of sentence it is. If you think it's a sentence with a period, I want you to clap your hands once, like this [clap hands together]. If you think it should have a question mark, I want you to tilt your head to one side and scrunch up your face like you're really, really confused—like this [make an exaggerated confused face]. Or, if you think the sentence should have an exclamation point, I want you to wave both of your hands in the air like you're really, super excited! [Demonstrate]

First let's practice! If you think the sentence needs a period, what are you going to do? [Wait for class to all clap hands once.] Good!

Now if you think it needs a question mark, how are you going to show me? [Wait for class to make confused faces.] Excellent!

Now the last one: If you think the sentence needs an exclamation point at the end, what are you going to do? Perfect!

OK, now let's give it a try. I'm going to show you a sentence and read it out loud. After I read the sentence, I want you to tell me if it should have a period, a question mark, or an exclamation point by using one of the signals we just practiced.

Display a sentence on chart paper, minus the end punctuation. Read the sentence out loud, exaggerating inflection, excitement, or monotone, depending on the sentence.

Great job! Most of you picked the right signal! This sentence needs a _____. [Add correct end punctuation to the displayed sentence.]

Ask one or two students how they knew the right answer.

Repeat this with three or four more sentences, or until students seem to get the hang of it. **ELL** Identify and Communicate Content and Language Objectives—Check for Understanding. Focus especially on your ELLs during this game—do they seem to understand the differences, or are they mostly looking around to their peers? Make sure you draw their attention to what makes a sentence a statement, question, or exclamation if they seem confused.

Clarify Briefly restate today's teaching objective and explain the practice task(s)

Praise students for their good work playing the game. Quickly review the symbol for each type of punctuation mark. Ask student volunteers to say a sentence that require each type of mark.

Connect this lesson to their work writing stories. Remind them to keep what they learned in mind as they write together as a class and on their own.

Practice Students work independently and/or in small groups to apply today's teaching objective

During group and independent reading and writing experiences, refer back to this lesson and support students in the appropriate reading and writing of end punctuation.

Wrap Up Check understanding as you guide students to share briefly what they have learned and produced today

When students read aloud to you, remind them to attend to the end punctuation. Periodically ask students to share their writing, and have them point out the end punctuation they used. Frequently encourage them to articulate why using end punctuation is important. **ELL** Assess for Content and Language Understanding—Formative Assessment. If your ELLs are struggling to apply the lesson, dig deep to find the source of the misunderstanding: Do they not know what the marks are for (content issue)? Do they use them correctly but struggle to articulate their reasoning (language issue)? Or are they unable to distinguish different types of sentences (content and language issue)?

GLOSSARY

adventures: journeys or other undertakings that involve risk, danger, or excitement.

character: a person in a story, play, or movie.

compare: to say or note how something is similar to or different from something else.

conclusion: the last part; ending.

contrast: to compare in order to show differences.

differences: the condition of being different from or not like.

ending: the last part; conclusion.

events: a special or important happening.

experiences: something that a person has done or lived through.

imagined: to form in the mind a thought, picture, or image.

narrative: a story, description, or account of events.

plot: the story line or order of events in a book, play, or movie.

real: not imagined; actually existing; true.

retell: to tell again, especially a story or account of events.

sentence: a complete unit of words in either writing or speech with a clear beginning and a full stop. A sentence usually has a subject and a verb. Sentences can state things, ask questions, give commands, or be exclamations.

setting: the surroundings in which an event takes place; environment.

similarities: the state or quality of being similar; resemblance.

story: an account of something that happened, either true or made up.

story elements: the basic parts that make up a story: character, setting, events, conclusion.

storytellers: people who tell stories or recount events.

Accompanying *Core Ready for Grades K–2*, there is an online resource site with media tools that, together with the text, provides you with the tools you need to implement the lesson sets.

The PDToolkit for Pam Allyn's *Core Ready* Series is available free for 12 months after you use the password that comes with the box set for each grade band. After that, you can purchase access for an additional 12 months. If you did not purchase the box set, you can purchase a 12-month subscription at **http://pdtoolkit.pearson.com**. Be sure to explore and download the resources available at the website. Currently the following resources are available:

- Pearson Children's and Young Adult Literature Database
- Videos
- PowerPoint Presentations
- Student Artifacts
- Photos and Visual Media
- Handouts, Forms, and Posters to supplement your Core-aligned lesson plans
- Lessons and Homework Assignments
- Close Reading Guides and Samples
- Children's Core Literature Recommendations

In the future, we will continue to add additional resources. To learn more, please visit **http://pdtoolkit.pearson.com.**

Grade 1

Could It Really Happen?:
An Introduction to Fantasy

Introduction

First graders are imaginative by nature. Watch them during recess and you'll see students transforming into superheroes, knights, princesses, and mythical creatures. Some of the greatest works of children's literature play with our imaginations, inviting us into a world filled with things that couldn't happen in our everyday lives. Some of the stories first graders fall in love with are filled with talking animals; dinosaurs that aren't extinct; and children who sail to faraway places, meet wild things, and become kings and queens. These stories are imaginative and fantastical but have themes that are still very much connected to the experiences and sensibilities of first graders.

In this lesson set, students will develop in their understanding of fiction through a focused study of fantasies. They will name story elements in reading and write their own fantasy stories that go beyond their realistic, everyday lives. Through this lesson set we want to release our first graders' imaginations and consider what's possible in a story. Literature should be full of joy and wonder at all ages, and it is with this spirit in mind that we have designed this lesson set to engage children.

Why This Lesson Set?

In this lesson set, students will:

- Discuss the structure of stories while building vocabulary
- Read closely and think analytically about fantasies
- Work collaboratively to retell stories orally and through writing and drawing
- Write their own fantasy stories
- Reflect upon and write about what they've learned
- Present their ideas using complete sentences

In grades K–2, children begin to master the decoding skills described in the standards for Reading Foundational Skills. As first graders strengthen their foundational skills from kindergarten by reading increasingly more complex texts, it is important to spend more time on the study of the structure of stories. By focusing on the structure, students have an opportunity to work, in a contextualized and engaging way, toward greater proficiency with improved decoding and deeper comprehension.

In support of the reading standards, students are taught within this unit to read closely and rely upon the text as evidence when describing or discussing what's real and what's not. Students will have many opportunities to discuss their thinking with both small groups and the larger class. By focusing on story structure, students will develop a deeper understanding of stories and apply that knowledge to writing stories of their own that play with imaginative elements. Through writing these original pieces, students will become better readers of narrative text.

Common Core State Standards Alignment

Reading Standards

RL.1.1 Ask and answer questions about key details in a text.

RI.1.1 Ask and answer questions about key details in a text.

RL.1.2 Retell stories, including key details, and demonstrate understanding of their central message or lesson.

RL.1.3 Describe characters, settings, and major events in a story, using key details.

RL.1.4 Identify words and phrases in stories or poems that suggest feelings or appeal to the senses.

RL.1.5 Explain major differences between books that tell stories and books that give information, drawing on a wide reading of a range of text types.

RL.1.7 Use illustrations and details in a story to describe its characters, setting, or events.

RL.1.9 Compare and contrast the adventures and experiences of characters in stories.

RL.1.10 With prompting and support, read prose and poetry of appropriate complexity for grade 1.

RI.1.10 With prompting and support, read informational texts appropriately complex for grade 1.

Writing Standards

W.1.3 Write narratives in which they recount two or more appropriately sequenced events, include some details regarding what happened, use temporal words to signal event order, and provide some sense of closure.

W.1.5 With guidance and support from adults, focus on a topic, respond to questions and suggestions from peers, and add details to strengthen writing as needed.

W.1.6 With guidance and support from adults, use a variety of digital tools to produce and publish writing, including in collaboration with peers.

W.1.8 With guidance and support from adults, recall information from experiences or gather information from provided sources to answer a question.

Speaking and Listening Standards

SL.1.1 Participate in collaborative conversations with diverse partners about grade 1 topics and texts with peers and adults in small and larger groups.

a. Follow agreed-upon rules for discussions (e.g., listening to others with care, speaking one at a time about the topics and texts under discussion).

b. Build on others' talk in conversations by responding to the comments of others through multiple exchanges.

c. Ask questions to clear up any confusion about the topics and texts under discussion.

SL.1.2. Ask and answer questions about key details in a text read aloud or information presented orally or through other media.

SL.1.3 Ask and answer questions about what a speaker says in order to gather additional information or clarify something that is not understood.

SL.1.4 Describe people, places, things, and events with relevant details, expressing ideas and feelings clearly.

SL.1.5 Add drawings or other visual displays to descriptions when appropriate to clarify ideas, thoughts, and feelings.

SL.1.6 Produce complete sentences when appropriate to task and situation.

Language Standards

L.1.1 Demonstrate command of the conventions of standard English grammar and usage when writing or speaking.

L.1.2 Demonstrate command of the conventions of standard English capitalization, punctuation, and spelling when writing.

L.1.5 With guidance and support from adults, demonstrate understanding of word relationships and nuances in word meanings.

L.1.6 Use words and phrases acquired through conversations, reading and being read to, and responding to texts, including using frequently occurring conjunctions to signal simple relationships (e.g., *because*).

Essential Skill Lenses (PARCC Framework)

The Partnership for Assessment of Readiness for College and Careers (PARCC) is a coalition of more than 20 states that has come together with "a shared commitment to develop an assessment system aligned to the Common Core State Standards that is anchored in college and career readiness" (http://www.parcconline.org). As part of its proposal to the U.S. Department of Education, PARCC has developed model content frameworks for English language arts to serve as a bridge between the Common Core State Standards and the PARCC assessments in development at the time of this publication. At the time of publication, PARCC has provided guidelines for grades 3 to 11. At the K to 2 grade levels, however, we expect students to engage in reading and writing through eight PARCC-specified skill lenses in order to build a foundation for future grades. The table below details how each skill lens is addressed across the lesson set (PARCC, 2012).

	Reading	Writing
Cite Evidence	There are many opportunities throughout the lesson set when students are encouraged to cite specific evidence about the structure of a story.	Students write short responses and are encouraged to include evidence from books read aloud.
Analyze Content	Students are asked to analyze how stories are alike and different.	Students write about their reading by analyzing how stories are alike and different.
Study and Apply Grammar	Students must demonstrate the ability to convey their ideas clearly, using language that is appropriate to the situation and audience.	Students work in partnerships to analyze their own writing to improve its clarity.
Study and Apply Vocabulary	Students will understand and apply vocabulary associated with stories, specifically fantasies.	Students identify important vocabulary in reading, which provides support for student writing. Students will think about words and phrases to describe the characters, setting, and events when creating their own stories.
Conduct Discussions	Throughout the lesson set, students engage in whole-group discussions, small-group discussions, and multiple opportunities to turn and talk one on one with a classmate. The teacher should emphasize following general rules and etiquette for discussions and review this as needed. It is crucial that students follow general rules and etiquette in order to have successful discussions.	Students discuss and share their developing stories. Students follow general rules and etiquette for discussions, which are crucial for the success of these discussions.
Report Findings	Students share with the class their investigations into the difference between fictional stories and informational texts.	Students share their final stories. In addition, throughout the lesson set students report back to the whole class about their process.
Phonics and Word Recognition	Plan opportunities for students to build Reading Foundational Skills by exploring grade-level appropriate skills in the context of the Core Texts from each lesson set and applying this knowledge to their independent reading and writing. Schools may also wish to acquire developmentally appropriate curricular materials specific to this area. *Words Their Way: Word Study in Action* by Donald Bear et al. is an excellent example of a program that addresses this need.	
Fluency	Fluency and stamina are emphasized throughout the lesson set. By providing independent reading selections that are at your students' reading levels, you are helping support their growing fluency and stamina. Repeated readings should be encouraged.	There are opportunities for short quick-writes as well as a longer, more extended focus on a particular piece. This balance gives students an opportunity to develop their writing stamina.

Core Questions

These questions should remain at the core of your teaching. Refer back to them often, encouraging your class to share their thinking as it evolves.

- What is a story?
- What are the key elements of a story?
- How do authors use their imaginations when they write stories?
- What is the difference between real and imaginary?
- What are clues that tell us a story couldn't really happen?
- When we compare stories, what do we look for?
- How can we use story elements to write our own fantasy stories?
- How can we work together to share our stories?

Ready to Get Started?

Let's release our students' imaginations . . .

First graders are coming into their own as readers and writers. While much of our reading and writing instruction now will be based in foundational skills, it is critical for first graders to explore and write stories that play with imaginative elements. Included in this lesson set are some of our favorite stories that ignite first graders' sense of how to play with what's realistic and what's fantastical—that their favorite stuffed bear could come alive, that dinosaurs might not be extinct after all, or that animals interact with each other just like you and I do. While many children's books for this age group appear on the surface to be simple stories, our first graders are ready to interpret and use what lies beneath. Read Leo Lionni's *Matthew's Dream* with a group of first graders and listen to them discuss how they are like Matthew, developing a sense of who they are and what they want to be. The texts we've chosen support readers of any age in their quest to think about themselves and the world differently. While the books recommended for this lesson set contain many elements of fantasy, they are stories with realistic themes about developing a sense of who you are, how to overcome adversity, and the struggles one faces to belong. Sometimes the characters are outcasts, misfits, victims, or heroes. In the end, these characters often overcome something and demonstrate for our first graders how to be resilient, hopeful, and kind. Yes, much of what's in these stories is imaginary, and it is through fantasy stories that we can fill our first graders with excitement for reading, observing, and considering a world that is different from their own.

Lesson Set Goals

Within this lesson set, there are many goals we want to help our students reach.

Lesson Set Goals Reading

- Build and demonstrate understanding of story elements through close reading of text, citing textual evidence to support thinking and ideas. (RL.1.1, RL.1.2, RL.1.3, RL.1.10, W.1.8, SL.1.1a, SL.1.1b, SL.1.1c, SL.1.2, SL.1.4, SL.1.5, SL.1.6, L.1.1, L.1.6)
- Identify and explain the differences between narrative stories and informational writing. (RL.1.1, RL.1.5, RL.1.10, RI.1.1, RI.1.10, SL.1.1a, SL.1.1b, SL.1.1c, SL.1.6, L.1.1, L.1.6)
- Use clues (story elements, words, and phrases) to identify what is possible (realistic) and what is not possible (fantasy) in a story. (RL.1.1, RL.1.3, RL.1.4, RL.1.5, RL1.10)
- Use information gained from illustrations and words to better understand a story. (RL.1.1, RL.1.2, RL.1.3, RL.1.7, RL.1.10, SL.1.1a, SL.1.1b, SL.1.1c, SL.1.2, SL.1.6, L.1.1, L.1.6)
- Compare and contrast stories with imaginative elements, citing textual evidence to support their thinking. (RL.1.1, RL.1.2, RL.1.3, RL.1.5, RL.1.9, RL.1.10, SL.1.1a, SL.1.1b, SL.1.1c, SL.1.2, SL.1.6, L.1.1, L.1.6)
- Analyze and discuss fantasy stories, using textual evidence. (RL.1.1, RL.1.2, RL.1.3, RL.1.10, SL.1.1a, SL.1.1b, SL.1.1c, SL.1.2, SL.1.6, L.1.1, L.1.6)
- Participate in the creation of a small-group story mural that contains elements of a fantasy story read together in class. (RL.1.1, RL.1.2, RL.1.3, RL.1.5, SL.1.1a, SL.1.1b, SL.1.1c, SL.1.5, L.1.6)
- Ask and answer questions about key details in a text. (RL.1.1, RI.1.1)

- With prompting and support, read prose and poetry of appropriate complexity for grade 1. (RL.1.10)

- In collaborative discussions, exhibit responsibility to the rules and roles and purpose of conversation. (SL.1.1a, SL.1.1b)

- In collaborative discussions, ask questions in a manner that enhances understanding of topic. (SL.1.1c)

- Speak in complete sentences when appropriate. (SL.1.6)

- Demonstrate knowledge of standard English and its conventions. (L.1.1, L.1.2)

- Use words and phrases acquired through conversations, reading and being read to, and responding to texts. (L.1.6)

Lesson Set Goals Writing

- Plan and write a fantasy story that includes the story elements and has a logical sequence of events (clear beginning, middle, and end). (RL.1.2, RL.1.3, RL.1.5, RL.1.7, RL.1.9, RL.1.10, W.1.3, W.1.5, SL.1.1a, SL.1.1b, SL.1.1c, SL.1.6, L.1.1, L.1.2, L.1.6)

- Include an imaginary character and setting that feels real. (W.1.3, SL.1.4, SL.1.5)

- Include temporal words to signal event order. (W.1.3)

- Add detailed illustrations that complement and enhance the story. (W.1.3, SL.1.5)

- Create a book jacket that shows what's most important in the story. (W.1.3, SL.1.1a, SL.1.1b, SL.1.1c, SL.1.6, L.1.1, L.1.2, L.1.6)

- Ask and answer questions about key details in a text. (RL.1.1)

- With prompting and support, read prose and poetry of appropriate complexity for grade 1. (RL.1.10)

- With guidance and support from adults, focus on a topic, respond to questions and suggestions from peers, and add details to strengthen writing as needed. (W.1.5)

- With guidance and support from adults and peers, share writing with others in meaningful ways. (W.1.6)

- In collaborative discussions, exhibit responsibility to the rules and roles and purpose of conversation. (SL.1.1a, SL.1.1b)

- In collaborative discussions, ask questions in a manner that enhances understanding of topic. (SL.1.1c)

- Speak in complete sentences when appropriate. (SL.1.6)

- Demonstrate knowledge of standard English and its conventions. (L.1.1, L.1.2)

- Use words and phrases acquired through conversations, reading and being read to, and responding to texts. (L.1.6)

Choosing Core Texts

Getting to know your students as readers—their interests, their likes, their dislikes, their goals and passions—is an important first step to teaching this lesson set and will help guide you as you choose read-alouds, shared reading texts, guided reading texts, and independent reading selections for your students. Conducting a student interest inventory is a great way to quickly get some input from your students, but we believe in the power of one-on-one conferring as an essential way of establishing relationships with each of your students and fostering an ethic of care in your classroom.

The following books are used within this lesson set:

- *Bear Has a Story to Tell* by Philip C. Stead
- *Cloudy with a Chance of Meatballs* by Judith Barrett
- *Corduroy* by Don Freeman
- *Dinosaurs* by Gail Gibbons
- *Edwina, the Dinosaur Who Didn't Know She Was Extinct* by Mo Willems
- *The Grouchy Ladybug* by Eric Carle
- *How Do Dinosaurs Count to Ten?* by Jane Yolen
- *If You Take a Mouse to School* by Laura Numeroff
- *Llama, Llama Misses Mama* by Anna Dewdney
- *Matthew's Dream* by Leo Lionni
- *Where the Wild Things Are* by Maurice Sendak

We also recommend having a selection of additional Leo Lionni books available for students to read, analyze, and enjoy in partnerships and independently, such as *Frederick*, *Tillie and the Wall*, *Swimmy*, and so on.

Recommended nonfiction texts to pair with fiction picture books:

- *Bears: Polar Bears, Black Bears and Grizzly Bears* by Deborah Hodge (to pair with *Corduroy*)
- *Eye Wonder: Weather* by DK Publishing
- *Weather* by Seymour Simon (to pair with *Cloudy with a Chance of Meatballs*)
- *Life-Size Zoo: From Tiny Rodents to Gigantic Elephants, an Actual Size Animal Encyclopedia* by Toyofumi Fukuda (to pair with *Matthew's Dream / Where the Wild Things Are*)

Recommended extended read-alouds:

- Little Bear series by Else Holmelund Minarik
- *Mr. Popper's Penguins* by Richard and Florence Atwater
- My Father's Dragon series by Ruth Stiles Gannett
- *The Jungle Book* by Rudyard Kipling
- *The Tales of Peter Rabbit* by Beatrix Potter
- *The Wonderful Wizard of Oz* by L. Frank Baum

A Note *about* Addressing Reading Standard 10: Range of Reading and Level of Text Complexity

This lesson set provides all students with opportunities to work with texts deemed appropriate for their grade level as well as texts at their specific reading level. Through shared experiences and focused instruction, all students engage with and comprehend a wide range of texts within their grade-level complexity band. We suggest a variety of high-quality, complex text to use within the whole-group lessons and recommend a variety of additional titles under Choosing Core Texts to extend and enrich instruction. During independent

practice and in small-group collaborations, however, research strongly suggests that all students need to work with texts they can read with a high level of accuracy and comprehension (i.e., at their developmentally appropriate reading level) in order to significantly improve their reading (Allington, 2012; Ehri, Dreyer, Flugman, & Gross, 2007). Depending on individual needs and skills, a student's reading level may be above, within, or below his or her grade-level band. It should also be noted that at times students can and should most certainly engage with complex texts above their levels when reading independently if they have been taught skills to grapple with texts and if they are confident in working with them.

Teacher's Notes

As you prepare for this lesson set, you will want to gather books from your classroom collection that you love and that will ignite your students' imaginations. We offer several suggestions in the Choosing Core Texts section, but any books you have with imaginative twists on our everyday lives would be appropriate. You will also want to gather books for independent reading, based on your students' reading levels. The lesson set begins with the general structure of stories following the CCSS but then shifts in Reading Lesson 4 to a more focused study of first grade–appropriate fantasy stories. You will want to assess your classroom library to determine if it is possible for students to independently read books that could be considered fantasy—that is, they have elements that couldn't really happen. If not, supply students with fictional stories to read independently and encourage them to consider how these stories could be different if they had fantasy twists. What would they add or change? Through the reading of any fictional text, students will have an opportunity to discuss key first-grade story structure terms—character, setting, and events.

This lesson set serves several critical purposes. First, it is designed to introduce your students to stories that we believe will ignite their imaginations as readers and inspire them as storywriters. Second, it is designed to equip your students with the academic vocabulary for discussing stories using text evidence. Through repeated practice, your students will be able to discuss with thoughtful detail the characters, settings, and events in stories.

In this lesson set, we want to encourage students to not only answer questions, but also to ask questions so that they can better understand stories. To begin their own story-writing process, they'll be writing their own "what if" questions. We want our first graders to write narratives that engage with their imaginations. For many of your students this will be second nature. When you watch students in this age group play, you will still see much of the imagined play they naturally took up in early childhood classrooms. This lesson set gives them an opportunity to explore this side of themselves that loves the imaginary. However, we recognize that for some students writing about their own lives in a realistic way is more comfortable. Notice which students are drawn to the fantasy stories we present in these lessons and which resist imaginative possibilities. Students who resist these stories may require extra support to ask "what if" questions. We believe that helping students imagine "what if" provides a cornerstone for their creative selves and impacts not only their lives as readers and writers, but also gives them a framework for thinking as a scientist, as a researcher, and as a global citizen. This lesson set may be about stories, but the impact of supporting our students as creative thinkers has limitless implications.

In this lesson set we are still solidifying for our first graders the basic structure of fictional stories, but do so with tales that are highly imaginative. The genre of fantasy generally has specific characteristics and classic motifs that this lesson set does not address at the young, first-grade level. These will be introduced in our fifth-grade lesson set. However, the imaginative stories used as Core Texts can be defined as "low fantasies"—that is, they have fantastical elements but take place in realistic settings.

Core Message to Students

What are some of your favorite stories? What do you like about them? Think for a moment of one of them. Could everything in your favorite story really happen? Does it have some things that could be real but also some things that aren't true but make it fun to read and think about? In this lesson set, we're going to read stories full of imagination. We're going to meet talking stuffed bears, a dinosaur who's alive, and mice who want to be artists! Not only are we going to read about these wonderful characters, but we're also going to write our own fantasy stories. What kind of character do you want to create? Where do you want your character to live? For these lessons, you need to have your imagination hats on.

See Appendix 1.1 for an enlarged version to reproduce and share with students.

Questions for Close Reading

The Core Ready lessons include many rich opportunities to engage students in close reading of text that require them to ask and answer questions, draw conclusions, and use specific text evidence to support their thinking (Reading Anchor Standard 1). These opportunities are marked with a close reading icon. You may wish to extend these experiences using our recommended Core Texts or with texts of your choosing. Use the following questions as a resource to guide students to read closely for exploring story structure in any narrative fiction text.

- What characters have you encountered in the story?
- Who are the main characters? Who are the supporting characters?
- Where and when does the story take place?
- What is happening in the story so far?
- What do you think will happen next? Why?
- Is there a problem that needs to be solved?
- Does the problem get solved? How?
- What in this story could really happen? What could not really happen? How do you know?
- What details in the illustrations show us something that is not real? What details in the illustrations show us something that is imagined?
- What words describe things we see, hear, and feel? Does this help the story feel real? In what ways?

Building Academic Language

Below is a list of academic language to build your students' comprehension of the focus of this lesson set and facilitate their ability to talk and write about what they learn. There are words and phrases listed below. Rather than introduce all the words at once, slowly add them to a learning wall as your teaching unfolds. See the glossary at the end of this lesson set for definitions of the words. Also listed are sentence frames that may be included on a sentence wall (Carrier & Tatum, 2006), a research-proven strategy for English language learners (Lewis, 1993; Nattinger, 1980), or as a handout to scaffold student use of the content words. Some students, especially English language learners, may need explicit practice in using the sentence frames. Encourage all students to use these words and phrases regularly in their conversations and writing.

Core Words

beginning	imagine
character	information
end	middle
events	plot
evidence	real
fantasy	realistic
fiction	setting
illustration	

Core Phrases

- I noticed that _____ seems real.

- _____ could really happen.

- _____ could not really happen.

- I see _____ in the illustrations. This shows me that _____.

- My favorite part of the story is _____ because _____.

- I think _____ because _____ (textual evidence to support your thinking).

Recognition

At the end of the lesson set, it is important to recognize the hard work your students have put into their learning and the way they've thought about themselves and others. The end of the writing lesson set offers the perfect opportunity for students to share their original narrative pieces incorporating imaginative elements. There are many other fun ways to make the end of the lesson set memorable, including:

- Students act out their favorite scenes from stories and have classmates share what seemed realistic and what couldn't be real.
- Students perform their own imaginative stories with classmates.
- Students add an imaginative class story to the school newspaper.
- Students add student writing to the classroom or school library.

Assessment

Assessment in this lesson set is both ongoing and culminating. As teachers we are constantly kid-watching and observing how students are making meaning and interpreting new material. Throughout this lesson set, look for performance-based assessments, called Milestone Performance Assessments, each marked with an assessment icon. Milestone Performance Assessments are opportunities to notice and record data on standards-aligned indicators during the course of the lesson set. Use the results of these assessments to determine how well students are progressing toward the goals of the lesson set. Adjust the pace of your teaching and plan instructional support as needed.

Also, we encourage you to use the Reading and Writing Rubrics, also marked with an assessment icon, with each lesson set to evaluate overall student performance on the standards-aligned lesson set goals. In this lesson set, the finalized character profiles are an important piece of summative assessment evidence that can be analyzed and then placed in a portfolio of student work.

In addition, we have provided a Speaking and Listening Performance Checklist (see the PDToolkit) that provides observable Common Core State Standards–aligned indicators to assess student performance as speakers and listeners. There are multiple opportunities in every Core Ready lesson set to make such observations. Use the checklist in its entirety to gather performance data over time or choose appropriate indicators to create a customized checklist to match a specific learning experience.

Core Support for Diverse Learners

This lesson set was created with the needs of a wide variety of learners in mind. Throughout the day-by-day lessons, you'll find examples of visual supports, graphic organizers, highlighted speaking and listening opportunities, and research-driven English language learner supports aimed at scaffolding instruction for all learners. However, we urge you to consider the following more specific challenges with which your students may need guided support. The following sections are written to spotlight important considerations as you move through the lesson sets.

Reading

Choosing texts that are at students' reading levels is essential for their reading success and reading identity. When searching for texts, make sure you have various levels represented in your classroom library. Your students, or some of them, may benefit from repeated exposure to a lesson's teaching point over several days. This can be accomplished with the whole class or in small-group settings.

Closely monitor your students who are reading below grade level to determine if they are reading with accuracy and fluency to support comprehension. Encourage students to use context to confirm or self-correct word recognition and understanding and to reread when necessary. Refer to the Common Core Foundational Skills Standards both at the grade 1 level as well as kindergarten for direct, explicit foundational skills support that your students reading below grade level may need.

As students dig into increasingly more difficult texts, they will encounter a growing number of multi-syllabic words that will require teacher support to decode. Consider organizing your students in story partnerships throughout the lesson set and playing with the roles these partnerships take. Refer to our Core Words guide for vocabulary, which you may want to frontload with small groups of students. Be cognizant of unfamiliar language embedded within the text selections you choose for both whole-class teaching as well as independent reading, and preview the texts you provide to students reading below grade level.

As you continue your work with students, use observational notes and reading assessment data to create two to three specific short-term goals for your students with diverse needs. For example, as stated above, these goals may be related to increasing word accuracy, building vocabulary, improving fluency, or enhancing comprehension. Throughout this lesson set, tailor your individualized and small-group instruction set so that it addresses and evaluates student progress toward these goals.

Writing

Inspired writers are motivated writers. Allowing students to choose the topic of their writing is critical for their ultimate success and their positive development of identity as a writer. When immersing your students in a new genre, form, or purpose for writing, be sure to emphasize the meaning and function this particular type of writing may have in their lives. Many of your students will also benefit from exposure to strong mentor texts, examples of your own writing, as well as the experience of sharing their own work—both the final product and versions in process.

Many of your students will benefit significantly from the opportunity to sketch their stories before adding text. For example, some students will require extra support to move from drawing to writing or to move from story mapping to sentences. You can also provide additional scaffolding by having students draw out the beginning, middle, and end of their story prior to writing it. This is especially helpful for visual learners and students who need to "sketch to stretch." Even your most proficient writers can benefit from this step, but many of your resistant writers especially will feel more comfortable with getting their ideas on paper through drawing first.

As your students move from determining their ideas for their stories and begin telling a sequential tale, provide them with a variety of paper choices that are first-grade appropriate. For students with fine motor control issues, providing a variety of paper choices that have handwriting lines with a dotted line in the middle can offer support, as letter formation may require significant energy for some writers. Also consider having some students type and electronically publish their stories rather than handwrite them if that is a medium more conducive to their writing success.

We want our first graders to communicate their stories to an audience, and supporting them as developing writers is essential. In addition to providing students with topic choice and the opportunity to draw prior to writing, we can provide further scaffolding by having students orally rehearse their stories to us or to a peer. For some students, the oral rehearsal will provide a springboard to writing. Others will have greater success dictating their stories to you.

As with the reading lessons, your students may benefit from several days on a single lesson's teaching point. This can be done with the whole class or in small-group settings.

English Language Learners

While it is always our goal as teachers to get to know all of our students deeply both in and out of the classroom setting, this work is perhaps more critical when considering our English language learners. Honoring families' cultural traditions and experiences is important in getting to know your students, understanding them, and working with them in meaningful ways.

We also encourage you to use your ELLs' home languages as a resource. Researchers on second language acquisition are nearly unanimous on this point: using the home language enhances learning—both content development *and* English language and literacy acquisition. Even if you don't speak your students' home languages, look for every opportunity to have them leverage what they already know as you teach new information. Multilingual practices, like asking students how to say something in their home language or encouraging students to discuss texts bilingually, also send welcoming messages that school is a place for people of all linguistic backgrounds.

English language learners are learning about story structure alongside native English speakers in your classroom, but they are also simultaneously learning English. For our English language learners, therefore, it is essential to simultaneously develop their ability to easily hold conversations about their reading and writing and build their academic language base. Goldenberg (2008) defines "academic English" as the more abstract, complex, and challenging language that permits us to participate successfully in mainstream classroom instruction. English language learners will over time be responsible for understanding and producing academic English both orally and in writing. However, language acquisition is a process, and our English language learners range in their development of English language acquisition. We urge you to consider your students along a spectrum of language acquisition: from students new to this country, to those who are proficient conversationally, to those who have native-like proficiency.

Refer to the English language learner icons **ELL** throughout this lesson set for ways to shelter instruction for English language learners. These elements will help English language learners participate successfully in the whole-group lesson and will support the development of their language skills. Although these moments during instruction are designed to support English language learners, many schools are adding a separate English language development (ELD) block targeted at oral English language development, to further support their students in language acquisition.

Students with growing English proficiency will benefit from a story word wall to build vocabulary (see Core Words and Phrases). A sentence word wall to give them sentence starters to help with conversation will also offer students another layer of support. Some students may benefit from having their own personalized copies of these words to keep in their reading or writing notebooks for quick reference. Visual aids will further support students and give them a reference to what words are important to this study and what they mean.

Some students will benefit from several days on the same teaching point. You may consider gathering small groups of readers or writers for repeated instruction or using one-on-one conferences as an opportunity to revisit teaching points.

Complementary Core Methods

Read Aloud

Take this opportunity to share a wide variety of picture books during your read-alouds. Consider multiple reads of the same text. In your first read, you are providing a foundation for the story as a whole, and your students may benefit from a read-aloud without repeated interruption. In your second read-aloud of the text, pausing to think aloud or asking for students' thoughts allows for deeper understanding of the text. Use your knowledge of students' interests to select texts that will inspire and excite your class. When appropriate, use your read-aloud as another chance for students to practice one or two of the following skills:

- Making a prediction about a text's message from the title
- Determining what's real and what's fantastical
- Asking and answering questions about a text, using the portions of the text as evidence in their responses
- Identifying and exploring the meaning of new vocabulary
- Looking for connections across stories by comparing which story elements are real and which are fantasy

Shared Reading

Shared reading provides a wonderful opportunity to look closely at excerpts from read-alouds for close reading. Use shared reading to reinforce the idea of reading to learn (versus learning to read). Use the Questions for Close Reading listed above as prompts for your conversation about these texts. Shared reading can also be a great place to specifically highlight the linking words found within a shared text and to discuss how they connect ideas.

Shared Writing

Shared writing also provides an opportunity to link your work in other subject areas. Use this time to do the following:

- Compose class questions to write to authors of their favorite fantasies.
- Craft answers to shared questions.
- Write a shared piece of fantasy.
- Revise shared writing to link ideas together, creating more-complex sentences, words, and phrases—such as *also, another, and, more, but.*

Core Connections at Home

Ask students to interview family members about their favorite stories that have elements of fantasy. This includes both stories that are in book form as well as oral traditions that have been passed down through families.

Invite families to come in and share their favorite fantasy stories from childhood. This could be done on a rotating basis or in a big culminating event.

Have students share their final writing projects with their families during a special recognition ceremony. Ask families to write a letter to their child sharing what they learned from their presentations. Display these letters alongside students' final stories.

Reading Lessons

The Core I.D.E.A. / Daily Reading Instruction at a Glance table highlights the teaching objectives and standards alignment for all 10 lessons across the four stages of the lesson set (Introduce, Define, Extend, and Assess). It also indicates which lessons contain special features to support English language learners, technology, speaking and listening, close reading opportunities, and formative ("Milestone") assessments.

The following CORE READY READING RUBRIC is designed to help you record each student's overall understanding across four levels of achievement as it relates to the lesson set goals. We recommend that you use this rubric at the end of the lesson set as a performance-based assessment tool. Use the Milestone Performance Assessments as tools to help you gauge student progress toward these goals. Reteach and differentiate instruction as needed. See the foundational book, *Be Core Ready: Powerful, Effective Steps to Implementing and Achieving the Common Core State Standards,* for more information about the Core Ready Reading and Writing Rubrics.

The Core I.D.E.A. / Daily Reading Instruction at a Glance

Grade 1 Could It Really Happen?: An Introduction to Fantasy

Instructional Stage	Lesson	Teaching Objective	Core Standards	Special Features
Introduce: *notice, explore, collect, note, immerse, surround, record, share*	1	Readers share what they know about stories.	RL.1.1 • RL.1.5 • RL.1.10 • SL.1.1a • SL.1.1b • SL.1.1c • SL.1.2 • SL.1.6 • L.1.1 • L.1.6	ELL S&L Close Reading Opportunity
Define: *name, identify, outline, clarify, select, plan*	2	Readers can tell the difference between stories and informational writing.	RL.1.1 • RL.1.5 • RL.1.10 • RI.1.1 • RI.1.10 • SL.1.1a • SL.1.1b • SL.1.1c • SL.1.2 • SL.1.6 • L.1.1 • L.1.6	ELL S&L Close Reading Opportunity
	3	Readers name elements of a story (characters, setting, major events).	RL.1.1 • RL.1.2 • RL.1.3 • RL.1.10 • W.1.8 • SL.1.1a • SL.1.1b • SL.1.1c • SL.1.2 • SL.1.4 • SL.1.5 • SL.1.6 • L.1.1 • L.1.6	ELL Milestone Assessment Close Reading Opportunity
Extend: *try, experiment, attempt, approximate, practice, explain, revise, refine*	4	Readers identify what makes a story a fantasy.	RL.1.1 • RL.1.2 • RL.1.3 • RL.1.5 • RL.1.10 • W.1.8 • SL.1.1a • SL.1.1b • SL.1.1c • SL.1.2 • SL.1.6 • L.1.1 • L.1.6	ELL S&L Close Reading Opportunity
	5	Readers notice specific words and phrases within a text that convey sensory images and feelings.	RL.1.1 • RL.1.4 • RL.1.10 • SL.1.1a • SL.1.1b • SL.1.1c • SL.1.2 • SL.1.6 • L.1.1 • L.1.5 • L.1.6	ELL Close Reading Opportunity
	6	Readers analyze how illustrations provide important details.	RL.1.1 • RL.1.2 • RL.1.3 • RL.1.7 • RL.1.10 • SL.1.1a • SL.1.1b • SL.1.1c • SL.1.2 • SL.1.4 • SL.1.6 • L.1.1 • L.1.6	ELL Close Reading Opportunity
	7	Readers discuss stories by answering key questions.	RL.1.1 • RL.1.2 • RL.1.3 • RL.1.10 • SL.1.1a • SL.1.1b • SL.1.1c • SL.1.2 • SL.1.4 • SL.1.6 • L.1.1 • L.1.6	ELL S&L Close Reading Opportunity
	8	Readers compare and contrast stories with imaginative elements.	RL.1.1 • RL.1.2 • RL.1.3 • RL.1.5 • RL.1.9 • RL.1.10 • W.1.8 • SL.1.1a • SL.1.1b • SL.1.1c • SL.1.2 • SL.1.4 • SL.1.6 • L.1.1 • L.1.6	ELL S&L Milestone Assessment Close Reading Opportunity
	9	Readers create story murals to share what they've read.	RL.1.1 • RL.1.2 • RL.1.3 • RL.1.7 • RL.1.10 • SL.1.1a • SL.1.1b • SL.1.1c • SL.1.5 • L.1.1 • L.1.2 • L.1.6	ELL Tech Close Reading Opportunity
Assess: *reflect, conclude, connect, share, recognize, respond*	10	Readers show what they know about reading fantasies.	RL.1.1 • RL.1.2 • RL.1.3 • RL.1.7 • RL.1.9 • RL.1.10 • W.1.8 • SL.1.1a • SL.1.1b • SL.1.1c • SL.1.4 • SL.1.5 • SL.1.6 • L.1.1 • L.1.2 • L.1.6	ELL S&L Milestone Assessment Close Reading Opportunity

Core Ready Reading Rubric

Lesson Set Goal	Emerging	Approaching	Achieving	Exceeding	Standards Alignment
Build and demonstrate understanding of story elements through close reading of text, citing textual evidence to support thinking and ideas.	Student is unable to identify or explain the story structure or genre of realistic fiction effectively. Consistently draws inaccurate or irrelevant conclusions. Little or no textual evidence to support thinking.	Student attempts to identify and explain the story structure and genre of realistic fiction. Some inaccuracies and irrelevant explanations may be present. Sometimes provides insufficient textual evidence to support thinking.	Student is able to identify and explain the story structure and genre of realistic fiction. Usually draws accurate and relevant conclusions. Provides sufficient textual evidence to support thinking.	Student effectively and insightfully identifies or explains the story structure and genre of realistic fiction. Provides detailed and thoughtful textual evidence to support thinking.	RL.1.1 RL.1.2 RL.1.3 RL.1.10 W.1.8 SL.1.1a SL.1.1b SL.1.1c SL.1.2 SL.1.4 SL.1.5 SL.1.6 L.1.1 L.1.6
Identify and explain the difference between stories and information writing.	Student is unable to accurately identify and/or explain the difference between stories and informational writing.	Student is able to identify and explain some differences between stories and information writing, with some scaffolding. May have some inaccuracies or lack evidence.	Student successfully identifies and accurately explains the difference between stories and information writing. Provides sufficient textual evidence to support thinking.	Student successfully identifies and explains with accuracy and in depth the difference between stories and information writing. Consistently provides detailed and relevant textual evidence.	RL.1.1 RI.1.1 RL.1.5 RL.1.10 RI.1.10 SL.1.1a SL.1.1b SL.1.1c SL.1.6 L.1.1 L.1.6
Use clues (story elements, words, and phrases) to identify what is possible (realistic) and what is not possible (fantasy) in a story.	Student demonstrates little or no understanding of how to use clues (story elements, words, and phrases) to identify what is possible (realistic) and what is not possible (fantasy) in a story.	Student attempts with some success to use clues (story elements, words, and phrases) to identify what is possible (realistic) and what is not possible (fantasy) in a story. Some misconceptions or inaccuracies may be present. May provide insufficient text evidence to support thinking.	Student is usually able to accurately use clues (story elements, words, and phrases) to identify what is possible (realistic) and what is not possible (fantasy). Cites relevant clues in the text and illustrations to support thinking.	Student is consistently able to use clues (story elements, words, and phrases) to identify what is possible (realistic) and what is not possible (fantasy). May be able to find and highlight exact words that support thinking.	RL.1.1 RL.1.3 RL.1.4 RL.1.5 RL.1.10

Lesson Set Goal	Emerging	Approaching	Achieving	Exceeding	Standards Alignment
Use information gained from illustrations and words to better understand a story.	Student struggles to use information gained from illustrations to better understand the story elements and what is real and what is imagined.	Student attempts with some success to describe understandings gained about the story elements and what is real and what is imagined by looking closely at the illustrations. May have some inaccuracies or lack evidence.	Student clearly describes understandings gained about the story elements and what is real and what is imagined by looking closely at illustrations. Provides accurate examples and relevant details from illustrations.	Student describes several insightful understandings gained about the story elements and what is real and what is imagined by looking closely at illustrations. Provides thorough, accurate, and relevant evidence. May attend to subtle clues or elements present in illustrations.	RL.1.1 RL.1.2 RL.1.3 RL.1.7 RL.1.10 SL.1.1a SL.1.1b SL.1.1c SL.1.2 SL.1.6 L.1.1 L.1.6
Compare and contrast stories with imaginative elements, citing textual evidence to support thinking.	Student struggles to identify the story elements and aspects of a story that is real and one that is imagined. Does not make comparisons between two stories with imaginative elements.	Student may be able to identify the story elements and aspects of a story that is real and one that is imagined but is unable to clearly compare and contrast two stories with imaginative elements. May provide insufficient text evidence to support thinking.	Student identifies the story elements and aspects of a story that is real and one that is imagined and accurately compares and contrasts two stories with imaginative elements. Cites relevant clues in the text and illustrations to support thinking.	Student can consistently and accurately identify the story elements and aspects of a story that is real and one that is imagined, with specific textual examples. Student compares and contrasts in detail stories with imaginative elements.	RL.1.1 RL.1.2 RL.1.3 RL.1.5 RL.1.9 RL.1.10 SL.1.1a SL.1.1b SL.1.1c SL.1.2 SL.1.6 L.1.1 L.1.6
Analyze and discuss fantasy stories using textual evidence.	Student demonstrates little or no success in analyzing and/or discussing fantasy stories. May be completely off task or topic. Little or no textual evidence to support thinking.	Student analyzes and discusses fantasy stories with some positive evidence of comprehension. At times, may lack focus or sense of purpose of discussion. May provide insufficient text evidence to support thinking.	Student analyzes and discusses fantasy stories with the focus and sense of purpose needed to deepen comprehension. Usually stays on topic and contributes to a meaningful discussion. Cites relevant clues in the text and illustrations to support thinking.	Student actively analyzes and discusses fantasy stories with the focus and sense of purpose needed to deepen comprehension. Consistently stays on topic and contributes to a deep and meaningful discussion. Provides detailed and relevant textual evidence.	RL.1.1 RL.1.2 RL.1.3 RL.1.10 SL.1.1a SL.1.1b SL.1.1c SL.1.2 SL.1.6 L.1.1 L.1.6
Participate in the creation of small-group story mural that contains elements of a fantasy story read together in class.	Student makes little or no attempt to participate in the creation of a small-group story mural.	Student shows some evidence of success participating in the creation of a small-group story mural. Some required elements of his/her contribution to the mural may be underdeveloped or unclear.	Student shows solid evidence of success in participating in the creation of a small-group story mural. All required elements of his/her contribution to the mural are clearly present.	Student shows exceptional evidence of actively and thoughtfully participating in the creation of a small-group story mural. Some required elements of his/her contribution to the mural may be very well developed or exceed grade-level expectations.	RL.1.1 RL.1.2 RL.1.3 RL.1.5 SL.1.1a SL.1.1b SL.1.1c SL.1.5 L.1.6

Core Ready Reading Rubric, Grade 1, *continued*

Lesson Set Goal	Emerging	Approaching	Achieving	Exceeding	Standards Alignment
Ask and answer questions about key details in a text.	Student demonstrates little or no evidence of understanding key details in the text through asking and/or answering questions about the text.	Student demonstrates some evidence of understanding key details in the text through asking and answering questions about the text.	Student shows solid evidence of understanding key details in the text through asking and answering questions about the text.	Student consistently shows solid evidence of understanding key details in the text through asking and answering high-level questions about the text and providing solid textual evidence to support thinking.	RL.1.1 RI.1.1
With prompting and support, read prose and poetry of appropriate complexity for grade 1.	Student shows little or no evidence of reading prose and poetry appropriate for the grade 1 text complexity band, with prompting and support, at this point of the school year.	Student shows inconsistent evidence of reading prose and poetry appropriate for the grade 1 text complexity band, with prompting and support, at this point of the school year.	Student shows solid evidence of reading prose and poetry appropriate for the grade 1 text complexity band, with prompting and support, at this point of the school year.	Student shows solid evidence of reading prose and poetry above the grade 1 text complexity band, with prompting and support, at this point of the school year.	RL.1.10
With prompting and support, read information texts of appropriate complexity for grade 1.	Student shows little or no evidence of reading information texts appropriate for the grade 1 text complexity band, with prompting and support, at this point of the school year.	Student shows inconsistent evidence of reading information texts appropriate for the grade 1 text complexity band, with prompting and support, at this point of the school year.	Student shows solid evidence of reading information texts appropriate for the grade 1 text complexity band, with prompting and support, at this point of the school year.	Student shows solid evidence of reading information texts above the grade 1 text complexity band, with prompting and support, at this point of the school year.	RL.1.10
In collaborative discussions, exhibit responsibility to the rules and roles and purpose of conversation.	Student makes little or no attempt to participate in collaborative discussions and build on the talk of others with multiple exchanges. Often disregards the rules and roles of conversation even with prompting.	Student inconsistently participates in collaborative discussions and builds on the talk of others with multiple exchanges. Student observes the rules and roles of conversation but needs frequent prompting.	Student usually participates in collaborative discussions and builds on the talk of others with multiple exchanges. Student observes the rules and roles of conversation. May need some prompting.	Student consistently participates in collaborative discussions and builds on the talk of others with multiple exchanges. Student observes the rules and roles of conversation with little or no prompting.	SL.1.1a SL.1.1b
In collaborative discussions, ask questions in a manner that enhances understanding of topic.	Student makes little or no attempt to ask questions that enhance understanding of the topic.	Student occasionally asks questions to clarify or build understanding of the topic or text under discussion but usually requires support or prompting.	Student asks questions that effectively clarify or build understanding of the topic or text under discussion. May need occasional support or prompting.	Student often asks effective and focused questions to clarify or build understanding of the topic or text under discussion. Proactively uses this strategy to support own learning.	SL.1.1c
Speak in complete sentences when appropriate.	Student shows little or no evidence of speaking in complete sentences when appropriate.	Student shows some evidence of attempting to speak in complete sentences when appropriate.	Student shows solid evidence of speaking in complete sentences when appropriate.	Student shows exceptional evidence of speaking in complete sentences when appropriate.	SL.1.6

Lesson Set Goal	Emerging	Approaching	Achieving	Exceeding	Standards Alignment
Demonstrate knowledge of standard English and its conventions.	Student demonstrates little or no knowledge of standard English and its conventions.	Student demonstrates some evidence of knowledge of standard English and its conventions.	Student consistently demonstrates knowledge of standard English and its conventions.	Student demonstrates an exceptional understanding of standard English and its conventions. Use of conventions is sophisticated for grade level and accurate.	L.1.1 L.1.2
Use words and phrases acquired through conversations, reading and being read to, and responding to texts.	Student shows little or no evidence of the acquisition and/or use of grade-appropriate words and phrases.	Student shows some evidence of acquiring and using grade-appropriate words and phrases.	Student shows solid evidence of acquiring and using grade-appropriate words and phrases.	Student shows a high level of sophistication and precision when using grade-appropriate words and phrases.	L.1.6

Reading Lesson 1

▼ Teaching Objective

Readers share what they know about stories.

Close Reading Opportunity

▼ Standards Alignment

RL.1.1, RL.1.5, RL.1.10, SL.1.1a, SL.1.1b, SL.1.1c, SL.1.2, SL.1.6, L.1.1, L.1.6

▼ Materials

- *Edwina, the Dinosaur Who Didn't Know She Was Extinct* by Mo Willems or our sample story, "The Dinosaur Who Couldn't Come for Tea" (see Appendix 1.2)

- Charting supplies or interactive whiteboard to create Our Favorite Stories . . . For Now Chart and What Stories Have In Common Chart

▼ To the Teacher

We kick off today's lesson with a contemporary picture book. Mo Willems is one of our favorite writers for this age group. Watch as your students become captivated by Edwina, a dinosaur who doesn't realize she is extinct. You may also find that some of your students side with Ronald von Hoobie Doobie (whose name will have them laughing out loud), proud to share their knowledge that dinosaurs are indeed extinct. As an alternative to Mo Willems's book, we have included a sample story that mirrors some of the whimsical, fantastical elements found in his work. Either text will support today's goal of introducing students to stories that have elements of fantasy.

Today's lesson is designed to springboard a discussion of stories, what's realistic, what can't really happen in our everyday worlds, and how writers create stories that make us want to read more and more. This lesson is also designed to informally assess what your students know about stories, what vocabulary they use to discuss stories, and whether they retell their favorite stories with details.

If you have conducted the first-grade character study lesson set from *The Journey to Meaning: Comprehension and Critique,* your students will already have a strong foundation in realistic fiction and this lesson will help them recall all that they learned during that series of lessons. But it is not necessary that your students have already completed that character study lesson set.

▼ Procedure

Warm Up Gather the class to set the stage for today's learning

Connect to students' prior experience with stories, and describe some of the stories they'll be reading in this lesson set.

> Today, we are going to dive into the world of stories. Have you ever read a story and thought to yourself, hmm . . . could this really happen? Or read about a character who goes on a wild and crazy adventure you wish you could have? Or read a story with a talking animal that makes you wonder what it would be like if dogs, cats, or your favorite stuffed animal could speak? For the next few weeks, we're going to spend a lot of time with stories that play with what's real and what's only possible in the world of stories.

> Who can tell me about of one of their favorite stories?

Take a moment and allow students to share the names of their favorite stories. Encourage students to think about both books they have read independently as well as books you have shared as read-alouds. Jot a quick list, titled "Our Favorite Stories . . . For Now" as students share. **ELL** Frontload the Lesson—Make Connections. By priming your ELLs to think about the lesson in terms of familiar stories, you are helping them get ready to mentally organize the new learning they're about to do.

Teach Model what students need to learn and do

Now that your students have identified their favorite stories, have them turn and talk to a partner to share what they think all these stories have in common. **ELL** Enable Language Production—Increasing Interaction. This is a time for ELLs to practice their oral English and to expand their thinking through the peer conversation.

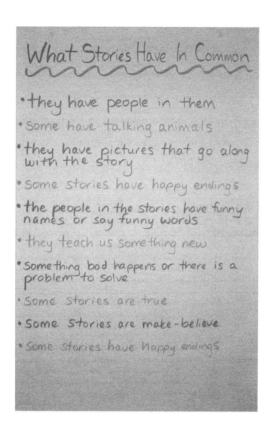

What Stories Have In Common

- they have people in them
- Some have talking animals
- they have pictures that go along with the story
- Some stories have happy endings
- the people in the stories have funny names or say funny words
- they teach us something new
- Something bad happens or there is a problem to solve
- Some stories are true
- Some stories are make-believe
- Some stories have happy endings

Invite students to share their thinking and begin a new chart titled "What Stories Have in Common."

> You have shared so many great stories. Let's see if we can list what these stories have in common.

> Your students may suggest such things as:

- There are people in them.
- Events happen.
- Some stories have happy endings.
- Some stories are from long ago.
- We have stories from our own lives.
- Some stories are true.
- There are make-believe stories.

At this introductory stage of the lesson set, allow for missing items and misconceptions. Today is all about generating initial ideas and focusing your students' attention on the main thrust of the lesson set: stories. Over the course of the lesson set, your students will learn how to discuss stories using vocabulary associated with the structure of a story—characters, setting, and events. They will also be able to discuss and compare stories that could be possible and stories that could not be possible. This conversation will help you determine what your students know and how you can specifically guide instruction in the lessons to come. **ELL** Assess for Content and Language Understanding—Diagnostic Assessment. This is an excellent opportunity for you to assess how much students already know about stories, and how well they are able to express this knowledge in English. Look for both strengths and opportunities for instruction.

Read aloud and discuss either *Edwina, the Dinosaur Who Didn't Know She Was Extinct* or our sample story, "The Dinosaur Who Couldn't Come for Tea." How do we know this is a story?

> I'm going to read a story about a dinosaur. Guess what? In this story, dinosaurs are not extinct. As I'm reading, I'm going to be thinking about how I know this is a story. As you listen, be ready to share what you think makes this a story.

As you read, pause to think aloud about who the characters are, how they talk to one another just like you and me, and what kinds of things happen to the characters along the way. **ELL** Identify and Communicate Content Objectives—Paraphrase, Repeat, Clarify. By discussing what is going on in the book as you read it, you give your ELLs a second point of entry—first, the text itself; second, your reexplanation of what is going on in the story.

After you finish reading the story, ask yourself aloud, "What made this a story?" using the list you created earlier in this lesson as a reference.

Use this opportunity to remind students of the importance of carefully listening for key details during a read aloud. Encourage them to ask and answer questions about specific details. (SL.1.2) **ELL** Provide Comprehensible Input—Models. By modeling your thought process, you make the task your students are about to complete on their own even more transparent for your ELLs.

Try Guide students to quickly rehearse what they need to learn and do in preparation for practice

In partnerships, have students continue to discuss what made your selection a story. Encourage them to discuss specific details from the story.

Ask students: *How did you know this was a story?*

 Turning and talking provides a wonderful opportunity for you to highlight the importance of the rules you have set for speaking and listening in the classroom, including taking turns, looking at the speaker, and staying on topic. (SL.1.1a, SL.1.1b, SL.1.1c)

Clarify Briefly restate today's teaching objective and explain the practice task(s)

Remind students of how the read-aloud you've shared today can be defined as a story.

Today we shared what we know about stories and how we knew this tale about a dinosaur was a story. When we gather together at the end of our independent reading time, I want each of you to bring a book you have identified as a story. Remember, you'll know that what you're reading is a story if there are characters and things happen to them. You might even find that the characters in your book talk to one another.

Practice Students work independently and/or in small groups to apply today's teaching objective

Students read independently at their seats. As students read, they should stop to identify details that indicate this is a story.

Wrap Up Check understanding as you guide students to share briefly what they have learned and produced today

Gather your class. Ask students to turn and share the book they chose from their independent reading. As they are talking, partners should share the title of the book, the author, and how they knew this book was a story. **ELL** Enable Language Production—Increasing Interaction. As students will have had ample time to make their selections and think about how they know they are stories, this is a perfect chance for your ELLs to shine by showing what they know. This is also another opportunity to check in with beginner ELLs to evaluate how comfortable they are speaking with their peers in English.

Once everyone has had a chance to share with their partner, ask several students to share their thinking with the entire class. Refer back to your chart from earlier, What Stories Have in Common. Do your students have anything to add to this list now?

Pressmaster/Fotolia

Reading Lesson 2

▼ Teaching Objective

Readers can tell the difference between stories and informational writing.

Close Reading
Opportunity

▼ Standards Alignment

RL.1.1, RL.1.5, , RL.1.10, RI.1.1, RI.1.10, SL.1.1a, SL.1.1b, SL.1.1c, SL.1.2, SL.1.6, L.1.1, L.1.6

▼ Materials

- *Edwina, the Dinosaur Who Didn't Know She Was Extinct* by Mo Willems
- *Dinosaurs* by Gail Gibbons, or another informational text on dinosaurs
- Sample Text: "The Dinosaur Who Couldn't Come for Tea" (see Appendix 1.2)
- Sample Text: Dinosaur Profile: The Stegosaurus (see Appendix 1.3)
- Charting supplies or interactive whiteboard for How Do I Know? Chart
- Variety of fiction stories and informational/explanatory picture books for students to explore

▼ To the Teacher

In Reading Lesson 1, your students shared their prior knowledge about stories. Today is about continuing to build knowledge of stories by comparing them to informational texts. While some of your students may already have this skill, we want to ensure that all first graders are able to distinguish comfortably between the two. If any of your students continue to have difficulty determining which books fall under which category, consider providing small-group or individual instruction to build mastery. This understanding is a necessary foundation for learning how readers approach each type of text. The remaining lessons within this lesson set focus on the world of stories.

Note that there are some informational texts, such as biographies, that are a combination of both story and factual information. Decide whether your class would benefit from discussing this at this point before you include any such examples in the mix. Once the students have a fairly firm grasp of what stories are, it can be beneficial to introduce them to biographies, with the mix of story and factual information providing another chance to reinforce their understanding of story by distinguishing between story and factual information.

▼ Procedure

Warm Up Gather the class to set the stage for today's learning

Remind students of the lesson on stories from Reading Lesson 1. Review with the class what they learned together.

> Did you know that writers of stories often use some real things to help them make their stories interesting? Mo Willems must have thought it was pretty interesting that dinosaurs are extinct and wanted to write a story where he got to imagine how it would be if they weren't.

> Yesterday we thought about what we know about stories. Who can remind us: How can we tell if what we are reading is in fact a story? How did we know the book about Edwina was a story?

Allow one or two students to share their thinking. Refer back to the charts you created in Reading Lesson 1 and the read-aloud you conducted of *Edwina, the Dinosaur Who Didn't Know She Was Extinct*. **ELL** Frontload the Lesson—Make Connections. Repeatedly using the same charts, books, and other resources builds common ground to which ELLs can continually refer back in order to make connections with future learning.

Teach Model what students need to learn and do

Discuss the idea that stories are different from informational writing by introducing an informational text on dinosaurs that students can compare to another story about dinosaurs.

Today I want us to think more about what makes something a story and compare that to another type of book we might find in our classroom—informational writing. Today, we are going to read a different book about dinosaurs. This book is an example of informational writing, which means it's full of information that is true about our natural world.

While I am reading this book, I want you to be thinking about the difference between stories such as *Edwina* and informational writing such as this book called *Dinosaurs*. What clues point us to the difference?

Read a few pages aloud from *Dinosaurs* by Gail Gibbons. Begin a chart titled How Do I Know? Think aloud one or two ways you know the difference between a fictional story and an informational text. Have the class help you determine clues we use to tell when a text is a story versus when it is a piece of informational writing. **ELL Enable Language Production—Listening and Speaking. When you explain how *you* can tell the difference between a story and informational text, you are modeling the language of such distinctions for your ELLs. When you have *students* offer the clues they've noticed, you're giving your ELLs a chance to practice this language themselves.**

Now that we've read these two books about dinosaurs, I need your help in adding to our chart.

ELL Provide Comprehensible Input—Visuals. ELLs can understand a lot by listening to their peers and teacher, but recoding this information in writing gives them another way to access it, using a different language mode.

Below is a sample of what may appear in the chart after this discussion. Content will vary depending on the discussion. Consider including simple drawings to help students read and recall the content of the charts.

How Do I Know?

Fictional Stories	Informational Writing
Sometimes realistic, sometimes not	Teaches true facts about the world
Characters, setting created by author	Real people, animals, places
Describes events in order: beginning, middle, end	Sometimes has sections with headings (ex: What Horses Eat)
Usually has drawings/illustrations that show the characters and what happened.	Sometimes there are photos of real things instead of drawings/illustrations.

Try Guide students to quickly rehearse what they need to learn and do in preparation for practice

Provide students with copies of Dinosaur Profile: The Stegosaurus (see Appendix 1.3), and have them read it to themselves or with a partner to decide whether it is a story or informational writing. Encourage students to point to specific sentences that led them to their decision. **ELL Enable Language Production—Reading and Writing. With this structured task completed in partners, ELLs of various levels of proficiency are getting support, guidance, and immediate feedback before moving on to less-structured practice.**

OK, friends, now I have a challenge for you. I'm going to give you two short readings, and you are going to need to decide which one is a story and which one is informational. How do you know?

The Amazing Starfish

Starfish, or sea stars, get their name from the unusual shape of their bodies. The five arms of a starfish remind people of stars. While most starfish have five arms, some may have as many as 50! Starfish come in many colors, some dull and some bright. Dull colors can help starfish hide. Bright colors often scare off enemies. It is true that some starfish can grow a new arm if one is injured or lost. Some types of starfish can completely regrow from just a small piece of an arm. Amazing!

Sammy the Starfish

It was a beautiful day at the seashore. The sun sparkled on the water and seagulls called out happily. Sammy the Starfish was all set to have a fantastic day. He and his friend Susie Scallop had big plans to have a picnic at the coral reef. He packed a basket full of delicious snacks and left to meet Susie at their favorite rock. When he arrived, he looked all over, but Susie was not to be found. Where could she be?

Have students share the details they found, and add these to your chart if new ideas are present. **ELL** Enable Language Production—Increasing Interaction. Whenever students are talking in your class, ELLs are getting a chance to develop both their speaking and listening skills. It is important that they frequently hear voices other than the teacher's and that they get a chance to practice putting their ideas into English words.

Clarify Briefly restate today's teaching objective and explain the practice task(s)

Direct students to their independent work for today, which will be to collaborate with a partner to sort books in their classroom library using the clues you've created together on a chart.

Today you are going to work with a partner to read some of the books in our classroom library. Work together to use the clues we talked about in our How Do I Know? Chart to point to specific moments in the text that told you, Yes, this is a story! or Yes, this is informational writing!

Practice Students work independently and/or in small groups to apply today's teaching objective

Rather than read independently, today students will be working collaboratively to determine whether texts are stories or informational.

Remind students of the speaking and listening skills needed for successful partnerships, such as how to hold the book between them and take turns with who is in charge of labeling the books. (SL.1.1a) If this is early in the school year, you might consider using this activity as a way to shelve your classroom library books into sorted baskets.

Have students use sticky notes to label whether a book is a story or an informational text. What clues did they use to determine this?

Wrap Up Check understanding as you guide students to share briefly what they have learned and produced today

Gather your class, asking students to hold up one example of a story and one example of informational writing. Revisit the How Do I Know? Chart and see if anyone has something to add to either column based on their reading today. **ELL** Assess for Content and Language Understanding—Formative Assessment. This is a chance for you to check both if your ELLs understand the distinction between stories and informational writing, and if they have the language to express their reasoning. Remember that gaps in vocabulary sometimes mask very solid content learning!

Reading Lesson 3 ·············

▼ Teaching Objective

Readers name elements of a story (character, setting, major events).

Close Reading Opportunity

▼ Standards Alignment

RL.1.1, RL.1.2, RL.1.3, RL.1.10, W.1.8, SL.1.1a, SL.1.1b, SL.1.1c, SL.1.2, SL.1.4, SL.1.5, SL.1.6, L.1.1, L.1.6

▼ Materials

- *Edwina, the Dinosaur Who Didn't Know She Was Extinct* by Mo Willems

- *Corduroy* by Don Freeman or another book with imaginative elements such as one of the following:

  If You Take a Mouse to School by Laura Numeroff

  Llama, Llama Misses Mama by Anna Dewdney

  The Grouchy Ladybug by Eric Carle

  Bear Has a Story to Tell by Philip C. Stead

- Charting supplies or interactive whiteboard to create Story Elements Chart

- Copies of Story Elements Graphic Organizer for students (Appendix 1.4)

▼ To the Teacher

In Reading Lesson 2, your students identified some books and short texts that are stories and others that are informational. Today we dive back into a focus on stories by helping students name the elements of a fictional story. Our Grade 1 lessons in *The Journey to Meaning: Comprehension and Critique* focus on characters, so if you have conducted that lesson set, your students have an in-depth understanding of character types. This lesson is designed to give students the academic vocabulary needed to discuss the basic structure of a story—that is, they all have characters, a setting, and events that occur. While any story could be used, we recommend continuing with *Edwina, the Dinosaur Who Didn't Know She Was Extinct* or another favorite fictional story from your read-aloud collection that students are adequately familiar with. And then introduce one new story that has imaginative elements. We've chosen *Corduroy*, but the world of children's literature is full of many wonderful choices. Some other excellent choices might be:

If You Take a Mouse to School by Laura Numeroff
Llama, Llama Misses Mama by Anna Dewdney
The Grouchy Ladybug by Eric Carle
Bear Has a Story to Tell by Philip C. Stead

Our Kindergarten Book 2 lesson set introduces students to the structure of a story through story strings, a kinesthetic tool designed to practice story elements. For students who need additional reinforcement, we recommend looking back at that grade level for additional lessons.

▼ Procedure

Warm Up Gather the class to set the stage for today's learning

Remind students of their success when asking themselves, "How do I know?" to determine whether what they were reading was a story or was informational.

Today builds on their developing vocabulary around stories by reinforcing the structure of a story. We want all of our first graders comfortable using the terms *character*, *setting*, and *events*. These terms may already be on a word wall you've created, or they may be on your What Stories Have in Common Chart. If so, refer to these.

> Today we're going to dive back into our world of stories. To help us better discuss these stories, we want to make sure we are all using some of the same words.

ELL Identify and Communicate Content and Language Objectives—Academic Vocabulary. These words may be translated into ELLs' home language to make their meaning clear and to support the transfer of vocabulary between languages.

Teach Model what students need to learn and do

Character	Setting	Event 1	Event 2	Event 3	Conclusion

Briefly define the basic story elements for students.

All fictional stories have certain key elements. They all have characters—the people or animals whom the story is about. They all have a setting—where the story takes place. Stories also have events that help keep the story moving. The last important event has a special name: the conclusion.

Begin a chart that documents the structural elements of the read-alouds you've used so far. **ELL** Provide Comprehensible Input—Graphic Organizers. Using graphic organizers offers another way to think about the information you are teaching. ELLS can use the graphic organizer to structure their thinking, and to make connections between the class discussion and the work they will do later.

Let's look back at Edwina, the Dinosaur Who Didn't Know She Was Extinct. *What were the elements of this story?*

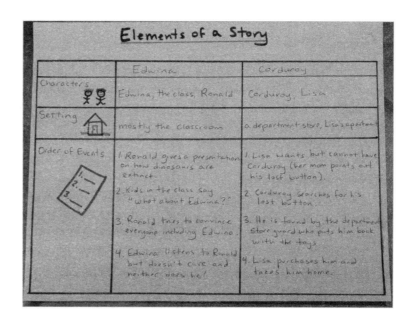

Story Elements

	Edwina	Corduroy
Characters	Edwina, the class, Ronald	
Setting	Mostly the classroom	
Events (in order, including conclusion)	1) Ronald gives a presentation on how dinosaurs are extinct. 2) Kids in class say, "What about Edwina?" 3) Ronald tries to convince everyone, including Edwina. 4) Edwina listens to Ronald but doesn't care, and neither does he!	

Try Guide students to quickly rehearse what they need to learn and do in preparation for practice

Now have students try identifying the elements of either a new story or another favorite story. We recommend reading aloud *Corduroy,* which is the beloved tale of a stuffed bear who comes to life in a department store. This book is also available in video form from Scholastic.

Story Elements

	Edwina	Corduroy
Characters	Edwina, the class, Ronald	Corduroy, Lisa
Setting	Mostly the classroom	Department store, then Lisa's apartment
Events (in order, including conclusion)	1) Ronald gives a presentation on how dinosaurs are extinct. 2) Kids in class say, "What about Edwina?" 3) Ronald tries to convince everyone, including Edwina. 4) Edwina listens to Ronald but doesn't care, and neither does he!	1) Lisa wants but cannot have Corduroy (her mom points out his lost button). 2) Corduroy searches for his lost button. 3) He is found by the department store guard, who puts him back with the toys. 4) Lisa purchases him and takes him home.

Clarify Briefly restate today's teaching objective and explain the practice task(s)

Explain to students how this applies to their independent reading. Remind students to ask themselves questions as they read about the characters, the setting, and what's happening. **ELL** Identify and Communicate Content Objectives—Repeat. With this final clarification, you help ELLs be sure they know what is expected of them during independent work.

> Today you are going to read independently and identify the elements in your own storybooks. Who are the characters? What is the setting? What events have happened so far? In what order?

Students should be encouraged to use writing and drawing to complete the Story Elements Graphic Organizer (Appendix 1.4). We want them to be able to identify, use, and discuss these elements. While writing about reading is important, some of your students will be better able to express themselves in this lesson through a combination of words and drawings. **ELL** Enable Language Production—Reading and Writing. Make sure students can see the whole-class chart on story elements, to support them in filling out their own chart. You should keep your content expectations high for all students, but know that your ELLs might need to use a combination of pictures, speaking, and writing (in English or in their home language) to make their meaning known.

Practice Students work independently and/or in small groups to apply today's teaching objective

Students will read independently and complete their own Story Elements Graphic Organizer, identifying key elements of their stories.

Wrap Up Check understanding as you guide students to share briefly what they have learned and produced today

Students retell their stories so far using their story organizer to help guide them. **ELL** Assess for Content and Language Understandings—Formative Assessment. This is an opportunity for you to assess your ELLs' language and content needs and then use this to inform upcoming lessons. Do they grasp the concepts of story elements but struggle to express their ideas? Or is the expressive language there, but something about the instruction has gone over their heads?

Collect and analyze the student Story Elements Graphic Organizer as a performance-based assessment to determine if students need additional instruction or support as a whole class, in small groups, or one on one.

Milestone Performance Assessment

Identifying the Story Elements

 Use this checklist to assess performance on the Story Elements Graphic Organizer.

Standards Alignment: RL.1.1, RL.1.2, RL.1.3, W.1.8, SL.1.5

	Achieved	Notes
Identify Character.		
Identify Setting.		
Three or more key events in order (including conclusion).		

Reading Lesson 4

▼ Teaching Objective

Readers identify what makes a story a fantasy.

Close Reading Opportunity

▼ Standards Alignment

RL.1.1, RL.1.2, RL.1.3, RL.1.5, RL.1.10, W.1.8, SL.1.1a, SL.1.1b, SL.1.1c, SL.1.2, SL.1.4, SL.1.6, L.1.1, L.1.6

▼ Materials

- *Edwina, the Dinosaur Who Didn't Know She Was Extinct* by Mo Willems
- *Corduroy* by Don Freeman
- Charting supplies or interactive whiteboard to create Could It Really Happen? Chart
- Story Cubes (Appendix 1.5 provides a template)

▼ To the Teacher

In Reading Lesson 3, your students began to use key terms for discussing stories. They did so by discussing two stories that are fantasies: *Edwina* and *Corduroy*. Today builds on yesterday's work, with more critical thinking as students specifically notice, analyze, and discuss what could really happen in these stories and what couldn't really happen. We've created story cubes to help reinforce the work from the previous lesson on the structure of a story, in addition to incorporating today's lesson. We believe this is a fun and interactive way to reinforce critical academic vocabulary and to continue to build students' understanding of how authors of fictional stories often play with what's real and what's not by using their imaginations to consider a world different from our own.

▼ Procedure

Warm Up Gather the class to set the stage for today's learning

Look back at the Story Elements Chart you created in Reading Lesson 3, identifying the story elements in *Edwina* and *Corduroy*. Your students now have a solid foundation in the basic elements of a story. Now they're ready to continue analyzing stories read aloud and read independently, by noticing what seems possible and what was imagined by the authors to create a world different from our own.

Connect to the work with story elements from Reading Lesson 3.

First graders, you really have a lot to say about the stories we're reading together and the stories you've been reading independently. We're going to continue using words such as character, setting, and events to describe with great detail the stories we're reading. Readers keep these elements in mind as they read to better understand the action of a story.

Teach Model what students need to learn and do

	Could really happen	Couldn't really happen
Edwina	• Children and teacher • Classroom • A boy who wants to be listened to	• A dinosaur that isn't extinct • A talking dinosaur • A dinosaur who bakes cookies
Corduroy	• A girl and her mom • The department store and apartment • Lots of toys in a toy store	• A walking, thinking stuffed bear goes on an adventure • The stuffed bear cares that his button is missing
Our independent reading books		

With background knowledge activated, introduce and define the term *fiction* for your class. For our first graders, we can define fiction as a story told from an author's imagination that didn't really happen. Within the world of fiction, we have both realistic stories in which everything truly exists and could really happen and fantasy stories that contain elements that couldn't really happen such as magic or talking animals.

You know a lot about what stories have in common. Fiction is the word we use when talking about stories that are made up by a writer.

Next, introduce and define the terms *realistic* and *fantasy*. **ELL** Identify and Communicate Content and Language Objectives—Key Content Vocabulary. This is an opportunity for you to help your ELLs expand their academic vocabulary. Modeling how to use these terms in sentences is also very effective for all your students, but especially so for ELLs.

Some fictional stories are realistic and full of things that could really happen. We also have stories that have things that couldn't happen the way they are described. We call those fantasies. We could tell a story about a rainy day. Could this really happen? Sure. That would be a realistic story. We could tell a story about a day it rained pancakes. Could this really happen? No, raining pancakes can only happen in our imaginations, and we would call that a fantasy.

Here are two examples. Can you decide which one is realistic and which one is fantasy? I could write a story about a boy who had a dog. I could also write a story about a boy who had a dog who could talk to him. Hmmm . . . which one is realistic? That's right, the story about the boy who had the dog. That could really happen. A story about a dog who could talk would be a fantasy—that couldn't really happen.

Today, we're going to analyze our read-alouds and independent reading books again, but this time we're going to be looking for what could really happen and what couldn't. Authors of fantasy stories usually mix things that could really happen with things that couldn't really happen. It's the parts that couldn't really happen that make them fantasies. Let's look back at Edwina and list for ourselves what in this fantasy story could really happen and what couldn't really happen.

Chart the realistic and fantasy elements of *Edwina*.

Now let's look back at *Corduroy*. What could really happen and what couldn't really happen?

Chart the realistic and fantasy elements of *Corduroy*. **ELL** Provide Comprehensible Input—Graphics. This chart helps clarify the content of the

conversation going on in your classroom about *Edwina* and *Corduroy*. ELLs can see how their and others' contributions fit into the two-part distinction (realistic and fantasy) that you are teaching about.

Could It Really Happen?

	Elements of the story that COULD happen	Elements of the story that COULD NOT happen
Edwina	Children and teacher Classroom A boy who wants to be listened to	A dinosaur that isn't extinct A talking dinosaur A dinosaur who bakes cookies
Corduroy	A girl and her mom The department store and apartment Lots of toys in a toy store	A walking, thinking stuffed bear goes on an adventure. The stuffed bear cares that his button is missing.
Our independent reading books		

Now we're going to try something a little bit different. To review our story elements and help us all discuss what's possible and what's imagined in the fiction books we've read, we're going to play with some story cubes. Listen to the prompts on our cubes and how, when they land on a side, I answer using a complete sentence.

Try Guide students to quickly rehearse what they need to learn and do in preparation for practice

Model how to use the story cube and how to answer using a complete sentence when discussing either *Edwina* or *Corduroy*. The labels on the six sides should be as follows: Title; Main characters; Setting; Three important events; What in this story could really happen?; What couldn't really happen? A template is available in Appendix 1.5.

This lesson provides a great opportunity to reinforce that students should use complete sentences when appropriate. (SL.1.6). **ELL** Provide Comprehensible Input—Models. Modeling the task at hand, rather than just explaining it, can help your ELLs feel confident that they know what is expected of them.

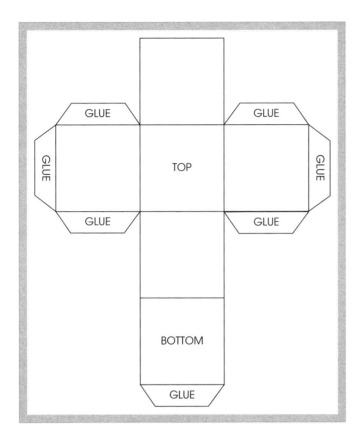

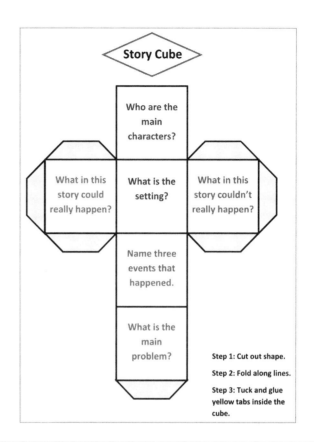

Have students practice discussing elements of a story and what could happen and what couldn't happen by using story cubes. If you modeled with *Edwina*, have students discuss *Corduroy* or vice versa.

Now it's your turn to try. Turn and talk to a partner about how you would answer this question on the story cube in a complete sentence.

Throw the story cube and have everyone answer the same question to a partner.

This provides not only practice with the content of today's lesson but also provides an opportunity for students to respond to the comments and thoughts of their partners and to ask thoughtful questions about the text. (SL.1.1b, SL.1.1c)

ELL Enable Language Production—Increasing Interaction. Using the story cube lets ELLs to hear their peers use language and demonstrate how they think about text evidence. The peer model may clarify the content focus (*Oh, that's what characters are!*), or clarify the language necessary to express the content (*Oh, that's how you make a sentence about a character!*), or both!.

Clarify Briefly restate today's teaching objective and explain the practice task(s)

Quickly review the main ideas of the lesson. Direct students to continue thinking about the story elements in their independent reading books, paying particular attention to what could really happen and what couldn't.

Practice Students work independently and/or in small groups to apply today's teaching objective

Students read independently or in a small-group setting for a sufficient amount of time to be able to answer the questions on the story cube, noticing the story elements, what could really happen, and what could not really happen. If you are not able to acquire fantasy stories at all of the independent reading levels represented in your class, consider the possibility of having students engage in fantasy stories through a listening center. After reading, instruct your students to use their story cubes to answer questions with a partner about their independent reading books. Remind them of the importance of answering in a complete sentence. **ELL** Enable Language Production—Listening and Speaking. ELLs have been reading their books and thinking about their assignment for 15–20 minutes now, so they have been given ample opportunity to get their words ready. This is a great chance for them to show off their good thinking in a low-pressure setting after having lots of time to prepare.

Wrap Up Check understanding as you guide students to share briefly what they have learned and produced today

Have students share any new story elements they noticed in their reading. What could really happen? What couldn't? Add some samples to the chart begun earlier in the lesson. **ELL** Assess for Content and Language Understanding—Formative Assessment. If some of your ELLs seem stuck, try to notice what the barrier is: do they not understand the difference between realistic and fantastic events? Or do they not have the words to express this understanding? Each requires a different instructional intervention.

Reading Lesson 5

▼ Teaching Objective

Readers notice specific words and phrases within a text that convey sensory images and feelings.

Close Reading Opportunity

▼ Standards Alignment

RL.1.1, RL.1.4, RL.1.10, SL.1.1a, SL.1.1b, SL.1.1c, SL.1.2, SL.1.6, L.1.1, L.1.5, L.1.6

▼ Materials

- Sample Text: "The Dinosaur Who Couldn't Come for Tea" (Appendix 1.2)
- Charting materials or interactive whiteboard to create Tickling Our Senses and Feelings Chart
- Small sticky notes

▼ To The Teacher

By now your students have been fully immersed in the world of stories, specifically fantasies that have elements that couldn't happen in the real world. They are deepening their awareness of story elements and tapping into their imaginations. They continue to build their sense of what makes up a story, noticing commonalities across them, as well as elements that could really happen and ones that couldn't. While the author of fantasy text wants the reader to imagine the impossible, he or she also wants to appeal to the readers' real senses and emotions. Writers may do this by including words and phrases with details that convey sensory images: sight, sound, smell, taste, and touch. It is also very common in fantasy texts for writers to include realistic character emotions to help the reader relate to a character; the character can feel happy or sad or jealous, even if he *is* a talking dinosaur. In this lesson, students will read closely to discover words and phrases that appeal to the senses or suggest characters' feelings. **ELL** Frontload the Lesson—Preview Text. Allowing beginner ELLs to preview and then revisit text is an excellent way to solidify language and content learning. The more they understand the arc of the story, the more they can focus on your teaching point rather than on understanding the text.

▼ Procedure

Warm Up Gather the class to set the stage for today's learning

Revisit the teaching point from Reading Lesson 4 and define again for your class what we mean by fiction, explaining that within fiction some stories are realistic (everything is possible), while others are fantasies (some things are impossible).

Yesterday, we learned a new word: fiction. Who can help me remember what a fiction story is? That's right—it's a story that a writer made up, that didn't really happen. We also learned that some fiction stories are realistic, which means everything in them could really happen. Sometimes fiction stories are fantasies, which means there's something about them that couldn't really happen. Edwina and Corduroy are fantasies—they had some things in the story that could happen, but they also had things that couldn't really happen.

Connect to this lesson's work on discovering sensory images and feelings in the text by reviewing the five senses and defining emotional feelings. Begin a chart called Tickling Our Senses and Feelings for your students to list and categorize words and phrases that appeal to the senses or suggest an emotional feeling. Draw symbols for each sense and emotional feeling on the chart (see right column for suggestions for symbols).

ELL Provide Comprehensible Input—Visuals. Charts offer a pathway to understanding the language used in the lesson without relying only on the words. Charts also provide a base that ELLs can refer back to later in the lesson when they are interacting with their peers.

Authors may want us to imagine things that are impossible, like a talking dinosaur, but they also want us to use our imagination in other ways. Everyone point to your eyes . . . your ears . . . your nose . . . your tongue . . . and wiggle your fingers. We use these body parts when we use our senses to see, hear, smell, taste and touch. [Draw symbols: an eye, an ear, a nose, a mouth, and a hand on the Tickling Our Senses and Feelings Chart.] Authors try to "tickle" our senses with their stories by describing things in the stories that may be seen, heard, smelled, tasted, and touched. Now, let's talk about one more way to use our imagination as we read. We may use our hands to feel things like a soft kitty or a cold ice cube. Touch is one way of feeling, but there is another kind of feeling we all experience, and that is emotional feeling. Emotional feelings include: happiness, sadness, anger, surprise, fright, and courage. Authors want us to imagine the emotions that characters feel in stories, too. [Draw a heart to symbolize emotional feeling on the chart. You should now have six symbols on the chart.]

Teach Model what students need to learn and do

Introduce today's teaching point of examining a story to find words and phrases that appeal to the senses or suggest a feeling. **ELL** Frontload the Lesson—Set a Purpose for Reading. Having a clear focus in mind as they begin to read can help ELLs zero in on the most essential parts of the story, rather than getting bogged down in unfamiliar language.

Today I'm going to read "The Dinosaur Who Couldn't Come for Tea" (see Appendix 1.2). We are going to read very closely to see if we can discover places that the author tries to "tickle" our senses or emotions.

Read the first part of "The Dinosaur Who Couldn't Come for Tea" with your students, up to where Rosie slams the door on Sharptail. Have students listen carefully for words and phrases that appeal to the senses or suggest an emotional feeling. Model a few that you notice. As you and the students notice examples, write the word or phrase on the chart and label it with the appropriate symbol. Some items may appeal to more than one sense or suggest both senses and emotional feeling. List more than one symbol, if appropriate.

Try Guide students to quickly rehearse what they need to learn and do in preparation for practice

Now have students continue these close reading skills, searching for evidence of words or phrases that appeal to the senses or suggest feelings with the remainder of the sample text "The Dinosaur Who Couldn't Come for Tea" (see Appendix 1.2). If students can read the text with a partner, allow them to do so, or you may continue reading aloud to scaffold the reading. Have students draw symbols on the text where they discover lines that the author included to appeal the senses or suggest emotion. **ELL** Enable Language Production—Increasing Interaction. Through strategic pairing of students, you could make this a chance for your ELLs to consolidate their new learning by using their *home* language to discuss an English text. Students should be encouraged to make use of all their linguistics resources as they try to acquire and express content learning.

Clarify Briefly restate today's teaching objective and explain the practice task(s)

Have students summarize what happened at the end of the story and share their discoveries from the close reading. Add to the Tickling Our Senses and Feelings Chart.

Direct students to their independent reading to look closely for places that the story appeals to the senses or suggests emotion. Whether your students are reading fantasies or realistic fiction, they should be able to find some examples.

Practice Students work independently and/or in small groups to apply today's teaching objective

Students will read independently or in teacher-led groups, using two small stickies to indicate words and phrases that appeal to the senses or suggest an emotion. **ELL** Identify and Communicate Content and Language Objectives—Check for Understanding. This is an ideal place to check if ELLs fully comprehend the five senses and, types of emotional feelings and how confident they feel expressing this.

Note that even students reading at very early levels can closely read illustrations for evidence of sensory imagery or emotions. Have them use small sticky notes to draw symbols and mark their discoveries directly on the text.

Some students, however, may be able to find and transcribe or highlight exact words in the text as evidence, as demonstrated earlier in the lesson. Differentiate accordingly.

Wrap Up Check understanding as you guide students to share briefly what they have learned and produced today

Ask a few students to share their findings. Prompt students to be specific about what words or illustrations in the text justify their thinking. **ELL** Enable Language Production—Listening and Speaking. Presenting after a long, supported practice session is the perfect situation for ELLs to speak publically. They have had ample opportunity to get their words ready and should be feeling confident.

Reading Lesson 6

▼ **Teaching Objective**

Readers analyze how illustrations provide important details.

Close Reading Opportunity

▼ **Standards Alignment**

RL.1.1, RL.1.2, RL.1.3, RL.1.7, RL.1.10, SL.1.1a, SL.1.1b, SL.1.1c, SL.1.2, SL.1.4, SL.1.6, L.1.1, L.1.6

▼ Materials

- *Where the Wild Things Are* by Maurice Sendak

▼ To the Teacher

Our first graders are continuously gaining skills as close readers of text. However, they have many years of closely reading illustrations under their belts. Today's lesson capitalizes on that close reading strength to help students slow down, analyze the illustrations, and become stronger text users. The illustrations of all of the stories read thus far through our Core Texts are critical to fully understanding the message of the story. We have often found that our students will notice details within illustrations that we may never have noticed despite having read the story dozens of times. Today is about slowing down, paying attention, and analyzing the power of pictures.

▼ Procedure

Warm Up Gather the class to set the stage for today's learning

Remind students of how they read closely by paying attention to words that indicated things could happen versus those that indicated things that could not happen in our everyday worlds.

> Yesterday we read stories closely by paying close attention to words that told us parts of the story could happen and parts couldn't really happen. Today we are going to continue our work on reading closely, but instead of focusing on the power of words, we're going to pay close attention to the power of the pictures to help tell the story.

Teach Model what students need to learn and do

Model close reading of a book cover. **ELL** Enable Language Production—Listening and Speaking. Your ELLs are likely as proficient as your other students in reading pictures—illustrations work in any language! However, they may not have the words to express what they see in pictures. Your teaching will provide them with a linguistic model for their own language production.

> Let's look at the cover of one of the most famous stories in all of children's literature, *Where the Wild Things Are*. I see a lot of important details on the cover that help me know what this story is going to be about. I see a jungle, which must be the setting of the story. I see a boat, which must have someone driving it. I wonder, who it could be? Finally, I see a giant monster on the bank of a river. This must be one of the wild things. When I look more closely, I notice that the monster is sleeping, which means it must be nighttime. Now I see that there are stars in the sky, which also confirms for me that it must be night.
>
> When I closely read illustrations, I ask myself, what are the elements of this story? Who are the characters? What is the setting? Then I go back and look again and ask myself, what other details do I notice? How does this help me better understand the story? What could happen? What couldn't really happen? If there are things that couldn't really happen, then this story must be a fantasy.

Try Guide students to quickly rehearse what they need to learn and do in preparation for practice

Begin reading aloud from *Where the Wild Things Are*. Pause at various times throughout the read-aloud to provide students with an opportunity to share what they notice as close readers of the illustrations. What elements of the story do they see? Urge them to look again and share other details they notice. What do the facial expressions of Max tell them about how he feels? What do the expressions of the wild things tell them? Are they friendly? How do they know? Are these wild things real? What within the illustrations lets us know this couldn't really happen? **ELL** Identify and Communicate Content and Language Objectives—Check for Undersatnding. Pausing and asking questions during the read-alouds lets you assess your ELLs' language and content needs through their answers. Do they understand what is expected of them? Do they have the words to communicate that understanding?

Clarify Briefly restate today's teaching objective and explain the practice task(s)

Draw your students' attention once again to the purpose of today—to closely read the illustrations of a story to better understand the characters, setting, and main events.

> Today we have been closely reading illustrations to better understand the elements of the story that could happen and those that couldn't happen.

In your independent reading today, take the time to notice the illustrations. How do they better help you understand the characters, where the story takes place, what could happen, and what couldn't really happen? When you find yourself reading the illustrations more closely and noticing new things, mark the page and be ready to share the important details you noticed.

Practice Students work independently and/or in small groups to apply today's teaching objective

Students read independently, noticing and marking illustrations that help them better understand the elements of the story, what could happen, and what couldn't really happen. **ELL** Enable Language Production—Listening and Speaking. Use this time to confer with your ELLs and offer language support where needed. You can help them prepare for the group share by discussing how they will express what they saw in their stories.

Wrap Up Check understanding as you guide students to briefly share what they have learned and produced today

Students will share an illustration that they read closely today. What details did they notice? How did it help them better understand the characters, setting, and events? What did they notice that could happen? What did they find that couldn't really happen?

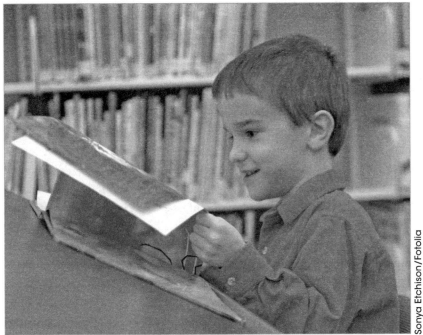

Sonya Etchison/Fotolia

Reading Lesson 7 · · · · · · · · · · · · · · · · · ·

▼ Teaching Objective

Readers discuss stories by answering key questions.

Close Reading Opportunity

▼ Standards Alignment

RL.1.1, RL.1.2, RL.1.3, RL.1.0, SL.1.1a, SL.1.1b, SL.1.1c, SL.1.2, SL.1.4, SL.1.6, L.1.1, L.1.6

▼ Materials

- *Cloudy with a Chance of Meatballs* by Judith Barrett
- Picture books read aloud so far (*Edwina, Corduroy, Where the Wild Things Are*)
- Charting supplies or interactive whiteboard

▼ To the Teacher

Throughout the year, it is important to focus our instruction on how to work together as readers in a group. Today's lesson reviews teaching objectives from previous lessons and focuses on the importance of speaking and listening behaviors when working as a collaborative group of readers. While many lessons in this lesson set implicitly reinforce these behaviors and give students the opportunity to practice them in partnerships or when discussing texts as a whole group, this lesson in particular explicitly teaches several of the speaking and listening skills valued by the Common Core State Standards.

While your students will discuss texts they have already been introduced to in this lesson set, we recommend modeling speaking and listening behaviors with a new fantasy story. In this lesson we'll be referring to *Cloudy with a Chance of Meatballs,* which is available as a book and an animated film. As always in this series, you can substitute another fantasy story if you do not have access to this book.

▼ Procedure

Warm Up Gather the class to set the stage for today's learning

Quickly review the stories you've read so far as a group.

> First graders, you've done a wonderful job reading and thinking about what makes stories such as *Edwina, Corduroy,* and *Where the Wild Things Are* so fun to read. Even though we've talked about what we've noticed about these stories as a group and in partnerships, today you are going to talk as a small group about one of our shared stories. Learning to listen and share your ideas are important skills for readers.

Teach Model what students need to learn and do

Model for students how to discuss a story together by focusing on key questions.

> While it is very exciting to work together, sometimes it can be difficult to know what to talk about and who should speak when. Today, we're going to talk about some rules and behaviors to help us have wonderful conversations about what makes these stories so special. Today is an opportunity to share with each other what you've noticed about these books: What could happen? What couldn't really happen? How do you know? Remember to look not only at the words of the story, but also the illustrations, to help you share your thinking. In these books, the words and pictures work together to tell an imaginative story.

> Today I'm going to share a new book, *Cloudy with a Chance of Meatballs.* In this story, we get to imagine what it would be like if food rained down from the sky. Would it be wonderful? Would it be messy? When I'm done reading, I'm going to ask for volunteers to help me talk about the book to share what could happen, what couldn't happen, and how we know that.

Read *Cloudy with a Chance of Meatballs* and invite a few students into a small inner circle so everyone can watch and listen to how you talk about this story. Remind everyone of the focus questions for today:

Focus Questions

1. What seemed real or could happen?

2. What couldn't really happen and shows us this is a fantasy?

3. How do we know?

You may need to begin the conversation and then have others respond. Encourage students to share within the circle without the need to raise their hands.

> **ELL** Provide Comprehensible Input—Models. By showing your students how to have a respectful academic discussion, you are giving them a clear picture of your expectations, rather than just telling them what you want. This example will be especially helpful for your ELLs.

Try Guide students to quickly rehearse what they need to learn and do in preparation for practice

After a few minutes of this modeled practice, review with the class what everyone did as speakers and listeners within the group. List these where everyone can see them. In parentheses are suggestions for icons to support developing readers:

 Group Rules

- Look at the speaker (eyes)
- Listen to the speaker (ears)
- Stay on topic (target)

- Give examples of your thinking (checkboxes)
- Add a new idea to the conversation (light bulb)
- Speak in complete sentences (period, question mark, exclamation point) (SL.1.1a, SL.1.1b, SL.1.1.c, SL.1.6)

Before students break up into their book groups, go over the logistics of working together, such as where each group will gather to work, how much time groups can expect to have, and so on.

Clarify Briefly restate today's teaching objective and explain the practice task(s)

Remind your students that today is all about working together to discuss their focus books. Everyone should get a turn to share his or her thinking. It is just as important to be an active listener as a speaker when learning together with a group. Review with the class their three questions for discussion: What could happen? What couldn't really happen? How do you know? **ELL** Enable Language Production—Increasing Interaction. ELLs are able to clarify and learn from their peers during this time in an informal forum. When you are forming groups, consider members who may speak an ELL's home language so that, if needed, the group discussion could be in English and the home language. Triad partnerships (one English speaker, one ELL, and one bilingual student) are often powerful for sharing and modeling language.

Practice Students work independently and/or in small groups to apply today's teaching objective

Today, students will be working collaboratively to discuss at least one of the three books they've previously heard read aloud as a class. We recommend giving groups about 10–15 minutes to discuss the book they've been given to focus on. If time permits, you may want groups to trade books and have an opportunity to discuss another fantasy story, giving all participants the chance to share. These are not permanent book clubs, but rather temporary discussion groups, so giving them the opportunity to discuss another book is a valuable use of time. Circulate and encourage students to stay centered around the focus question and observant of the group rules.

Wrap Up Check understanding as you guide students to share briefly what they have learned and produced today

Gather your class and ask a few students to share briefly what they discussed. Then turn the discussion to their group work. What went well? What was hard about working together? What could you do better next time? Allow students time to reflect and share their successes and struggles.

Reading Lesson 8 ·

▼ Teaching Objective

Readers compare and contrast stories with imaginative elements.

Close Reading
Opportunity

▼ Standards Alignment

RL.1.1, RL.1.2, RL.1.3, RL.1.5, RL.1.9, RL.1.10, W.1.8, SL.1.1a, SL.1.1b, SL.1.1c, SL.1.2, SL.1.4, SL.1.6, L.1.1, L.1.6

▼ Materials

- Picture books read aloud so far (*Edwina, Corduroy, Where the Wild Things Are, Cloudy with a Chance of Meatballs*)
- Enlarged copy of a Comparing Characters, Setting, Events Graphic Organizer
- Student copies of Comparing My Story to *Corduroy* (see Appendix 1.6)

▼ To the Teacher

Today builds on all of the previous lessons within this lesson set. Your students have heard several fantasies read aloud. They've been introduced to the power of words and the power of pictures to make the fantastical elements feel real. They've discussed at least one of the fantasies, with textual evidence, as a small group. Now we want our first graders to explicitly put it all together and compare and contrast these stories.

▼ Procedure

Warm Up Gather the class to set the stage for today's learning

Review what your students have focused on thus far in their learning around fantasy stories.

> You've learned a lot about stories, especially fantasies that play with what could happen and what couldn't really happen. You've noticed the power of words and the power of pictures. We've noticed that these stories have a lot in common, but they are also different from one another in important ways.

Teach Model what students need to learn and do

Tell the class that today you're going to be looking for more similarities and differences between the imaginative stories you have been reading, using a Comparing Characters, Setting, Events Graphic Organizer. Model how to fill out a graphic organizer, comparing two of the books read aloud, such as *Edwina* and *Corduroy*. **ELL** Provide Comprehensible Input—Graphic Organizers. The organizer offers a strong support for your ELLs. It makes your thinking more transparent and helps students plan what they are going to say. You can use the organizer to help students practice responding to prompts before or after a lesson.

Be sure to rely on the text as evidence as you begin the graphic organizer.

> When Mo Willems and Don Freeman wrote these imaginative stories, they relied on making sure their stories had elements that all fictional stories have—characters, a setting, and events that happen. These two imaginative stories have a lot in common, but the authors made specific choices to make their stories different from other stories.

Try Guide students to quickly rehearse what they need to learn and do in preparation for practice

> What do you notice when you think about these two stories? What is the same? What is different about them? Turn and talk with a partner.

As partners discuss the similarities and differences between *Edwina* and *Corduroy*, circulate and listen in to their conversations. Take this opportunity to review and reinforce essential speaking and listening behaviors you want to see used during practice. For example, focus on the skills of staying on topic, taking turns, and looking at the speaker. (SL.1.1a, SL.1.1b, SL.1.1c)

Gather your class once partners have had an adequate amount of time to talk, and then ask them to share their thinking. Plot student contributions on your enlarged class copy of the Comparing Characters, Setting, Events Graphic Organizer.

Here is what your chart might look like at this point in the lesson.

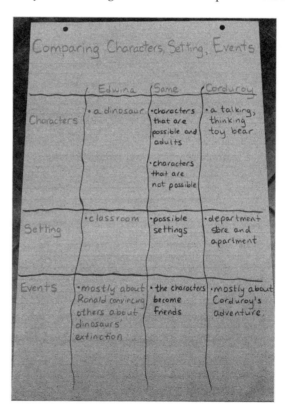

Comparing Characters, Setting, Events

	Edwina	Corduroy
Characters	A dinosaur Ronald Von Hoobie Doobie Other children Teacher	A talking, thinking toy bear Lisa Lisa's mom Saleslady
Setting	Classroom	Department store and apartment
Things that CAN happen	A boy COULD try to convince others of why dinosaurs are extinct	A girl COULD buy a stuffed teddy bear and take it home.
Things that CAN'T happen	Living talking dinosaur	A stuffed teddy bear goes on an adventure in a store.

Ask a follow-up question with your students: What things do the stories have in common? How are they different? Responses could include but are not limited to:

SAME:

- They both have some details that are real and some that are fantasy.
- They both have characters who could not talk in real life.
- They both have characters who could talk in real life.
- Realistic characters interact with fantasy characters in both stories.
- The settings could be real in both stories.
- They both have children in the story.
- They both are fun stories that we love to read!

DIFFERENT:

- One has a dinosaur and one has a bear.
- One is about a boy and one is about a girl.
- One has a teacher and one has a salesperson.
- They have different settings (school/store and apartment).
- They have different events.

ELL Identify and Communicate Language Objectives—Language Form and Function. ELLs may have all the words to express these facts about *Edwina* and *Corduroy*, but comparing and contrasting requires special linguistic forms. Notice the differences between the sentences in the sample sentences above: the "same" sentences start "They both . . . " and then use generalized terms to describe the books; the "different" sentences take the form "One is/has a _____, one is/has a _____," filled in with parallel specifics from the stories. Help ELLs to form their sentences, while honoring the good ideas that might be hidden behind "imperfect" language.

Clarify Briefly restate today's teaching objective and explain the practice task(s)

Direct students to think about the story elements in their own independent reading books and how they can compare them to other stories they've read so far.

> Today we are comparing how some stories are the same and how they are different. Together, we compared two different stories using a graphic organizer. Today you are going to continue reading your own stories. After some time to read, you are going to complete your own organizer. When you are done, think about your story and *Corduroy*. How is your story similar to *Corduroy*? How is it different? Think about the characters, setting, and events that can happen and those that can't happen.

Comparing My Story to *Corduroy*

Title of my story	
Characters	
Setting	
Things that CAN happen	
Things that CAN'T happen	
How my story is the SAME as *Corduroy*	
How my story is DIFFERENT than *Corduroy*	

Practice Students work independently and/or in small groups to apply today's teaching objective

Students read independently. Then distribute the graphic organizers. Students should be prepared to share their work at the end of the workshop. **ELL** Provide Comprehensible Input—Graphic Organizers. The time to speak with peers using their graphic organizers lets ELLs clarify their thinking and vocabulary about ideas that they wrote, as well as expand thinking through the peer conversation.

Wrap Up Check understanding as you guide students to share briefly what they have learned and produced today

Gather your class, asking students to have Comparing My Story handy. Ask students to share how their independent reading selections were the same as or different from one of the shared texts, using their organizers to guide and focus their thinking.

Collect and analyze students' Comparing My Story to *Corduroy* Graphic Organizer as a performance-based assessment to determine if students need additional instruction or support as a whole class, in small groups, or one on one. **ELL** Assess for Content and Language Understandings—Formative Assessment. This is an opportunity for you to assess your ELLs' language and content needs and then use this to inform upcoming lessons. Remember to look for both content and language strengths and challenges.

Milestone Performance Assessment

Comparing and Contrasting Imaginative Stories

 Use this checklist to assess student work on Comparing My Story to *Corduroy* Graphic Organizer.

Standards Alignment: RL.1.1, RL.1.2, RL.1.3, RL.1.9, W.1.8

Task	Achieved	Notes
Accurately identify one or more characters in the story.		
Accurately identify one or more settings in the story.		
Accurately identify one event that could really happen.		
Accurately identify one event that could not happen (if applicable to his or her book).		
Accurately identify one way his or her book is similar to *Corduroy*.		
Accurately identify one way his or her book is different from *Corduroy*.		

Reading Lesson 9

▼ Teaching Objective

Readers create story murals to share what they've read.

Close Reading Opportunity

▼ Standards Alignment

RL.1.1, RL.1.2, RL.1.3, RL.1.7, RL.1.10, SL.1.1a, SL.1.1b, SL.1.1c, SL.1.6, L.1.1, L.1.6

▼ Materials

- Picture books read aloud so far (*Edwina, Corduroy, Where the Wild Things Are, Cloudy with a Chance of Meatballs*)
- Materials needed to create student story mural
- Images of story murals from sites such as Google Images
- Charting supplies or interactive whiteboard

▼ To the Teacher

This lesson kicks off a collaborative class project in which your students will work together to create a story mural depicting what's real and what's imagined. You will notice both a low-tech and high-tech option for this project below that follows. Regardless of your choice, this lesson is best taught across several days to allow your students adequate time to create a thoughtful visual representation of the stories they've read. We recommend breaking your class up into small groups, with each group focusing on one of the shared stories. One important goal of the lesson is for students to work collaboratively to create a shared artistic representation of how the fantasy stories they've read use elements that could happen and elements that couldn't really happen. We want to emphasize with students that drawings/paintings should be large so that people can see them from a distance when they're all done. Consider hanging paper on the wall of the classroom or speaking with your administrators about displaying the mural in a public place at the school if this is something that you think might be possible.

By working together, these murals encourage social development, language and literacy skills, and the creative arts. In addition, these projects serve as a part of a Milestone Performance Assessment during Reading Lesson 10, when students use their murals to reflect on what they now know about the fiction stories they've read that include possible and imaginary elements. As the projects are collaborative, you will be evaluating your students' ability to work together in a group to create a shared product. However, we also want to assess individual students' understanding of the stories studied. Students will be sharing their individual contributions in a written response in Lesson 10.

▼ Procedure

Warm Up Gather the class to set the stage for today's learning

Connect to prior concepts from this lesson set, such as what makes a story a fantasy, what students have noticed that the stories read aloud have in common and what they don't share, and the importance of closely reading words and illustrations to make meaning.

ELL Frontload the Lesson—Activate Prior Knowledge. By connecting back to previous lessons, you help students activate their prior knowledge and build on vocabulary and content already covered. This is an excellent opportunity to assess how best to support their language and content needs.

> First graders, we've spent the last couple of weeks focusing on the structure of stories and how many authors use a combination of elements that make their stories fun and interesting to read. By now, you know a great deal about these stories. We've considered what they have in common, how they are different, and the impact of both the words and the illustrations on how we make meaning.

Teach Model what students need to learn and do

Define for students what a mural is and how this art form will be the vehicle for how they share what they've learned with each other and possibly the rest of the school.

> Today we are going to share what we've learned about these stories we've read by creating story murals. A mural is a big painting or image that is as big as a wall.

> Let's look at some images of murals together and think about the steps an artist would take to make this kind of giant painting.

ELL Provide Comprehensible Input—Visuals. ELLs will better understand the assignment if they can see real examples in addition to hearing your oral explanation.

> What steps would we take to make this mural?

> First, we would need to decide on what we wanted to paint.

> Next, we'd plan our ideas.

> Then we would choose colors and materials.

> Finally, we'd make sure to use the whole surface.

You are going to work with some partners in small groups to make a mural on one of the stories we've read together. For our mural we need to include some important elements from the stories we've read. What are the elements all fictional stories have? [Provide wait time to have your students respond.]

ELL Enable Language Production—Listening and Speaking. All students, but especially ELLs, benefit from being given several moments to pull together their thoughts before being asked to speak. Wait a few seconds longer than you usually would before calling on anyone, and watch your ELLs' hands start to fly up.

That's right, characters, a setting, and events that happen. The stories we've read are special because not everything in them could really happen, so we want our murals to show that too. We need to decide some things: Who would like to help create the characters? Who would like to do the big background of the mural showing the setting? Who would like to make sure that the mural shows some events that couldn't really happen?

Try Guide students to quickly rehearse what they need to learn and do in preparation for practice

Help your students make decisions as a class. Then work with students to list what they need to include in their mural. Students working on characters will need materials for creating large images of the characters. Students working on the background will need support mapping out the setting. Is it outdoors? Where will the sky be? Are there trees, a road, and so on? If it's an indoor setting, what are important images to include?

Direct students to follow a simple step-by-step checklist for working together to complete a story mural.

- First, we decide what to paint. We must include lots of details from the story.
  - Who are the characters?
  - What is the setting?
  - What events couldn't really happen?
- Next, we plan our ideas.
- Then we choose colors and materials.
- Finally, we make sure to use the whole surface.

Clarify Briefly restate today's teaching objective and explain the practice task(s)

Remind your class that the goal of the mural is that they represent the elements of the story, including what couldn't really happen, and that they work together by listening respectfully to one another. Every contribution to the mural is important.

Practice Students work independently and/or in small groups to apply today's teaching objective

Contrastwerkstatt/Fotolia

The class works collaboratively to create a story mural. Support students by reminding them of their checklist for working together on the mural. As students work, compliment them on their teamwork and incorporation of story elements.

Well done, first graders! You worked well together and included all of the story elements that show the characters, the setting, and the things that make this story a fantasy—the things that couldn't really happen.

Wrap Up Check understanding as you guide students to share briefly what they have learned and produced today

Gather the class to discuss and share their progress daily. Check in: How is each group doing? Where are they on the checklist? Does anyone need help? What's going well? What can we work on more?

Goal	Low-Tech	High-Tech
Students create a collaborative visual display that outlines their learning and thinking about imaginative stories.	Students create a mural, using materials such as: • Construction paper • Glue • Drawings or paintings • Handwritten text	Students create a mural, using computer-based materials such as: • Scanned images • Photographs • Scanned or typed text • Clip art images • Images from the Internet

Reading Lesson 10

▼ Teaching Objective

Readers show what they know about reading fantasies.

Close Reading Opportunity

▼ Standards Alignment

RL.1.1, RL.1.2, RL.1.3, RL.1.7, RL.1.9, RL.1.10, W.1.8, SL.1.1a, SL.1.1b, SL.1.1c, SL.1.4, Sl.1.5, SL.1.6, L.1.1, L.1.2, L.1.6

▼ Materials

• Story mural created in Reading Lesson 9

▼ To the Teacher

Today is an opportunity for your students to reflect on all the new knowledge they've gained about stories. They'll be working independently to share the vocabulary they've learned, what stories have in common, and how stories differ, as well how they displayed that knowledge as part of their story murals.

In order to give students ample time to think, write about, and discuss these ideas, this lesson may require an additional day of instruction.

▼ Procedure

Warm Up Gather the class to set the stage for today's learning

Compliment the class on a job well done creating a beautiful mural by working together.

> Wow, when I stand before our mural I'm reminded of the hard work you put into working together to make this masterpiece. I'm also reminded of how much we've all learned about stories that play with things that could happen and things that couldn't really happen in our everyday lives. Today we're going to look back and think about all that we've learned. There is so much to be proud of.

Teach Model what students need to learn and do

Tell the class that today you want them to think about the power of words and pictures to tell a story. As readers, it is important to take the time to reflect on the power of literature to ignite our own imaginations.

Chart the following questions for the class to consider:

• What do I know about stories? Why is this important to think about as a reader?

• What makes fantasies a special kind of story?

• How did I help with our story mural?

Now, begin a shared response by recalling the key ideas about stories from this lesson set. Then model for the class how to respond to these questions in writing by composing a shared piece about imaginative stories.

ELL Provide Comprehensible Input—Models. Provide By physically showing ELLs what you want them to do, you help them feel confident as they transition to independent work.

There is no need to make your piece lengthy or overly academic; rather, it is important that the language, length, and style be at or slightly above grade-level expectations for your students. Remember, in shared writing, you are the scribe who has the ultimate control over the format of the piece. However, your students should be active participants in the content of the writing. Here is what your piece might look like after a class discussion:

> We have learned a lot about stories. First, we learned that stories have many things in common, such as characters, a setting, and events that happen. We also learned that there are some stories called fantasies that include things that couldn't really happen, like the one about Edwina, the talking dinosaur. Finally, we also learned that pictures help make the stories come alive, like when Max met the wild things.
>
> What I will remember most of all about reading these stories is _____. This is important for me as a reader because _____.
>
> Our story mural showed _____. I helped make the mural by _____. This was important because _____.

ELL Identify and Communicate Content and Language Objectives—Language Form and Function. Through this model, you show ELLs how they can use language as a tool to express their learning. The sentence frames, in particular, can be a powerful tool for ELLs struggling to put their thinking into words.

Shared writing provides a wonderful opportunity to highlight several key speaking and listening skills such as producing complete sentences. (SL.1.6)

Try Guide students to quickly rehearse what they need to learn and do in preparation for practice

Support students to share with a partner what they've learned over the course of the past lessons by providing them with simple questions to guide their brief discussion.

Let's help each other remember all that we've learned. Take a moment to turn and talk to a partner about these questions:

- What you will most remember about stories from this lesson set?
- What did these lessons teach you about reading?
- What important thing did you contribute to the mural?

Allow students ample time to consider these questions together.

ELL Enable Language Production—Increasing Interaction. This is a great chance for ELLs to consolidate what they know about stories while drawing on all their linguistic resources. Consider pairing ELLs with classmates who speak the same home language so they can rehearse their learning in a comfortable way before attempting to record their thinking in English.

Clarify Briefly restate today's teaching objective and explain the practice task(s)

Guide students to compose their own reflection through drawing and writing.

> I am proud of all of you for your perseverance as readers and your great teamwork in creating our class masterpiece(s). Now I want to hear from each of you.

- What you will most remember about stories from this lesson set?
- What did these lessons teach you about reading?
- What important thing did you contribute to the mural?

Practice Students work independently and/or in small groups to apply today's teaching objective

Students will write reflections on what they enjoyed and learned during the study and how they helped create the class mural. Encourage students to share their thoughts through words and pictures. They may frame their responses as follows:

- I remember . . .
- I learned . . .
- When I worked on the mural, I was proud of . . .

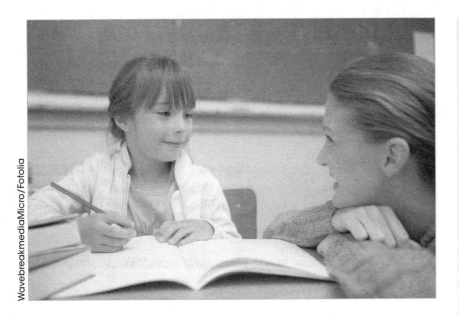

WavebreakmediaMicro/Fotolia

Wrap Up Check understanding as you guide students to share briefly what they have learned and produced today

Gather your class and have them share their reflections. Note similarities and differences in their responses. Do certain things stand out for many students? Consider why this might be so. **ELL** Identify and Communicate Content and Language Objectives—Check for Understanding. Pay close attention to your ELLs' understandings and gaps: Are they struggling with a misunderstanding of the content, or do they lack the language needed to show what they know in English?

Observe and collect student work as a performance-based assessment to determine if students need additional instruction or support as a whole class, in small groups, or one on one. **ELL** Assess for Content and Language Understandings—Summative Assessment. This is an opportunity for you to assess your ELLs' language and content needs and then use this information to plan upcoming lessons. You may need to spend some extra time with your ELLs, discussing their work, to get at the root of any misunderstandings you notice.

Milestone Performance Assessment

Lesson Set Reflection

 Use this checklist to assess students reflections.

Standards Alignment: RL.1.1, W.1.8, SL.1.5, SL.1.6, L.1.1, L.1.6

	Achieved	Notes
Describe a strong memory from the lesson set.		
Describe something he/she learned that will help him/her be a stronger reader.		
Explain a contribution to the mural that makes him/her proud.		

Grade 1

Writing Lessons

The Core I.D.E.A. / Daily Writing Instruction at a Glance table highlights the teaching objectives and standards alignment for all 10 lessons across the four stages of the lesson set (Introduce, Define, Extend, and Assess). It also indicates which lessons contain special features to support English language learners, technology, speaking and listening, close reading opportunities, and formative ("Milestone") assessments.

The following CORE READY WRITING RUBRIC is designed to help you record each student's overall understanding across four levels of achievement as it relates to the lesson set goals. We recommend that you use this rubric at the end of the lesson set as a performance-based assessment tool. Use the Milestone Performance Assessments as tools to help you gauge student progress toward these goals. Reteach and differentiate instruction as needed. See the foundational book, *Be Core Ready: Powerful, Effective Steps to Implementing and Achieving the Common Core State Standards,* for more information about the Core Ready Reading and Writing Rubrics.

The Core I.D.E.A. / Daily Writing Instruction at a Glance

Instructional Stage	Lesson	Teaching Objective	Core Standards	Special Features
Introduce: *notice, explore, collect, note, immerse, surround, record, share*	1	Writers ask "what if" to generate fantasy story topics.	RL.1.1 • RL.1.2 • RL.1.3 • RL.1.10 • W.1.3 W.1.5 • SL.1.1a • SL.1.1b • SL.1.1c • SL.1.2 • SL.1.4 • SL.1.6 • L.1.1 • L.1.2 • L.1.6	ELL S&L Milestone Assessment Close Reading Opportunity
	2	Writers create imaginary characters.	RL.1.1 • RL.1.10 • W.1.3 • W.1.5 • SL.1.1a • SL.1.1b • SL.1.1c • SL.1.2 • SL.1.4 • SL.1.5 • SL.1.6 • L.1.1 • L.1.2 • L.1.6	ELL S&L Close Reading Opportunity
Define: *name, identify, outline, clarify, select, plan*	3	Writers create settings that feel real.	RL.1.1 • RL.1.10 • W.1.3 • W.1.5 SL.1.1a • SL.1.1b • SL.1.1c • SL.1.4 • SL.1.5 • SL.1.6 • L.1.1 • L.1.2 • L.1.6	ELL S&L Close Reading Opportunity
Extend: *try, experiment, attempt, approximate, practice, explain, revise, refine*	4	Writers create beginnings that hook the reader.	RL.1.1 • RL.1.10 • W.1.3 • W.1.5 • SL.1.1a • SL.1.1b • SL.1.1c • SL.1.6 • L.1.1 • L.1.2 • L.1.6	ELL Close Reading Opportunity
	5	Writers add important events to stories.	RL.1.1 • RL.1.3 • RL.1.10 • W.1.3 • W.1.5 • SL.1.1a • SL.1.1b • SL.1.2 • SL.1.4 • SL.1.6 • L.1.1 • L.1.2 • L.1.6	ELL Close Reading Opportunity
	6	Writers add detailed illustrations.	RL.1.1 • RL.1.7 • RL.1.10 • W.1.3 • W.1.5 • SL.1.1a • SL.1.1b • SL.1.1c • SL.1.5 • SL.1.6 • L.1.1 • L.1.2 • L.1.6	ELL S&L Close Reading Opportunity
	7	Writers revise their stories for story elements.	W.1.3 • W.1.5 • SL.1.1a • SL.1.1b • SL.1.1c • SL.1.6 • L.1.1 • L.1.2 • L.1.6	ELL Milestone Assessment
	8	Writers create book jackets that show what's most important in their story.	W.1.3 • W.1.6 • SL.1.1a • SL.1.1b • SL.1.1c • SL.1.4 • SL.1.6 • L.1.1 • L.1.2 • L.1.6	ELL Tech
Assess: *reflect, conclude, connect, share, recognize, respond*	9	Writers share their stories with pride.	W.1.6 • SL.1.1a • SL.1.1b • SL.1.1c • SL.1.2 • SL.1.3 • SL.1.4 • SL.1.6 • L.1.1 • L.1.6	ELL S&L Tech Milestone Assessment
	10	Writers reflect on what they've learned by saying thanks.	W.1.8 • SL.1.1a • SL.1.1b • SL.1.1c • SL.1.5 • SL.1.6 • L.1.1 • L.1.2 • L.1.6	ELL

 Core Ready Writing Rubric

Grade 1   Could It Really Happen?: An Introduction to Fantasy

Lesson Set Goal	Emerging	Approaching	Achieving	Exceeding	Standards Alignment
Plan and write a fantasy story that includes the story elements and has a logical sequence of events (clear beginning, middle, and end).	Student shows little or no evidence of planning or writing a story with the required story elements or a logical sequence of events.	Student plans and writes a fantasy story. Some of the required elements (story elements and a logical sequence of events) may be missing or underdeveloped.	Student plans and writes a fantasy story with all required elements (story elements and a logical sequence of events). Some components may be more effective than others.	Student plans and writes fantasy story with all required elements (story elements and a logical sequence of events). Narrative is well developed and some elements may be particularly effective or advanced for the grade level.	RL.1.2 RL.1.3 RL.1.5 RL.1.7 RL.1.9 RL.1.10 W.1.3 W.1.5 SL.1.1a SL.1.1b SL.1.1c L.1.1 L.1.2 L.1.6
Include an imaginary character and a setting that feel real.	Student shows little or no success creating an imaginary character and a setting that feel real.	Student shows some evidence of success creating an imaginary character and a setting that feel real. Some elements of may be underdeveloped or unclear.	Student shows solid evidence of creating an imaginary character and a setting that feel real. All elements are clearly present.	Student shows exceptional evidence of creating an imaginary character and a setting that feel real. Some elements may be very well developed or exceed grade-level expectations.	W.1.3 SL.1.4 SL.1.5
Include temporal words to signal event order.	Student writing does not include temporal words to signal event order.	Student attempts to include temporal words to signal event order. Some of the uses of temporal words may be unclear or lack obvious connection to event order.	Student includes temporal words to signal event order. Most uses of temporal words are clear and help connect events in a logical order.	Student includes several examples of temporal words. The uses of temporal words are clear and relevant and effectively serve to connect events in a logical order.	W.1.3
Add detailed illustrations that complement and enhance the story.	Student does not add illustrations or illustrations do not complement or enhance the story in any meaningful way.	Student attempts to include some illustrations to enhance the story. Some may be unclear or underdeveloped.	Student adds illustrations that in most or all instances complement and enhance the story.	Student adds outstanding illustrations that effectively enhance the story with well-developed details and elements.	W.1.3 SL.1.5
Create a book jacket that shows what's most important in the story.	Student does not create a book jacket that shows what's most important in the story. Book jacket may be inaccurate or irrelevant.	Student attempts to create a book jacket that shows what's most important in the story. May have some inaccuracies or may not have all the required components (front and back cover and a blurb that explains what the story is about).	Student creates a book jacket that shows what's most important in the story. Includes all of the required components (front and back cover and a blurb that explains what the story is about), but some may be stronger than others.	Student creates a thoughtful, relevant, and detailed book jacket that includes strong examples of all the required components (front and back cover and a blurb that explains what the story is about).	W.1.3 W.1.6 SL.1.1a SL.1.1b SL.1.6 L.1.1 L.1.2 L.1.6

Core Ready Writing Rubric, Grade 1, *continued*

Lesson Set Goal	Emerging	Approaching	Achieving	Exceeding	Standards Alignment
With guidance and support from adults and peers, share writing with others in meaningful ways.	Student shows little or no evidence of attempting to share writing with others in meaningful ways.	Student attempts to share writing with others but may lack focus and sense of purpose at times.	Student successfully shares writing with others in meaningful ways. In most or all instances student uses a variety of tools and effective collaboration to prepare the piece for presentation.	Student clearly, thoroughly, and effectively shares writing with others in a meaningful way. Student accurately uses a variety of tools and proactively seeks collaboration, when necessary, in order to prepare the piece for presentation.	W.1.6
Ask and answer questions about key details in a text.	Student demonstrates little or no evidence of understanding key details in the text through asking and/or answering questions about the text.	Student demonstrates some evidence of understanding key details in the text through asking and answering questions about the text.	Student shows solid evidence of understanding key details in the text through asking and answering questions about the text.	Student consistently shows solid evidence of understanding key details in the text through asking and answering high-level questions about the text and providing solid textual evidence to support thinking.	RL.1.1
With prompting and support, read prose and poetry of appropriate complexity for grade 1.	Student shows little or no evidence of reading prose and poetry appropriate for the grade 1 text complexity band, with prompting and support, at this point of the school year.	Student shows inconsistent evidence of reading prose and poetry appropriate for the grade 1 text complexity band, with prompting and support, at this point of the school year.	Student shows solid evidence of reading prose and poetry appropriate for the grade 1 text complexity band, with prompting and support, at this point of the school year.	Student shows solid evidence of reading prose and poetry above the grade 1 text complexity band, with prompting and support, at this point of the school year.	RL.1.10
With guidance and support from adults, focus on a topic, respond to questions and suggestions from peers, and add details to strengthen writing as needed.	Student makes little or no attempt to strengthen writing as needed by responding to feedback, focusing on a topic, or adding details, even with extensive prompting and support from adults.	Student attempts to strengthen writing as needed by responding to feedback, focusing on a topic, and/or adding details. Revisions may not connect to suggestions or strengthen piece effectively.	Student strengthens writing as needed by responding to feedback, focusing on topic, and/or adding details. Revisions usually connect to feedback and enhance the piece. Some areas of writing may be more developed than others.	Student effectively strengthens writing as needed by responding to feedback, focusing on a topic, and/or add details. Revisions are relevant and thoughtful and consistently serve to enhance piece. May proactively seek feedback to improve writing.	W.1.5
In collaborative discussions, exhibit responsibility to the rules and roles and purpose of conversation.	Student makes little or no attempt to participate in collaborative discussions and build on the talk of others with multiple exchanges. Often disregards the rules and roles of conversation even with prompting.	Student inconsistently participates in collaborative discussions and builds on the talk of others with multiple exchanges. Student observes the rules and roles of conversation but needs frequent prompting.	Student usually participates in collaborative discussions and builds on the talk of others with multiple exchanges. Student observes the rules and roles of conversation. May need some prompting.	Student consistently participates in collaborative discussions and builds on the talk of others with multiple exchanges. Student observes the rules and roles of conversation with little or no prompting.	SL.1.1a SL.1.1b
In collaborative discussions, ask questions in a manner that enhances understanding of topic.	Student makes little or no attempt to ask questions that enhance understanding of the topic.	Student occasionally asks questions to clarify or build understanding of the topic or text under discussion but usually requires support or prompting.	Student asks questions that effectively clarify or build understanding of the topic or text under discussion. May need occasional support or prompting.	Student often asks effective and focused questions to clarify or build understanding of the topic or text under discussion. Proactively uses this strategy to support own learning.	SL.1.1c

Lesson Set Goal	Emerging	Approaching	Achieving	Exceeding	Standards Alignment
Speak in complete sentences when appropriate.	Student shows little or no evidence of speaking in complete sentences when appropriate.	Student shows some evidence of attempting to speak in complete sentences when appropriate.	Student shows solid evidence of speaking in complete sentences when appropriate.	Student shows exceptional evidence of speaking in complete sentences when appropriate.	SL.1.6
Demonstrate knowledge of standard English and its conventions.	Student demonstrates little or no knowledge of standard English and its conventions.	Student demonstrates some evidence of knowledge of standard English and its conventions.	Student consistently demonstrates knowledge of standard English and its conventions.	Student demonstrates an exceptional understanding of standard English and its conventions. Use of conventions is sophisticated for grade level and accurate.	L.1.1 L.1.2
Use words and phrases acquired through conversations, reading and being read to, and responding to texts.	Student shows little or no evidence of the acquisition and/or use of grade-appropriate words and phrases.	Student shows some evidence of acquiring and using grade-appropriate words and phrases.	Student shows solid evidence of acquiring and using grade-appropriate words and phrases.	Student shows a high level of sophistication and precision when using grade-appropriate words and phrases.	L.1.6

Writing Lesson 1

▼ Teaching Objective

Writers ask "what if" to generate fantasy story topics.

▼ Standards Alignment

RL.1.1, RL.1.2, RL.1.3, RL.1.10, W.1.3, W.1.5, SL.1.1a, SL.1.1b, SL.1.1c, SL.1.2, SL.1.4, SL.1.6, L.1.1, L.1.2, L.1.6

Close Reading Opportunity

▼ Materials

- *Matthew's Dream* by Leo Lionni (We recommend having a collection of Leo Lionni books for students to preview, read, analyze, and enjoy.)
- Sample story "Maple's Dream" (Appendix 1.7)

▼ To the Teacher

Our first graders are budding writers eager to tell stories that play with what's real and what's completely their own idea—something they might wish for but know couldn't really happen. This first lesson is an introduction to how authors of fantasy stories get their ideas—by simply asking "what if?" Throughout this lesson set, it will be important to model the writing process through a shared writing experience. Creating a fantasy story as a class will be a memorable experience for your students and will help support their individual stories. While developing the content you also have an opportunity to feature the use of the period, capitalization, and the use of common nouns and action verbs as you support your first graders in their evolving understanding of the conventions of standard English.

If your students have written realistic fiction stories through our Book 1 first-grade lesson set (*Getting to Know You: Discovering Characters in Narrative Stories*), then they will already have a foundation in writing narrative fiction. These lessons do not require the Book 1 lesson set to have been done, though, and can stand alone or extend that lesson set.

Finally, throughout this writing lesson set we refer to working with students to create a fantasy story as a class. As an alternative, you can use our sample story "Maple's Dream" (in Appendix 1.7) to model the writing process—choosing a character, determining a setting, and crafting a beginning. Although this story is available, we encourage teachers to write a class story together as a shared writing process. Not only will it be worthwhile instruction, but it will also build classroom community.

▼ Procedure

Warm Up Gather the class to set the stage for today's learning

First graders, today we are going to start a new writing adventure together. We're going to write stories, but here's the twist: They're going to have some things in them that couldn't really happen. One famous author who has written lots of books that have imaginative twists is Leo Lionni. He writes stories about animals who do amazing things—like talk, and visit museums, and have dreams of what they want to be one day, just like you and me.

Teach Model what students need to learn and do

Provide your students with a brief summary of *Matthew's Dream* and then read aloud from the text, considering what the "what if" question is that drives this story. **ELL** Provide Comprehensible Input—Summaries. Summaries are an ideal way to provide ELLs with a concise text that they can easily understand. By highlighting the key points of the text beforehand, you remove some of the burden of basic comprehension and allow them to focus on asking, "what if?" (This is a good strategy when your lesson focus is on content rather than on reading, but be careful not to over-use it—when reading is the focus, we should not pre-empt the text and take the work away from students by telling them everything that is going to happen.)

Today we're going to read one of Leo Lionni's stories called *Matthew's Dream*, about a mouse named Matthew who wondered a lot about what he wanted to be when he grew up. As I'm reading, think about what Leo Lionni must have asked himself to come up with this story. He probably started with a "what if" question such as "What if mice had dreams?" See if you can think of any other "what if?" questions Leo Lionni would have asked himself as he wrote this story.

Read aloud *Matthew's Dream*. Pause intermittently to see if anyone has a "what if?" question they think Leo Lionni must have asked himself. Some possibilities include:

- What if mice grew up to have jobs like doctors or painters?
- What if mice went on school field trips to museums?
- What if mice fell in love and got married?
- What if mice could become famous?

Keep a list of the "what if" questions your students come up with after listening to *Matthew's Dream*. Use that as a springboard into generating "what if" questions the students can come up with to write their own class story.

As students listen to the read aloud, reinforce the importance of carefully listening for key details in the text and asking questions about those details. (SL.1.2)

Try Guide students to quickly rehearse what they need to learn and do in preparation for practice

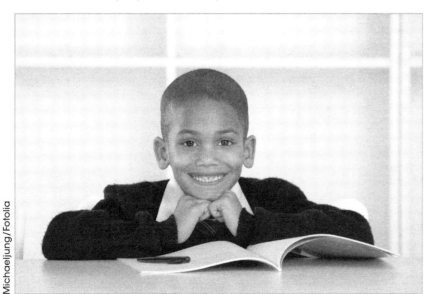

Michaeljung/Fotolia

Engage students in generating "what if" questions that might inspire their fantasy writing pieces.

> Leo Lionni has a big imagination. He asked himself a lot of "what if" questions to make Matthew's Dream really fun to read. As I look at the other books Leo Lionni wrote, he always had a "what if" question about animals. That was a good strategy for writing stories that couldn't really happen in our world. I think we can ask ourselves "what if" questions to write our own fantasy stories. Let's start by coming up with some together.

While anything is possible, the best fantasy stories for this age group combine unrealistic elements within the actual experiences of children in this age group (home, school, playgrounds, and so on). In addition, while students could write "what if" questions about anything, we recommend encouraging your students to write imaginative stories for which there are mentor texts available.

The Core Texts we've chosen for this lesson set focus on animals (Leo Lionni), stuffed animals (Don Freeman), dinosaurs (Mo Willems, Jane Yolen), and monsters (Maurice Sendak). As such, some example "what if" questions include:

- What if _____ could talk?
- What if lions, tigers, etc., could be loveable pets?
- What if cats went to school?
- What if dogs played on the playground?
- What if dolphins played games with their families?
- What if my stuffed bunny was alive?
- What if dinosaurs still lived today but were friendly?
- What if monsters really existed?

Decide on one or several "what if" questions to compose a class story over the next few lessons. This will provide an ongoing model for students as they write their own fantasy tales. **ELL** Provide Comprehensible Input— Models. Charting examples of strong "what if?" questions will help your ELLs understand what sort of questions they should generate on their own.

Clarify Briefly restate today's teaching objective and explain the practice task(s)

Direct students to write their own "what if" questions and star their favorite.

> Today you are going to think like Leo Lionni and write some "what if" questions of your own. When you're done, put a star next to the question you most want to write a story about.

Practice Students work independently and/or in small groups to apply today's teaching objective

Students will compose their own "what if" questions to help them generate fantasy story topics. They should star one that inspires them to write a story.

Wrap Up Check understanding as you guide students to share briefly what they have learned and produced today

Have students share the "what if" question they starred. Encourage them to share why this is a topic they are interested in writing a story about. **ELL** Enable Language Production—Listening and Speaking. This is a good time to have your ELLs share in front of the class, especially if they were reluctant during the whole-group lesson. At this point, they have had lots of time to get their words ready and likely feel more confident about sharing their ideas.

Collect and analyze student writing as a performance-based assessment to determine if students need additional instruction or support as a whole class, in small groups, or one on one. **ELL** Assess for Content and

Language—Formative Assessment. This is an opportunity for you to assess your ELLs' language and content needs and then use this information to plan upcoming lessons. Try to zero in on the source of any gaps you notice: Is the content going over students' heads? Then you may need to explain the lesson focus in simpler language, using the home language, and/or with pictures. Do students grasp the content but struggle to form their "what if?" questions in English? Then you may need to support their expressive language.

Milestone Performance Assessment
Asking "What If" Questions to Inspire Writing

 Use this checklist to assess student work generating "what if" questions.

Standards Alignment: W.1.3, W.1.5

Task	Achieved	Notes
Generate three or more "what if" questions.		
Choose one question that inspires him/her to write a story.		

Writing Lesson 2

▼ Teaching Objective
Writers create imaginary characters.

▼ Standards Alignment
RI.1.1, RI.1.10, W.1.3, W.1.5, SL.1.1a, SL.1.1b, SL.1.1c, SL.1.2, SL.1.4, SL.1.5, SL.1.6, L.1.1, L.1.2, L.1.6

Close Reading Opportunity

▼ Materials

- Leo Lionni picture books
- If possible, video clip of Leo Lionni discussing his inspiration (you can find the clip at the Random House website, www .randomhouse.com)

▼ To the Teacher

The heart of Leo Lionni's stories is his characters. Now that your students have an introduction to his work through *Matthew's Dream*, today is a great time to view a video clip of Lionni discussing his inspiration and which of his characters he most identifies with. Students of all ages love to see who the writers are of their favorite stories.

▼ Procedure

Warm Up Gather the class to set the stage for today's learning

Remind students of their work from Writing Lesson 1 on generating "what if" questions to guide their fantasy writing.

> Yesterday, we read *Matthew's Dream* by Leo Lionni and thought about how he must have asked himself some "what if" questions to create such an imaginative story about a mouse who becomes a famous painter. We then wrote our own "what if" questions to help us choose an imaginative story topic to write about. We're now ready to think about the main characters in our stories.

ELL Frontload the Lessons—Make Connections. By reminding students of yesterday's lesson, you are helping them find a mental space to put today's lesson. This is especially useful for your ELLs, as it creates a clear context for the language they are about to hear. If they already know, roughly, what's going on, they can interpret new language more easily. If you are able to show your students the video of Leo Lionni sharing his inspirations, this will help inspire their own writing.

As students watch the video, have them carefully listen for key details and encourage them to ask questions about the key details. (SL.1.2) If the video is unavailable, consider sharing your own inspiration for writing stories that couldn't really happen.

> Let's listen to what Leo Lionni has to say about his inspirations for his stories and the characters he's created.

View the video clip of Leo Lionni speaking about his stories, where he discusses how he loves animals and how everyone identifies easily with animals. Use this as a springboard for students to create their own imaginary characters. **ELL** Provide Comprehensible Input—Audiovisual Aids. Multimedia is an excellent way to offer a pathway to understanding without relying only on words.

Teach Model what students need to learn and do

Choose a "what if" question as a class. With suggestions from your students, create a class character to star in your story. Draw inspiration from Leo Lionni's characters. We recommend a character who is an animal with some human qualities. Sketch your character and give him or her a name.

> Today we're going to create our own exciting new characters to use when we write a fantasy story. Before we create our own characters, let's decide on a character for our very own class story. First, we need to choose a "what if" story of our own. Who has an idea for our class "what if" story? OK, good. Now, let's think about a character who can star in our story. Leo Lionni uses animals. Is there an animal we'd like to star in our story who we can imagine does things just like you and me?

Try Guide students to quickly rehearse what they need to learn and do in preparation for practice

Direct students to think about their own character for their fantasy story.

Take a moment and think about the character you would like to star in your stories. Just like we did as a group, start with your "what if" question. If your question is "What if there were a talking dinosaur?" you would have a talking dinosaur star in your story. Maybe his name would be Sam. Before you start writing and drawing, turn and share with a partner what you're thinking about right now.

Allow partnerships to share their initial ideas. Circulate as partners are talking, listening in to their conversations for possibilities to share with the larger group. Listen for students who are already beginning to plan how they might represent this character through their drawing. Gather your students once again and share with the class two or three tidbits you overheard. **ELL** Enable Language Production—Increasing Interaction. ELLs are able to clarify and learn from their peers during this time in an informal forum. They also get to rehearse their own ideas before they start to write and draw. This is an opportunity to whisper in when needed or listen in to understand how best to support their language or content needs.

Clarify Briefly restate today's teaching objective and explain the practice task(s)

Remind students of the importance of their "what if" question to drive the creation of their character.

Your job today is to create a fun and exciting new character to star in your fantasy story. Based on your "what if" question, create a detailed drawing of your character.

Practice Students work independently and/or in small groups to apply today's teaching objective

Students work independently to draw and describe the main character that will be central to their "what if" question. **ELL** Identify and Communicate Content and Language Objectives—Check for Understanding. This is a great chance to check in with your ELLs to see if anything about the content or language is throwing them off. If students are able to create detailed drawings of their characters, then they are probably clear on the content; you can extend their learning by helping them talk about their drawings.

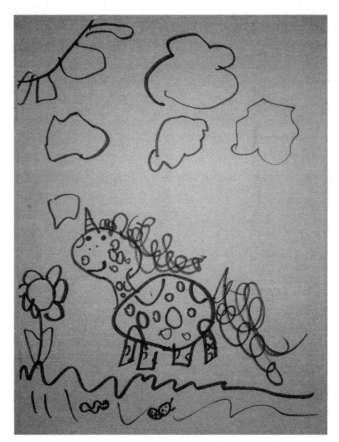

Student's detailed drawing of a main character for her fantasy story. Talking unicorn.

Wrap Up Check understanding as you guide students to share briefly what they have learned and produced today

Gather the class and have a few students share their drawings with the class. Discuss the range of characters your students have created and how much you are looking forward to reading their imaginative stories.

Writing Lesson 3

▼ Teaching Objective

Writers create settings that feel real.

Close Reading
Opportunity

▼ Standards Alignment

RL.1.1, RL.1.10, W.1.3, W.1.5, SL.1.1a, SL.1.1b, SL.1.1c, SL.1.4, SL.1.5, SL.1.6, L.1.1, L.1.2, L.1.6

▼ Materials

- *Matthew's Dream* by Leo Lionni

▼ To the Teacher

Matthew's Dream is an imaginative story with a character who does things that mice can't do in real life, but the setting feels quite real throughout the story. We encourage students to use this approach in their fantasy stories. Matthew lives in the corner of an attic vividly described by Lionni and then he spends time in a museum on a class field trip just like your students may have experienced. Today is about helping your students plan for where their fantasy stories take place. Whether they choose places they've been to or places they'd like to go to, they can describe the setting in ways that make the places in which their characters roam feel real.

▼ Procedure

Warm Up Gather the class to set the stage for today's learning

Use this time to have students review their character drawings.

> Let's look back at our character drawings from yesterday. I am so excited about these imaginary characters and all they can do. Just like Matthew, they can do anything you want them to do. That's the fun of writing stories that have imaginative twists. Today we're going to look at where Matthew's story took place so that we can make decisions about where we want our characters to roam. Will your characters live somewhere we could go, or will they live somewhere you wish you could travel?

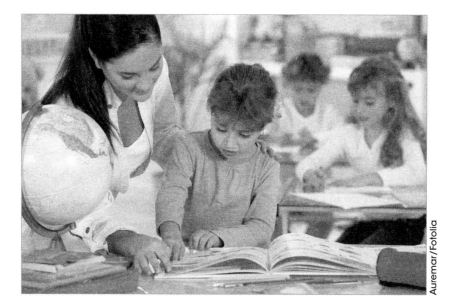

Auremar/Fotolia

Teach Model what students need to learn and do

Look back through *Matthew's Dream* for descriptions of the setting.

> Let's take a close look at where Matthew lives and where he travels throughout the book. Where a story takes place is called the setting. As we're doing a picture walk, keep your eyes peeled on where the description of the setting begins and how the setting changes. Even though lots of things happen to Matthew that couldn't really happen, how did Leo Lionni make the settings feel real?

ELL Identify and Communicate Content Objectives—Avoid Idioms. Note that the phrase "keep your eyes peeled" is idiomatic. While you need not avoid it altogether—children must learn it eventually—make sure you clarify this meaning for your ELLs.

Conduct a picture walk of *Matthew's Dream*. Pause throughout to first think aloud about what you notice about the setting, how it's described by Leo Lionni and how it feels real. Then ask your students to comment on what they notice about the changing settings. **ELL** Enable Language Production—Listening and Speaking. Through this discussion of the story, ELLs

After looking through *Matthew's Dream* with a focus on setting, create a setting for your class "what if" story. In Writing Lesson 2, you chose an imaginary character for this class story. Where would this character most likely live? Decide as a class on a setting that is familiar to first graders, such as a classroom, a playground, the park, and so on. Model how to sketch the chosen setting(s) and how to write a sentence that describes what you've chosen.

Try Guide students to quickly rehearse what they need to learn and do in preparation for practice

Move students to begin thinking about their own story settings.

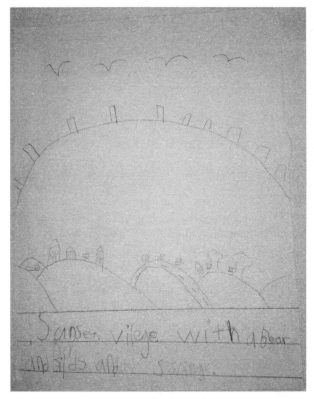

Student's fantasy story drawing. A detailed setting and explanatory sentence. Demonstrates use of conventional spelling of common words and the spelling of untaught words phonetically. (L.1.2d, L.1.2e)

Take a moment and think about the setting you would like your character to roam in throughout your story. Turn and share with a partner what you're thinking about right now.

Allow partnerships to share their initial ideas. Circulate as partners are talking, listening in to their conversations for things you may want to share with the larger group. Listen for students who are already beginning to plan how the setting will be described. Gather your students once again and share with the class two or three things you overheard.

Use this opportunity to remind them of the important speaking and listening skills including: carefully listening to their partners and taking turns speaking. (SL.1.1a) **ELL** Enable Language Production—Increasing Interaction. ELLs may already have great ideas for the settings of their imaginative stories. Through peer sharing, they hear examples of how one might *talk* about settings, and get to rehearse their own descriptions before going off to write.

Clarify Briefly restate today's teaching objective and explain the practice task(s)

Remind students of the goals for today of creating a drawing with a detailed setting and sentence that provides an explanation.

> Our job today is to decide on the setting or settings for our fantasy stories. Create a detailed drawing of your setting with a sentence describing what you've drawn. We want our settings to feel real for our readers. Be ready to share your thinking with the class when you're finished.

Practice Students work independently and/or in small groups to apply today's teaching objective

Students will sketch where they want their characters to live and include a caption that explains the drawing. **ELL** Enable Language Production— Reading and Writing. Realize that some ELLs may not yet have the words in English to describe their beautiful drawings. Consider a variety of accommodations and supports: they could write or dictate a sentence in their home language (to you or a peer) and then get help to translate it; they could dictate a sentence to you in English if writing is holding them up; or you could support them to be their own advocates, encouraging them to ask you the English names of things in their pictures.

Wrap Up Check understanding as you guide students to briefly share what they have learned and produced today

Have students share their drawings and captions with the class. What do you notice about their choices as writers?

The story takes place inside a carved pumpkin. The eyes of the pumpkin are windows and the front door is a tooth!

Writing Lesson 4

▼ Teaching Objective
Writers create beginnings that hook the reader.

Close Reading Opportunity

▼ Standards Alignment
RL.1.1, RL.1.10, W.1.3, W.1.5, SL.1.1a, SL.1.1b, SL.1.1c, SL.1.6, L.1.1, L.1.2, L.1.6

▼ Materials

- *Matthew's Dream* by Leo Lionni and other Leo Lionni selections
- Charting supplies or interactive whiteboard to create Story Beginnings Chart

▼ To the Teacher

Today your students will take their ideas about their characters and chosen settings and start writing their stories. We want to encourage first graders to write their beginnings with confidence. Gather several fantasy stories for analysis prior to having students set off on their writing. How do these authors begin?

▼ Procedure

Warm Up Gather the class to set the stage for today's learning

Introduce the idea that writers make decisions about how they want to begin their stories.

> You have worked hard to plan your fantasy stories. Now we're ready to turn our drawings and ideas into writing. Today I'm going to share with you the ways other writers often begin their stories.

Teach Model what students need to learn and do

Explain the importance of the beginning of the story to hook the reader, and provide some examples. Then model this technique with your class story.

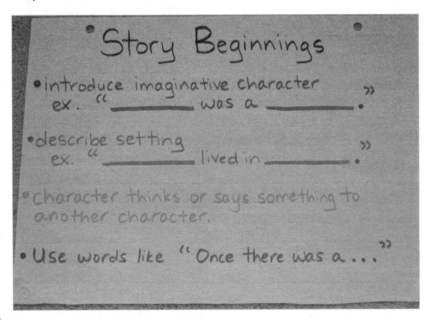

One of the most important jobs writers have is to hook their reader right from the beginning. Listen to some beginnings Leo Lionni wrote for his fantasy stories about animals. Here are some ways that authors often begin fiction stories.

ELL Identify and Communicate Content Objectives—Avoid Idioms. Note that the phrase "hook their readers" is idiomatic—no one is actually hooking anyone. Make sure you clarify this meaning for your ELLs.

Create a chart that includes ways in which authors often start stories.

ELL Identify and Communicate Language Objectives—Language Form and Function. Note that by providing examples and sentence frames, you are demystifying the language that your ELLs will need in order to try out the types of story beginnings.

Story Beginnings

Type of Beginning	Example
Introduce imaginative character: "_____ was a _____"	Mel was a little white dog.
Describe setting: "_____ lived in _____"	Daisy Lou lived on a farm.
Character thinks or says something to another character	Abby wondered, "What will happen at school today?"
Classic beginnings, words such as "Once there was . . ."	Once there was a fish named Finn.

Decide on one way you'd like to begin your class story. Choose one of the story beginnings and then model for students how to add on to it by choosing another technique from the list. If you start your first sentence with a description of the character, for example, you can then have your character say something to another character or you can describe the setting.

Try Guide students to quickly rehearse what they need to learn and do in preparation for practice

Have students quickly rehearse their ideas by sharing how they want to begin their fantasy story. Have partnerships share their thoughts.

> Today we are going to start our stories. Before we start writing, let's turn and share with a partner what you're thinking. How do you want to begin? Use our Story Beginnings Chart to help guide your thinking.

Clarify Briefly restate today's teaching objective and explain the practice task(s)

Remind students to use the Story Beginnings Chart to help guide them as they start their stories. **ELL** Provide Comprehensible Input—Visuals. Charts offer visual support for ELLs to refer back to when they are working independently.

> In your practice today, you are going to start your story. Remember to use our Story Beginnings chart to help you. When you have your beginning down, keep writing your story. I am looking forward to reading what you write.

Practice Students work independently and/or in small groups to apply today's teaching objective

Students will draft the beginnings of their stories using one of the techniques listed on your Story Beginnings Chart. As you roam around the room, have handy some of the Leo Lionni picture books you used as Core Texts. This will help students remain true to the genre and give them models for how to proceed when they get stuck. **ELL** Provide Comprehensible Input—Models. Visuals and models offer a pathway to understanding the language of the lesson without relying only on the words. If you are not able to provide the actual texts, use pictures; include hand-drawn pictures or clip art to illustrate parts of the stories.

Wrap Up Check understanding as you guide students to share briefly what they have learned and produced today

Have a few students share their "unrealistic" beginnings. Compliment the class on making you as a reader say, "Hmmm . . . could this really happen?"

Writing Lesson 5

▼ Teaching Objective

Writers add important events to stories.

Close Reading Opportunity

▼ Standards Alignment

RL.1.1, RL.1.13, RL.1.10, W.1.3, W.1.5, SL.1.1a, SL.1.1b, SL.1.1c, SL.1.2, SL.1.4, SL.1.6, L.1.1, L.1.2, L.1.6

▼ Materials

- *Matthew's Dream* by Leo Lionni
- Charting supplies or interactive whiteboard to create Hmmm . . . Could This Really Happen? Chart for *Matthew's Dream*
- Beginning, Middle, and End Planning Paper (Appendix 1.8)

▼ To the Teacher

Today's work builds on Writing Lesson 4. Today you want your students to continue writing their stories with their "what if" question in mind. We want our first graders to be thoughtful in their writing process and to learn that writers make careful choices. We want to avoid stories that read, "and then . . . and then . . . and then . . . and then . . . ," where the story goes far off course. Instead, we want students to write logical adventures for their imaginary characters. Telling them to say what happens first, next, and finally is one way to help ensure that students are thinking sequentially about the events that their imaginative characters get into.

▼ Procedure

Warm Up Gather the class to set the stage for today's learning

As I read each of your stories yesterday, I wondered, Hmmm . . . could this really happen? and I was immediately drawn into the world of your imaginative stories. Writers such as Leo Lionni keep their readers asking this question by having a sequence of events happen to their main characters. Today we're going to look back at what happened to Matthew to think about what's going to happen to your imaginary characters.

Teach Model what students need to learn and do

> Hmm...Could This Really Happen?
> 1. Matthew sits in the corner of his attic.
> 2. The class is on a field trip at the museum.
> 3. Matthew meets Nicoletta.
> 4. Matthew dreams he is in a painting!
> 5. Matthew becomes a famous painter and marries Nicoletta.

We have read Matthew's Dream many times over the past few days, so I know you are all experts on what happens to Matthew. Today we're going to walk through the story one more time and notice what happens first, in the middle, and at the end. These are called the main events of the story.

Conduct a picture walk with your students, having them share the events in the beginning, in the middle, and in the end. **ELL** Frontload the Lesson—Activate Prior Knowledge. As students are already experts on Matthew, walking through the pictures before generating the list that follows will help them get ready to actively participate in documenting the events. When you're

done, work with the class to list the events in order. Also model adding words such as next, while, then, later and finally to signal event order and provide a sense of closure. (Appendix 1.8). The events could include the following:

> 1) Matthew sat in the corner of the attic.
> 2) His parents wondered what he would be when he grows up.
> 3) Next, he class went on a field trip to the museum.
> 4) While they were there, Matthew met Nicoletta.
> 5) Then, Matthew dreamed he was in a painting!
> 6) Finally, Matthew became a famous painter and married Nicoletta.

Next, decide as a class what will happen in the beginning, middle, and end of your class story. Model how to sketch out the events of the story using a large sheet of paper with three boxes clearly marked Beginning, Middle, and End. Then, use the sketch to help you continue writing the middle and end of your class story. **ELL** Enable Language Production—Reading and Writing. Using the sketch as a base from which to continue writing will assist ELLs to develop their stories. Drawing pictures lets ELLs get down their ideas before diving into the more challenging process of finding words to express those ideas.

Sketch the events of your story below.

Beginning	Middle	End

Try Guide students to quickly rehearse what they need to learn and do in preparation for practice

Direct students how to sketch the events in their story, following the model of your class story.

> Now that we've read closely for how Leo Lionni includes events in a particular order and we've tried it with our class story, we're ready to write our own story events. Before we begin, let's sketch what we want our characters to do in the beginning, in the middle, and in the end. Remember, because we are writing fantasies, some of the events should make your reader wonder, "Hmmm . . . could this really happen?"

Provide students with paper folded three ways. The first box will be for the beginning of the story, etc. Students should sketch what will happen in the beginning, middle, and end of their story. **ELL** Provide Comprehensible Input—Organizers. Offering students this folded paper helps make clear that their stories are to have three parts. ELLs benefit from having this point reinforced multiple times in different formats—first, from your explanation; then, from your model; finally, from the three-part handout.

Clarify Briefly restate today's teaching objective and explain the practice task(s)

Have students use their drawing paper to help guide their writing of fantasy stories.

> In your practice today, you are going to add events to your story. Remember to look back at your sketches to include important details about what is going to happen in the beginning, in the middle, and in the end. Don't forget to use temporal words like next, then, and finally to help suggest the order of your events.

Temporal Words

In the beginning
At first
During
Next
Before
After
Then
In the end
Finally

Practice Students work independently and/or in small groups to apply today's teaching objective

Students will continue writing their stories. To fully develop the events may require more than one lesson. **ELL** Enable Language Production—Reading and Writing. Remember that your ELLs may struggle in two different areas: language and/or content. They may be bursting with story ideas but may be unsure how to express them in English. Help them use all the tools at their disposal—pictures, speaking, writing, the home language, and English—to make their meaning known. (On the other hand, ELLs may truly be confused about story parts, if the language of the lesson was over their heads; use paraphrasing, simpler language, and pictures to help them understand what they are meant to do.)

Wrap Up Check understanding as you guide students to briefly share what they have learned and produced today

Have a few students share several events from their story so far. Have students share what they notice in the stories that is real and is fantasy.

Writing Lesson 6 . . . .

▼ **Teaching Objective**

Writers add detailed illustrations.

Close Reading Opportunity

▼ **Standards Alignment**

RL.1.1, RL.1.7, RL.1.10, W.1.3, W.1.5, SL.1.1a, SL.1.1b, SL.1.1c, SL.1.5, SL.1.6, L.1.1, L.1.2, L.6

▼ Materials

- *Matthew's Dream* by Leo Lionni

▼ To the Teacher

By this lesson your students should have fully developed fantasy stories that include imaginary characters, a somewhat realistic setting, and a sequence of events. During the planning phase of writing, your students used quick but detailed sketches to help capture and organize their thinking. Now it is time for your students to create illustrations that capture the strength of their writing and help to tell the story. Beginning in kindergarten and continuing into first grade, we emphasize the importance of illustrations in the process of storytelling. This lesson guides students toward thinking about the kinds of details they include in their drawings and how those details can help tell their story in powerful ways. In order to provide your students with an adequate amount of time to create truly dynamic illustrations, this lesson is best taught across several days.

Reading Lesson 6 is designed to complement this writing lesson. In that lesson, your students will be examining illustrations closely to better understand the real and imagined elements of the story. The core text in that lesson is *Where the Wild Things Are* by Maurice Sendak. For this writing lesson, we continue with *Matthew's Dream,* but you may want students to review the illustrations from previous read-alouds to enhance their understanding of how to use illustrations as a writer.

▼ Procedure

Warm Up Gather the class to set the stage for today's learning

Congratulate the class on their hard work as writers. Introduce today's aim of illustrating their stories to enhance their readers' understanding of the imaginative elements they've created and to make their stories incredibly interesting to read.

First graders, your stories include all the important components fiction stories need, including characters, a setting, and a sequence of events. But your fantasy stories also have an imaginative twist.

Congratulations on your hard work thus far. Today you have the chance to add illustrations to your story, to help the reader better picture the story elements you've created.

Teach Model what students need to learn and do

Focus on key illustrations from *Matthew's Dream*. For the purposes of this lesson, we've chosen the illustration that shows Matthew's parents imagining he's a doctor. **ELL** Provide Comprehensible Input—Visuals. Visuals offer students a pathway to understanding the text without relying only on the words. If you are not able to provide pictures, include hand-drawn pictures or clip art to illustrate your story. Take a moment to think aloud about all the details you notice, such as how Leo Lionni uses a thought bubble to show what Matthew's parents are thinking and how he dresses up Matthew as a doctor with great detail.

Leo Lionni does a wonderful job of illustrating *Matthew's Dream*; his drawings help us understand what in this story could happen and what couldn't really happen. Take a look at this picture of Matthew's parents imagining he's a doctor. Let's read the words on this page to see how the picture and the words work together to tell the story.

Read aloud the words that correspond with this illustration. Think aloud about how the illustration includes all the details mentioned in the text.

I'm really impressed with how Leo Lionni added each and every detail from the words into his drawings. We know from this picture who Matthew's parents are. They certainly look like everyday mice, don't they? But then, his picture shows us important details that let us know that this is an imaginative story full of things that can't really happen. Notice how Leo Lionni uses a thought bubble to show us what Matthew's parents are dreaming for him. That's a useful tool when you want to show what a character is thinking. Then let's look at how Matthew is dressed. Isn't that funny? He's dressed up as a doctor! How do we know? That's right. He has on a white lab coat and a stethoscope. Well, that certainly is imaginative isn't it? I don't know of any mice who could actually become doctors. Do you?

Try Guide students to quickly rehearse what they need to learn and do in preparation for practice

Choose another illustration from the story. Ask partners to turn and talk to one another to discuss how this illustration shows us what's real and what's imagined.

 Remind students to ask their partner questions about the text to clarify any areas of confusion. (SL.1.1c) **ELL** Enable Language Production—Increasing Interaction. Now that they have heard you talk about the illustrations, ELLs get a chance to hear their peers do the same, and to practice describing illustrations themselves.

Clarify Briefly restate today's teaching objective and explain the practice task(s)

Today we've noticed how Leo Lionni did two important things with his drawings. First, he made sure his pictures matched the words on the page. Next, he wanted to help us better picture what could happen and what couldn't really happen in this story. As you plan and illustrate your writing today, think about showing everything you've included in your writing on a given page *and* think about ways to make it clear to your readers that some things are realistic, while others couldn't really happen.

Practice Students work independently and/or in small groups to apply today's teaching objective

Students work independently to create illustrations that capture realistic and fantasy elements in their writing and that match the corresponding text.

Wrap Up Check understanding as you guide students to briefly share what they have learned and produced today

Gather your class, asking students to have one completed (or nearly completed) illustration handy for sharing. Ask several students to share their work, highlighting how they showed elements that could happen and elements that couldn't really happen, and explaining how those details help to tell their story. **ELL** Language Production—Listening and Speaking. Your ELLs are probably as proficient as any of your students in drawing; this sharing time gives them a chance to extend their learning by applying language to their pictures. They may feel more confident if you have met with them in advance to help them get their words ready.

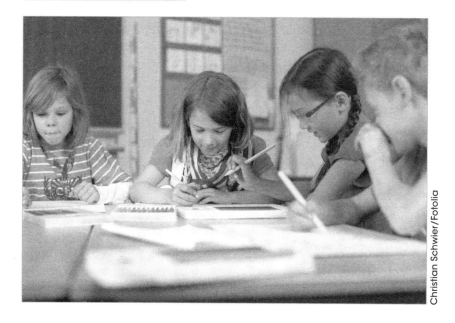

Christian Schwier/Fotolia

Writing Lesson 7 ·

▼ **Teaching Objective**

Writers revise their stories for story elements.

▼ **Standards Alignment**

W.1.3, W.1.5, SL.1.1a, SL.1.1b, SL.1.1c, SL.1.6, L.1.1, L.1.2, L.1.6

▼ Materials

- Imaginative Stories Checklist (Appendix 1.9)

▼ To the Teacher

This lesson may be best taught over two days—one day for revision and one day for editing of conventions. Revision means to "see again," and you will want your students to focus on how they've created imaginative stories that combine realistic and unrealistic elements. Editing is about conventions. Do all of the sentences end in punctuation? Is *I* always capitalized? Because this piece of writing was genre specific and involved a heavy emphasis on weaving realistic and unrealistic elements, the Imaginative Stories Checklist in Appendix 1.9 will serve as an important tool for students to account for the story elements they've included as well as the conventions that will be most critical to this piece of writing, consistent with the first-grade Common Core State Standards. **ELL** Provide Comprehensible Input—Graphic Organizers/Outlines.

▼ Procedure

Warm Up Gather the class to set the stage for today's learning

Review your work from the last few days and orient your students to their job for today, which is to reread their stories for final revisions and the conventions of standard English.

> You have accomplished a lot as storywriters during this lesson set. For the past few days, we've focused on making our writing more exciting for our readers by adding important events and detailed drawings. Now we're ready to do a final read of our stories and check to make sure we've done our job as writers of writing an imaginative story and writing in an understandable way.

Teach Model what students need to learn and do

Describe for students what an editor does. Tell them that they are going to reread their writing with the purpose of revising to make sure that it has all the components of an imaginative piece of fiction. They are also going to edit their writing, paying attention to conventions such as spelling and punctuation.

Revising	Yes/No
Did I compare own story elements with the checklist?	
Did I include strong character(s)?	
Did I include a setting?	
Did I include a sequence of events?	
Did I use temporal words?	
Did I include things that CAN happen?	
Did I include things that CAN'T happen?	
Did I include a good ending?	
Editing	
Did I check and correct my capitalization?	
Did I check and correct my order and usage of words?	
Did I check and correct my punctuation?	
Did I check and correct my spelling?	

When writers go to publish their pieces, they have an editor read over their work to make sure it's clear for the reader. An editor is someone who rereads with a purpose in mind. Today, we are going to reread our stories and use an Imaginative Stories Checklist (Appendix 1.9) to make sure we've included strong characters, created a setting, and written events that include things that could be real as well as things that couldn't really happen.

Show students the Imaginative Stories Checklist and go over each item included for clarity. As you work your way through each item, locate moments or sentences within the shared piece of writing you created over the past several days that satisfy each component. **ELL** Provide Comprehensible Input—Organizers. The checklist will help all your students, but your ELLs in particular, understand how to revise their writing. The checklist provides an anchor students can carry with them after the lesson to support their independent work.

Try   Guide students to quickly rehearse what they need to learn and do in preparation for practice

> Let's take a look together at these next few items on our checklist. Here it says that _____. Turn and talk with your partner: How did we do? Can you find moments where we _____ in our class story?

Allow partners sufficient time to turn and talk with one another. **ELL** Enable Language Production—Increasing Interaction. Peer discussion gives your ELLs a low-pressure environment to hear another example of how to revise and to practice the language they need to express their own ideas about revision. Listen in for moments in conversations that you would like to share with the entire class. Then gather students' attention and highlight the places where you did indeed include _____, modeling for students the process you would like them to utilize independently with this checklist.

Clarify   Briefly restate today's teaching objective and explain the practice task(s)

Remind students to use their Imaginative Stories Checklist when revising their story.

> When reading your story today, use your Imaginative Stories Checklist to ensure that your story includes all the things you need.

Practice   Students work independently and/or in small groups to apply today's teaching objective

Students will reread their stories using the Imaginative Stories Checklist.

Some students may need extra support with this stage of the writing process in order to know how to revise their piece when they see an element missing. Guide these students to revisit the stories they've read so far, and refer back to charts created that offer specifics on the elements of fantasy stories. In addition, other students may need support with basic writing conventions such as capitalization and punctuation. The Imaginative Stories Checklist is designed to help students revise for content as well as conventions of standard English.

Collect and analyze student writing as a performance-based assessment to determine if students need additional instruction or support as a whole class, in small groups, or one on one. **ELL** Assess for Content and Language Understanding—Formative Assessment. This is an opportunity for you to assess

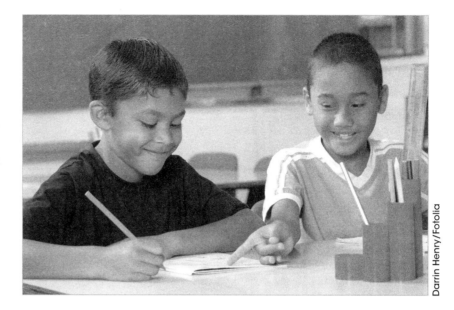

Darrin Henry/Fotolia

your ELLs' language and content needs. How effectively are your ELLs using the checklist? Do they need more support to understand the ideas contained in the checklist, or do they need help applying those ideas to their own writing? This information can be used to plan upcoming lessons.

Milestone Performance Assessment

Revising Writing

 Use this checklist to assess student revisions.

    Standards Alignment: W.1.3, W.1.5, SL.1.5, L.1.1, L.1.2, L.1.6

Task	Achieved	Notes
Compare elements of story with checklist.		
Include a main character.		

Task	Achieved	Notes
Revising		
Include a setting.		
Include a sequence of events.		
Use temporal words to suggest order of events and closure.		
Include things that could happen.		
Include things that couldn't happen.		
Include a good ending.		
Include detailed illustrations that match the words on each page.		

Task	Achieved	Notes
Editing		
Capitalization.		
Sentences.		
Punctuation.		
Spelling.		

Wrap Up Check understanding as you guide students to briefly share what they have learned and produced today

Have students share one thing they revised or edited today to make their writing stronger.

Writing Lesson 8 •

▼ Teaching Objective

Writers create book jackets that show what's most important in their story.

▼ Standards Alignment

W.1.3, W.1.6, SL.1.1a, SL.1.1b, SL.1.1c, SL.1.4, SL.1.6, L.1.1, L.1.2, L.1.6

▼ Materials

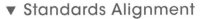

- *Matthew's Dream* by Leo Lionni
- Sample book jackets
- Book cover materials

▼ To the Teacher

Your students' stories are complete! Now is the opportunity for them to design their own book jacket by creating a front cover, a back cover, and a blurb about their story. This lesson will not only support your students as growing writers, but also continue to familiarize them with features of books that they can apply to their reading lives.

▼ Procedure

Warm Up Gather the class to set the stage for today's learning

Well done, first graders. Just like Leo Lionni you've written and illustrated stories that have an imaginative twist. We're almost ready to share them with a live audience. First, we're going to create book jackets that help explain to our audience what our stories are about.

Teach | Model what students need to learn and do

Gather from your classroom some books with book jackets to provide models for your class.

> Let's look at some examples of book jackets from our classroom. What kinds of things do you notice?

Provide some wait time for your students to respond. Listen to and list what they notice about book jackets. **ELL** Enable Language Production—Listening and Speaking. Give ample wait time for students to formulate their answers. ELLs in particular might need a moment more to put their noticing into words—waiting a few extra seconds increases their confidence and participation.

Examples include:

- front cover
  - title
  - big picture (usually of main character)
  - author
- back cover
  - tells what the book is about (also called the blurb)
  - sometimes another picture

Use your class story as a guide. Map out for your students what you would include on the front cover and back cover for this shared story. Leo Lionni often uses the main character's name as the title of his stories. This is a simple technique for helping first graders generate titles. When writing the short summary for the back cover, keep your blurb to one or two sentences that simply introduce the character and asks the original "what if" question you used to generate the story back in Writing Lesson 1. This will help your students remember what the big idea of their story is.

A blurb for *Matthew's Dream* could read, "What if mice had dreams like you and me? In this story, meet Matthew, a mouse who discovers that he wants to be a painter." **ELL** Enable Language Production—Listening and Speaking. Give ample wait time for students to formulate their answers. ELLs in particular might need a moment more to put their noticing into words—waiting a few extra seconds increases their confidence and participation.

Try | Guide students to quickly rehearse what they need to learn and do in preparation for practice

Before setting out to design their book jackets, have students rehearse sharing with a partner what they're going to include on the front cover and back cover. Remind students that to write their blurbs they want to introduce the main character and ask their original "what if" question. **ELL** Enable Language Production—Reading and Writing. This oral rehearsal with partners sets ELLs up to be successful in the writing task ahead of them.

Clarify | Briefly restate today's teaching objective and explain the practice task(s)

Remind students to look at classroom examples when designing their book jackets.

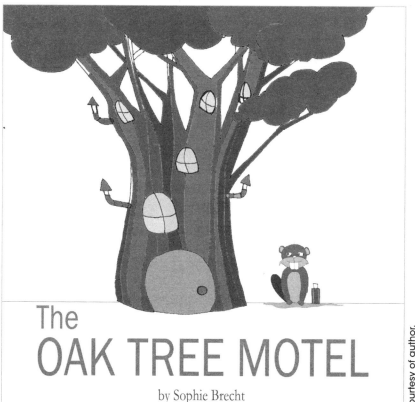

The OAK TREE MOTEL

by Sophie Brecht

Courtesy of author.

Courtesy of author.

Where will Beaver Gus stay this winter?

A terrible storm has swept his dam down the riverbank! Thankfully he finds The Oak Tree Motel, where he meets many animals from all over the forest.

In your independent practice today, you are going to create a book jacket for your story by creating a front cover and back cover. Remember to look back at our chart, take a look at our sample, or review some of the book jackets from our classroom library for ideas.

Provide Comprehensible Input—Visuals, Models. Displaying the jackets of familiar books can help ELLs who might not find it easy to interpret the words on the chart.

Practice Students work independently and/or in small groups to apply today's teaching objective

Students will create book jackets by focusing on what's included on the front and back covers. To generate their own short summary for the back cover, they should include the name of the character and ask their original "what if" question to pull in readers. In the left column and on the previous page are examples of book jackets.

Wrap Up Check understanding as you guide students to briefly share what they have learned and produced today

Have students share the back-cover short summaries. Listen carefully for those who have successfully used a complete sentence or two to include the main character's name and asks "what if?"

Goal	Low-Tech	High-Tech
Students write and illustrate book jackets that include a front cover and back cover with a blurb that explains what the story is about.	Use a variety of materials such as pencils, colored pencils, crayons, markers, magazine cutouts, tissue paper, and so on.	Use digital art and typing tools such as child painting programs (e.g., Tux Paint or Paint Slate).

Writing Lesson 9 . . . .

▼ Teaching Objective

Writers share their stories with pride.

▼ Standards Alignment

W.1.6, SL.1.1a, SL.1.1b, SL.1.1c, SL.1.2, SL.1.3, SL.1.4, SL.1.6, L.1.1, L.1.6

▼ Materials

- Student writing
- Charting supplies or interactive whiteboard to create Sharing our Stories with Pride Chart

▼ To the Teacher

Today is a celebratory day! Your students have written and illustrated wonderful stories with a focus on combining real and fantasy story elements. Today is all about sharing their stories with pride. As such, we recommend calling today an Author's Fair and encourage you to consider inviting other classrooms, grades, or your students' families to enjoy this culminating occasion. On the day of the Author's Fair, set up your classroom into a series of author's booths. A simple setup for this is to turn the desks or tables into a large open rectangle, with your students standing behind the tables so the audience can roam from one booth to the next in any order. At the booths, the students will have their stories available for reading and their book jackets on display. Encourage your audience to share what they liked about each story as they make their way around the room. To prepare for the Author's Fair, we want to give our first graders ample time to practice reading their stories aloud with pride. Today's lesson is about that focused practice in reading clearly, slowly, and with purpose.

Monkey Business/Fotolia

Goal	Low-Tech	High-Tech
Students share and discuss their writing with an audience through an Author's Fair.	• Invite other classes, staff, and/or parents to an Author's Fair of imaginative stories. • Students will read their work aloud to the audience, taking time to show their illustrations.	• Record students as they read their stories aloud, including up-close shots of their illustrations. • Upload these recordings online for a virtual Author's Fair, asking viewers to respond in detail to what they liked about the stories.

▼ Procedure

Warm Up Gather the class to set the stage for today's learning

Compliment the class on a job well done. They are authors and have much to be proud of!

Congratulations, first graders, on your imaginative stories, illustrations, and book jackets. Today is the day that we get to prepare for how we'll share our hard work with others. We want to share our stories with pride because there is so much to be proud of.

Teach Model what students need to learn and do

Using your class story, model for students how to read a story with pride by expressing your ideas loudly and clearly. They need to make sure they project their voice, speak in complete sentences, and use standard English grammar. In addition, model for students how to stand up straight and tall when sharing their writing out loud. Following your reading, ask students what they noticed about the way you read the story. Create a class chart on Sharing Our Stories with Pride. **ELL** Enable Language Production—Listening and Speaking. Modeling the type of language you expect students to use, rather than just telling them what to do, can be very helpful for ELLs.

Your chart might look like this:

Sharing Our Stories with Pride

- Speak loudly and clearly.
- Read complete sentences.
- Pause at periods.
- Stand tall.
- Listen carefully to the stories of others.
- Smile and be proud.

Try Guide students to quickly rehearse what they need to learn and do in preparation for practice

Ask students to work with a partner to practice reading their stories aloud. **ELL** Enable Language Production—Listening and Speaking. Practicing with peers is a great way to make sure your ELLs feel ready to share their stories with the world in English. Bear in mind also that if you have invited families to the Author's Fair, you should encourage students to practice telling their original stories in their home language as well. That way, their parents can be part of the celebration. This also shows respect for all the linguistic and cultural skills your students bring to the classroom.

 Circulate and listen in to partnerships, offering gentle reminders about the key speaking and listening skills, including expressing ideas clearly, producing complete sentences, and asking and answering questions about what a speaker says. (SL.1.3, SL.1.4, SL.1.6).

Clarify Briefly restate today's teaching objective and explain the practice task(s)

Nice work reading your stories with pride. You are working hard to read clearly and with expression. Today we're going to continue practicing and preparing for our Author's Fair by reading our stories aloud to a partner. In your next reading, make sure you offer your partner a specific compliment about what you love about their story.

Practice Students work independently and/or in small groups to apply today's teaching objective

Students work in partnerships, reading their stories aloud to one another with a focus on fluency and expression. In addition, have students give each other a specific compliment using sentence starters such as "I like how you _____" or "_____ was my favorite part because _____." **ELL** Enable Language Production—Listening and Speaking. Consider creating a group of bilingual students who can alternately practice reading their stories in English and then retelling them in their common home language, so they are ready to share them with families.

Wrap Up Check understanding as you guide students to briefly share what they have learned and produced today

Ask students to share their favorite moments from friends' stories. Also, have students share what they learned by listening to each other's stories. This will help them think more deeply and critically about how they will share their own stories with pride.

Analyze students' presentations of stories as a performance-based assessment to determine if students need additional instruction or support as a whole class, in small groups, or one on one. **ELL** Assess for Content and Language Understandings—Summative Assessment. This is an opportunity for you to assess your ELLs' language and content needs through their performance of stories. This information can then be used to plan upcoming lessons.

Milestone Performance Assessment

Sharing Own Stories

Use this checklist to assess student performances of stories.

Standards Alignment: SL.1.1a, SL.1.1b, SL.1.1c SL.1.3, SL.1.4, SL.1.6

Task	Achieved	Notes
Speak loudly and clearly.		
Read complete sentences.		
Pause at appropriate moments such as at end punctuation.		
Listen carefully to the stories of others.		

Writing Lesson 10

▼ Teaching Objective

Writers reflect on what they've learned by saying thanks.

▼ Standards Alignment

W.1.8, SL.1.1a, SL.1.1b, SL.1.1c, SL.5, SL.1.6, L.1.1, L.1.2, L.1.6

▼ Materials

- Thank-you letter materials

▼ To the Teacher

The Author's Fair is intended to be a shared community event to celebrate the fantasy writers your first graders have become. As such, you may have invited another class, another grade, or your students' families. Today's lesson is designed to have your first graders reflect on what they've learned about writing imaginative stories. It's also designed to be an opportunity to say thank you to the audience that shared in the Author's Fair, whether they came in person or viewed your students' writing online. In this way, we hope to inspire first graders to not only continue celebrating a job well done, but also to recognize the importance of saying thanks to others when the time is right.

We recommend that you write a shared thank-you letter if you are writing to another class that visited your Author's Fair, and then have students create thank-you drawings to accompany the letter. If students' families attended, we suggest that you write a shared thank-you as a model and then have students write brief, individualized thank-you notes to their families.

▼ Procedure

Warm Up Gather the class to set the stage for today's learning

Applaud your class for their performances during the Author's Fair, and let them know that their success was thanks to their hard work and creativity

as writers. However, we have other people to thank for making the event a success.

> First graders, you have shared your stories with pride. In fact, I wanted to thank you for sharing your stories with me. You ignited my imagination by showing me just how imaginative you can be. When someone affects your life in big or small ways, it's always nice to thank them. So, today we're going to write thank-you notes to our Author's Fair visitors to thank them for joining us yesterday. Without them, our fair wouldn't have been nearly as exciting.

Teach Model what students need to learn and do

Use this letter as an opportunity for the class to share what they learned about writing imaginative stories and how the visitors helped make the sharing so much fun.

With your class, create a list of all the things they learned about writing imaginative stories and what they are most proud of. Use this list to create a shared letter to use as either a model for students as they write individual thank-yous and/or as a springboard for student illustrations of what they learned and what they are most proud of. **ELL** Enable Language Production—Reading and Writing. The list and the accompanying group discussion offer a strong support for your ELLs as they get ready to write independently.

> Date
>
> Dear _____,
>
> Thank you for joining us yesterday for our Author's Fair. We were happy you got a chance to see all that we learned about writing imaginative stories such as _____ and _____. We are proud of how we _____. You really helped make our sharing event extra special.
>
> With thanks,

Try Guide students to quickly rehearse what they need to learn and do in preparation for practice

Before students compose their own letters and/or accompanying illustrations, have them turn and share with a partner one thing they learned and what they are most proud of as a writer. Listen in on these conversations. Does everyone have something to share? **ELL** Enable Language Production—Reading and Writing. ELLs should be encouraged to write thank-you notes in the language of their audience—if their parents or others who speak their home language attended the fair, they should try to write in that language. Pair students with others who speak their home language for this conversation, so they can rehearse what they will write.

Clarify Briefly restate today's teaching objective and explain the practice task(s)

Today in your practice you are going to _____ (*either* write your own thank-you note using ours as a guide *or* help us send our thank-you note with drawings made by each of you or both). Remember to include what you learned about writing imaginative stories and what you are most proud of. I can't wait to see your contribution.

Practice Students work independently and/or in small groups to apply today's teaching objective

Students will reflect on what they learned and what they are most proud of through writing and/or drawing. **ELL** Enable Language Production—

Reading and Writing. If ELLs have never learned to read and write in their home language, they might feel reluctant to try. Encourage them to use what they know about reading and writing in English to help them spell in their home language. Reassure them that the final product doesn't have to be perfect. So that you have something to assess, have them do two versions: one in English and one in the home language.

Wrap Up Check understanding as you guide students to briefly share what they have learned and produced today

Have students share with the group one detail from their letter or drawing. **ELL** Enable Language Production—Increasing Interaction. The more students actively use language, the better it will develop!

Once again, let your class know how proud you are of them for their hard work writing imaginative stories, listening to one another, and sharing their ideas with an audience. Much has been accomplished over these past few weeks!

Language Companion Lesson

Note: This lesson is best taught early in the lesson set so that students may have the opportunity to apply these spelling strategies to their written work.

▼ Teaching Objective

We are able to use three different strategies to help us spell correctly.

▼ Standards Alignment

L.1.2d, L.1.2e

▼ Materials

- Charting supplies or interactive whiteboard
- Individual whiteboards and dry-erase markers

▼ To the Teacher

The writers in your class are at varying stages of writing and spelling development. For some, getting words down on paper will feel easy. For others, it may feel like a monumentally challenging task. Sometimes young writers let the "I can't spell it" roadblock stand between them and expressing their ideas on paper. This lesson is designed to build courage and capacity to spell words strategically to keep the writing flowing.

Keep in mind that spelling every word correctly is not the goal at this point—getting words down on paper is. Developmental spelling (spelling that is not yet conventionally accurate but reflects the spelling knowledge of the individual student) is appropriate at this level and should be encouraged, especially for challenging words. That said, don't hesitate to expect students to spell selected words correctly such as those you have studied as a class and/or posted accurately on a word wall.

▼ Procedure

Warm Up Gather the class to set the stage for today's learning

Introduce to students the need for spelling strategies.

Everyone loves to share their stories and ideas with others. Sometimes we do this by talking. Sometimes we do this through writing. We write down our stories or ideas so other people can read them. Yet if we want people to be able to read our writing, we need to try to spell our words as correctly as possible. We never want to say, "I can't spell this" and just give up! Luckily, there are spelling strategies we can use to help us.

Teach Model what students need to learn and do

Model three spelling strategies.

Today I am going to show you how to use three tools that you have to help you spell words correctly.

Draw three simple pictures on the board or chart:

153

1. An eye

2. An ear

3. A poster with a tack in it

Refer to the first picture, of an eye. Model spelling a common word next to the eye. What does it look like? Say a word and close your eyes to try to remember what it looks like, after you have seen it. Write the letters that you remember. It is OK to model approximate as well as accurate spellings. **ELL** Enable Language Production—Reading and Writing. Remember that ELLs are still getting used to the sounds of English. They may understand how to use this strategy and still spell words differently than their English-speaking peers would (e.g., is the "g" in *dog* the same as the "g" in *goat*, or is one quieter? English groups them as one sound, so your English speakers might say so, but they are subtly different, so your ELLs might not realize they are spelled the same way). Encourage the use of the strategy anyway, and work on phonemic awareness with them when necessary.

Refer to the second picture, of an ear. Model spelling a common word next to the ear. What does it sounds like? Say a word slowly to listen to the sounds you hear. Write down the sounds you hear. It is OK to model approximate as well as accurate spellings.

Refer to the third picture, of a poster. Model using resources around the room, such as word walls, posters, and so on, as a reference for spelling. Point out where students can find commonly used words such as names, colors, numbers, or high-frequency words to aid their spelling. If the word is visible, students should be able to spell it accurately. Model this.

Try Guide students to quickly rehearse what they need to learn and do in preparation for practice

Provide students with whiteboards. Guide them to spell common words using the three tools above—spelling by ear, spelling by eye, and using the print in the room.

Prompt students with a word. Have them practice spelling the word on their whiteboards using all three strategies—first by ear, then by eye, and then by looking for it in the room.

Repeat this practice 2–3 times.

Clarify Briefly restate today's teaching objective and explain the practice task(s)

Encourage students to use these three strategies during their independent writing.

Practice Students work independently and/or in small groups to apply today's teaching objective

Students write independently using spelling strategies to "keep the words flowing."

Wrap Up Check understanding as you guide students to briefly share what they have learned and produced today.

Students share their writing and talk about which spelling strategies helped them the most in their independent writing.

GLOSSARY

beginning: the first part of something (a sentence, a chapter, a story).

character: a person in a story, play, or movie.

ending: how a story stops or finishes; the last part. Also called the conclusion.

events: things that happen, especially important things.

evidence: something that gives proof of or a reason to believe something.

fantasy: a type of fiction that contains elements that couldn't really happen such as magic or talking animals.

fiction: writing that tells a story from an author's imagination; it didn't really happen.

illustration: a picture or drawing used to explain or decorate written material.

imagine: to form a picture in the mind of something that is dreamed up.

information: knowledge or facts about any thing or event.

middle: the place, point, or position that is in the center of something or halfway from each end of it.

plot: the story line or order of events in a book, play, or movie.

real: actual or true.

realistic: truly existing, real.

setting: the time and place in which something happens.

Accompanying *Core Ready for Grades K–2*, there is an online resource site with media tools that, together with the text, provides you with the tools you need to implement the lesson sets.

The PDToolkit for Pam Allyn's *Core Ready* Series is available free for 12 months after you use the password that comes with the box set for each grade band. After that, you can purchase access for an additional 12 months. If you did not purchase the box set, you can purchase a 12-month subscription at **http://pdtoolkit.pearson .com.** Be sure to explore and download the resources available at the website. Currently the following resources are available:

- Pearson Children's and Young Adult Literature Database
- Videos
- PowerPoint Presentations
- Student Artifacts

- Photos and Visual Media
- Handouts, Forms, and Posters to supplement your Core-aligned lesson plans
- Lessons and Homework Assignments
- Close Reading Guides and Samples
- Children's Core Literature Recommendations

In the future, we will continue to add additional resources. To learn more, please visit **http://pdtoolkit.pearson.com.**

Grade 2

Once Upon a Time: A New Look at Fairy Tales

Introduction

The magic of fairy tales has the power to capture the imagination of all second-grade readers and writers. From classic tales that have been told and re-told for hundreds of years to more modern adaptations that tickle our funny bones, the genre of fairy tales is rich and full of potential for engaging study. In this lesson set, students come to know both the classic versions of a variety of fairy tales as well as more contemporary adaptations of the same tales, sometimes referred to as "fractured fairy tales."

In grades K–2, children begin to master the decoding skills described in the standards for reading foundational skills. As more sophisticated readers, many second graders are able to read longer, more complex pieces, yet often struggle with comprehending their reading on a deeper level and demonstrating this understanding through fluent reading and rich conversation. Helping students understand what they read is always one of our ultimate

Why This Lesson Set?

In this lesson set, students will:

- Identify key story elements, using them to compare and contrast different versions of the same tale
- Conduct close readings of illustrations to support comprehension
- Trace character change across one tale, using this information to determine the central theme or lesson
- Write an original adaptation of a classic fairy tale
- Elevate their writing by adding details such as character dialogue and descriptive character action

goals as teachers. By focusing on these engaging and classic tales, students have an opportunity to work toward greater proficiency with these goals.

In support of the reading standards, students engage with the elements of story to determine the central theme or lesson included in the tale as well as to compare and contrast different versions of the same tale. In addition, students honor the oral tradition of fairy tales by performing familiar tales for an authentic audience with a focus on fluency and expression in their delivery.

In support of the writing standards, students compose an original fairy tale with an eye on including a variety of details aimed at making their writing more dynamic and sophisticated. More specifically, students experiment with the use of internal thought, dialogue, descriptive action, and powerful endings to engage their audience.

Common Core State Standards Alignment

Reading Literature Standards

RL.2.1 Ask and answer such questions as *who, what, where, when, why,* and *how* to demonstrate understanding of key details in a text.

RL.2.2 Recount stories, including fables and folktales from diverse cultures, and determine their central message, lesson, or moral.

RL.2.3 Describe how characters in a story respond to major events and challenges.

RL.2.5 Describe the overall structure of a story, including describing how the beginning introduces the story and the ending concludes the action.

RL.2.7 Use information gained from the illustrations and words in a print or digital text to demonstrate understanding of its characters, setting, or plot.

RL.2.9 Compare and contrast two or more versions of the same story (e.g., Cinderella stories) by different authors or from different cultures.

RL.2.10 By the end of the year, read and comprehend literature, including stories and poetry, in the grades 2–3 text complexity band proficiently, with scaffolding as needed at the high end of the range.

Writing Standards

W.2.3 Write narratives in which they recount a well-elaborated event or short sequence of events, include details to describe actions, thoughts, and feelings, use temporal words to signal event order, and provide a sense of closure.

W.2.5 With guidance and support from adults and peers, focus on a topic and strengthen writing as needed by revising and editing.

W.2.6 With guidance and support from adults, use a variety of digital tools to produce and publish writing, including in collaboration with peers.

W.2.8 Recall information from experiences or gather information from provided sources to answer a question.

Speaking and Listening Standards

SL.2.1 Participate in collaborative conversations with diverse partners about *grade 2 topics and texts* with peers and adults in small and larger groups.

a. Follow agreed-upon rules for discussions (e.g., gaining the floor in respectful ways, listening to others with care, speaking one at a time about the topics and texts under discussion).

b. Build on others' talk in conversations by linking their comments to the remarks of others.

c. Ask for clarification and further explanation as needed about the topics and texts under discussion.

SL.2.2 Recount or describe key ideas or details from a text read aloud or information presented orally or through other media.

SL.2.3 Ask and answer questions about what a speaker says in order to clarify comprehension, gather additional information, or deepen understanding of a topic or issue.

SL.2.4 Tell a story or recount an experience with appropriate facts and relevant, descriptive details, speaking audibly in coherent sentences.

SL.2.5 Create audio recordings of stories or poems; add drawings or other visual displays to stories or recounts of experiences when appropriate to clarify ideas, thoughts, and feelings.

SL.2.6 Produce complete sentences when appropriate to task and situation in order to provide requested detail or clarification.

Language Standards

L.2.1 Demonstrate command of the conventions of standard English grammar and usage when writing or speaking.

L.2.2 Demonstrate command of the conventions of standard English capitalization, punctuation, and spelling when writing.

L.2.3 Use knowledge of language and its conventions when writing, speaking, reading, or listening.

L.2.4 Determine or clarify the meaning of unknown and multiple-meaning words and phrases based on grade 2 reading and content, choosing flexibly from an array of strategies.

L.2.6 Use words and phrases acquired through conversations, reading and being read to, and responding to texts, including using adjectives and adverbs to describe (e.g., *When other kids are happy that makes me happy*).

Essential Skill Lenses (PARCC Framework)

The Partnership for Assessment of Readiness for College and Careers (PARCC) is a coalition of more than 20 states that has come together with "a shared commitment to develop an assessment system aligned to the Common Core State Standards that is anchored in college and career readiness" (http://www.parcconline.org). As part of its proposal to the U.S. Department of Education, PARCC has developed model content frameworks for English language arts to serve as a bridge between the Common Core State Standards and the PARCC assessments in development at the time of this publication. At the time of publication, PARCC has provided guidelines for grades 3 to 11. At the K to 2 grade levels, however, we expect students to engage in reading and writing through eight PARCC-specified skill lenses in order to build a foundation for future grades. The table below details how each skill lens is addressed across the lesson set. (PARCC, 2012).

	Reading	Writing
Cite Evidence	There are many opportunities throughout this lesson set for students to cite specific portions of a given text as evidence to support their thinking, particularly about elements of a fairy tale, character, and theme.	As writers, students work collaboratively, citing their own writing as well of that of a partner as evidence of specific teaching objectives.
Analyze Content	Students identify various elements of fairy tales, find specific evidence of a central theme or lesson, and compare and contrast two versions of the same fairy tale.	Students revisit their own writing multiple times throughout this lesson set, looking closely at their drafts to make purposeful revisions.
Study and Apply Grammar	Students demonstrate the ability to convey their ideas clearly, using language that is appropriate to the situation and audience.	Students work in partnerships to analyze their own writing to improve its clarity.
Study and Apply Vocabulary	Students apply the vocabulary and specific language associated with fairy tales.	Identifying important vocabulary in reading provides support for student writing. When creating their own stories, students think carefully about words and phrases to describe the characters, setting, and events.
Conduct Discussions	Throughout the lesson set, students engage in whole-group discussions, small-group discussions, and multiple opportunities to turn and talk one on one with a classmate. The teacher should emphasize following general rules and etiquette for discussions and review this as needed.	Students discuss and share their developing stories. Students follow general rules and etiquette for discussions, which are crucial for the success of these discussions.
Report Findings	In many lessons, students share with the class their investigations into various fairy tales.	As writers, students bring back their writing to share with the class their successes and struggles. In many instances, children lift a line of text from their own writing as a means of collecting excellent writing examples.
Phonics and Word Recognition	Plan opportunities for students to build Reading Foundational Skills by exploring grade-level appropriate skills in the context of the Core Texts from each lesson set and applying this knowledge to their independent reading and writing. Schools may also wish to acquire developmentally appropriate curricular materials specific to this area. *Words Their Way: Word Study in Action* by Donald Bear et al. is an excellent example of a program that addresses this need.	

	Reading	Writing
Fluency	By providing independent reading selections that are at your students' reading levels, you are helping support their growing fluency and stamina. Repeated readings should be encouraged.	This lesson set provides students with the opportunity to revisit their work multiple times, improving their ability to stick with a piece of writing and see it through to completion. Students also may choose to pursue and balance working on a number of drafts of adapted fairy tales at once.

Core Questions

Before getting started with the day-to-day lessons, it's important to consider the core questions that drive this lesson set. These questions remain the core of our teaching throughout the lesson set, and each lesson should come back to these overarching ideas.

- What are the key elements in a story?
- What are the characteristics of a fairy tale?
- How do classic versions of fairy tales compare to the more modern adaptations?
- How does knowledge of story elements help students to write an adaptation of a classic story?
- What types of details help to enhance our writing?

Ready to Get Started?

Your second graders are going to fall in love with the magic and excitement of fairy tales. Both the classic and reimagined versions are packed with imaginative creatures, magical moments, and exciting twists and turns. However, fairy tales offer more opportunities for our readers than just a good story. Not only do fairy tales contain a deeper lesson or message for readers to uncover, they present us with a chance to encourage students to question the content of their reading. By contrasting classic versions of fairy tales with more-modern adaptations, we open up the possibility for students to pursue a high level of critical thinking by addressing issues of power, gender, and social class presented in fairy tales. For

instance, why do classic fairy tales typically portray the female character as the one in need of saving? Why are the wealthy often described as wicked? What does it mean to truly live "happily ever after"?

Lesson Set Goals

Lesson Set Goals Reading

- Build and demonstrate understanding of traditional literature (fairy tales) through close reading of text, citing textual evidence to support thinking and ideas. (RL.2.1, RL.2.2, RL.2.3, RL.2.10, W.2.8, SL.1.1a, SL.1.1b, SL.1.1c, SL.2.2, SL.2.4, SL.2.6, L.2.1, L.2.3, L.2.6)
- Identify and define the features and elements of fairy tales (magic, good vs. evil, problem, solution, key events, lesson). (RL.2.1, RL.2.2, RL.2.5, RL.2.10, SL.2.1a, SL.2.1b, SL.2.1c, SL.2.2, SL.2.4, SL.2.6, L.2.1, L.2.3, L.2.6)
- Infer the message or lesson in a fairy tale and use text evidence to defend their interpretations. (RL.2.1, RL.2.2, RL.2.10, W.2.8, SL.2.1a, SL.2.1b, SL.2.1c, SL.2.2, SL.2.4, SL.2.6, L.2.1, L.2.3, L.2.6)
- Use strategies to determine or clarify the meaning of new words and phrases in fairy tales. (L.2.4)
- Use information gained from illustrations to better understand a fairy tale. (RL.2.1, RL.2.7, RL.2.10)
- Identify and explain how and why a character changes throughout a fairy tale. (RL.2.1, RL.2.3, RL.2.10, SL.2.1a, SL.2.1b, SL.2.1c, SL.2.2, SL.2.4, SL.2.6, L.2.1, L.2.3, L.2.6)

- Compare and contrast two versions of the same fairy tale to recognize similarities and differences. (RL.2.2, RL.2.9, RL.2.10, W.2.8, SL.2.1a, SL.2.1b, SL.2.1c, L.2.1, L.2.3, L.2.6)

- Ask and answer such questions as who, what, where, when, why, and how to demonstrate understanding of key details in a text. (RL.2.1)

- By the end of year, read and comprehend a variety of literature texts in the grades 2–3 text complexity band proficiently, with scaffolding as needed at the high end of the range. (RL.2.10)

- In collaborative discussions, exhibit responsibility for the rules and roles and purpose of conversation. (SL.2.1a, SL.2.1b)

- In collaborative discussions, ask questions in a manner that enhances understanding of topic. (SL.2.1c)

- Speak in complete sentences when appropriate. (SL.2.6)

- Demonstrate knowledge of standard English and its conventions. (L.2.1, L.2.2, L.2.3)

- Use words and phrases acquired through conversations, reading and being read to, and responding to texts. (L.2.6)

Lesson Set Goals Writing

- Plan and write an original adaptation of a classic fairy tale that includes the elements common to fairy tales and a logical sequence of events. (RL.2.1, RL.2.2, RL.2.3, RL.2.10, W.2.3, W.2.5, W.2.8, SL.1.1a, SL.1.1b, SL.1.1c, SL.2.2, SL.2.4, SL.2.6, L.2.1, L.2.2, L.2.3, L.2.6)

- Include strong details such as dialogue, descriptive language, inner thoughts, and feelings. (W.2.3, SL.2.1a, SL.2.1b, SL.2.1c, SL.2.6, L.2.1, L.2.2, L.2.3, L.2.6)

- Write narratives in which they recount a well-elaborated event or short sequence of events, include details to describe actions, thoughts, and feelings, use temporal words to signal event order, and provide a sense of closure. (W.2.3)

- With guidance and support from adults and peers, focus on a topic and strengthen writing as needed by revising and editing. (W.2.5)

- With guidance and support from adults and peers, share writing with others in meaningful ways. (W.2.6)

- In collaborative discussions, exhibit responsibility for the rules and roles and purpose of conversation. (SL.2.1a, SL.2.1b)

- In collaborative discussions, ask questions in a manner that enhances understanding of topic. (SL.2.1c)

- Speak in complete sentences when appropriate. (SL.2.6)

- Demonstrate knowledge of standard English and its conventions. (L.2.1, L.2.2, L.2.3)

- Use words and phrases acquired through conversations, reading and being read to, and responding to texts. (L.2.6)

Choosing Core Texts

To prepare for the teaching in this lesson set, you'll need to gather enough fairy tales for your students to read during independent practice. Be sure to gather classic versions, adapted or reimagined versions (sometimes referred to as fractured fairy tales), and versions from other cultures. There are many wonderful collections of fairy tales available for students at all ranges of reading levels. The texts listed below are specifically referenced in the expanded core teaching for this lesson set.

- *Cinderella* retold by Barbara Karlin
- *Cinderella, or, The Little Glass Slipper* translated by Marcia Brown
- *The Egyptian Cinderella* by Shirley Climo
- *Good Little Wolf* by Nadia Shireen
- *The Korean Cinderella* by Shirley Climo
- *The Paper Bag Princess* by Robert Munsch
- *Prince Cinders* by Babette Cole
- *The Princess and the Pea* by Rachel Isadora
- *Red Riding Hood* retold by James Marshall
- *Yeh Shen: A Cinderella Story from China* by Ai-Ling Louie

We encourage you to seek out and use other fairy tales as well. Fairy tales make for fun and engaging read-alouds—so tuck them into your teaching as often as you'd like, and fill your room with the joy and magic of these stories! Many popular folktales are widely available in your school or public library. You can also find both text and video versions of many popular folktales online with a quick search of Google or YouTube.

Here are a few additional texts we recommend. These have been chosen because they represent both classic and contemporary versions of the genre.

- *Bigfoot Cinderrrrrella* by Tony Johnston
- *Cinder Edna* by Ellen Jackson
- *Cindy-Ellen: A Wild Western Cinderella* by Susan Lowell
- *Cinder-Elly* by Frances Minters
- *Goldilocks and the Three Bears* by James Marshall
- *Little Red Riding Hood: A Newfangled Prairie Tale* by Lisa Campbell Ernst
- *Tell the Truth, B.B. Wolf* by Judy Sierra
- *The Three Bears* by Paul Galdone
- *The Three Little Wolves and the Big Bad Pig* by Eugene Trivizas
- *The Wolf Who Cried Boy* by Bob Hartman

A Note *about* Addressing Reading Standard 10: Range of Reading and Level of Text Complexity

This lesson set provides all students with opportunities to work with texts deemed appropriate for their grade level as well as texts at their specific reading level. Through shared experiences and focused instruction, all students engage with and comprehend a wide range of texts within their grade-level complexity band. We suggest a variety of high-quality, complex text to use within the whole-group lessons and recommend a variety of additional titles under Choosing Core Texts to extend and enrich instruction. During independent practice and in small-group collaborations, however, research strongly suggests that all students need to work with texts they can read with a high level of accuracy and comprehension (i.e., at their developmentally appropriate reading level) in order to significantly improve their reading (Allington, 2012; Ehri, Dreyer, Flugman, & Gross, 2007). Depending on individual needs and skills, a student's reading level may be above, within, or below his or her grade-level band. It should also be noted that at times students can and should most certainly engage with complex texts above their levels when reading independently if they have been taught skills to grapple with texts and if they are confident in working with them.

Teacher's Notes

Have you ever had a moment where something familiar appeared to you in a whole new light? Perhaps it was a time when you saw an event from a completely different perspective or took a new and unexpected adventure that you had never considered before. These are the moments that can shake up our view of ourselves and make us question what was. They are exhilarating.

In this lesson set, we have the opportunity to shake up our students' perspectives on some classic and widely known stories—fairy tales! Don't worry if your students are unfamiliar with these tales; just reading a classic tale in juxtaposition with a more modern version of the same tale will give them a taste of actively questioning as they read. Whose version of the tale is correct? Is the wolf really all that bad? And what does it really mean to live happily ever after? In order to tackle these more abstract ideas, the lessons build upon students' knowledge of key story elements, using them as a springboard to more closely question their reading, analyze characters, infer lessons, and compare and contrast two versions of the same tale.

The adaption of an original fairy tale students create as part of this lesson set will make an excellent selection for their writing portfolios. Not only will it show a command of a new genre, but it will also demonstrate students' ability to craft highly detailed narrative complete with well-developed characters. Finally, students' commentary about their writing provides an interesting look into their emergent ability to self-critique and reflect on their own learning.

To best support students who may be unfamiliar with these sorts of traditional texts, spend time preparing for this lesson set by reading aloud to the class several classic fairy tales. In addition, when possible, build in time to read and enjoy a variety of fairy tales alongside your formal instruction.

Core Message to Students

Close your eyes and imagine a magical land. Maybe it's a castle. Maybe it's beside the ocean. Maybe it's on a wintry mountaintop. Now, imagine the characters and other magical creatures who might fill that land. In a fairy tale, all magical things are possible—talking wolves, fire-breathing dragons, and fairy godmothers are just the beginning! What kind of magic do you want to create?

See Appendix 2.1 for an enlarged version to reproduce and share with students.

Questions for Close Reading

The Core Ready lessons include many rich opportunities to engage students in close reading of text that require them to ask and answer questions, draw conclusions, and use specific text evidence to support their thinking (Reading Anchor Standard 1). These opportunities are marked with a close reading icon. You may wish to extend these experiences using our recommended Core Texts or with texts of your choosing. Use the following questions as a resource to guide students through close reading experiences in traditional literature, particularly fairy tales.

- What characters have you encountered in the story?
- Where and when does the story take place?
- What is happening in the story so far?
- What do you think will happen next? Why?
- What is the problem that needs to be solved?
- Does the problem get solved? How?
- What characteristics of a fairy tale are present in this story? Where?
- How does this version of the fairy tale compare to _____ (another version of the same tale)? Which parts are most similar?

- How has _____ (a particular character) changed over the course of this story? How do you know?
- What is the message or lesson readers can take from this tale? How does the author teach you this lesson?

Building Academic Language

On the next page is a list of academic language to build your students' comprehension of the focus of this lesson set and facilitate their ability to talk and write about what they learn. There are words and phrases listed there. Rather than introduce all the words at once, slowly add them to a learning wall as your teaching unfolds. See the glossary at the end of this chapter for definitions of the words. Also listed are sentence frames that may be included on a sentence wall (Carrier & Tatum, 2006), a research-proven strategy for English language learners (Lewis, 1993; Nattinger, 1980), or as a handout to scaffold student use of the content words. Some students, especially English language learners, may need explicit practice in using the sentence frames. Encourage all students to use these words and phrases regularly in their conversations and writing.

Recognition

At the end of the lesson set, it is important to recognize the hard work your students have put into their learning and the way they've thought about themselves and others. The end of the writing lesson set offers the perfect opportunity for students to share their original adaptations of classic fairy tales. There are also many other fun ways to make the end of the lesson set memorable, including:

- Students act out their favorite scenes from a fairy tale.
- Students perform their own fairy tales with classmates.
- Class creates an anthology of student work to reproduce and share with families.
- Add student writing to the classroom or school library alongside the classic versions that served as inspiration.

Core Words

characters	good	
dialogue	illustration	
emotion	internal thinking	
event	message/lesson	
evil	plot	setting
fairy tale	problem	solution

Core Phrases

- I see _____ in the illustrations. This shows me that _____.

- The main characters in this fairy tale are _____.

- The good characters are _____. I know this because _____ (text as evidence).

- The evil characters are _____. I know this because _____ (text as evidence).

- This fairy tale takes place in _____ (setting).

- The problem in this fairy tale is _____.

- The solution is _____.

- _____ (character's name) was _____, and now he or she is _____. I think this is because _____.

- The lesson of this fairy tale is _____.

Assessment

Assessment in this lesson set is both ongoing and culminating, meaning that as teachers we are constantly kid-watching and observing how students make meaning and how they are interpret new material. Throughout this lesson set, look for performance-based assessments, called Milestone Performance Assessments, each marked with an assessment icon. Milestone Performance Assessments are opportunities to notice and record data on standards-aligned indicators during the course of the lesson set. Use the results of these assessments to determine how well students are progressing toward the goals of the lesson set. Adjust the pace of your teaching and plan instructional support as needed.

Also, we encourage you to use the Reading and Writing Rubrics, also marked with an assessment icon, with each lesson set to evaluate overall student performance on the standards-aligned lesson set goals. In this lesson set, the original adaptation of a classic fairy tale students write will be an essential piece of summative assessment evidence that can be analyzed and placed in a portfolio of student work.

In addition, we have provided a Speaking and Listening Checklist (see PDToolKit) that provides observable Common Core State Standards–aligned indicators to assess student performance as speakers and listeners. There are multiple opportunities in every Core Ready lesson set to make such observations. Use the checklist in its entirety to gather performance data over time or choose appropriate indicators to create a customized checklist to match a specific learning experience.

Core Support for Diverse Learners

This lesson set was created with the needs of a wide variety of learners in mind. Throughout the day-by-day lessons, you'll find examples of visual supports, graphic organizers, highlighted speaking and listening opportunities, and research-driven English language learner supports aimed at scaffolding instruction for all learners. However, we urge you to consider the following more specific challenges with which your students may need guided support. The following sections are written to spotlight important considerations as you move through the lesson sets.

Reading

Choosing texts that are at students' reading levels is essential for their reading success and reading identity. When searching for texts make sure you have various levels represented in your classroom library. Some of your students may benefit from repeated exposure to a lesson's teaching point over several days. This can be accomplished with the whole class or in small-group settings.

Closely monitor your students who are reading below grade level to determine if they are reading with accuracy and fluency to support comprehension. Encourage students to use context to confirm or self-correct word recognition and understanding and to reread when necessary. Refer to the Common Core Foundational Skills Standards at the grade 2 level as well as at the kindergarten and grade 1 levels for direct, explicit foundational skills support that your students reading below grade level may need.

Second graders reading below grade level may have a difficult time with certain versions of fairy tales as well as some of the more sophisticated or antiquated language contained within many classic tales. Look for a variety of versions of the same tale at lower reading levels. "The Three Little Pigs" is a classic example of a fairy tale that has been told and retold in many variations at a range of different independent reading levels. Be cognizant of unfamiliar language embedded within the text choices for both whole-class teaching and independent reading, and preview the texts you provide to students reading below grade level.

As you continue your work with students, use observational notes and reading assessment data to create two to three specific short-term goals for your students with diverse needs. For example, as stated above, these goals may be related to increasing word accuracy, building vocabulary, improving fluency, or enhancing comprehension. Throughout this lesson set, tailor your individualized and small-group instruction set so that it addresses and evaluates student progress toward these goals.

Writing

Inspired writers are motivated writers. Allowing students to choose the topic of their writing is critical for their ultimate success and their positive development of identity as a writer. When immersing your students in a new genre, form, or purpose for writing, be sure to emphasize the meaning and function this particular type of writing may have in their lives. Many of your students will also benefit from exposure to strong mentor texts, examples of your own writing, as well as the experience of sharing their own work—both the final product and versions in process.

Many students may benefit from extended illustration work prior to writing. Illustration can be a pathway to deeper thinking about characters, their actions, and their feelings. In addition, consider the accessibility your students have to word walls of fairy tale language as well as examples of strong writing details created and curated by members of the class. Some students will require extra support in writing to move from drawing to writing or to move from story mapping to sentences. You can also provide additional scaffolding by having students draw out their fairy tale prior to writing it. This is especially helpful for visual learners and students who need to "sketch to stretch." Even your most proficient writers can benefit from this step, but many of your resistant writers will feel more comfortable with getting their ideas on paper through drawing first.

As your students move from determining their ideas for their stories and begin telling a sequential tale, provide them with a variety of paper choices that are second-grade appropriate. For students with fine motor control issues, providing a variety of paper choices that have handwriting lines with a dotted line in the middle can offer support, as letter formation may require significant energy for some writers. Also consider having some students type and electronically publish their stories rather than handwrite them if that is a medium more conducive to their writing success.

We want our second graders to communicate their stories to an audience, and supporting them as developing writers is essential. In addition to providing students with topic choice and the opportunity to draw prior to writing, we can provide further scaffolding by having students orally rehearse their stories to us or to a peer. For some students, the oral rehearsal will provide a springboard to writing. Others will have greater success dictating their story to you.

As with the reading lessons, your students may benefit from several days on a single lesson's teaching point. This can be done with the whole class or in small-group settings.

English Language Learners

While it is always our goal as teachers to get to know all of our students deeply both in and out of the classroom setting, this work is perhaps more critical when considering our English language learners. Honoring families' cultural traditions and experiences is important in getting to know your students, understanding them, and working with them in meaningful ways.

We also encourage you to use your ELLs' home languages as a resource. Researchers on second language acquisition are nearly unanimous on this point: using the home language enhances learning—both content development *and* English language and literacy acquisition. Even if you don't speak your students' home languages, look for every opportunity to have them leverage what they already know as you teach new information. Multilingual practices, like asking students how to say something in their home language or encouraging students to discuss texts bilingually, also send welcoming messages that school is a place for people of all linguistic backgrounds.

English language learners are learning about characters alongside native English speakers in your classroom, but they are also simultaneously learning English. For our English language learners, therefore, it is essential to simultaneously develop their ability to easily hold conversations about their reading and writing and build their academic language base. Goldenberg (2008) defines "academic English" as the more abstract, complex, and challenging language that permits us to participate successfully in mainstream classroom instruction. English language learners will over time be responsible for understanding and producing academic English both orally and in writing. However, language acquisition is a process, and our English language learners range in their development of English language acquisition. We urge you to consider your students along a spectrum of language acquisition: from students new to this country, to those who are proficient conversationally, to those who have native-like proficiency.

Refer to the English language learner icons ELL throughout this lesson set for ways to shelter instruction for English language learners. These elements will help English language learners participate successfully in the whole-group lesson and will support the development of their language skills. Although these moments during instruction are designed to support English language learners, many schools are adding a separate English language development (ELD) block targeted at oral English language development, to further support their students in language acquisition.

Students with growing English proficiency will benefit from a fairy tales word wall to build vocabulary (see Core Words and Phrases). A sentence word wall to give them sentence starters to help with conversation will also offer students another layer of support. Some students may benefit from having their own personalized copies of these words to keep in their reading or writing notebooks for quick reference. Visual aids will further support students and give them a reference to what words are important to this study and what they mean. Consider forming small, flexible groups of students with similar needs in fairy tale clubs—particularly native English speakers with English language learners. Each group can focus on a particular fairy tale and its related versions throughout the lesson set, and you can use the group as a platform for reinforcing individual lessons on reading and writing fairy tales.

Some students will benefit from several days on the same teaching point. You may consider gathering small groups of readers or writers for repeated instruction or using one-on-one conferences as an opportunity to revisit teaching points.

Complementary Core Methods

Read-Aloud

Take this opportunity to share a wide variety of fairy tales during your read-alouds. Consider multiple reads of the same text. In your first read, you are providing a foundation for the story as a whole, and your students may benefit from a read-aloud without repeated interruption. In your second read-aloud of the text, pausing to think aloud or asking for students' thoughts allows for deeper understanding of the text. Use your knowledge of students' interests to select texts that will inspire and excite your class. When appropriate, use your read-aloud as another chance for students to practice one or two of the following skills:

- Determining the characteristics included in fairy tales
- Identifying the elements of a fairy tale

- Asking and answering questions about a text, using portions of the text as evidence in the responses
- Identifying and exploring the meaning of new vocabulary
- Looking for similarities and differences between different versions of the same tale
- Stating opinions about a particular version of a fairy tale

Shared Reading

Shared reading provides a wonderful opportunity to look closely at excerpts from read-alouds for close reading. Use shared reading to reinforce the idea of reading to learn (versus learning to read). Below are some prompts you may want to use in your conversations about these texts:

- What portions of this fairy tale are magical? How do we know?
- Who are the main characters? Who are the supporting characters?
- Which characters are good? Which characters are evil? How do you know?
- What is the setting, or where does the fairy tale take place?
- What are the major events that happen?
- What new vocabulary or fairy tale language did we take away from this text? How can we use this new vocabulary?
- What lesson or message can we take away from this fairy tale?
- Let's look for examples of strong character dialogue . . .
- Let's look for evidence of characters' emotions . . .
- Let's look for examples of internal thinking . . .
- Let's look for examples of descriptive character action . . .

Shared reading can also be a great time to specifically highlight the linking words found within a shared text and discuss how they connect ideas.

Shared Writing

Shared writing also provides an opportunity to link your work in other subject areas. Use this time to do the following:

- Compose class questions to write to authors of their favorite fairy tales.
- Rewrite the ending to a fairy tale—What happens after "happily ever after"?
- Write a class adaptation of an original fairy tale.
- Revise shared writing to link ideas together, creating more-complex sentences, words, and phrases with such additions as *also, another, and, more, but.*
- Revise shared writing to add interesting details such as character dialogue, descriptive character action, internal thinking, and character emotion.

Core Connections at Home

Ask students to interview family members about their favorite fairy tales. What are their memories of reading these tales? What makes these fairy tales so special? Invite families to come in and share their favorite fairy tales. This could be done on a rotating basis or in a big culminating event.

Another possibility is to provide families with a Fairy Tales Graphic Organizer, used in Writing Lesson 4 and found in Appendix 2.7, and simple directions, in order for them to write an original adaptation of a family favorite.

Have students share their final writing projects with their families during a special recognition ceremony. Ask families to write a letter to their child sharing what they learned from their presentations. Display these letters alongside students' final stories.

Reading Lessons

The Core I.D.E.A. / Daily Reading Instruction at a Glance table highlights the teaching objectives and standards alignment for all 10 lessons across the four stages of the lesson set (Introduce, Define, Extend, and Assess). It also indicates which lessons contain special features to support English language learners, technology, speaking and listening, close reading opportunities, and formative ("Milestone") assessments.

The following CORE READY READING RUBRIC is designed to help you record each student's overall understanding across four levels of achievement as it relates to the lesson set goals. We recommend that you use this rubric at the end of the lesson set as a performance-based assessment tool. Use the Milestone Performance Assessments as tools to help you gauge student progress toward these goals. Reteach and differentiate instruction as needed. See the foundational book, *Be Core Ready: Powerful, Effective Steps to Implementing and Achieving the Common Core State Standards,* for more information about the Core Ready Reading and Writing Rubrics.

Grade 2   Once Upon a Time: A New Look at Fairy Tales

Instructional Stage	Lesson	Teaching Objective	Core Standards	Special Features
Introduce: *notice, explore, collect, note, immerse, surround, record, share*	1	Readers explore fairy tales.	RL.2.1 • RL.2.2 • RL.2.3 • RL.2.10 • SL.2.1a • SL.2.1b • SL.2.1c • SL.2.2 • SL.2.4 •SL.2.6 • L.2.1 • L.2.3 • L.2.6	ELL S&L Close Reading Opportunity
Define: *name, identify, outline, clarify, select, plan*	2	Readers notice specific features of fairy tales.	RL.2.1 • RL.2.2 • RL.2.3 • RL.2.10 • SL.2.1a • SL.2.1b • SL.2.1c • SL.2.6 • L.2.1 • L.2.3 • L.2.6	ELL Close Reading Opportunity
	3	Readers identify key story elements in fairy tales.	RL.2.1 • RL.2.2 • RL.2.5 • RL.2.10 • W.2.8 • SL.2.1a • SL.2.1b • SL.2.1c •SL.2.2 • SL.2.4 • SL.2.6 • L.2.1 •L.2.3 • L.2.6	ELL Milestone Performance Assessment Close Reading Opportunity
	4	Readers find and figure out unfamiliar language in fairy tales.	RL.2.1 • RL.2.10 • SL.2.1a • SL.2.1b • SL.2.1c • SL.2.2 • SL.2.4 • SL.2.6 • L.2.1 • L.2.3 • L.2.4 • L.2.6	ELL S&L Tech Close Reading Opportunity
Extend: *try, experiment, attempt, approximate, practice, explain, revise, refine*	5	Readers study illustrations to aid in their comprehension.	RL.2.1 • RL.2.2 • RL.2.3 • RL.2.7 • RL.2.10 • SL.2.1a • SL.2.1b • SL.2.1c • SL.2.6 • L.2.1 • L.2.3 • L.2.6	ELL Close Reading Opportunity
	6	Readers notice how characters change across a story.	RL.2.1 • RL.2.3 • RL.2.10 • W.2.8 • SL.2.1a • SL.2.1b • SL.2.1c • SL.2.2 • SL.2.6 • L.2.1 • L.2.3 • L.2.6	ELL Milestone Performance Assessment Close Reading Opportunity
	7	Readers determine the lesson of a fairy tale.	RL.2.1 • RL.2.2 • RL.2.3 • RL.2.10 • W.2.8 • SL.2.1a • SL.2.1b SL.2.1c • SL.2.2 • SL.2.4 •SL.2.6 • L.2.1 • L.2.3 • L.2.6	ELL S&L Tech Close Reading Opportunity
	8	Readers compare and contrast different versions of the same tale.	RL.2.1 • RL.2.2 • RL.2.3 • RL.2.9 • RL.2.10 • W.2.8 • SL.2.1a • SL.2.1b • SL.2.1c • SL.2.2 • SL.2.4 • SL.2.6 • L.2.1 • L.2.3 • L.2.6	ELL S&L Milestone Assessment Close Reading Opportunity
Assess: *reflect, conclude, connect, share, recognize, respond*	9	Readers engage in the oral tradition of fairy tales by performing favorite tales aloud.	RL.2.1 • RL.2.2 • RL.2.10 • SL.2.1a • SL.2.1b • SL.2.1c • SL.2.2 • SL.2.4 • SL.2.5 • SL.2.6 • L.2.1 • L.2.3 • L.2.6	ELL Close Reading Opportunity
	10	Readers respond to the Core Questions.	RL.2.1 • RL.2.2 • RL.2.3 • RL.2.5 • RL.2.9 • RL.2.10 • W.2.8 • SL.2.1a • SL.2.1b • SL.2.1c • SL.2.6 • L.2.1 • L.2.2 • L.2.3 • L.2.6	ELL S&L Milestone Assessment Close Reading Opportunity

 **Core Ready Reading Rubric**

Lesson Set Goal	Emerging	Approaching	Achieving	Exceeding	Standards Alignment
Build and demonstrate understanding of traditional literature (fairy tales) through close reading of text, citing textual evidence to support thinking and ideas.	Student is unable to use clues (the story elements, language common to fairy tales, and illustrations) to gain and demonstrate understanding of traditional literature (fairy tales). Consistently draws inaccurate or irrelevant conclusions. Little or no textual evidence to support thinking.	Student attempts to develop and demonstrate an understanding of fairy tales using clues (the story elements, language common to fairy tales, and illustrations). Some inaccuracies and irrelevant explanations may be present. Sometimes provides insufficient textual evidence to support thinking.	Student develops and demonstrates understanding of fairy tales by using clues (the story elements, language common to fairy tales, and illustrations). Usually draws accurate and relevant conclusions. Provides sufficient textual evidence to support thinking.	Student effectively uses clues (the story elements, language common to fairy tales, and illustrations) to develop and demonstrate insightful understanding of fairy tales. Provides detailed and thoughtful textual evidence to support thinking.	RL.2.1 RL.2.2 RL.2.3 RL.2.10 W.2.8 SL.2.1a SL.2.1b SL.2.1c SL.2.2 SL.2.4 SL.2.6 L.2.1 L.2.3 L.2.6
Identify and define the features and elements of fairy tales (magic, good vs. evil, problem, solution, key events, lesson).	Student is unable to accurately identify and/or define the features and elements of fairy tales (magic, good vs. evil, problem, solution, key events, lesson). Little or no textual evidence to support thinking.	Student is able to identify and define some features and elements of fairy tales (magic, good vs. evil, problem, solution, key events, lesson) with some scaffolding. May have inaccuracies or lack evidence.	Student successfully identifies and defines the features and elements of fairy tales with accuracy (magic, good vs. evil, problem, solution, key events, lesson). Provides sufficient textual evidence.	Student successfully identifies and defines with accuracy and depth the features and elements of fairy tales (magic, good vs. evil, problem, solution, key events, lesson). Consistently provides detailed and relevant textual evidence.	RL.2.1 RL.2.2 RL.2.5 RL.2.10 SL.2.1a SL.2.1b SL.2.1c SL.2.2 SL.2.4 SL.2.6 L.2.1 L.2.3 L.2.6
Infer the message or lesson in a fairy tale and use text evidence to defend their interpretations.	Student shows little or no evidence of inferring the message or lesson in a fairy tale. Little or no textual evidence to support thinking.	Student attempts to infer life lessons suggested by the study of character but may require significant scaffolding to name a lesson or struggle to connect lesson to relevant evidence to support thinking.	Student successfully infers logical life lessons suggested by the study of characters and provides sufficient relevant evidence to support thinking.	Student successfully infers logical life lessons suggested by the study of characters and provides specific and thoughtful supporting details to support thinking.	RL.2.1 RL.2.2 RL.2.10 SL.2.1a SL.2.1b SL.2.1c SL.2.2 SL.2.4 SL.2.6 L.2.1 L.2.3 L.2.6

Lesson Set Goal	Emerging	Approaching	Achieving	Exceeding	Standards Alignment
Use strategies to determine or clarify the meaning of new words and phrases. in fairy tales.	Student struggles to apply any strategies to determine or clarify the meaning of new words and phrases in fairy tales.	Student uses some strategies to determine or clarify the meaning of new words and phrases in fairy tales. May have some inaccuracies.	Student uses several strategies to determine or clarify the meaning of new words and phrases in fairy tales. Is consistently accurate.	Student uses multiple strategies to determine or clarify the meaning of new words and phrases in fairy tales. May use subtle clues to determine or clarify meaning of sophisticated words and phrases.	L.2.4
Use information gained from illustrations to better understand the fairy tale.	Student struggles to describe what is conveyed in an illustration and is unable to explain the connection to the text of the fairy tale.	Student attempts with some success to describe information gained about the fairy tale by looking closely at the illustrations. With some scaffolding, may explain some connections between the illustration and the text. May have some inaccuracies or lack evidence.	Student clearly describes information gained about the fairy tale by looking closely at illustrations. Makes connections between information in illustrations and the accompanying text. Provides accurate examples and relevant details from illustrations.	Student describes several insightful examples of information gained about the fairy tale by looking closely at illustrations. Provides thorough, accurate, and relevant evidence. May attend to subtle clues or elements present in illustrations and make insightful connections between the text and the illustrations.	RL.2.1 RL.2.7 RL.2.10
Identify and explain how and why a character changes throughout a fairy tale.	Student is unable to identify and explain how and why a character changes throughout a fairy tale.	Student identifies and explains with some success how and why a character changes throughout a fairy tale. May have some inaccuracies or lack evidence.	Student accurately identifies how and why a character changes throughout a fairy tale. Provides sufficient textual evidence.	Student consistently identifies how and why a character changes throughout a fairy tale and provides accurate and thorough textual evidence. May notice subtle or sophisticated changes or text clues.	RL.2.1 RL.2.3 RL.2.10 SL.2.1a SL.2.1b SL.2.1c SL.2.2 SL.2.4 SL.2.6 L.2.1 L.2.3 L.2.6
Compare and contrast two versions of the same fairy tale to recognize similarities and differences.	Student struggles to identify the elements of either fairy tale. Does not demonstrate capacity to compare and contrast two versions of the same tale even with significant support.	Student identifies with some success the elements of two versions of the same fairy tale. Needs support to compare and contrasts two versions of the same tale. May have some inaccuracies or lack evidence.	Student accurately identifies the elements of two versions of the same fairy tale. Compares and contrasts two versions of the same tale with sufficient accurate examples.	Student accurately identifies the elements of two versions of the same fairy tale. Compares and contrasts two versions of the same tale in detail. Provides subtle or detailed textual examples.	RL.2.2 RL.2.9 RL.2.10 W.2.8 SL.2.1a SL.2.1b SL.2.1c SL.2.6 L.2.1 L.2.3 L.2.6
Ask and answer such questions as who, what, where, when, why, and how to demonstrate understanding of key details in a text.	Student demonstrates little or no evidence of understanding key details in the text through asking and/or answering questions about the text.	Student demonstrates some evidence of understanding key details in the text through asking and answering questions about the text.	Student shows solid evidence of understanding key details in the text through asking and answering questions about the text.	Student consistently shows solid evidence of understanding key details in the text through asking and answering high-level questions about the text and providing solid textual evidence to support thinking.	RL.2.1

Core Ready Reading Rubric, Grade 2, *continued*

Lesson Set Goal	Emerging	Approaching	Achieving	Exceeding	Standards Alignment
By the end of year, read and comprehend a variety of literature texts in the grades 2–3 text complexity band proficiently, with scaffolding as needed at the high end of the range.	Student shows little or no evidence of reading and comprehending texts appropriate for the grade 2–3 text complexity band.	Student shows inconsistent evidence of reading and comprehending texts appropriate for the grade 2–3 text complexity band.	Student shows solid evidence of reading and comprehending independently and proficiently texts appropriate for the grade 2–3 text complexity band. May need scaffolding at the grade 3 level.	Student shows solid evidence of reading and comprehending independently and proficiently complex texts above the grade 2–3 text complexity band.	RL.2.10
In collaborative discussions, exhibit responsibility for the rules and roles and purpose of conversation.	Student makes little or no attempt to participate in collaborative discussions and build on others' talk by linking their comments to others. Often disregards the rules and roles of conversation even with prompting.	Student inconsistently participates in collaborative discussions and builds on others' talk by linking their comments to others. Student observes the rules and roles of conversation but needs frequent prompting.	Student usually participates in collaborative discussions and builds on others' talk by linking their comments to others. Student observes the rules and roles of conversation. May need some prompting.	Student consistently participates in collaborative discussions and builds on others' talk by linking their comments to others. Student observes the rules and roles of conversation with little or no prompting.	SL.2.1a SL.2.1b
In collaborative discussions, ask questions in a manner that enhances understanding of topic.	Student makes little or no attempt to ask questions that enhance understanding of the topic.	Student occasionally asks questions to clarify or build understanding of the topic or text under discussion but usually requires support or prompting.	Student asks questions that effectively clarify or build understanding of the topic or text under discussion. May need occasional support or prompting.	Student often asks effective and focused questions to clarify or build understanding of the topic or text under discussion. Proactively uses this strategy to support own learning.	SL.2.1c
Speak in complete sentences when appropriate.	Student shows little or no evidence of speaking in complete sentences when appropriate.	Student shows some evidence of attempting to speak in complete sentences when appropriate.	Student shows solid evidence of speaking in complete sentences when appropriate.	Student shows exceptional evidence of speaking in complete sentences when appropriate.	SL.2.6
Demonstrate knowledge of standard English and its conventions.	Student demonstrates little or no knowledge of standard English and its conventions.	Student demonstrates some evidence of knowledge of standard English and its conventions.	Student consistently demonstrates knowledge of standard English and its conventions.	Student demonstrates an exceptional understanding of standard English and its conventions. Use of conventions is sophisticated for grade level and accurate.	L.2.1 L.2.2 L.2.3
Use words and phrases acquired through conversations, reading and being read to, and responding to texts.	Student shows little or no evidence of the acquisition and/or use of grade-appropriate words and phrases.	Student shows some evidence of acquiring and using grade-appropriate words and phrases.	Student shows solid evidence of acquiring and using grade-appropriate words and phrases.	Student shows a high level of sophistication and precision when using grade-appropriate words and phrases.	L.2.6

Reading Lesson 1

▼ Teaching Objective

Readers explore fairy tales.

Close Reading
Opportunity

▼ Standards Alignment

RL.2.1, RL.2.2, RL.2.3, RL.2.10, SL.2.1a, SL.2.1b, SL.2.1c, SL.2.2, SL.2.4, SL.2.6, L.2.1, L.2.3, L.2.6

▼ Materials

- Charting supplies or interactive whiteboard
- A collection of related fairy tales, such as a variety of Cinderella stories
  - *Cinderella* by Barbara Karlin
  - *Cinderella, or, The Little Glass Slipper* by Marcia Brown
  - *The Egyptian Cinderella* by Shirley Climo
  - *The Korean Cinderella* by Shirley Climo
  - *Prince Cinders* by Babette Cole
  - *Yeh Shen* by Ai-Ling Louie

▼ To the Teacher

The purpose of this first reading lesson is to immerse students in the genre. We want to build students' familiarity with the classic versions of these tales. We also want to provide students with an opportunity to interact with versions of fairy tales from other cultures as well as those that have been reimagined in interesting ways. Finally, we want to allow our students time to explore and enjoy the magic and wonder of these imaginative tales. For these reasons, you may want to extend this lesson and its related exploration of stories across more than one day.

In advance of this lesson set, you will want to put together collections of fairy tales that are related to one another. For example, a group of Cinderella tales, a group of Three Little Pigs tales, and a group of versions of Little Red

Riding Hood. Please see the Choosing Core Texts section of the lesson set for examples and suggestions of texts and groupings. **ELL** Frontload the Lesson—Make Connections. Try to find out if your ELLs know any stories from their home cultures that are similar to the ones you will be studying as a class. Make this connection explicit for them, so that they can already begin the process of comparing different versions of stories that is the focus of this lesson set.

▼ Procedure

Warm Up Gather the class to set the stage for today's learning

Get your students excited about your new reading adventure.

> Today we are going to begin to study a special kind of story—fairy tales. Fairy tales can take us on magical adventures and really get our imaginations going. We're going to read classic versions of tales you may have heard before as well as exciting new versions of those same tales that will really surprise you.

Ask students to share the name of a fairy tale with which they are familiar. Keep a quick list of these titles on a chart titled "Fairy Tales We Know . . . for Now." **ELL** Frontload the Lesson—Activate Prior Knowledge. This is an excellent way to gauge your ELLs' understanding of the concept of a fairy tales and begin to shape that understanding with examples. This forms the base from which vocabulary knowledge can develop. Your ELLs might know many fairy tales already but not be familiar with that term; they might know fairy tales from other cultures and not recognize the examples their peers are giving! Work hard to draw out their knowledge without defining "fairy tale" too much, as this is the focus of the next lesson.

Teach Model what students need to learn and do

Explain to the class that many familiar, classic versions of fairy tales have been updated and rewritten in imaginative ways. You will begin this new reading adventure by exploring sets of both classic and reimagined tales. Take a moment to ensure that your students understand the terms *classic* and *reimagined*. **ELL** Identify and Communicate Content and Language

Objectives—Key Content Vocabulary. This is an excellent opportunity for you to model the use of key content vocabulary for your students.

We are going to look at a lot of different fairy tales together in this lesson set. There are a lot of fairy tales out there to read—and often you will find many versions of the same fairy tale. Take a look at all these versions of *Cinderella*. (Show the class a variety of Cinderella stories, such as those suggested previosly in the Materials section of this lesson set.) Some of the fairy tales can be considered classic. A classic is an original version of the story as it is told here in the United States. Other cultures and other people who live in different countries may have a different version of the same story. Regardless of where it comes from, the classic version means an old or original version—the way the story has been told for many years. This version of *Cinderella* is a classic version of the story as we tell it here. However, there are also reimagined versions of *Cinderella*. These versions take the *Cinderella* story and make several big changes to create a new way to tell the tale. **ELL** Frontload the Lesson—Build Background. Remember that a story that is classic to you might be brand-new to your ELLs. You may want to meet with your ELLs before the whole-group lesson to familiarize them with the "classic" versions of the stories the class will study. *Prince Cinders* will make little sense for children who don't know *Cinderella*!

Model browsing through a collection of Cinderella stories, both old and new. Look through the covers and read the titles, thinking aloud about which book represents the classic version, which represents the same tale as it is told in another country, and which represents a newer version of the classic tale. Select a new version of the tale to share with the class. For the purposes of this lesson, we have chosen *Prince Cinders* by Babette Cole, a twist on the Cinderella story (you can use any nonclassic version of a well-known fairy tale). **ELL** Provide Comprehensible Input—Models. By watching you physically go through the process of examining versions of stories, ELLs get another point of access to the lesson focus, beyond the basic explanation of the task.

> Here's an interesting looking book: *Prince Cinders*. Based on the title, I think this is a reimagined version of Cinderella, but instead of a girl, the main character is a boy.

Now read aloud a portion of *Prince Cinders* to the class, stopping at an interesting point that will encourage students to want to hear the rest later. You will resume reading at the end of this lesson, during the Wrap Up.

Try Guide students to quickly rehearse what they need to learn and do in preparation for practice

Once you have read a portion of the fairy tale, allow your students to discuss their thoughts about what they noticed about the tale. Encourage a collaborative conversation with prompts, for example:

- What has happened in this tale so far? Retell to a partner what we have read so far.
- Do you think this is a classic version of a tale, a version from another country, or a reimagined version? How do you know? What line or images from the text support your thinking?
- What do you think might happen next? Why?
- Did you like this version? Why or why not?

Holding a whole-class conversation provides a wonderful opportunity to reinforce and encourage several key speaking and listening behaviors such as listening to others with care, appropriately signaling a desire to speak, staying on topic, and building on the talk of others. (SL.2.1a, SL.2.1b)

ELL Enable Language Production—Increasing Interaction. Speaking with peers is an excellent way for ELLs to hear more models of English and to practice their own use of English. When you are forming groups, consider members who may speak an ELL's home language so that, if needed, the group discussion could be in English and the home language.

Clarify Briefly restate today's teaching objective and explain the practice task(s)

Explain to the class that today's reading work is about exploring fairy tales—both classic and reimagined.

> We are going to explore all sorts of fairy tales together. We'll take another look at some classic versions and discover some new or reimagined fairy tales. Today, as you read, pay attention to the one fairy tale that captured your attention the most and think about why. At the end of our reading time today, I'd like each of you to share with a partner one fairy tale as well as your favorite part of that story.

Restate your method for exploring fairy tales. First, you browsed through a collection of books, thinking aloud about the titles while trying to recognize classic versions, versions from other countries, and reimagined versions of classic tales. Then you chose a fairy tale that seemed interesting. Finally, you read the tale and prepared to share your thinking with a partner.

Practice Students work independently and/or in small groups to apply today's teaching objective

Students independently explore collections of classic and reimagined fairy tales, grouped in sets. Once students have had ample independent reading time to explore these tales, direct them to share with a partner their favorite tale of the day. Chart and review the following questions with students, instructing partners to use them to guide their conversations:

- What happened in this tale? Retell the tale to a partner.

- Do you think this is a classic version of a tale, a version from another country, or a reimagined version? How do you know? What lines or images from the text support your thinking?

- Did you like this version? Why or why not?

Circulate and listen in to several partnerships to support their talk about fairy tales. For yourself, note if your class generally prefers the classic versions or the newer fairy tales. **ELL** Identify and Communicate Content and Language Objectives—Check for Understanding. Use this time to listen in on your ELLs' conversations to see how they may need support for their responses. Notice where they are struggling: Are they confused about how to distinguish the different categories of stories? Is this because the language of the lesson was over their heads or because their background knowledge does not include familiarity with these stories? Or do they understand the distinctions,

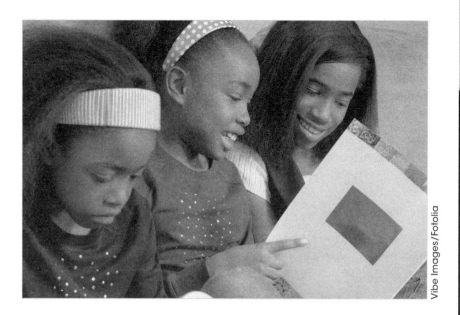

Vibe Images/Fotolia

but lack the English to express their thoughts and reasoning? Each situation will require a different instructional response.

Wrap Up Check understanding as you guide students to briefly share what they have learned and produced today

Gather your class, asking students to bring the fairy tale that sparked their interest in the most exciting ways. Ask students to share their selected fairy tale with the class, as well as their answers to the questions charted for partner work.

Then finish reading aloud *Prince Cinders* (or the book you have selected) to the class.

Reading Lesson 2

▼ Teaching Objective

Readers notice specific features of fairy tales.

Close Reading
Opportunity

▼ Standards Alignment

RL.2.1, RL.2.2, RL.2.3, RL.2.10, SL.2.1a, SL.2.1b, SL.2.1c, SL.2.6, L.2.1, L.2.3, L.2.6

▼ Materials

- Charting supplies or interactive whiteboard

▼ Procedure

`Warm Up` Gather the class to set the stage for today's learning

Explain to the class that there are certain features many fairy tales have in common. Not only do these features help define a story as a fairy tale, but they are also fun to search for as you read.

> There are certain features that most fairy tales have in common—features that help identify a particular story as being a fairy tale. One feature that many fairy tales have in common is the presence of magic. Usually there is something magical happening in the story, as we noticed in our story from yesterday, *Prince Cinders*.

Ask students to take a moment to remember the fairy tales they have read so far during this unit of study or other fairy tales with which they may be familiar.

> Can you think of a magical feature in any of the fairy tales you know of or have read?

Have students share their examples of a magical feature from a familiar fairy tale. Be sure to ask them to name the fairy tale as well as the magic feature. **ELL** Enable Language Production—Listening and Speaking. This is a great chance for your ELLs to show off their prior knowledge, and teach their peers something new, by naming stories with magic elements that they know from their home cultures.

`Teach` Model what students need to learn and do

Begin a chart titled "Features of Fairy Tales." Add *magic* to the chart. Now, introduce the other common features of fairy tales, adding each idea to the chart as you teach. As you introduce each element, be sure to give examples of its presence in familiar fairy tales. Add these examples to your chart as well. **ELL** Provide Comprehensible Input—Graphic Organizers. Charts can help ELLs access the content you are teaching by turning the oral discussion, which may be moving fast, into stable, written bullet points that highlight key take-away information. The chart will give ELLs something concrete to refer back to during independent work.

Here is a list of several features—in addition to the presence of magic—common to most fairy tales:

- happy endings
- the battle of good versus evil
- the use of groups of three or seven

Here is one way your modeling might unfold as you explain and give examples (for the use of groups) of happy endings in fairy tales:

> Many fairy tales have a happy ending. A happy ending means that good characters usually get rewarded and evil characters are punished in some way. For example, in *Prince Cinders*, the main character, ends up finding someone who makes him very happy, while his stepbrothers are left alone and unhappy.

Here is what your chart might look like at this point in your lesson. Notice that the examples of good versus evil are intentionally left blank for students to discuss during the Try portion of this lesson.

Features of Fairy Tales

Presence of magic	Cinderella: fairy godmother
Happy endings	Cinderella: marries the prince
Groups of three or seven	Snow White and the Seven Dwarfs: seven dwarfs as important characters Three Little Pigs: three pigs as main characters
Good versus evil	

`Try` Guide students to quickly rehearse what they need to learn and do in preparation for practice

Instruct students to turn and talk with a partner about an example of good versus evil from a familiar fairy tale. As students work together to come up with an example, circulate and listen in to support their conversations. Encourage students to be specific in their examples, citing a particular text as evidence. **ELL** Enable Language Production—Increasing Interaction. Consider pairing your ELLs with peers who share their home culture, so that they can refer to stories from that culture that might be unfamiliar to the rest of the class but are more likely to be recognized by their partner. At the same time, know that two students from the same cultural background do not necessarily have knowledge of the same stories. No matter what stories your ELLs share, make sure they identify the title and give a clear example of good versus evil (and support them with the meaning of this phrase, if needed).

Gather the class and have several partnerships share their examples. Add these examples to the chart. If students struggle to identify a relevant example, lead the class in a discussion of *Prince Cinders* (or the fairy tale your read aloud during Reading Lesson 1) to determine a solid example to add to the chart.

Clarify Briefly restate today's teaching objective and explain the practice task(s)

Tell the class that today they will look for and mark examples of the common features of fairy tales as they read. Be clear that each student must have at least one example marked and ready to share with a partner.

FEATURES OF FAIRY TALES

Magic		• Cinderella - fairy godmother • Snow White - magic mirror
Patterns of 3s or 7s		• Snow White and the Seven Dwarfs – 7 dwarfs as important characters • Three little pigs with three houses
Happy endings		• Beauty and the Beast – The beast becomes a prince and marries Beauty • Little Red Riding Hood – Red escapes the wolf
Good versus evil		• Snow White-The evil Queen tries to kill Snow White with a poisoned apple • The Little Mermaid battles with an evil Ursula over a prince and control of the sea kingdom

Practice Students work independently and/or in small groups to apply today's teaching objective

Students read fairy tales independently, focusing on identifying examples of the various features of fairy tales discussed in today's lesson. Encourage students to refer for support to the chart created during today's lesson. **ELL** Frontload the Lesson—Set a Purpose for Reading. Independent reading time will be a great opportunity for your ELLs to familiarize themselves with classic U.S. versions of stories, if they do not know them already. By clearly stating what students are to look for as they read, you are helping your ELLs zero in on what is most important in their stories, so they don't get bogged down trying to understand *all* the unfamiliar language.

Wrap Up Check understanding as you guide students to briefly share what they have learned and produced today

Gather the class, asking students to bring with them the examples of the features of fairy tales discussed in today's lesson. Provide time for students to share their examples with one another. Encourage students to share their discoveries, relying on the text itself as evidence of their thinking.

> As you share your example with your partner, be sure to show him or her specific evidence from the fairy tale you have chosen. Turn to the page and read a line or two from the story to support your thinking.

Listen in as partners work together, supporting students as they use specific evidence from the text in their discussions. Then have several students share their thinking with the entire class, adding their ideas to the class chart as necessary. **ELL** Enable Language Production—Increasing Interaction. This is a time for ELLs to practice their thinking out loud in English and clarify any issues they may be struggling with.

Reading Lesson 3

▼ Teaching Objective

Readers identify key story elements in fairy tales.

Close Reading
Opportunity

▼ Standards Alignment

RL.2.1, RL.2.2, RL.2.5, RL.2.10, W.2.8, SL.2.1a, SL.2.1b, SL.2.1c, SL.2.2, SL.2.4, SL.2.6, L.2.1, L.2.3, L.2.6

▼ Materials

- Features of Fairy Tales Chart (created during Reading Lesson 2)
- Elements of Fairy Tales Graphic Organizer (Appendix 2.2)
- *Good Little Wolf* by Nadia Shireen

▼ Procedure

Warm Up Gather the class to set the stage for today's learning

Remind the class of the work they did during Reading Lesson 2.

> Yesterday, we learned that many fairy tales share certain features—such as the presence of magic, the battle of good versus evil, and happy endings.

Take a moment to go over the Features of Fairy Tales Chart that you created during Reading Lesson 2. **ELL** Identify and Communicate Content and Language Objectives—Repeat. By going over the familiar chart from the day before, you are helping your ELLs get ready to mentally organize the new learning they're about to do. This repetition reinforces yesterday's teaching points while priming them for today's work.

Teach Model what students need to learn and do

Explain to the class that fairy tales also have the same story elements as other works of fiction: characters, a setting, a problem, key events, and a solution. Take a moment to discuss and define each of these story elements, focusing in particular on the idea of *key events*. **ELL** Identify and Communicate Content and Language Objectives—Key Content Vocabulary.

Elements of Fairy Tales

Title:	Author:
Characters:	
Setting:	
Problem:	
Key Event 1:	
Key Event 2:	
Key Event 3:	
Solution:	

Knowing and using these terms will be an important part of mastering the content of this lesson set. By introducing them explicitly here, you are giving your ELLs a base from which they will build a rich understanding of story elements in the coming days. Identifying key events encourages students to choose those events that factor more heavily into the outcome or dramatic action of the story. For example, in *Cinderella*, a list of key events might include Cinderella going to the ball and Cinderella leaving behind her glass slipper but probably not Cinderella sweeping the ashes in the fireplace.

> Today we're going to focus on identifying various story elements in the fairy tales we read. One element that might be more challenging to identify is the key events. When you identify the key events in a story, think about the

moments that are most important. Look for big events, not small details. Think about the events that would be essential to include if you were retelling the story to a friend.

Introduce the Elements of Fairy Tales Graphic Organizer (Appendix 2.2). Tell the class that you are going to use this graphic organizer to record the elements of a new fairy tale, *Good Little Wolf* by Nadia Shireen (you can use another fairy tale of your choice, preferably one that is a modern version of a classic tale). Read *Good Little Wolf* aloud to the class. Then model using the graphic organizer to record the characters, setting, problem, and solution. **ELL** Provide Comprehensible Input—Graphic Organizers. The oral discussion you have been having can be made more transparent for your ELLs through this graphic organizer.

Here is what your graphic organizer might look like at this point in the lesson:

Elements of Fairy Tales

Title: Good Little Wolf	Author: Nadia Shireen
Characters: Rolf, Mrs. Boggins and the Big Bad Wolf	
Setting: Rolf and Mrs. Boggins' house, the forest	
Problem: Rolf meets the Big Bad Wolf who bullies him, and tells him he is not a real wolf if he doesn't do bad things.	
3 Key Events: 1. Rolf tried to blow a pig's house down and couldn't. 2. Rolf, the Big Bad Wolf and Mrs. Boggins all celebrate when Rolf tied up the Big Bad Wolf. 3. The Big Bad Wolf ate Rolf and Mrs. Boggins.	
Solution: The Big Bad Wolf says he will start being good tomorrow, from the illustration, it looks like he has just eaten Rolf and Mrs. Boggins.	

Try Guide students to quickly rehearse what they need to learn and do in preparation for practice

Now, turn to the class to identify the key events together.

Take a moment and think about the key events from this story. What are the most important things that happened to Rolf? What are the most important scenes from the story that would be essential to retelling it successfully?

Allow students several minutes to discuss these questions with a partner. **ELL** Enable Language Production—Increasing Interaction. The time to speak with peers using the questions as a prompt lets ELLs hear another language model, get more clarity on the content of the lesson, and rehearse the language and ideas they will need their independent work.

Work with student partnerships to guide their conversations toward identifying key events, rather than focusing on small details. Then gather the class to share the relevant events, adding them to your class graphic organizer as you go. Phrase the key events in the language used by your students, to increase ownership of ideas and make the chart more readable for students. Several key events your students may identify from *Good Little Wolf* include:

- Rolf tried to howl at the moon but couldn't.
- Rolf tried to blow a pig's house down and couldn't.
- Rolf and Mrs. Boggins all celebrated when Rolf tied up the Big Bad Wolf.
- The Big Bad Wolf ate both Rolf and Mrs. Boggins.

If your students struggle to identify key events successfully, as opposed to small details, consider listing both big events and small details individually on cards or creating similar cards for your interactive whiteboard. Then work with the class to sort the cards into the appropriate categories.

Clarify Briefly restate today's teaching objective and explain the practice task(s)

Today we are identifying the story elements included in fairy tales. The story elements we are focusing on include the characters, setting, the problem, two or three key events, and a solution. Use your Elements of Fairy Tales Graphic Organizer to record these elements from one fairy tale you read today.

Elements of Fairy Tales

Title:	The little Mermaid	Author:	Hans Christian Anderson

Characters:
The Little Mermaid
The Prince
The evil Witch

Setting: The Beatiuful deep sea!

Problem: She wants to marry a Prince but she's a mermaid.

3 Key Events:
1. She meets the prince and
2. She makes a deal with the evil Witch to be human.
3. She saves the prince and becomes a angel.

Solution: The mermaid gets a Soul and turns into a angle and helps people.

Student's completed Elements of Fairy Tales graphic organizer.

ELL Identify and Communicate Content Objectives—Repeat, Clarify. By restating your directions one more time, you are sending your ELLs off to independent work confident that they know what is expected of them.

Practice Students work independently and/or in small groups to apply today's teaching objective

Students read and work independently. Students choose one fairy tale for filling out the Elements of Fairy Tales Graphic Organizer.

Wrap Up Check understanding as you guide students to briefly share what they have learned and produced today

Gather the class. Ask them to use their Elements of Fairy Tales Graphic Organizer to retell to a partner the fairy tale they read today.

Collect and analyze the Elements of Fairy Tales Graphic Organizer as a performance-based assessment to determine if students need additional instruction or support as a whole class, in small groups, or one on one. **ELL** Assess for Content and Language Understanding—Formative Assessment. This is an opportunity for you to assess your ELLs' language and content needs, especially identifying the key elements of stories. Take care to notice whether they are confused about content (either because they are unfamiliar with the stories or because they simply didn't understand the language of the lesson) or whether they get the point but struggle to find the words to express their understanding. Use this information to plan upcoming lessons.

Milestone Performance Assessment

Identifying the Key Elements of a Fairy Tale

 Use this checklist to assess student work on the Elements of Fairy Tales Graphic Organizer.

Standards Alignment: RL.2.1, RL.2.2, RL.2.5, W.2.8

Task	Achieved	Notes
Identify character(s).		
Identify setting.		
Identify problem.		
Identify 3 key events.		
Identify solution.		

Reading Lesson 4

▼ Teaching Objective

Readers find and figure out unfamiliar language in fairy tales.

Close Reading
Opportunity

▼ Standards Alignment

RL.2.1, RL.2.10, SL.2.1a, SL.2.1b, SL.2.1c, SL.2.2, SL.2.4, SL.2.6, L.2.1, L.2.3, L.2.4, L.2.6

▼ Materials

- Features of Fairy Tales chart created during Reading Lesson 2
- Charting supplies or interactive whiteboard
- *Cinderella* retold by Barbara Karlin (or another modern retold version of a classic fairy tale)

▼ To the Teacher

This lesson provides your students with strategies for discovering the meaning of unfamiliar words they may encounter in their reading. Fairy tales often contain sophisticated or old-fashioned language that is not widely used in conversation today. Your students will encounter a variety of interesting and potentially new words such as *horrid, wicked, royal, vain, cottage, hag, porridge, cinders, slipper, peasant, maiden, troll,* and *coach.* However, we do not want to limit their word explorations to fairy tale language alone, nor can we predict which words or phrases will cause our students confusion. Rather, we want to open up their exploration to be inclusive of all words and phrases that may feel new or unfamiliar. **ELL** **Identify and Communicate Content and Language Objectives—Academic Vocabulary. This lesson is important for all your students, but especially for your ELLs, who will likely find more words unfamiliar than their English-speaking peers do. Practicing vocabulary acquisition strategies is a powerful way for your ELLs to become their own advocates for their English development.**

Celebrate your students' word discoveries by creating a Word Collection Wall. Your Word Collection Wall is simply a place for students to record, display, share, and preserve the new and interesting words they have discovered in their reading work. Below are low-tech and high-tech options for creating this space in your classroom. Choose a method and prepare in advance of teaching this lesson.

Goal	Low-Tech	High-Tech
Students record, display, and share their word discoveries on a Word Collection Wall.	Use a pocket chart or bulletin board titled "Word Collection Wall." Students record their word discoveries (including the word, an illustration when appropriate, and a student-crafted definition) on index cards or sentence strips.	Create a PowerPoint or Prezi presentation of word discoveries. Students create a slide for each word they discover, including the word, an illustration when appropriate, and a student-crafted definition. Share this presentation with students and families via a classroom website. Collect words in a graphically visual way by using a digital application such as Wordle.

▼ Procedure

Warm Up Gather the class to set the stage for today's learning

Explain that fairy tales, new and old, often use uncommon words and phrases to describe characters, settings, and events. Many of these terms may be unfamiliar to your students and difficult to understand. In fact, some of these words and phrases are old-fashioned and rarely used in common conversations today.

> You may have already noticed that fairy tales often use fancy words and phrases to describe a character or a setting. A lot of these words may be unfamiliar. Today we're going to learn some strategies for finding the meaning of these new words or phrases and build a Word Collection Wall of the new words we find.

Teach Model what students need to learn and do

Begin a chart called "Figuring Out Unfamiliar Words." **ELL** **Provide Comprehensible Input—Graphic Organizers. The chart helps ELLs follow the**

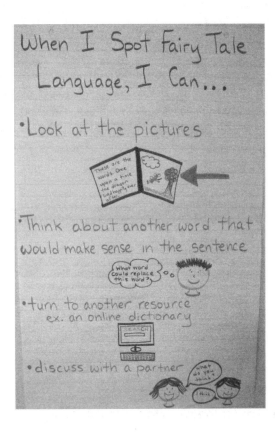

For the purposes of this lesson, we have chosen to read aloud from *Cinderella*; however, you may substitute a fairy tale of your choice that is packed with new vocabulary and the types of descriptive words common to many fairy tales. Read the first page of *Cinderella*, pausing to note the following fairy tale language as you read: *vain* and *horrid*. As you think aloud, make concrete connections to your use of the Figuring Out Unfamiliar Words Chart.

> Vain and horrid sound unfamiliar to me. I know the author is describing Cinderella's new stepmother and stepsisters, so it's important that I have an idea of what these words might mean. Let's see . . . I'll start by looking at the picture. The illustration sure gives a lot of detail, but there is so much detail that I'm not really sure I can pinpoint the meaning of these two words. OK, so next I'll try to come up with other words that will make sense in their place . . .

Once you have determined the general meaning of these new words, add them to the Word Collection Wall (see the suggestions listed above for creating the wall). Below is an example of a Word Collection Wall using a word cloud created on Wordle.net. **ELL** Identify and Communicate Content and Language Objectives—Academic Vocabulary. ELLs in particular will benefit from having this visible, stable, student-created reference source as they build their understanding of new words. It will support their English development as well as their content learning.

discussion and provides a visual anchor for them to refer back to during independent work.

Introduce and discuss each of the following ideas, adding them to your Figuring Out Unfamiliar Words Chart as your teaching unfolds.

- . . . look at the picture
- . . . think about another word that would make sense in the unfamiliar word's place
- . . . turn to another resource (such as an online dictionary)
- . . . discuss with a partner

Demonstrate reading a short passage from a fairy tale and identifying new and unfamiliar fairy tale language. Model working through each of these ideas to determine the meaning of the new word or phrase. **ELL** Provide Comprehensible Input—Models. ELLs will benefit from hearing

hag
duke saber squire stroll
coach gourd
bridle courting potion tapestry
chamberlain smoldering vessel
cast coachman porridge spindle vain
cinders lair spell stallion
horrid raven

Courtesy of the author.

Try Guide students to quickly rehearse what they need to learn and do in preparation for practice

Read aloud the next two pages of *Cinderella*, asking students to listen carefully for new and unfamiliar words. When you have finished reading these two pages, stop and ask your students to volunteer the words or phrases they noticed. Some words that will most likely stand out include *widower*, *ragged*, and *cinders*.

Ask partners to choose a word or phrase to investigate together. Instruct them to use the suggestions included on the Figuring Out Unfamiliar Words Chart to try and determine the meaning of this new word or phrase. Circulate and listen in to partnerships as they work, noting moments or conversations that should be shared for the benefit of the entire class. **ELL** Enable Language Production—Increasing Interaction. Partner work helps ELLs understand the content while giving them someone with whom to practice their English. This conversation provides an opportunity to support student conversation by reinforcing several key speaking and listening skills such as listening with care, taking turns speaking, staying on topic, and building upon the comments of others. (SL.2.1)

Then gather the class, asking several partnerships to share their thinking and adding relevant words to your Word Collection Wall.

Clarify Briefly restate today's teaching objective and explain the practice task(s)

Review the strategies for figuring out unfamiliar words with the class. Tell them to rely upon these strategies to determine the meanings of new words and phrases that they encounter in their own reading.

> As you read today, pay close attention to the language of your fairy tales. Are there any special words or phrases that seem unfamiliar? Do you know what these new words and phrases mean? Use the strategies we've listed here on our Figuring Out Unfamiliar Words Chart to help you determine the meaning of the words and phrases you encounter. Be prepared to contribute at least one word or phrase to our Word Collection Wall.

Practice Students work independently and/or in small groups to apply today's teaching objective

Students read from a variety of fairy tales independently. Students jot down or note various words or phrases that are unfamiliar. When necessary, students utilize the strategies listed in the lesson's Figuring Out Unfamiliar Words Chart to determine the meaning of these new words or phrases. **ELL** Enable Language Production—Reading and Writing. Encourage ELLs who are using the "other word" strategy to use terms from their home language, which might be more easily accessible than an English synonym. This affirms that their home language has a place in the classroom and can be a resource for academic learning.

Student's list of unknown words in preparation to use strategies to determine or clarify the meaning of the unknown words. (L.2.4)

Wrap Up Check understanding as you guide students to briefly share what they have learned and produced today

Ask students to share with a partner at least one word or phrase they gathered for the Word Collection Wall. Be specific in your expectations for partner talk, charting the following expectations for partners to refer to during their conversations. Partners should:

- share the word or phrase they encountered
- read the passage or page that includes this language
- share their thinking about its meaning
- discuss what strategy helped them uncover this particular meaning

Once partners have shared their work with one another, ask several students to share their observations with the entire class. Add appropriate words and phrases to the Word Collection Wall. **ELL** Identify and Communicate Content and Language Objectives—Key Content Vocabulary. By listing the words and phrases from the lesson set you assist ELLs with their vocabulary acquisition. Encourage ELLs to include home-language translations for new words as part of their contributions to the Word Collection Wall, and honor these contributions publically—use them as a chance for the class to learn *two* new words!

Reading Lesson 5 . . . .

▼ Teaching Objective

Readers study illustrations to aid in their comprehension.

Close Reading Opportunity

▼ Standards Alignment

RL.2.1, RL.2.2, RL.2.3, RL.2.7, RL.2.10, SL.2.1a, SL.2.1b, SL.2.1c, SL.2.6, L.2.1, L.2.3, L.2.6

▼ Materials

- Charting supplies or interactive whiteboard
- *Good Little Wolf* by Nadia Shireen
- *The Paper Bag Princess* by Robert Munsch
- *Prince Cinders* by Babette Cole

▼ Procedure

Warm Up Gather the class to set the stage for today's learning

Discuss the following question as a class:

Why do you think illustrations are important?

Student responses might include:

- They show what's happening in a story.
- They let us know what the characters look like.
- They make reading more fun.
- They tell us things the words don't.

Jot down their ideas to refer to later in this lesson.

Teach Model what students need to learn and do

Begin a chart called "Why Are Illustrations Important?" Explain to your students that illustrations are a key part of the story for many reasons, some of which you have just discussed. **ELL** Provide Comprehensible Input—Graphic Organizers. The chart helps ELLs follow the discussion by highlighting key takeaway points. It also provides a visual anchor for ELLs to refer back to during independent work

Sometimes, readers become too focused on the words in a story and don't spend enough time with the illustrations. Other times, readers only look at the pictures and don't pay enough attention to the words. It's important to understand that the illustrations and the words in a story work *together* to tell the story. If you don't pay attention to both the illustrations and the words, and how they work together, you may only be getting half of the story.

Outline the ways in which illustrations help tell a story and, therefore, can aid in student comprehension. As you introduce each of the following ideas, take the time to explain it thoroughly, providing examples wherever possible. If during the Warm Up for this lesson a student mentioned one of the items on this list, or another item that you believe would be a welcome addition to this list, be sure to highlight that student's contribution—it never hurts to make a student "famous" and give him or her ownership over great ideas!

- *Illustrations contain important information.* Often there is an event, emotion, or clue related to the story that occurs only in the illustration, not in the words.

- *Illustrations give you something to picture in your head.* Illustrations can bring a story to life. They can help to confirm what is already in a reader's mind or to revise a reader's misunderstanding of the action.

- *Illustrations can help in determining the key events.* Often, illustrations depict key moments within a story and can help a reader decide which events are essential to understanding the story being told.

- *Illustrations catch our eye.* As much as we don't like to admit it, many of us judge a book by its pictures. If the illustrations are intriguing, we are more likely to pick up a book and check it out.

- *Illustrations can help in discovering the meaning of new vocabulary.* Readers may encounter unfamiliar words as they read. Using the illustrations wisely may help support readers to discover the meaning of new vocabulary through visual representation.

- *Illustrations give you important details about characters and the setting.* Often, illustrators include key or interesting details about the characters and setting that are not mentioned in the text itself. These details not only provide visual interest, but can also contain key information for making inferences about the story being told.

Following are a few ideas for illustrations to use as examples to support your teaching. These examples are drawn from fairy tales listed in the Choosing Core Texts section of this lesson set.

Idea	Example
Illustrations contain important information.	*Good Little Wolf:* Page 28 shows that the Big Bad Wolf ate Rolf and Mrs. Boggins (information that is not contained explicitly in the text).
Illustrations give you something to picture in your head.	*Prince Cinders:* Page 13 includes a nice visual of Prince Cinders as a monkey looking in the mirror.
Illustrations can help in determining the key events.	*The Paper Bag Princess:* Page 4 zooms in on the princess in her paper bag, which is the most important event from the beginning of the story.
Illustrations catch our eye.	*The Paper Bag Princess:* The cover shows a princess in a paper bag standing in front of a dragon, which makes a reader wonder if she is going to get eaten or not.
Illustrations can help in discovering the meaning of new vocabulary.	*Prince Cinders:* On page 15, "bash" is illustrated clearly.

Try Guide students to quickly rehearse what they need to learn and do in preparation for practice

Show students illustrations from a familiar fairy tale. **ELL** Provide Comprehensible Input—Visuals. Seeing a familiar picture will help ELLs recall what they already know about the story; from there, they can examine the illustration for more details. Ask students to discuss with a partner how this particular illustration helps them to better understand the story. Direct students to use specific evidence from the illustration to support their thinking. For example, "This illustration shows the prince trying the slipper on Cinderella in her house while the stepsisters and stepmother watch angrily." Circulate as students talk, pushing them to consistently support their thinking by providing specific evidence from the text. In this case, the text is the illustration. **ELL** Enable Language Production—Increasing interaction. Your ELLs are likely as proficient as your other students in reading pictures—illustrations work in any language! However, they may not have the words to express what they see in pictures. Peer interaction will help ELLs find the language they need.

After students have had a moment to discuss this question, gather the class's attention and share several of their ideas aloud.

Christian Schwier/Fotolia

ELL Identify and Communicate Content Objectives—Repeat. With this final clarification, you help ELLs be sure they know what is expected of them during independent work.

Practice Students work independently and/or in small groups to apply today's teaching objective

Students read fairy tales independently, focusing on the relationship between illustrations and text. Students study illustrations, looking for an example to share of an illustration that aided in their comprehension. **ELL** Enable Language Production—Listening and Speaking. Use this time to confer with your ELLs and offer language support where needed. You can help them prepare for the group share by discussing how they will express what they saw in their stories.

Wrap Up Check understanding as you guide students to briefly share what they have learned and produced today

Gather the class, asking students to have their chosen illustration handy. Instruct students to share their illustration with a partner. Students should share the illustration and specifically how that illustration helped them better understand the fairy tale. Remind students to rely on the chart you created earlier in the lesson. Check in with partnerships as they share, to determine if students are successfully identifying strong examples of the ways in which illustrations aid in comprehension. Then ask two or three students to share their thinking with the entire class, adding their thinking to the class chart as appropriate. **ELL** Enable Language Production—Listening and Speaking. Be sure to encourage your ELLs to share. Some may have felt more reluctant during the whole-group lesson; however, now they have had ample time to study pictures and get their words ready. This preparation time should increase confidence—and success!

Clarify Briefly restate today's teaching objective and explain the practice task(s)

Today as you are reading, your job is to pay careful attention to how the illustrations and words work together to tell the fairy tale. How do the illustrations help you better understand your reading? Find an example of an illustration to share with the class that helped you better understand the story (if it's helpful, you can use our chart as a reference as you work).

Reading Lesson 6 ·

▼ **Teaching Objective**

Readers notice how characters change across a story.

Close Reading
Opportunity

▼ **Standards Alignment**

RL.2.1, RL.2.3, RL.2.10, W.2.8, SL.2.1a, SL.2.1b, SL.2.1c, SL.2.2, SL.2.6, L.2.1, L.2.3, L.2.6

▼ Materials

- *Good Little Wolf* by Nadia Shireen
- Tracing Character Change Graphic Organizer (Appendix 2.3)

▼ Procedure

Warm Up Gather the class to set the stage for today's learning

Ask students to describe the difference between *main characters* and *supporting characters*. Students may have learned this concept in first grade. **ELL** Frontload the Lesson—Activate Prior Knowledge. Connecting prior learning to today's objective helps ELLs focus their listening (so the important parts stand out) and mentally organize the new learning they are about to do.

Use this portion of the lesson to review this content for students and/or to clear up any confusion. As you discuss these definitions, be sure to incorporate examples of both main characters and supporting characters from familiar texts. For example, in *Prince Cinders*, Prince Cinders can be considered a main character, while his three stepbrothers are considered supporting characters.

Teach Model what students need to learn and do

Tracing Character Change

Title:		
Character:		
Beginning	Middle	End

How did the character change?

_____

_____

Why did the character change?

_____

_____

Discuss with the class how characters can change over time. Explain that as the events unfold in a story, main characters often change in response to these events. Use the graphic organizer Tracing Character Change to frame your modeling. **ELL** Provide Comprehensible Input—Graphic Organizers. The graphic organizer helps make your teaching point clear by presenting it visually. It will help your ELLs keep track of what you are saying, and it will serve as a base for them to organize their own thinking during independent work.

> Main characters in our story rarely stay the same the entire way through the story. It wouldn't be a very interesting story if everything stayed the same! Characters often change in response to the different events in a story. For example, in *The Paper Bag Princess*, Elizabeth was at first very determined to save Prince Ronald so they could be married. However, as the events of the story unfolded and Prince Ronald reprimanded Elizabeth for wearing a paper bag, Elizabeth changed, no longer wanting to marry the prince at all. Elizabeth changed in response to Prince Ronald's actions and the way he treated her. This sort of character change is important for readers to notice as a story unfolds.

Prepare the class for a new read-aloud. For the purposes of this lesson set, we have chosen *Good Little Wolf*; however, you may substitute any fairy tale of your choice that includes strong examples of character change. Before you begin, instruct students to pay careful attention to how Rolf, the little wolf, changes across the story. **ELL** Frontload the Lesson—Set a Purpose for Reading. This gives your ELLs a focus for their listening and helps them avoid getting bogged down in unfamiliar language. Now, read aloud to the class *Good Little Wolf*.

Introduce the Tracing Character Change Graphic Organizer (Appendix 2.3) and explain that you will use this organizer to trace how Rolf changed in the story. Model for students how to draw, in the first box of the graphic organizer, a quick sketch of Rolf from the beginning of the story. Then add a sentence or two about Rolf to match the picture. For example, you might write, "Rolf was an obedient, sweet wolf who was afraid of the Big Bad Wolf." Now, think aloud about how Rolf begins to change during the course of the story. He runs into the Big Bad Wolf and tries his hand at being bad. In the second box on your graphic organizer, illustrate this change, perhaps adding a quick sketch of Rolf unsuccessfully trying to blow down the pig's house. Then add two or three sentences to detail this change, in words. Be sure to model sentences that include information about *how* and *why* Rolf changed. **ELL** Enable Language Production—Listening and Speaking. Here you are modeling *how* to talk about characters' changes. This may be very helpful for your ELLs, some of whom can probably tell quite well how a character is changing but may not be sure how to express this understanding clearly in English.

> As you think about character change across a story, it is important to notice both HOW a character changes as well as WHY the character changes. Readers pay attention to the events in the story that motivate or cause the character to change.

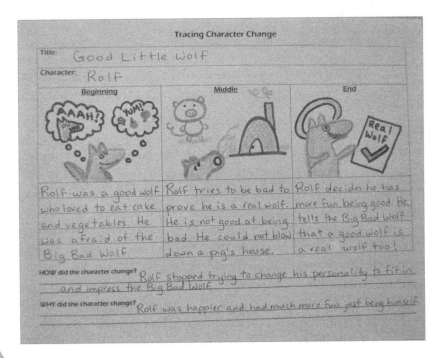

Try Guide students to quickly rehearse what they need to learn and do in preparation for practice

Turn to your class for help with completing the final box on your graphic organizer. Ask your students:

> Did Rolf change again during this story? Turn and talk to your partner. How did Rolf change? Why did he change?

Circulate as students work with a partner, supporting their talk. This is an excellent opportunity to reinforce the importance of citing specific textual evidence to support one's thinking. Students should not only be able to explain how and why Rolf changed, but they should also be able to give a specific example of this change from the text. **ELL** Enable Language Production—Increasing Interaction. By exchanging ideas with peers, ELLs are hearing additional models of English and getting a chance to practice the language of the objective before heading off to work independently.

Gather the class's attention and discuss Rolf's final change. Add your thinking to the graphic organizer in both picture and words. It is important to work with the class to craft sentences that explain both *how* and *why* Rolf changed, using evidence from the text to support their answer. Possible responses:

- Rolf changes by actually doing something mean. He tied up the Big Bad Wolf. On page 24, he tells the Big Bad Wolf that he can be a proper wolf, he just chooses to be a good wolf. This shows me that Rolf changes to prove to the Big Bad Wolf that he really is a wolf.

- Rolf changes from being a good little wolf, to being a little bit more like the Big Bad Wolf. The book says that a strange feeling came over Rolf after the Big Bad Wolf made fun of him for not being able to blow the pig's house down. I think Rolf changed because he was tired of the Big Bad Wolf telling him that he isn't a real wolf. That made him angry. On pages 19 and 20, you can see the illustration shows Rolf going from being little and cute to being big, with angry eyes and sharp teeth. He looks more like a Big Bad Wolf now.

Clarify Briefly restate today's teaching objective and explain the practice task(s)

> Today, each of you should follow how a main character changes across a fairy tale. Use the Tracing Character Change Graphic Organizer to record

your thinking. Be sure to include information about HOW the character changed as well as WHY the character changed. What event(s) in the story caused this change?

Practice Students work independently and/or in small groups to apply today's teaching objective

Distribute copies of the Tracing Character Change Graphic Organizer to the class. Students work in small groups with a fairy tale of their choice to trace the change of a main character across the story, recording their thinking both in pictures and words on the graphic organizer. **ELL** Enable Language Production—Increasing interaction. Group work can be a good way for ELLs to gain entry to the lesson. If they are still unsure of what is expected of them, their peers can help. Consider putting ELLs in groups with bilingual students who share their home language as well as with monolingual English-speaking peers, so that the discussion can occur in both languages.

Wrap Up Check understanding as you guide students to briefly share what they have learned and produced today

Gather the class and ask two or three students to share their work and thinking with the entire class. As students share, encourage their use of specific textual evidence to support their thinking. Ask students to show moments from their story that illustrate the character changes being discussed.

Collect and analyze the Tracing Character Change Graphic Organizer as a performance-based assessment to determine if students need additional instruction or support as a whole class, in small groups, or one on one. **ELL** Assess for Content and Language Understandings—Formative Assessment. This is opportunity for you to assess your ELLs' language and content needs, especially their ability to (a) recognize changes in character and (b) express that recognition. Use this to inform how you will support them in upcoming lessons.

Milestone Performance Assessment

Identifying Change in Character

 Use this checklist to assess student work on the Tracing Character Change Graphic Organizer.

Standards Alignment: RL.2.1, RL.2.3, W.2.8

Task	Achieved	Notes
Identify character who changes.		
Identify how a main character changes.		
Infer why a main character changes.		

Reading Lesson 7 · · · · · · · · · · · · · · · ·

▼ Teaching Objective

Readers determine the lesson of a fairy tale.

Close Reading Opportunity

▼ Standards Alignment

RL.2.1, RL.2.2, RL.2.3, RL.2.10, W.2.8, SL.2.1a, SL.2.1b, SL.2.1c, SL.2.2, SL.2.4, SL.2.6, L.2.1, L.2.3, L.2.6

▼ Materials

- Charting supplies or interactive whiteboard
- *The Paper Bag Princess* by Robert Munsch

▼ Procedure

Warm Up Gather the class to set the stage for today's learning

Review the Features of Fairy Tales Chart you created during Reading Lesson 2. You will be adding a new feature to this chart.

> I have a new feature of fairy tales to share with you today. Fairy tales often include a lesson for the reader to take away from the story.

Add "teach a lesson" to your Features of Fairy Tales Chart.

Teach Model what students need to learn and do

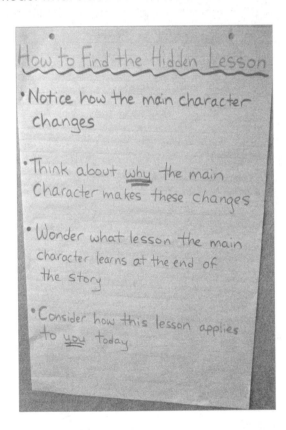

Explain to the class that there are a few steps readers can take to figure out the lesson a fairy tale is trying to teach. Readers can determine the lesson of a fairy tale by noticing how the main character changes across the

story, inferring why the character changed, and thinking about what lesson the main character may have learned by the end of the story. Begin a How to Find the Hidden Lesson Chart to outline these steps for students. **ELL** Provide Comprehensible Input—Graphic Organizers. Charts can help ELLs access the content you are teaching by turning the oral discussion, which may be moving fast, into stable, written bullet points that highlight key take-away information. The chart will give ELLs something concrete to refer back to during independent work.

Introduce and discuss the following steps:

- Notice how the main character changes.
- Think about *why* the main character makes these changes.
- Wonder what lesson the main character learns at the end of the story.
- Consider how this lesson might apply to you today.

Introduce *The Paper Bag Princess* by Robert Munsch. Before you read the story aloud, instruct your students that their job is to listen carefully and keep track of how the main character, Elizabeth, changes over the course of the story.

Read aloud to the class *The Paper Bag Princess*. Then demonstrate walking through the steps listed above to determine a possible lesson to be learned from this fairy tale. **ELL** Provide Comprehensible Input—Models. Modeling a strategy allows ELLs to actually see what you want them to do, rather than just listening to your directions and explanations.

First, think aloud about how Elizabeth changes over the course of the story. You might notice the following changes in Elizabeth:

- In the beginning of the story, Elizabeth wanted to marry Prince Ronald.
- After her castle burned down, Elizabeth was determined to save Prince Ronald, even if she only had a paper bag to wear.
- When Elizabeth rescued Ronald and he was rude to her, Elizabeth no longer wanted to marry Ronald.

Now, think aloud about *why* Elizabeth changed so much at the end of the story.

> Elizabeth must be very smart and brave if she outsmarted the dragon so easily. I think at the end of the story she is smart enough to realize that Ronald isn't very nice and wouldn't make a very good husband. So she walks away.

Finally, wonder about what Elizabeth may have learned from this experience.

> I think Elizabeth has learned that it is important to marry someone who is kind and appreciates her. Ronald doesn't even say thank you to her for rescuing him. Elizabeth learns that she doesn't have to marry someone just because he is a prince.

Try Guide students to quickly rehearse what they need to learn and do in preparation for practice

Instruct your class to turn and consider this with a partner:

> What can you learn from Elizabeth? How does the lesson she learned apply to you?

Circulate as partners discuss these questions, taking the opportunity to reinforce the importance of key speaking and listening skills such as staying on topic and building on the comments of others. (SL.2.1)

Gather the class to discuss the questions as a larger group. If necessary, guide students toward recognizing some of these possible lessons:

- You should choose friends who are kind and appreciate you.
- You should appreciate the efforts of your friends.
- It is important to be brave and stand up for people you love.
- It is important to be brave and stand up for yourself.

Lead the class in a shared writing that summarizes the lesson they have learned from this fairy tale. **ELL** Enable Language Production—Reading and Writing. Here you are showing your ELLs what a strong response to literature looks like. They can refer back to this example when they write their own summaries of lessons learned.

For example, together you might write the following:

> *The Paper Bag Princess* teaches us that it is important to be brave and to stand up for ourselves. When Elizabeth rescues Ronald and he is rude to her, Elizabeth stands up for herself by walking away and not marrying him. She knows she deserves better than someone who is not nice to her. We can stand up for ourselves by not being friends with people who are unkind.

Clarify Briefly restate today's teaching objective and explain the practice task(s)

Review the chart you created for students during this lesson.

> Today we learned a few steps that can help us determine the lesson a fairy tale is attempting to teach. As you are reading today, I want you to use these steps to try and discover a lesson to be learned from a new fairy tale. Be ready to share all of your thinking in some creative ways.

Practice Students work independently and/or in small groups to apply today's teaching objective

Students read independently. Students focus on determining the lesson of at least one fairy tale, using the steps outlined in this lesson as a guide. Once students have had sufficient independent reading time, ask them to record their thinking in one of the following ways suggested in the low-tech/high-tech box.

Goal	Low-Tech	High-Tech
Students determine and share the lesson of a fairy tale, applying it to their own lives.	Students write a short paragraph to be displayed in the classroom. Their writing should include: • the title of the fairy tale • the lesson learned by the main character • how the lesson might apply to their own lives	Students post on a classroom blog. Blog entries should include: • the title of the fairy tale • the lesson learned by the main character • how the lesson might apply to their own lives Students can then comment on other entries and/or share them with their families via the classroom blog as a homework connection.

Wrap Up Check understanding as you guide students to briefly share what they have learned and produced today

Gather the class, asking them to share their writing with a partner. **ELL** Assess for Content and Language Understanding—Formative Assessment. Listen as your ELLs share with their peers. If they seem to be struggling, listen and use thoughtful questioning to try to diagnose the source of their challenge: Have they misunderstood the teaching point because the language of it went over their heads? Have they read a book that they cannot comprehend independently? Do they understand the story's lesson but struggle to put it in words? Each of these will require a different instructional response from you.

Reading Lesson 8

▼ Teaching Objective

Readers compare and contrast different versions of the same tale.

Close Reading Opportunity

▼ Standards Alignment

RL.2.1, RL.2.2, RL.2.3, RL.2.9, RL.2.10, W.2.8, SL.2.1a, SL.2.1b, SL.2.1c, SL.2.2, SL.2.4, SL.2.6, L.2.1, L.2.3, L.2.6

▼ Materials:

- Comparing and Contrasting Fairy Tales Graphic Organizer (Appendix 2.4)
- *Cinderella* retold by Barbara Karlin
- *Prince Cinders* by Babette Cole

▼ Procedure

Warm Up Gather the class to set the stage for today's learning

Introduce and define for the class the terms *compare* and *contrast*. Practice comparing and contrasting two simple objects using a blank Venn diagram. For example, you might lead the class in comparing and contrasting apples and bananas. Or you might want to have some fun comparing something related to fairy tales, such as castles and cottages.

> When we compare and contrast two things, we look at them closely to see how they are the same and how they are different. One way to record these ideas is to use a Venn diagram. Watch me as I label one circle "apples" and the other circle "bananas." We write all the things that are the same right here, where the two circles overlap. We write all the things that are specific to apples in this circle and all the things that are specific to bananas in this circle.

Teach Model what students need to learn and do

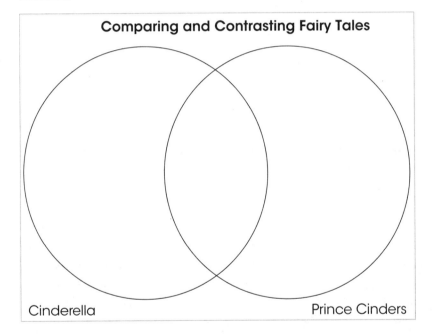

Comparing and Contrasting Fairy Tales

Cinderella   Prince Cinders

Introduce the idea of comparing and contrasting two versions of the same fairy tale. For the purposes of this lesson, we have chosen to compare two versions of Cinderella—the classic version retold by Barbara Karlin and the alternative version *Prince Cinders*. These two fairy tales provide a wide range of elements for students to compare and contrast, both concrete and abstract. Of course you may choose to use two other versions or versions

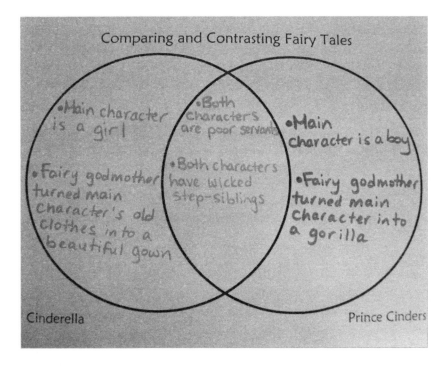

Comparing and Contrasting Fairy Tales

- Main character is a girl
- Fairy godmother turned main character's old clothes into a beautiful gown

- Both characters are poor servants
- Both characters have wicked step-siblings

- Main character is a boy
- Fairy godmother turned main character into a gorilla

Cinderella   Prince Cinders

Regardless of your choice of tales, guide the class toward using the elements of story as an entry point into this type of more abstract thinking. By relying on these familiar aspects of story, we provide students with an accessible method for making a direct comparison, which will foster a higher level of success.

> Just like we looked closely at apples and bananas to see how they are the same and how they are different, we can use a Venn diagram to help us compare and contrast two versions of the same fairy tale. Today we are going to take a closer look at a classic version of *Cinderella* and also *Prince Cinders*, to see how these two tales are the same and how they are different. To organize our thinking, we're going to use the elements of a fairy tale as our guide.

Take a moment to review with your class the elements of a fairy tale (character, setting, problem, key events, and solution). These are key ideas from your teaching in Reading Lesson 3. **ELL** Identify and Communicate Content and Language Objectives—Key Content Vocabulary. This offers ELLs an opportunity to refresh their memories and deepen their understanding of these core terms.

Now, guide your class through thinking about each of these elements one at a time, beginning with the characters. As you think about a particular element as it is included in each of the two tales, record your thinking on a large, blank Venn diagram. Here is how your modeling might unfold:

> Let's start by thinking about the characters in each of these fairy tales. The main character in *Cinderella* is Cinderella, a poor servant girl. The main character in *Prince Cinders* is Prince Cinders. One thing that is different about these characters is that Cinderella is a girl and Prince Cinders is a boy. Because that is a difference between the two tales, I'm going to record that in the separate circle for each fairy tale. However, they were both poor servants who had to serve their wicked step-siblings. Let me record that idea in the middle, where we write down the things about the fairy tales that are the same. Now I'll think about the supporting characters . . .

Continue to think aloud about the setting, problem, and solution, comparing and contrasting how they are included in each of these two tales and recording your observations on the Venn diagram.

of another tale. One popular choice in many classrooms is to compare and contrast two fairy tales as they are told in two different cultures, such as the classic version of *Little Red Riding Hood* and *Lon Po Po*, the Chinese version of the same tale. **ELL** Frontload the Lesson—Make Connections. This is an ideal opportunity to assist ELLs to connect different fairy tales from different cultures. Try to find printed versions of fairy tales that students named earlier in the lesson set that have analogues in U.S. culture, and compare and contrast these stories. This is a powerful exercise for showing ELLs that their home language and culture can help them learn at school, and that school is a place where more languages than just English are welcome.

Label a large, blank Venn diagram with the titles of each fairy tale. **ELL** Provide Comprehensible Input—Graphic Organizers. The Venn diagram can help make the thinking behind comparing and contrasting more transparent. ELLs can watch you physically sort aspects of the stories into different categories, and will refer to this when working on their own later.

Try Guide students to quickly rehearse what they need to learn and do in preparation for practice

Invite the class to help you think through the similarities and differences between the key events in the plot of each of these two tales. Have partners turn and talk with one another to identify a key event from one of the tales and consider if it is the same or different than a key event from the other tale.

Circulate as partners talk, listening in to determine if students need additional support with accurately identifying a key event and/or comparing and contrasting this event against the events in the other tale. As partners discuss this, take the opportunity to reinforce the importance of several key speaking and listening skills such as staying on topic and building on the comments of others. (SL.2.1)

Gather the class's attention once again, and record ideas on the Venn diagram.

Clarify Briefly restate today's teaching objective and explain the practice task(s)

Tell the class that readers often compare and contrast two versions of the same story. Instruct each student to choose two versions of the same fairy tale to work with, recording their thinking about the similarities and differences on a blank Venn diagram.

> When we encounter different versions of the same story, it's interesting to think about how they are similar and how they differ. Today, we're comparing and contrasting two versions of a fairy tale. I'd like each of you to choose two versions of a fairy tale. Then use a Venn diagram to record your thinking about how the two tales are similar and how they are different. Remember, use the elements of a fairy tale to help guide your thinking.

Distribute blank Comparing and Contrasting Fairy Tales Graphic Organizer (Appendix 2.4) to the class.

Practice Students work independently and/or in small groups to apply today's teaching objective

Students choose two versions of a fairy tale. Students compare and contrast these tales using the elements of story as a guide. Students should record

their thinking on the Comparing and Contrasting Fairy Tales Graphic Organizer (Appendix 2.4). **ELL** Enable Language Production—Reading and Writing. Try to have the stories available for students to consult as they write. This support is especially important for your ELLs, who might be less familiar with the stories than their peers or might want to double-check the language of the book.

Wrap Up Check understanding as you guide students to briefly share what they have learned and produced today

Ask students to share their comparisons with a partner. Then partners should discuss which version of the fairy tale they preferred and why. If you choose, students can record their responses on the back of their graphic organizers.

Collect and analyze the Comparing and Contrasting Fairy Tales Graphic Organizer as a performance-based assessment to determine if students need additional instruction or support as a whole class, in small groups, or one on one. **ELL** Assess for Content and Language Understandings—Formative Assessment. This is opportunity for you to assess your ELLs' language and content needs, especially in comparing and contrasting fairy tales. Do a close reading of their work, and possibly follow up with them one on one to, to determine the source of any confusion you notice: Do they understand the lesson but struggle to put their ideas into words? Or do they truly not understand the assignment? Use this information to inform upcoming lessons.

Milestone Performance Assessment

Comparing and Contrasting Fairy Tales

 Use this checklist to assess student work on the Comparing and Contrasting Fairy Tales Graphic Organizer.

Standards Alignment: RL.2.1, RL.2.2, RL.2.3, RL.2.9, W.2.8

Task	Achieved	Notes
Identify two versions of the same tale.		
Correctly identify each element of the fairy tale.		

Task	Achieved	Notes
Accurately articulate elements that are similar and different about the two tales.		

Reading Lesson 9

▼ Teaching Objective

Readers engage in the oral tradition of fairy tales by performing favorite tales aloud.

Close Reading Opportunity

▼ Standards Alignment

RL.2.1, RL.2.2, RL.2.10, SL.2.1a, SL.2.1b, SL.2.1c, SL.2.2, SL.2.4, SL.2.5, SL.2.6, L.2.1, L.2.6

▼ Materials

- Charting supplies or interactive whiteboard
- Reader's Theater Fairy Tale Scripts (Appendix 2.5)
  - Jack and the Beanstalk
  - The Princess and the Pea
  - The Little Red Hen

▼ To the Teacher

Today's lesson challenges students to engage in the oral tradition of fairy tales by analyzing, rehearsing, and performing a key scene from a tale as reader's theater. Using the reader's theater scripts provided in Appendix 2.5, students do a close reading of a key scene from a fairy tale, analyzing the scene to determine the lesson being taught. Students should then work collaboratively to rehearse and perform this scene for the class, focusing on appropriate expression and fluency.

This lesson is best taught across multiple days. On the first day, small groups can read and analyze their scene. They may then need one or two additional days to rehearse their scenes before performing for the class. All together, including time for each small group to perform, this lesson can and should stretch between four and six days.

In advance of teaching this lesson, review the scripts included in Appendix 2.5. Organize your students into small groups, assigning each group a script and taking care to consider individual students' independent reading levels. **ELL** Enable Language Production—Reading and Writing. When you are forming groups, consider grouping ELLs with others who speak their home language so that, if needed, the group discussion could be in English and the home language.

▼ Procedure

Warm Up Gather the class to set the stage for today's learning

Without showing students the pictures, do a dramatic read-aloud of a fairy tale that has been a favorite in your class. Keep your read-aloud restricted to a short, familiar scene. The goal is for students to be exposed to the power of a fluent, expressive performance of a fairy tale as an entry point to discussing and engaging with the oral tradition behind these classic texts.

Teach | Model what students need to learn and do

Explain the oral tradition behind fairy tales. They have roots in the oral tradition and have been told by generations as a mechanism for emphasizing and sharing various cultural lessons and values.

> Did you know that fairy tales began as stories that were told out loud? They are part of what is called an oral tradition, meaning that originally fairy tales were shared by storytellers and were not written down as books until many years later. Fairy tales were one way for various cultures to share their values with future generations. They were used as a way to teach important lessons to young children and can still teach us valuable lessons today.

Tell the class that you would like them to engage in the oral tradition of fairy tales by performing in small groups. Show the class an enlarged or projected copy of a reader's theater script included in Appendix 2.5. Discuss the logistics of how to read a script, indicating how each speaker knows when it is his or her turn to talk.

Now turn your attention to expression and fluency. Underscore the importance of reading fluently and with dynamic expression. One way students can show that they understand a story on a deeper level is to read with appropriate expression that reflects the emotional twists and turns of a particular tale.

Model for students, reading a portion of the reader's theater script with no expression. Then model reading the same portion of the script in a dynamic fashion, full of facial and vocal expression. **ELL** Enable Language Production—Listening and Speaking. Here you are showing your students how to use what the text says to inform an expressive reading. This will be especially helpful for your ELLs, who may initially struggle just to comprehend the text; thanks to your model, they will know to look for textual clues regarding emotion and to aim for an expressive reading like yours.

For the purposes of this lesson, you could read the first seven lines of The Princess and the Pea. In your first reading, use a flat, expressionless voice for both characters. Then, in your second reading, read with exaggerated excitement (such as a shaky voice and wide eyes). Lead the class in a discussion of the difference, relying on the following prompts and encouraging students to stay close to the text in their analysis:

- How did I make my reading more dynamic in the second reading?
- What lines sounded dynamic or interesting to you?
- How did I change my voice or use my face when reading those lines?
- How did my voice and face help you understand the text?

Try | Guide students to quickly rehearse what they need to learn and do in preparation for practice

Draw students' attention to the first six lines of the Jack and the Beanstalk script, where Jack and his mother talk about the beans. Work together with the class to analyze this section, discussing how you might use your voice and facial expressions to clearly convey the emotions contained in this scene. Do this by first asking students to focus on a few specific lines from the text. Then ask students to describe how they would use their voices and faces to clearly express and support the emotion contained in these lines, relying on the text as their guide. For example, take the following lines from that section:

> Jack: Mother! Look what I got at the market when I sold our cow! Four magical beans!
>
> Mother: Shame on you, Jack! These are plain old lima beans.
>
> Reader 1: Jack's mother was so angry that she threw the beans out the window. Jack went to bed without any supper.

Use the following prompts to guide your conversation:

- How might Jack sound in his line? What makes you think that? What evidence from the text supports your thinking?
- How might the mother sound in her line? What makes you think that? What evidence from the text supports your thinking?

Below are some examples of solid responses to these questions:

- In the first line, Jack should sound very excited because he found beans that he believes are magical. There are also exclamation marks after everything he says.
- In the mother's line, she should sound angry and maybe a little bit mean. She scolds Jack and then makes Jack go to bed without

supper, and her words have an exclamation point after them. She also throws the beans out the window, showing she is angry.

Finally, ask students to practice with a partner reading these lines aloud with adequate expression.

Clarify Briefly restate today's teaching objective and explain the practice task(s)

Reiterate the importance of *expression* while reading.

> As we read, it is important to consider how something should be read. How can we use our faces and bodies to reflect the emotion and action happening in the words?

Instruct students to work in small groups to analyze and rehearse selected scenes as reader's theater. Remind students to return to the text itself to help determine how they should use their voices and bodies.

Practice Students work independently and/or in small groups to apply today's teaching objective

Students work in small groups to analyze and rehearse short scenes from a variety of fairy tale scripts (provided in Appendix 2.5), focusing on reading with dynamic expression. **ELL** Identify and Communicate Content and Language Objectives—Language Form and Function. Reading scripts aloud gives ELLs a chance connect the words and sentences to oral expression and emotions; this builds their comprehension of English. Their peers' acting will also help them better understand the language of the text.

Wrap Up Check understanding as you guide students to briefly share what they have learned and produced today

Small groups perform their selected scenes for the class (see our low-tech and high-tech options below). After each performance, lead the class in a discussion regarding the choices made by that particular group. Use the following prompts as a guide for your conversation.

- What part of this group's performance was the most expressive? What lines stood out to you?
- How did this group's performance help you better understand the scene?
- Can you connect the performers' expressions with the text being read?

Goal	Low-Tech	High-Tech
Students perform short scenes from a selection of fairy tale scripts.	Invite other classes or students' families to watch students perform their short scenes.	Create a digital video of students performing their short scenes or create animated characters who speak the script. Share creations with students' families and other classes via the internet.

Reading Lesson 10

Close Reading Opportunity

▼ Teaching Objective

Readers respond to the Core Questions.

▼ Standards Alignment

RL.1, RL.2.2, RL.2.3, RL.2.5, RL.2.9, RL.2.10, W.2.8, SL.2.1a, SL.2.1b, SL.2.1c, SL.2.6, L.2.1, L.2.2, L.2.3, L.2.6

▼ Materials

- Charting supplies or interactive whiteboard

▼ To the Teacher

Today is an opportunity for your students to reflect on all the new knowledge they've gained about fairy tales. They'll be working independently to respond in writing to one of the Core Questions. These questions address key aspects of the instruction presented and represent ideas or understandings we would like students to carry forward with them across genres and grade levels.

In order to give students ample time to think, write about, and discuss these ideas, this lesson may require an additional day of instruction.

▼ Procedure

Warm Up — Gather the class to set the stage for today's learning

Remind the class of the good work they have been doing, and ask them to recall some of the things they have learned about fairy tales and some of their favorite tales. **ELL Frontload the Lesson—Make Connections. Reminding students of all the work they have recently done will help ELLs in particular call up what they have learned and get their minds ready for this lesson.**

> Over the past few weeks, we have done a lot of reading of fairy tales—old and new—and learned what fairy tales are all about. What are some things we learned about this type of story? Who has a favorite? Why?

Allow a short time for students to share things they have learned about fairy tales and some of their favorite tales.

Teach — Model what students need to learn and do

Tell the class that today you want them to think about the power of fairy tales as a form of traditional literature that has been shared for generations. As readers, it is important to take the time to reflect on the power of literature to ignite our imaginations.

Chart the following questions for the class to consider:

• What are the key elements in a story?

• What are the characteristics of a fairy tale?

Now, choose a question and begin a shared response by recalling the key ideas about stories from this lesson set. Then model for the class how to respond to these questions in writing by composing a shared piece about fairy tales. For the purposes of this lesson, we have chosen to focus on the following Core Question: What are the key elements in a story? There is no need to make your piece lengthy or overly academic; rather, it is important that the language, length, and style reflect grade-level expectations for your students. Remember, in shared writing you are the scribe who has

the ultimate control over the format of the piece. However, your students should be active participants in the content of the writing. **ELL Enable Language Production—Reading and Writing. Modeling the composition process offers ELLs a chance to see the language of a strong literary reflection. Note that the sample shared writing piece below features age-appropriate academic language conventions: topic sentences, transition (e.g., "First . . . Then . . .") and linking (e.g., "These elements are . . ."; "Here is an example . . .") words, and introductory phrases (e.g., "The problem is . . ."). This writing model will become the structure your students will refer to when writing their own reflections.**

Here is what your piece might look like after a class discussion:

What are the key elements in a story?

Stories have five key elements. These elements are characters, setting, key events, problem, and solution. Here is an example of each of these elements from a fairy tale we read together.

In *Prince Cinders*, the characters are Prince Cinders; his three big, hairy brothers; the dirty fairy; and Princess Lovelypenny. This fairytale is set in Prince Cinders's house and at a bus stop where Prince Cinders meets Princess Lovelypenny. There are a few key events that lead up to the big problem in this story. First, Prince Cinders's brothers were not kind to him. They never let him go to the disco. Then a dirty fairy comes along and tries to help Prince Cinders, but ends up turning him into a hairy gorilla. Next, Prince Cinders meets Princess Lovelypenny at the bus stop on his way home from the disco. Princess Lovelypenny was scared, but just then the clock struck midnight and Prince Cinders turned back into himself. Princess Lovelypenny thought Prince Cinders had saved her from the gorilla. He is shy and runs away, leaving his pants behind. The problem in this story is that Princess Lovelypenny wants to find the man who fits into the pants, so she can marry him. The solution is that, finally, Prince Cinders tries on the pants and they fit. The prince and the princess get married and live happily ever after.

Shared writing provides a wonderful opportunity to highlight several key speaking and listening and language skills such as producing complete sentences and demonstrating a command of standard English conventions and grammar. (SL.2.6)

Try Guide students to quickly rehearse what they need to learn and do in preparation for practice

Let's help each other remember all that we've learned. You will respond to our other Core Question: What are the features of fairy tales? Now, take a moment to turn and talk to a partner about how you might answer that question.

Allow students ample time to consider this question together. **ELL** Enable Language Production—Listening and Speaking. Be sure you allow plenty of "think" time before students turn to talk with their partners. ELLs in particular benefit from this wait time, as it gives them a chance to collect their thoughts and get their words ready.

Clarify Briefly restate today's teaching objective and explain the practice task(s)

Today we are reflecting on our learning together, sharing with one another what we now know about fairy tales.

Direct students to choose one of the remaining Core Questions and write a response.

Practice Students work independently and/or in small groups to apply today's teaching objective

Students will respond to one of the Core Questions in writing.

Wrap Up Check understanding as you guide students to briefly share what they have learned and produced today

Gather your class and have them share their reflections on each of the questions. Note similarities and differences in their responses. Do certain things stand out for many students? Consider why this might be so.

Collect and analyze student responses to the Core Questions as a performance-based assessment to determine if students need additional instruction or support as a whole class, in small groups, or one on one. **ELL** Assess for Content and Language Understandings—Summative Assessment. This is an ideal opportunity for you to assess your ELLs' language and content needs by checking their ability to express themselves through their writing. Remember to check for the root of any misunderstandings you notice: Are they struggling with content or language (or both)? Use this information to inform upcoming lessons.

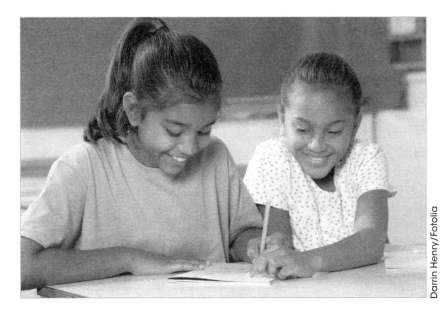

Darrin Henry/Fotolia

Milestone Performance Assessment

Expressing Yourself Clearly

 Use this checklist to assess student work on answering the Core Questions.

Standards Alignment: RL.2.2, RL.2.5, RL.2.9, W.2.8

Task	Achieved	Notes
Accurately articulate the features or elements of a fairy tale.		
Include as examples complete and accurate details from a story.		

Grade 2

Writing Lessons

The Core I.D.E.A. / Daily Writing Instruction at a Glance table highlights the teaching objectives and standards alignment for all 10 lessons across the four stages of the lesson set (Introduce, Define, Extend, and Assess). It also indicates which lessons contain special features to support English language learners, technology, speaking and listening, close reading opportunities, and formative ("Milestone") assessments.

The following CORE READY WRITING RUBRIC is designed to help you record each student's overall understanding across four levels of achievement as it relates to the lesson set goals. We recommend that you use this rubric at the end of the lesson set as a performance-based assessment tool. Use the Milestone Performance Assessments as tools to help you gauge student progress toward these goals. Reteach and differentiate instruction as needed. See the foundational book, *Be Core Ready: Powerful, Effective Steps to Implementing and Achieving the Common Core State Standards*, for more information about the Core Ready Reading and Writing Rubrics.

Grade 2 Once Upon a Time: A New Look at Fairy Tales

Instructional Stage	Lesson	Teaching Objective	Core Standards	Special Features
Introduce: *notice, explore, collect, note, immerse, surround, record, share*	1	Writers imagine magical characters and settings.	RL.2.1 • RL.2.7 • RL.2.10 • W.2.3 • SL.2.1a • SL.2.1b • SL.2.1c • SL.2.4 • SL.2.6 • L.2.1 • L.2.3 • L.2.6	ELL Tech Close Reading Opportunity
	2	Writers consider alternative endings to classic fairy tales.	RL.2.1 • RL.2.10 • W.2.3 • W.2.8 • SL.2.1a • SL.2.1b • SL.2.1c • SL.2.2 • SL.2.4 • SL.2.6 • L.2.1 • L.2.3 • L.2.6	ELL S&L Close Reading Opportunity
	3	Writers imagine how alternative story elements change familiar tales.	RL.2.1 • RL.2.2 • RL.2.3 • RL.2.10 • W.2.3 • W.2.8 • SL.2.1a • SL.2.1b • SL.2.1c, • SL2.2 • SL.2.4 • SL.2.6 • L.2.1 • L.2.3 • L.2.6	ELL S&L Close Reading Opportunity
Define: *name, identify, outline, clarify, select, plan*	4	Writers plan an organized sequence of events to include in a tale.	RL.2.1 • RL.2.2 • RL.2.3 • R.2.10 • W.2.3 • W.2.5 • W.2.8 • SL.2.1a • SL.2.1b • SL.2.1c • SL2.2 • SL.2.4 • SL.2.6 • L.2.1 • L.2.2 • L.2.3 • L.2.6	ELL Milestone Assessment Close Reading Opportunity
Extend: *try, experiment, attempt, approximate, practice, explain, revise, refine*	5	Writers create dynamic stories by including character thought and dialogue.	RL.2.1 • RL.2.10 • W.2.3 • W.2.5 • SL.2.1a • SL.2.1b • SL.2.1c • SL.2.2 • SL.2.4 • SL.2.6 • L.2.1 • L.2.2 • L.2.3 • L.2.6	ELL S&L Close Reading Opportunity
	6	Writers create dynamic stories by describing characters' actions.	RL.2.1 • RL.2.3 • RL.2.10 • W.2.3 • W.2.5 • SL.2.1a • SL.2.1b • SL.2.1c • SL.2.2 • SL.2.4 • SL.2.6 • L.2.1 • L.2.2 • L.2.3 • L.2.6	ELL Close Reading Opportunity
	7	Writers create dynamic stories by describing characters' feelings.	RL.2.1 • RL.2.3 • RL.2.10 • W.2.3 • W.2.5 • SL.2.1a • SL.2.1b • SL.2.1c • SL.2.2 • SL.2.4 • SL.2.6 • L.2.1 • L.2.2 • L.2.3 • L.2.6	ELL Milestone Assessment Close Reading Opportunity
	8	Writers craft strong endings.	RL.2.1 • RL.2.10 • W.2.3 • W.2.5 • SL.2.1a • SL.2.1b • SL.2.1c • SL.2.4 • SL.2.6 • L.2.1 • L.2.2 • L.2.3 • L.2.6	ELL Close Reading Opportunity
Assess: *reflect, conclude, connect, share, recognize, respond*	9	Writers improve their writing by revising and editing their writing collaboratively.	W.2.3 • W.2.5 • W.2.6 • SL.2.1a • SL.2.1b • SL.2.1c • SL.2.5 • SL.2.6 • L.2.1 • L.2.2 • L.2.3 • L.2.6	ELL Milestone Assessment
	10	Writers share their work with pride.	W.2.6 • SL.2.1a • SL.2.1b • SL.2.1c • SL.2.2 • SL.2.3 • SL.2.4 • SL.2.5 • SL.2.6 • L.2.1 • L.2.3 • L.2.6	ELL S&L Tech

Core Ready Writing Rubric

Lesson Set Goal	Emerging	Approaching	Achieving	Exceeding	Standards Alignment
Plan and write an original adaptation of a classic fairy tale that includes the elements common to fairy tales and a logical sequence of events.	Student shows little or no evidence of planning or writing an original adaption of a classic fairy tale with the required plot elements.	Student plans and writes an original adaption of a classic fairy tale. Some of the required elements (elements common to fairy tales and a logical sequence of events) may be missing or underdeveloped.	Student plans and writes a narrative with all required elements (a main character who experiences a series of realistic and imagined events in a logical sequence with a clear beginning, climax, and end). Some components may be more effective than others.	Student plans and writes narrative with all required elements (a main character who experiences a series of realistic and imagined events in a logical sequence with a clear beginning, climax, and end). Narrative is well developed and some elements may be particularly effective or advanced for the grade level.	RL.2.1 RL.2.2 RL.2.3 RL.2.10 W.2.3 W.2.5 W.2.8 SL.2.1a SL.2.1b SL.2.1c SL.2.4 SL.2.6 L.2.1 L.2.2 L.2.3 L.2.6
Include strong details such as dialogue, descriptive language, inner thoughts, and feelings.	Student writing lacks details such as dialogue, descriptive language, inner thoughts, and feelings.	Student attempts to include details such as dialogue, descriptive language, inner thoughts, and feelings. Some details may be unclear or lack obvious connection to fairy tale development.	Student includes strong details such as dialogue, descriptive language, inner thoughts, and feelings. Most details are clear and relevant to the fairy tales.	Student includes several examples of strong details such as dialogue, descriptive language, inner thoughts, and feelings. Details are clear and relevant and effectively serve to develop the fairy tale for the reader.	W.2.3 SL.2.1a SL.2.1b SL.2.1c SL.2.6 L.2.1 L.2.2 L.2.3 L.2.6
Write narratives in which they recount a well-elaborated event or short sequence of events, include details to describe actions, thoughts, and feelings, use temporal words to signal event order, and provide a sense of closure.	Student shows little or no evidence of composing a narrative that recounts a well-elaborated event or short sequence of events. May not have or may inaccurately use details to describe actions, thoughts, and feelings; temporal words to signal event order; and a sense of closure.	Student shows inconsistent evidence of composing a narrative piece that recounts a well-elaborated event or short sequence of events. Student attempts to include details to describe actions, thoughts, and feelings; temporal words to signal event order; and a sense of closure.	Student shows solid evidence of successfully composing a narrative piece that recounts a well-elaborated event or short sequence of events. Student includes details to describe actions, thoughts, and feelings; temporal words to signal event order; and a sense of closure. Some components may be more developed than others.	Student shows outstanding evidence of composing a successful narrative piece that recounts a well-elaborated event or short sequence of events. Student includes accurate and insightful details to describe actions, thoughts and feelings; appropriate temporal words to signal event order; and a clear sense of closure. Ideas may be particularly thoughtful or sophisticated.	W.2.3

Lesson Set Goal	Emerging	Approaching	Achieving	Exceeding	Standards Alignment
With guidance and support from adults and peers, focus on a topic and strengthen writing as needed by revising and editing.	Student makes little or no attempt to strengthen writing as needed by responding to feedback, focusing on a topic, or revising and editing, even with extensive adult prompting and support.	Student attempts to strengthen writing as needed by responding to feedback, focusing on a topic, and revising and editing. Revisions may not connect to suggestions or strengthen piece effectively.	Student strengthens writing as needed by responding to feedback, focusing on a topic, and revising and editing. Revisions usually connect to feedback and enhance the piece. Some areas of writing may be more developed than others.	Student effectively strengthens writing as needed by responding to feedback, focusing on a topic, and revising and editing. Revisions are responsive and thoughtful and consistently serve to enhance piece. May proactively seek feedback to improve writing.	W.2.5
With guidance and support from adults and peers, share writing with others in meaningful ways.	Student shows little or no evidence of attempting to share writing with others in meaningful ways.	Student attempts to share writing with others but may lack focus and sense of purpose at times.	Student successfully shares writing with others in meaningful ways. In most or all instances student uses a variety of tools and effective collaboration to prepare the piece for presentation.	Student clearly, thoroughly, and effectively shares writing with others in a meaningful way. Student accurately uses a variety of tools and proactively seeks collaboration, when necessary, in order to prepare the piece for presentation.	W.2.6
In collaborative discussions, exhibit responsibility for the rules and roles and purpose of conversation.	Student makes little or no attempt to participate in collaborative discussions and build on others' talk by linking their comments to others. Often disregards the rules and roles of conversation even with prompting.	Student inconsistently participates in collaborative discussions and builds on others' talk by linking their comments to others. Student observes the rules and roles of conversation but needs frequent prompting.	Student usually participates in collaborative discussions and builds on others' talk by linking their comments to others. Student observes the rules and roles of conversation. May need some prompting.	Student consistently participates in collaborative discussions and builds on others' talk by linking their comments to others. Student observes the rules and roles of conversation with little or no prompting.	SL.2.1a SL.2.1b
In collaborative discussions, ask questions in a manner that enhances understanding of topic.	Student makes little or no attempt to ask questions that enhance understanding of the topic.	Student occasionally asks questions to clarify or build understanding of the topic or text under discussion but usually requires support or prompting.	Student asks questions that effectively clarify or build understanding of the topic or text under discussion. May need occasional support or prompting.	Student often asks effective and focused questions to clarify or build understanding of the topic or text under discussion. Proactively uses this strategy to support own learning.	SL.2.1c
Speak in complete sentences when appropriate.	Student shows little or no evidence of speaking in complete sentences when appropriate.	Student shows some evidence of attempting to speak in complete sentences when appropriate.	Student shows solid evidence of speaking in complete sentences when appropriate.	Student shows exceptional evidence of speaking in complete sentences when appropriate.	SL.2.6
Demonstrate knowledge of standard English and its conventions.	Student demonstrates little or no knowledge of standard English and its conventions.	Student demonstrates some evidence of knowledge of standard English and its conventions.	Student consistently demonstrates knowledge of standard English and its conventions.	Student demonstrates an exceptional understanding of standard English and its conventions. Use of conventions is sophisticated for grade level and accurate.	L.2.1 L.2.2 L.2.3
Use words and phrases acquired through conversations, reading and being read to, and responding to texts.	Student shows little or no evidence of the acquisition and/or use of grade-appropriate words and phrases.	Student shows some evidence of acquiring and using grade-appropriate words and phrases.	Student shows solid evidence of acquiring and using grade-appropriate words and phrases.	Student shows a high level of sophistication and precision when using grade-appropriate words and phrases.	L.2.6

Writing Lesson 1

▼ Teaching Objective

Writers imagine magical characters and settings.

Close Reading
Opportunity

▼ Standards Alignment

RL.2.1, RL.2.7, RL.2.10, W.2.3, SL.2.1a, SL.2.1b, SL.21.c, SL.2.4, SL.2.6, L.2.1, L.2.3, L.2.6

▼ Materials

- *Cinderella* retold by Barbara Karlin
- *Good Little Wolf* by Nadia Shireen
- *The Paper Bag Princess* by Robert Munsch
- Drawing paper or drawing software program

▼ To the Teacher

Today's lesson is intended to get students' creative juices flowing as they prepare to craft an original adaptation of a classic fairy tale of their choosing. Drawing and sketching are often the most developmentally appropriate entry points for young students attempting to work in a new and unfamiliar genre. Think about how you will preserve and display the drawings that result from students' independent practice. Consider a Fairy Tale Inspiration Wall or mounting the drawings on cardstock and using them as storytelling cards. Simply shuffle the cards, drawing one or more original character and a setting to spark some creative oral storytelling.

Below are low-tech and high-tech options for student work in today's lesson.

Goal	Low-Tech	High-Tech
Students create one magical character and one magical setting to inspire a fairy tale.	Students draw a magical character and a magical setting on separate pieces of drawing paper, using supplies such as magic markers, oil pastels, colored pencils, or crayons to breathe additional life into their work.	Students create one magical character and one magical setting using drawing or doodling software or app.

▼ Procedure

Warm Up Gather the class to set the stage for today's learning

Display an illustration from a fairy tale that depicts a magical character as well as realistic characters. For the purposes of this lesson, we have chosen the illustration on page 12 of *Cinderella* retold by Barbara Kelfin; however, you can certainly substitute with another fairy tale illustration of your choosing. **ELL** Provide Comprehensible Input—Visuals. ELLs benefit from nonlinguistic forms of representation (pictures, sketches, copies from scenes in books). The pictures can provide another point of access to the teaching point you are making orally.

> Which character is magical? How do you know?

As students respond, encourage them to utilize specific details from the illustration to support their answer.

Teach Model what students need to learn and do

Get your class excited about embarking on a new journey as authors of fairy tales. As part of this journey, it will be necessary for them to stretch their imaginations to dream up magical characters and detailed settings for their stories.

> Today is an exciting day! Today is our first day in becoming authors of fairy tales! Authors of fairy tales have a fun and creative job; they get to dream up magical characters and detailed settings to capture the imaginations of their readers. Are you ready to dive with me into this exciting new type of storytelling?

Refer back to the conversation you had with students during the Warm Up. Study specific illustrations from other Core Texts that show examples of magical characters, to get students' imaginations going. Here are some suggestions for texts:

- *Cinderella* (depicts a fairy godmother)
- *Good Little Wolf* (depicts talking wolves)
- *The Paper Bag Princess* (depicts a talking dragon)

Now it's time to model for students how to sketch an original magical character. **ELL** Provide Comprehensible Input—Models. By watching you physically sketch a magical character, ELLs get another point of access to the lesson focus, beyond the oral explanation of the task. This will make it easier for them to transition to independent work.

Think aloud about your character as you sketch, asking yourself questions such as:

- Should my character be some sort of magical person or a talking animal?
- How can I show in my illustration that my character is magical?
- What magical powers or objects do I want my character to have?

Your character could truly take any form. For example, you might choose a dragon, a talking animal, or some sort of prince or princess.

Try Guide students to quickly rehearse what they need to learn and do in preparation for practice

Turn to the class for help generating ideas for a detailed setting.

> Think for a moment about where this character might live. What details can we add to our illustration to clearly show that place? Then turn and share your ideas with a partner.

Circulate and listen in to various partnerships as they brainstorm together. Encourage students to name a place as well as brainstorm specific details to add to the illustration to clearly show this location. Once students have shared their ideas with one another, gather the class and share several ideas with the whole class and do some quick sketching. **ELL** Enable Language Production—Increasing Interaction. Conversing with peers gives ELLs yet another point of entry into this lesson. If they were unsure of the task at hand, hearing their partners' contributions can solidify their understanding. At the same time, peer conversation aids ELLs' English acquisition.

Clarify Briefly restate today's teaching objective and explain the practice task(s)

Direct each student to dream up (at least) one magical character to draw today. Once students create a character, they should decide on where that character lives, adding detailed setting clues to their illustration. Get students organized with the necessary supplies based on your choice of a low-tech or high-tech option for student work.

> Today we are going to get our imaginative juices flowing by dreaming up magical characters and settings for fairy tales. As authors of fairy tales, we need to let our imaginations run free. Take today to imagine stories for these characters and settings as you draw.

Practice Students work independently and/or in small groups to apply today's teaching objective

Christian Schwier/Fotolia

Students work independently to create (at least) one magical character and a detailed setting for that character. As students work, circulate and check in with various students, asking them for more detail about their characters or settings. Also, prompt students to begin thinking about what sorts of adventures they can imagine for their character. What tales can they dream up for the setting they have created? **ELL** Enable Language Production—Reading and Writing. Your ELLs are likely as proficient as any of your students in imagining and drawing. You can help them get ready for the writing portion of subsequent lessons by having them tell you orally about their pictures and by getting them to

My Magical Character

by Maya Thunder

THe Three little girls and the big bad bully

Students' magical characters with detailed settings.

The queen
Evil step mother

start thinking about the adventures they will write about. This creates a bridge to increasing linguistic complexity: from their thoughts, to pictures, to oral language, to their written stories.

Wrap Up Check understanding as you guide students to briefly share what they have learned and produced today

Gather your class. Have students share with one another their magical characters and detailed settings. Encourage students to articulate exactly what makes their character magical and what sorts of details they chose to include in their setting. Consider displaying student work on a Fairy Tale Inspiration Board. **ELL** Enable Language Production—Listening and Speaking. This oral sharing time is a great opportunity for ELLs to practice turning their ideas into English sentences, using drawings of their own creation as an anchor. Visuals can help ELLs with both comprehension and with language production.

Writing Lesson 2

Close Reading
Opportunity

▼ Teaching Objective

Writers consider alternative endings to classic fairy tales.

▼ Standards Alignment

RL.2.1, RL.2.10, W.2.3, W.2.8, SL.2.1a, SL.2.1b, SL.21.c, SL.2.2, SL.2.4, SL.2.6, L.2.1, L.2.2, L.2.3, L.2.6

▼ Materials

- Fairy Tales We Know . . . for Now Chart (created during Reading Lesson 1)
- Charting supplies or interactive whiteboard
- Happily Ever After Graphic Organizer (Appendix 2.6)

▼ To the Teacher

One goal of this lesson set is to immerse students in the genre of fairy tales, familiarizing them with a variety of stories from this type of traditional text. Some students will enter our classrooms with rich knowledge of these stories, while others will be discovering them for the first time. **ELL** Frontload the Lesson—Make Connections. Try to find out if your ELLs know any stories from their home cultures that are similar to the ones you will be studying as a class. Make this connection explicit for them, so they can feel more confident that they understand the stories that are new to them.

Therefore, in advance of teaching this lesson (and throughout this entire lesson set), read aloud to your class many classic versions of fairy tales. Some classic fairy tales to consider:

- "The Princess and the Pea"
- "Cinderella"
- "Little Red Riding Hood"
- "Rapunzel"
- "Goldilocks and the Three Bears"
- "Rumpelstiltskin"

ELL Frontload the Lesson—Build Background. Remember that a story that is classic to you might be brand-new to your ELLs. You may want to meet with your ELLs before the whole-group lesson to familiarize them with the "classic" versions of the stories the class will study.

▼ Procedure

Warm Up Gather the class to set the stage for today's learning

Review the Fairy Tales We Know . . . for Now Chart you created with students during Reading Lesson 1. Ask students if there are any other classic or familiar fairy tales they would like to add to the list. Add any relevant student suggestions.

Then direct each student to choose one fairy tale with which they are familiar to retell to a partner. Have partners turn and retell one fairy tale to each other. **ELL** Enable Language Production—Increasing Interaction. When partnering ELLs with other students, think of how partners can support language acquisition through sharing in the home language, translation, and modeling. ELLs should be encouraged to tell stories they know well and to use their home language as a resource. If there are no students who share an ELL's home language, you will need to provide individual support to help that child retell a familiar story in English.

If students are unfamiliar with fairy tales as a genre, direct them to retell the fairy tale they explored during their reading work or a fairy tale you have read aloud to the entire class, giving students a moment to flip through that particular tale and refresh their memory. Take this opportunity to circulate amongst your students and informally assess students' ability to orally recount a familiar tale with accuracy and appropriate details. (SL.2.4)

Teach Model what students need to learn and do

Invite your class to think more deeply about the endings to these familiar fairy tales. Begin a chart titled Happily Ever After. Divide your chart into three columns. Use the far left column to list the titles of several familiar fairy tales. Use the middle column to jot down a quick description of the fairy tale's current ending. Leave the far right column for ideas for an alternative ending. **ELL** Provide Comprehensible Input—Graphic Organizers.

Here is what your chart should look like (in your chart, you will substitute the titles with those that are most familiar to your class):

Happily Ever After

Title	How it ends now . . .	Another ending could be . . .
Cinderella	The prince finds Cinderella; they get married and live happily ever after.	Cinderella sells the other glass slipper to the highest bidder and uses the money to buy her own house. She moves out and is rid of her wicked stepsisters forever.
The Princess and the Pea		
Little Red Riding Hood		

Work with the class to jot down a quick sentence or two about how each fairy tale currently ends. For example, when discussing "Cinderella," you might jot, "Cinderella fits into the glass slipper, marries the prince, and lives happily ever after."

Now, model for students imagining an alternative ending for these familiar tales. Here is one way your modeling could unfold if you choose to use "Cinderella":

> How else could "Cinderella" end? In the story as it is written now, Cinderella marries the prince. But what if she didn't? What if she tried on the glass slipper and it fit, but then she said, "No thank you" and went off to live with her fairy godmother? That could be an interesting twist . . .

Jot "Cinderella says no thank you and goes to live with her fairy godmother" as an idea for an alternative ending on your chart.

Try Guide students to quickly rehearse what they need to learn and do in preparation for practice

Challenge students to think about additional alternatives for endings of the same fairy tale. We want to challenge students to think of a variety of endings, rather than a single alternative.

Let's think a bit more about "Cinderella." Is there yet another way this story could end differently? Turn and discuss some ideas with your partner.

Students turn and share ideas with one another. Listen in to students, jotting down ideas to share with the entire class. Gather the class once partners have had sufficient time to talk and share several ideas you overheard. **ELL** Enable Language Production—Increasing Interaction. Conversing with peers offers a host of benefits to your ELLs: they can practice speaking in a low-pressure environment, they can hear proficient language models aside from the teacher, and they can clarify and practice their understanding of the lesson content. Allow ELLs (especially beginners) to tell their alternate endings in their home language. They are still practicing the content, and it will help them get ready to write in English later.

Clarify Briefly restate today's teaching objective and explain the practice task(s)

Instruct students to work with a partner. Each partnership should choose a fairy tale. Then the partnership should work together to generate three ideas for an alternative ending to that tale. Distribute copies of the Happily Ever After Graphic Organizer (Appendix 2.6).

Happily Ever After?

Title
How it ends now . . .
Another ending could be . . . 1. 2. 3.

Today we're imagining new endings for familiar fairy tales. I'd like each of you to work with a partner. Choose a fairy tale to focus on. Jot down the current ending to the fairy tale, and then work together to imagine three

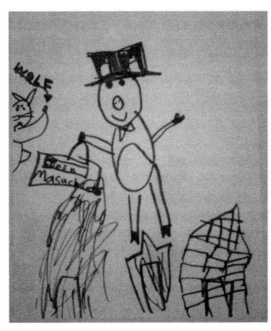

Student's sketch of an alternate ending to a fairy tale.

different endings to that same story. You can organize and record your thinking on the graphic organizer.

Practice Students work independently and/or in small groups to apply today's teaching objective

Students work in partnerships. Focusing on one fairy tale, each partnership records the current ending to the fairy tale as well as three alternative endings for this same tale. **ELL** Enable Language Production—Reading and Writing. The graphic organizer provides a scaffold for ELLs' writing: it makes transparent the structure of the task they are to complete, so they can focus on their ideas. When partnering ELLs with other students, think of how partners can support language acquisition and content understanding through sharing in native language, translation, and modeling.

Wrap Up Check understanding as you guide students to briefly share what they have learned and produced today

Gather the class and have several partnerships share their work with the whole class. Add student ideas to the chart you created earlier. Then, if time allows, pick an ending to write as a shared writing exercise.

Writing Lesson 3 . . . .

▼ Teaching Objective

Writers imagine how alternative story elements change familiar tales.

Close Reading Opportunity

▼ Standards Alignment

RL.2.1, RL.2.2, RL.2.3, RL.2.10, W.2.3, W.2.8, SL.2.1a, SL.2.1b, SL.2.1c, SL.2.2, SL.2.4, SL.2.6, L.2.1, L.2.2, L.2.3, L.2.6

▼ Materials

- Elements of Fairy Tales Graphic Organizer (also used in Reading Lesson 3) (Appendix 2.2)
- Fairy Tales We Know . . . for Now Chart (created during Reading Lesson 1)

▼ To the Teacher

This lesson pushes students to rely on the key elements of story to reimagine a classic fairy tale. Students must spend time reading and thinking deeply about a classic fairy tale, considering how it might be adapted in interesting ways by changing a key story element. Then we want students to put their ideas to the test by attempting to draft this revised tale. Therefore, this lesson will be best taught across at least two days—one for reading and using the graphic organizer to think about how to best adapt the tale and another for attempting to draft this new version. You may want to consider extending students' work time beyond two days in order to increase their volume of writing during this lesson set.

▼ Procedure

Warm Up Gather the class to set the stage for today's learning

In Reading Lesson 1, you shared with your class an alternative version of a classic fairy tale. We suggested using the classic version of *Cinderella* and the alternative tale *Prince Cinders*. **ELL** Frontload the Lesson—Build Background. Remember that a story that is classic to you might be brand-new to your ELLs. You may want to meet with your ELLs before the whole-group lesson to familiarize them with the "classic" versions of the stories the class will study. In order to put a twist on a classic tale, they *must* be thoroughly familiar with the tale.

Display both of these books for the class to see and recall. **ELL** Provide Comprehensible Input—Visuals. Showing the books under discussion will give ELLs a nonlinguistic cue about what's going on, so they can orient themselves to the content of this lesson.

Discuss what elements of the classic tale were changed to create the alternative version. For example, in *Prince Cinders*, the author changed several of the characters to create a completely new twist on the story.

Teach Model what students need to learn and do

Review the elements of a fairy tale that you introduced during Reading Lesson 3. These elements include character(s), setting(s), problem, solution, and key events.

Now, take out the Fairy Tales We Know . . . for Now Chart that you created during Reading Lesson 1. Review this list with the class, choosing one title to focus on today. For the purposes of this lesson, we have chosen to work with *Cinderella*; however, you may choose to use any other classic fairy tale that is familiar to the majority of your class.

Using a blank Elements of Fairy Tales Graphic Organizer, work collaboratively with the class to determine the elements of this tale. Now model for students, changing *one* of these essential elements. Be bold in your changes. Put an X through the element you wish to change, and jot your ideas right on the same graphic organizer. For example, you might choose to set the tale in a city. Or you might choose to change a key event. Perhaps the prince breaks the glass slipper. **ELL** Provide Comprehensible Input— Organizers, Modeling. The act of physically crossing out one element in the organizer and changing it will make clear to your ELLs how to add a twist to a story. This makes the assignment transparent for students who may not understand all your oral directions.

Here is one way your modeling could unfold:

Changing just one of these elements could make for an entirely different story, just like changing the character made a big difference in Prince Cinders. Hmmmm . . . let me think of a few possibilities. I could change the setting and have the story take place in a city. Or I could change one of these key events. Maybe the glass slipper breaks while the prince is traveling around the kingdom asking girls to try it on. Let's see . . . which change would make for the most interesting new tale? I think I might make the glass slipper break. That could change the story a lot!

Try Guide students to quickly rehearse what they need to learn and do in preparation for practice

Invite your class to join in the fun. Instruct them to choose a different element from *Cinderella* to change. Then ask students to turn and share their idea with a partner.

What element could you change?

Circulate as partners talk, listening in for interesting ideas to share with the entire class. This type of student conversation provides a wonderful opportunity to reinforce speaking with clarity and questioning the speaker for additional detail when necessary. (SL.2.1c)

ELL Identify and Communicate Content and Language Objectives— Check for Understanding. Use this time to confer with your ELLs to see how they may need support for their responses. Are they clear on the assignment? Do they have the words to express their ideas? Listen closely so that the support you offer meets their language *and* content needs.

Once students have had ample time to share, gather everyone's attention and share several ideas. Choose one to pursue further. Discuss how that change would impact the remainder of the tale. Use the following prompts to help guide your conversation:

- How would this new element change the story?
- What other parts of the story would need to change so that this new element makes sense?
- Let's tell this new version of the story out loud right now.

Clarify Briefly restate today's teaching objective and explain the practice task(s)

Instruct each student to choose a classic fairy tale to work with. Distribute copies of the Elements of Fairy Tales Graphic Organizer.

Today I'd like each of you to change ONE element in a classic fairy tale. Begin by filling out the Elements of Fairy Tales Graphic Organizer for the fairy tale as it is now. Then cross out one element and jot down your changes, just like I did here. Then get some writing paper and take a stab at writing this new version. Let's see what new and interesting tales we can create with just one new element.

ELL Identify and Communicate Content and Language Objectives—Avoid Idioms. Note that the expressions "jot down" and "take a stab at" are idiomatic and may be confusing for your ELLs. Be aware of idioms when you give directions.

Practice Students work independently and/or in small groups to apply today's teaching objective

Students work independently to fill out the Elements of Fairy Tales Graphic Organizer. Students then cross out and change one element of this tale. Each student should then attempt to draft the new version of a classic fairy tale

for themselves. **ELL** Enable Language Production—Reading and Writing. Use this time to confer with your ELLs to see how they may need support for their writing. Some students, especially recent arrivals with prior schooling in their home language, may need to begin their work in their home language, just to get their ideas out; they can work on translating into English later. Some students may need to tell you orally about their ideas before attempting to get them down on paper.

Allow students ample time to complete this task, perhaps stretching the lesson out across two or three days. In Writing Lesson 4, students will start a new tale.

Wrap Up Check understanding as you guide students to briefly share what they have learned and produced today

Gather the class, asking them to share their work. Choose two or three students to share their graphic organizers and/or read aloud to the class their newly drafted tales. **ELL** Enable Language Production—Listening and Speaking. If you have given your students ample time to compose their ideas, your ELLs in particular may feel more confident about sharing with the group than they felt earlier in the lesson. Writing and conferring with you have allowed them to get their words ready, and they should be encouraged to take this moment to shine!

Writing Lesson 4

▼ Teaching Objective

Writers plan an organized sequence of events to include in a tale.

Close Reading Opportunity

▼ Standards Alignment

RL.2.1, RL.2.2, RL.2.3, R.2.10, W.2.3, W.2.5, W.2.8, SL.2.1a, SL.2.1b, SL.21.c, SL.2.2, SL.2.4, SL.2.6, L.2.1, L.2.2, L.2.3, L.2.6

▼ Materials

- Planning a Fairy Tale Graphic Organizer (Appendix 2.7)
- Adaptation of "The Princess and the Pea" (Appendix 2.8)

▼ To the Teacher

In today's lesson, students will plan an original fairy tale. While this lesson encourages students to reimagine a classic tale by changing at least one story element in significant ways, there is also room for students to create an entirely original tale. Use your judgment to decide which students may benefit from the support of altering a familiar tale and which students are capable of and interested in creating something entirely from scratch.

This lesson asks students to plan and draft their fairy tale. Students begin by working with a graphic organizer. Allow at least one full day of planning for students to organize their thinking. You will want to allow students ample time to delve into drafting this tale, relying on their graphic organizer. Therefore, this lesson is best taught across multiple days. If several students plan and complete thoughtful drafts of a fairy tale before the class is ready to move on to the next writing lesson, direct those students to plan and draft an entirely new tale.

▼ Procedure

Warm Up Gather the class to set the stage for today's learning

Review the work you did during Writing Lesson 3. Students worked to change one element of a classic tale and then created a draft of their new twist on the fairy tale.

Teach Model what students need to learn and do

Name: _____   Date: _____

Planning a Fairy Tale

Title:		
Setting:	Good Characters:	Evil Characters:

Introduction	Problem	Key Event 1	Key Event 2	Solution

Remind the class that it is important for authors to carefully plan the stories they wish to write, even if they are adaptations of familiar tales. Authors

think ahead and often have an entire story in their heads before they lift the pen to write. Young writers will certainly benefit from planning ideas in advance of writing.

Introduce the class to the Planning a Fairy Tale Graphic Organizer (Appendix 2.7). Point out and describe each portion of the graphic organizer. It has places for students to sketch and name the good and evil characters, as well as space to sketch and quickly describe the setting. In addition, the organizer contains five boxes, each with room for a quick sketch and some notes, for students to plan the introduction, the problem, two key events, and the solution to their fairy tale. As you go over the graphic organizer with the class, be sure to make concrete connections between the different parts of the graphic organizer and the elements of a fairy tale. **ELL** Provide Comprehensible Input—Graphic Organizers. Providing an organizer makes the task at hand clearer for your ELLs; it will allow them to follow the instruction better and to organize their ideas more easily when they begin to write.

Model for the class how to plan an adaptation of an original fairy tale using the graphic organizer. First, choose a classic fairy tale you would like to adapt. For the purposes of this lesson, you will notice that we have chosen "The Princess and the Pea"; however, you can certainly choose to focus on another classic tale. Then quickly retell the story. Next, think aloud about the element you would like to change. Now, move to recording your plan on the Planning a Fairy Tale Graphic Organizer. You can plan your own original adaptation as part of this lesson or use the adaptation of "The Princess and the Pea" that we have included for your convenience in Appendix 2.8. If you choose to use this tale as your demonstration piece, here is what your graphic organizer might look like:

This example represents a completed graphic organizer. However, be sure to begin with a blank organizer (Appendix 2.7) and demonstrate thinking through and filling out the sheet in front of the class. Here is what your modeling might sound like as you think aloud about the changes you wish to make to the ending of this classic tale:

> Remember, I decided to change the ending or solution of this fairy tale. In the original version, the princess marries the prince and they live happily ever after. In my version, the princess is going to say, "No thank you" when the prince proposes. I want her to think that discovering a pea under a pile of mattresses is ridiculous and no reason to marry someone.

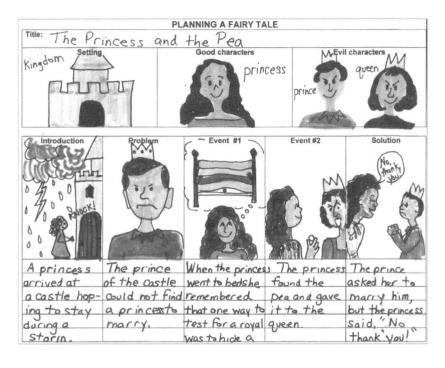

PLANNING A FAIRY TALE

Title: The Princess and the Pea

Setting	Good characters	Evil characters
Kingdom	princess	prince, queen

Introduction	Problem	Event #1	Event #2	Solution
A princess arrived at a castle hoping to stay during a storm.	The prince of the castle could not find a princess to marry.	When the princess went to bed she remembered that one way to test for a royal was to hide a	The princess found the pea and gave it to the queen.	The prince asked her to marry him, but the princess said, "No thank you!"

Sketch this ending in the box labeled "solution" on your graphic organizer. Jot a note or two, such as "The princess says, 'No thank you.'"

Reiterate the process of your thinking and planning once your graphic organizer is complete. **ELL** Identify and Communicate Content and Language Objectives—Repeat. By reiterating your thought process one more time, you give your ELLs another chance to understand your language and your instruction. This will help them get ready for independent practice.

> Did you see how I planned a new version of a classic fairy tale? First, I picked a classic fairy tale to adapt. Then I retold the story quickly to myself. After that, I thought about the element I wanted to change. Then I planned out my fairy tale using this graphic organizer.

Try Guide students to quickly rehearse what they need to learn and do in preparation for practice

Ask students to take a moment to choose a classic fairy tale they would like to adapt on their own. Have students quickly turn and share with a partner which fairy tale they have chosen and which element they are considering changing.

Listen in as partners talk, jotting down a few examples of student thinking to share with the entire group once all the partnerships have had ample time to share. **ELL** Enable Language Production—Increasing Interaction. During this time, ELLs are able to learn from their peers and practice their English in an informal forum. This is an opportunity to whisper in when needed or listen in to understand how best to support their language and content needs

Clarify Briefly restate today's teaching objective and explain the practice task(s)

Explain that students will be using their own Planning a Fairy Tale Graphic Organizer to map out their stories during Practice. Then students should move on to using their organizer to help them draft their fairy tale.

> Authors map out the details of their stories to keep them organized. Today, we are using the Planning a Fairy Tale Graphic Organizer to help us plan a new version of a classic fairy tale. Remember, once you've chosen a tale to use, retell that fairy tale to yourself, choose an element to change, and then get planning. Once you've completed your Planning a Fairy Tale Graphic Organizer, it's time to get started drafting your new fairy tale!

Take a moment to demonstrate how to move from a plan to a draft. Using your the graphic organizer that you created during the Teach portion of this lesson, model for students how to get started drafting by turning your plan into sentences. **ELL** Provide Comprehensible Input—Models. This demonstration of how to move from planning to drafting will be crucial for your ELLs, if they did not fully understand your oral explanation of this transition.

Practice Students work independently and/or in small groups to apply today's teaching objective

Students work independently to plan an original adaptation to a classic fairy tale. Each student should choose a tale, retell that tale, and then choose one element to change. Students should complete the Planning a Fairy Tale Graphic Organizer before beginning to draft their tale. Once students have a plan, they should move on to drafting their tale during this lesson.

Check in with students as they continue with this work for a second day. Some students may need guidance with moving from planning their fairy tale to beginning their draft. Consider gathering small groups to support students who may struggle moving from the Planning a Fairy Tale Graphic Organizer to drafting. `ELL` Enable Language Production—Reading and Writing. Ideas often come faster than words—ELLs in particular may need support to get started writing. When partnering ELLs with other students, think of how partners can support language acquisition through sharing in native language, translation, and modeling. Use this time to confer with your ELLs to see how they may need support for their responses—are they struggling with content, or language, or both?

`Wrap Up` Check understanding as you guide students to briefly share what they have learned and produced today

Gather the class, guiding students to share their Planning a Fairy Tale Graphic Organizer with a partner, orally telling their tale as they share.

Then ask the class if there are any writers who are struggling with any part of their writing and would like help from the class. If so, allow that student to present his or her issue and then lead the class in helping brainstorm possible solutions. Cultivate a writer's group feel, where all struggles are taken seriously and all involved work to learn from one another. `ELL` Enable Language Production—Increasing Interaction. It is important to create an atmosphere of supportive sharing in your classroom, so that your ELLs in particular feel comfortable sharing their struggles with their peers, and can benefit from collective support.

Collect and analyze the Planning a Fairy Tale Graphic Organizers as a performance-based assessment to determine if students need additional instruction or support as a whole class, in small groups, or one on one. `ELL` Assess for Content and Language Understandings—Formative Assessment. This is opportunity for you to assess your ELLs' language and content needs and then use this information to inform upcoming lessons. If students are struggling to write adaptations, be sure to thoughtfully consider the root of the problems: Are they working with an unfamiliar story? Did they misunderstand your directions to change something? Do they have good ideas but struggle to find the English words to express them? Each issue will require a different instructional response.

Milestone Performance Assessment

Sequence and Key Elements

 Use this checklist to assess student work on the Planning a Fairy Tale Graphic Organizer.

Standards Alignment: RL.2.1, RL.2.2, RL.2.3, W.2.3, W.2.5, W.2.8

Task	Achieved	Notes
Plan a sequential tale.		
Identify key elements of a classic tale.		
Change one key element of a classic tale.		

Writing Lesson 5 ·

▼ Teaching Objective

Writers create dynamic stories by including character thought and dialogue.

Close Reading Opportunity

▼ Standards Alignment

RL.2.1, RL.2.10, W.2.3, W.2.5, SL.2.1a, SL.2.1b, SL.21.c, SL.2.2, SL.2.4, SL.2.6, L.2.1, L.2.2, L.2.3, L.2.6

▼ Materials

- Original adaptation of "The Princess and the Pea" (Appendix 2.8)
- Student writing
- Charting supplies or interactive whiteboard
- *Good Little Wolf* by Nadia Shireen

▼ To the Teacher

As you move into teaching this lesson, your students should have at least one draft developed from their Fairy Tale Planning Graphic Organizers. While the draft does not have to be entirely complete by this point, it is beneficial for students to have a fair amount of writing to work with in order to truly be able to practice today's objective. If you have students with multiple drafts, have them select one draft to work with initially, and then encourage them to revisit other drafts with this teaching in mind.

This lesson includes extensive practice within the lesson itself, as it asks students to examine their own work and practice revising to add dialogue or internal thinking during the Try. Therefore, this lesson may run longer than your typical writing lesson. If you find students are not left with ample time to work independently on their own drafts, extend this lesson another day.

▼ Procedure

Warm Up Gather the class to set the stage for today's learning

Choose for reading aloud to the class a short portion of a fairy tale that includes interesting dialogue and/or internal thought. For the purposes of this lesson, we have chosen to use a section of *Good Little Wolf*, in which Rolf is talking to the Little Pig. Read these pages aloud to the class.

> The author could have just written that Rolf tried to blow down the Little Pig's house and couldn't. But these pages are more interesting than that. What techniques or tricks did the author use to make these pages more interesting? Find an example from the text to support your thinking.

Some details from the text that your students might notice include:

- character dialogue
- descriptive character action

Teach Model what students need to learn and do

Connect your discussion during the Warm Up to your teaching objective for today.

> Writers are usually avid readers. They read to study and enjoy the writing of other people and are often inspired to try new ideas in their own writing. Today we noticed that the author of *Good Little Wolf* used talking and thinking details to make this part of the story more interesting. As writers, we are going to use what we noticed as inspiration and try our hand at adding similar details to our own writing.

Specifically define for students the terms *dialogue* and *internal thinking*.

ELL Identify and Communicate Content and Language Objectives—Key Content Vocabulary. Demystifying, defining, visualizing, and translating key content vocabulary are all ways to meet ELLs' language needs and to help them begin to build an understanding of these key terms.

> Dialogue refers to conversation between two or more characters—or more simply, what the characters are actually *saying*. Internal thinking refers to the thoughts that occur to a character but that are not said out loud—or what the character thinks to himself or herself.

Provide an example of writing that includes dialogue and internal thinking. You can choose a moment from a familiar fairy tale or your own writing. For the purposes of this lesson, we have chosen to use an original version of "The Princess and the Pea," which is included for your convenience in Appendix 2.8.

Before you reread this fairy tale aloud to the class, charge your students with a specific listening task. Ask students to listen specifically for examples of dialogue or internal thinking. Instruct students to raise their hand when they have just heard this type of detail read. (This listening task provides an excellent opportunity to informally assess students' ability to recount details from material read aloud.) (SL.2.2) Now, reread aloud to the class the original adaptation of "The Princess and the

Pea" (Appendix 2.8). Pause in your reading as students raise their hands. Discuss each example identified by the class. Are these indeed examples of dialogue and internal thinking or teachable moments to clarify students' misunderstanding? **ELL** Identify Content and Language Objectives—Check for Understanding. ELLs in particular may struggle with this language-heavy task, as they may not be familiar with the phrases authors use to signal dialogue or internal thinking, or they may be focused on just figuring out what the text means. Listen carefully to the contributions they make, and check in with them to ensure they're following the lesson. While dialogue is more easily identified, below are several examples of how internal thinking is shown in this story:

- "Maybe I should leave," she thought, . . .
- "But how silly," she thought. "That wouldn't tell you anything about someone."

Demonstrate for students how to include and create character dialogue and internal thinking. Begin by helping students identify the most relevant places to insert dialogue or internal thinking into their own writing. As a general rule, authors include dialogue or internal thinking at the most important point in their stories.

> Writers include details such as dialogue and internal thinking at the most important parts of their stories. In "The Princess and the Pea," one of the most interesting and important parts is the first key event, when the princess is invited inside the castle. Take a closer look at that part of the story. The author added a lot of dialogue, or talking, between the princess and the servant. (Highlight the second, third and fourth paragraphs of this story.) What does the dialogue do here? The added dialogue draws out the suspense of this event: Will the princess get invited inside or not? This makes the reader get excited wondering what will happen. You can add dialogue at the most important parts of your stories too.

Now, model for students how to conceive of what their character might say or think. Guide students to imagine themselves in their character's shoes—What might they say or think in the same situation?

> Turn students' attention to the following important moment from "The Princess and the Pea" (Appendix 2.8).

> After dinner, the princess was shown into a guest chamber. The bed was piled with mattresses and featherbeds nearly to the ceiling. She climbed up the pile and sat on top of it, feeling ridiculous.

Think aloud about what you might think to yourself if you were in the character's shoes.

> Let me imagine I am in the princess's shoes. I am sleeping at a stranger's house. I am shown to a bedroom with a pile of mattresses and blankets that reaches almost to the ceiling. I actually have to climb up into bed—maybe even on a ladder. I might think to myself, "This place is getting crazier by the second." Watch me as I add that into this story.

Demonstrate adding this piece of internal thinking into the story, modeling a system for inserting additional text (such as a caret) and proper use of quotation marks. **ELL** Identify and Communicate Content and Language Objectives—Language Form and Function. Through this model of written language conventions, you are demystifying a common literary practice and helping your ELLs participate in a community of authors.

Try Guide students to quickly rehearse what they need to learn and do in preparation for practice

Reiterate the importance of dialogue and internal thinking as key details of a dynamic tale. Then direct students to turn to their own writing. Each student should determine an important moment in his or her fairy tale.

> Take a moment and reread your work to find an important event in your own fairy tale.

Give students a moment to identify this section of their tale.

Now encourage students to think about what the characters might say or think at this point in the story, guiding them to place themselves in the shoes of their character. Once students have a moment to gather their thoughts, instruct them to turn and share their plans for these revisions with a partner. Circulate as students discuss their ideas, coaching students who struggle to come up with relevant dialogue or internal thinking for their characters. Keep watch for examples of student work to share with the whole class. **ELL** Enable Language Production—Increasing Interaction. Peer discussion lets ELLs hear more examples of dialogue from English-proficient peers and gives them a low-pressure environment in which to rehearse their own ideas. This is an opportunity to whisper in when needed or listen in to understand how best to support their language and content needs.

Once students have had ample time to discuss their ideas, gather the class's attention and share one or two examples of successful student revisions with the entire class.

Direct students to make these changes in their writing right now. Take a moment to once again give students practical suggestions on how they might add additional sentences into an already-existing draft. Use a piece of student work as an example, demonstrating methods of making revisions directly on the draft. Model using a caret to indicate the place where additional sentences are to be inserted. Then demonstrate how to add more writing in the margins—on a sticky note or a revision strip that can be taped to the margin of the draft. **ELL** Enable Language Production—Reading and Writing. Modeling through student work is another important scaffolding strategy for ELLs. It lets them see how the strategy you are teaching could be applied to their own work and sets them up for success during independent practice.

Goodluz/Fotolia

Clarify Briefly restate today's teaching objective and explain the practice task(s)

Briefly review the definitions of dialogue and internal thinking. Reiterate that including these two types of details makes writing more dynamic and interesting for the reader. Writers add these sorts of details to the most important parts of their stories. Then instruct the class to work to include both dialogue and internal thinking in their current fairy tale as well as any other fairy tales they might have drafted during this lesson set.

Reread your writing today. What did the characters say to each other? What were they thinking during the most important moments of your fairy tale?

Practice Students work independently and/or in small groups to apply today's teaching objective

Students reread their drafts independently, with a focus on adding character dialogue and internal thinking. Students should also attempt to correctly use quotation marks in their work. Mastery of this, however, is not expected of second graders.

At the end of Practice, ask each student to pick one example from their work to share with the class.

Wrap Up Check understanding as you guide students to briefly share what they have learned and produced today

Ask students to share their examples with a partner. Then have several students share their work with the entire class. Be sure to specifically highlight and praise creative thinking as well as correct use of quotation marks. **ELL** Enable Language Production—Increasing Interaction. This is an excellent time for ELLs to solidify their understanding of this language-heavy lesson by sharing their written work aloud and by hearing their peers' examples as well.

Writing Lesson 6

▼ Teaching Objective

Writers create dynamic stories by describing characters' actions.

Close Reading
Opportunity

▼ Standards Alignment

RL.2.1, RL.2.3, RL.2.10, W.2.3, W.2.5, SL.2.1a, SL.2.1b, SL.21.c, SL.2.2, SL.2.4, SL.2.6, L.2.1, L.2.2, L.2.3, L.2.6

▼ Materials

- Original adaptation of "The Princess and the Pea," projected or enlarged for easy student access (Appendix 2.8)
- Student writing

▼ To the Teacher

In first grade, Core Ready writers are exposed to the idea of adding more specific and descriptive character actions as a way to make their writing more exciting. In this lesson (which builds on that prior teaching for those who have had it and introduces the concept to students who have not yet), we focus exclusively on these types of character details: how they enhance a piece of writing, what they sound like, and how to strategically pick and choose moments to include them.

▼ Procedure

Warm Up Gather the class to set the stage for today's learning

Gather students with their fairy tale drafts and introduce your focus for today's teaching.

> Today we are going to spice up your writing by adding descriptions of the characters' movements and actions: How are the characters in your fairy tales moving their bodies? What exactly are they doing?

Teach Model what students need to learn and do

Revisit the writing you shared as an example during Writing Lessons 5, reinforcing for students that authors return to and revise their writing many times. **ELL** Frontload the Lesson—Make Connections. Reminding ELLs of the work you have already been doing will help them orient themselves to this new lesson and get their minds ready to learn. For the purposes of this lesson, we will revisit the original version of "The Princess and the Pea" included in Appendix 2.8.

Before you read your example aloud to the class, charge your students with a specific listening task. Ask students to listen specifically for moments in which the characters' movements and actions—when the characters actually do something with their bodies—are described clearly. Instruct students to raise their hand when they have just heard this type of detail read. **ELL** Frontload the Lesson—Set a Purpose for Reading. Assigning a specific listening task helps your ELLs focus on the most important information as you read aloud. Now, read aloud to the class "The Princess and the Pea." Pause in your reading as students raise their hands. Discuss each example identified by the class. Are they indeed identifying character action as opposed to other details related to the character? If needed, take a moments to address students' misunderstanding. **ELL** Identify Content and Language Objectives—Check for Understanding. This is another language-heavy task: ELLs might not be familiar with the words the author uses to describe actions. As they offer contributions, listen carefully for any content or language misunderstandings. Below are several examples of descriptive character action included in this story:

- "... a young woman knocked on the door of a castle."
- "The servant whispered into the queen's ear ..."
- "She climbed up the pile and sat on top of it. ..."
- "The prince dropped to one knee."
- "The princess bridled her horse and rode off into the dewy, shining countryside."

Highlight each example within the text, using a bright color. Think aloud about the location of these phrases and sentences—they are sprinkled throughout the entire story, not just in one particular scene or moment.

> I want you to take a minute and look at the sentences we highlighted. Notice where they are within the story. They are not simply at the beginning or the end or even in just one scene. They are sprinkled throughout the entire story, giving us a clear idea of what each character is doing in the most important moments. Think about this as you decide where and how often to add these types of details to your own work. In each important moment in your writing, ask yourself, "Did I clearly describe what the character is doing with his or her body?"

Introduce the term *verb* to the class, taking a moment to define verbs for the class. **ELL** Identify and Communicate Content and Language Objectives—Academic Vocabulary. Naming and describing parts of speech gives ELLs access to discussions of grammar and language in use. This information will be helpful to them as they acquire and use English.

Verbs are action words, commonly referred to as "doing words," and can often be the most exciting part of a sentence. We want to draw students' attention to the active verbs used in this piece. Work with students to circle the verb in each example from "The Princess and The Pea" (knocked, whispered, climbed, dropped, bridled, rode). Remark on how dynamic and descriptive each verb is. The verbs provide the reader with a clear picture of what the character is doing.

> These verbs really pack a punch! Each one is different and clearly describes what the character is doing with his or her body in that moment. These are the types of verbs you want to use throughout your writing so that readers are able to get a clear picture in their minds of the action.

ELL Identify and Communicate Language and Content Objectives—Avoid Idioms. Note that expressions like "pack a punch" are idiomatic—no one is punching anyone—and may be confusing for your ELLs. Be aware of such expressions as you explain content and give directions.

Try Guide students to quickly rehearse what they need to learn and do in preparation for practice

Direct students to reread their own drafts in order to find one place to add more-descriptive character action.

As you reread your draft, look for one moment to add in a more detailed description of what your character is doing with his or her body. Remember, these details usually show up during the most important moments in a story. These types of details also include active and dynamic verbs. When you find a place to add in this type of detail, go ahead and do it right now.

Give students several moments to work. As students delve into their drafts, circulate among the group and support their efforts. You may need to give on-the-spot direction about how students should physically add these details. **ELL** Enable Language Production—Reading and Writing. Check in with your ELLs to help them think of appropriate, interesting verbs. They may have found good places to describe action but lack the English vocabulary they need. Take a moment to review practical suggestions (first introduced in Writing Lesson 5) on how students might add additional sentences into an already-existing draft. Model using a caret to indicate the place where additional sentences are to be inserted. Then demonstrate how to add more writing in the margins—on a sticky note or a revision strip that can be taped to the margin of the draft. If necessary, stop and give a quick demonstration of using a caret to insert a sentence into the middle of a piece of writing.

Have several students share their work with the entire class. Highlight and praise the use of dynamic verbs.

Clarify Briefly restate today's teaching objective and explain the practice task(s)

Reinforce several key ideas for students:

- Descriptive details about a character's actions make writing more interesting.
- These details usually include dynamic, active verbs.
- Look for the important moments in a story and ask, "Did I clearly describe the characters' actions?"

> Reread your writing today, looking for the most important moments or events in your fairy tales. In those moments, ask yourself if you included specific descriptions of the characters' actions. Remember, these details include active and exciting verbs and will definitely make your writing more enjoyable.

Practice Students work independently and/or in small groups to apply today's teaching objective

Students reread their drafts independently, with a focus on finding moments to add more descriptive details about characters' actions. Students should find at least three moments within their fairy tales in which to include these types of descriptions and attempt to use specific, dynamic verbs. If students complete this objective with writing time to spare, direct them to continue drafting or to plan and draft another version of a classic fairy tale. **ELL** Enable Language Production—Reading and Writing. Consider keeping some kind of class list of dynamic, interesting verbs. That way, your ELLs have a resource to turn to when they struggle to put their ideas into words, and they won't always have to seek your help.

While it is not the expectation that every student completes drafts of multiple fairy tales, many second graders are prolific writers, capable of producing several stories during a lesson set. We want to allow room for those writers to flourish, while providing the necessary support and encouragement for more-reluctant writers to complete at least one draft of a fairy tale during this lesson set. All students will publish only one tale at the end of this lesson set.

At the end of Practice, ask each student to pick one example from his or her work to share with the class.

Wrap Up Check understanding as you guide students to briefly share what they have learned and produced today

Ask students to share their examples with a partner. Then have several students share their work with the entire class. Be sure to specifically highlight and praise the use of character action phrases with dynamic verbs. **ELL** Enable Language Production—Listening and Speaking. This is a great chance for your ELLs to hear other examples of interesting verbs from their peers and get ideas for how they can describe their own characters' actions. Finally, transcribe several student examples to display in the classroom so that this type of detailed writing might transcend the genre of fairy tales and find its place in all types of student writing. **ELL** Identify and Communicate Content and Language Objectives—Language Form and Function. ELLs can refer back to these examples of excellent work to get ideas for how to express action in writing.

Writing Lesson 7

▼ Teaching Objective

Writers create dynamic stories by describing characters' feelings.

Close Reading Opportunity

▼ Standards Alignment

RL.2.1, RL.2.3, RL.2.10, W.2.3, W.2.5, SL.2.1a, SL.2.1b, SL.21.c, SL.2.2, SL.2.4, SL.2.6, L.2.1, L.2.2, L.2.3, L.2.6

▼ Materials

- Original adaptation of "The Princess and the Pea" (Appendix 2.8)
- Student writing
- Charting supplies or interactive whiteboard

▼ To the Teacher

Today we build upon students' repertoire of engaging details by focusing on how to add in details that show how a character is feeling. Rather than asking students to add to their work details such as "He or she felt sad," we want to push them to be more creative and compelling as writers. Therefore, this lesson focuses on adding in details such as "The king frowned"—as a way of *showing*, not just *telling*, how a character is feeling.

▼ Procedure

Warm Up Gather the class to set the stage for today's learning

Have students think back to the work they did as writers during Writing Lessons 5 and 6. Can students articulate the objectives from these lessons and discuss how these objectives can impact their lives as writers? Students reread drafts to find important moments within their fairy tales in which to add specific details describing character action, as a way to make their writing more exciting. Today, students will revisit their drafts yet again, but this time with a focus on incorporating details about characters' feelings.

> Authors rarely read their writing only once. They read and reread and then reread again, each time adding new and exciting details that help tell their story better. Yesterday, we added details that described your characters' actions in exciting ways. Today, we are going to revisit our drafts yet again—just like true authors—and look for moments in which to add in details that show readers how our characters are feeling.

Teach Model what students need to learn and do

Specifically define for students what it means, as writers, to *show* rather than *tell* how a character is feeling. Set up a simple two-column grid on a chart titled "How Do We Show Our Feelings?" **ELL** Provide Comprehensible

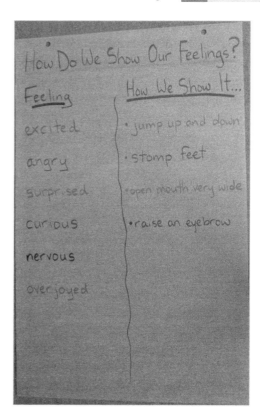

Input—Graphic Organizers. Graphic organizers and charts will be a strong anchor that your ELLs refer to when reading and writing independently. This chart will also help make your teaching point clearer than words alone would. Offer visuals and graphics whenever applicable to represent strategies and enhance vocabulary acquisition.

Use the left column to list a variety of emotions. Reserve the right column to collect a variety of examples of how individuals show these emotions. Here are examples of what your chart should look like:

How Do We Show Our Feelings?

Feeling or Emotion	How We Show It . . .

Begin by brainstorming with your class a list of emotion words to add to the left-hand column. Take a moment to ensure that students understand the meaning of each emotion, using real-life examples as needed. Encourage your class to suggest a wide range of interesting emotions, rather than relying on *happy* and *sad* alone. **ELL** Identify and Communicate Content and Language Objectives—Key Content Vocabulary. Bear in mind that your ELLs might be stuck on "happy" and "sad" because they don't know many other words for feelings in English. This list will be great resource for them. Be sure to help them develop a nuanced understanding of these terms (e.g., "excited" is not the same as "happy") by acting them out and giving examples. Here is a brief list of dynamic emotions. Use these as needed to get students' thinking flowing.

- excited
- angry
- surprised
- jealous

- curious
- disappointed
- overjoyed
- nervous

Now, choose one or two emotion words to focus on. Think aloud about how you might *show* that you are feeling this way with your facial expression or body movements. Dramatically act out this emotion. Don't hold back—the class will love it! **ELL** Provide Comprehensible Input—Visuals. By acting out key terms, you are helping your ELLs build a deep understanding of their meaning. Then record your thinking on the chart. For example, for *curious* you might raise an eyebrow.

Here are a few examples:

How Do We Show Our Feelings?

Feeling or Emotion	How We Show It ...
excited	jump up and down
angry	stomp feet
surprised	opened wide mouth and eyes
curious	raise an eyebrow
nervous	
sad	

Transition the class to thinking about how and where to add these types of details into their writing. Revisit the writing you shared during Writing Lessons 5 and 6, reinforcing for students that authors return to and revise their writing many times. For the purposes of this lesson, we will revisit the original version of "The Princess and the Pea" included in Appendix 2.8.

Before you read your example aloud to the class, charge your students with a new listening task. Ask them to listen specifically for moments in which the characters' feelings are described clearly. Instruct students to raise their hand when they have just heard this type of detail read. **ELL** Frontload the Lesson—Set a Purpose for Reading. Giving your ELLs a focus for listening helps them zero in on the most important information and avoid getting overwhelmed by the language they don't understand. Now, reread aloud to the class "The Princess and the Pea." Pause in your reading as students raise their hands. Discuss each example identified by the class. Are these indeed examples of "showing, not telling" or moments to correct students' misunderstanding? **ELL** Identify and Communicate Content and Language Objectives—Check for Understanding. Again, ELLs might not be familiar with the words the author uses to show feelings, and may struggle to find examples of "showing not telling." Listen thoughtfully to their contributions, direct their attention to strong models from their peers (and act out the examples if necessary), and check in with them to make sure they understand the teaching point and have the language to enact it.

Below are several examples of how feelings are shown in this story:

- "The servant whispered into the queen's ear, and her eyes lit up."
- "The queen smiled."
- "The queen clapped her hands."
- "The queen and the prince sat with their jaws open."

Highlight each example within the text using a bright color. Think aloud about the location of these phrases and sentences—again, they are sprinkled throughout the entire story, not just in one particular scene or moment.

> I want you to take a minute and look at the sentences we highlighted. Notice where they are within the story. Just like we noticed when looking at details that describe characters' actions, details about characters' feelings are not simply at the beginning or the end or in just one scene. They are sprinkled throughout the entire story, giving us a clear idea of how characters are feeling during the most important moments. Think about this as you decide where and how often to add these types of details to your own work. In each important moment in your writing, ask yourself, "Did I show how my character is feeling at this moment?"

Try Guide students to quickly rehearse what they need to learn and do in preparation for practice

Direct students to reread their own drafts to look for places that show how a character is feeling.

> As you reread your draft, look for one moment to show us how a character is feeling. Remember, these details usually show up during the most important moments in a story. When you find a place to add in this type of detail, go ahead and do it.

Have several students share their work with the whole class. Highlight and praise original and creative ideas, adding relevant ones to the How Do We Show Our Feelings? Chart. **ELL** Enable Language Production—Increasing Interaction. ELLs will benefit from hearing more examples of "showing not telling" from their peers, so they get more exposure to the vocabulary and structure of this aspect of author's craft. They can also benefit from sharing their ideas and receiving feedback.

Clarify Briefly restate today's teaching objective and explain the practice task(s)

Reinforce several key ideas for students

- Descriptive details about a character's feelings make writing more interesting.

- These details usually show how a character is feeling.

- Look for the important moments in a story and ask, "Did I show how the characters are feeling?"

Reread your writing, looking for the most important moments or events in your fairy tales. In those moments, ask yourself if you showed us how the characters are feeling. Remember, simply telling the reader how a character feels is less exciting; push yourself to think about how the character might show his or her emotions with facial expressions or body movements. Act it out at your seat if you have to! Then come up with a way to add those details into your story.

Practice Students work independently and/or in small groups to apply today's teaching objective

Students reread their drafts independently, with a focus on finding moments to add details that show how characters are feeling. Students should find at least three moments within their fairy tales in which to include these types of details. If students complete this objective with writing time to spare, direct them to continue drafting or to plan and draft another version of a classic fairy tale. **ELL** Enable Language Production—Reading and Writing. Check in with your ELLs to see if they need support to find the words to show how their characters feel. Additionally, they may need support to craft appropriate sentences to show their characters' feelings.

At the end of student practice, ask students to pick one example from their work to share with the whole class.

Wrap Up Check understanding as you guide students to briefly share what they have learned and produced today

Ask students to share their examples with a partner. Then have several students share their work with the entire class. Be sure to specifically highlight

and praise creative thinking, adding original ideas to the class chart as appropriate. **ELL** Enable Language Production—Increasing Interaction.

Collect and analyze student writing as a performance-based assessment to determine if students need additional instruction or support as a whole class, in small groups, or one on one. **ELL** Assess for Content and Language Understandings—Formative Assessment. This is opportunity for you to assess your ELLs' language and content needs and then use this information to inform upcoming lessons. Note in particular if students (a) have the vocabulary to show feelings and (b) are able to put that vocabulary together into clear sentences.

Milestone Performance Assessment

Additional Character Information

 Use this checklist to assess student ability to accurately include additional information about characters.

Standards Alignment: W.2.3

Task	Achieved	Notes
Accurately add descriptive character action.		
Include character dialogue.		
Include character internal thinking.		
Accurately add reference to character emotion.		

Writing Lesson 8

▼ Teaching Objective

Writers craft strong endings.

Close Reading Opportunity

▼ Standards Alignment

RL.2.1, RL.2.10, W.2.3, W.2.5, SL.2.1a, SL.2.1b, SL.21.c, SL.2.2, SL.2.4, SL.2.6, L.2.1, L.2.2, L.2.3, L.2.6

▼ Materials

- Original adaptation of "The Princess and the Pea" (Appendix 2.8)
- *The Paper Bag Princess* by Robert Munsch
- Student writing
- Completed student Fairy Tale Planning Graphic Organizers

▼ Procedure

Warm Up — Gather the class to set the stage for today's learning

Ask the class, *What is the most common ending to a fairy tale?*

Once students have identified "and they all lived happily ever after" as the most common ending to fairy tales, question this ending. Do all fairy tales need to end this way? Ask students if anyone has an alternative idea for the ending of their original adaptation of a fairy tale. **ELL** Frontload the Lesson—Set a Purpose for Reading. Your ELLs in particular will benefit from your using a text they already know well. That frees them up to think about alternative endings without getting bogged down by basic comprehension of the story.

Teach — Model what students need to learn and do

Direct the class's attention to the endings of at least one of the Core Texts you have used throughout this lesson set. You may wish to pull from a variety of the nontraditional fairy tales you have shared with your class, but for the purposes of this lesson set, we have chosen to work with *The Paper Bag Princess* precisely because it does not end happily ever after—or at least not in the same way as most classic fairy tales.

Revisit the ending of *The Paper Bag Princess* by rereading the final two pages of text. As in many classic fairy tales, the princess does not ending up marrying the prince and living happily ever after. Rather, the princess, Elizabeth, realizes that the prince, Ronald, is not marriage material and ends up happily ever after all by herself. Lead the class in a brief discussion of this ending. Use the following prompts to guide your conversation:

- Does this fairy tale end "happily ever after?" How do you know?
- How is this ending different from the ending of many classic fairy tales?
- As a reader, are you happy with the way this fairy tale ended? Why?

Point out to the class that this is a strong ending. A strong ending is satisfying to the reader and brings closure to the key events of the story by presenting a clear solution to the story's problem.

A strong ending requires more than just writing, ". . . and then they all went home" or ". . . and they all went to sleep." A strong ending is an ending that feels good to the reader. As an author, you want to make sure that the problem in your story is addressed. Did it get solved? How?

Turn to the example you have been using throughout this lesson set. For the purposes of this lesson set, we have relied upon an original adaptation of "The Princess and the Pea" included in Appendix 2.8.

Reread the ending to "The Princess and the Pea," reproduced below:

The queen smiled. The test had worked again.

"Oh, but I found this," said the princess. She placed the pea on the table.

The queen clapped her hands. The prince dropped to one knee. "Will you marry me?" he asked.

"No, thank you," said the princess. "It was a test. I don't believe either of you passed."

The queen and the prince sat with their jaws open. The princess bridled her horse and rode off into the dewy, shining countryside.

Explain specifically how this represents a strong ending.

Did you notice how this fairy tale ends "happily ever after" for the princess? Not because she ended up marrying the prince, but because she was smart enough to walk away from his silly test. In the last moment of this tale, we are given an image of the princess proudly riding away on her horse as the queen and the prince stare after her. What a fantastic last picture to have in your mind as a reader!

ELL Enable Language Production—Model Language. By sharing a strong ending and identifying what makes it strong, you are helping your ELLs get ready to craft their own endings. You are showing them how "story language" is different from "talking language," and thereby inducting them into the world of authors.

Reiterate that a strong ending provides readers with a solution to the story's problem, leaving them with a strong last image in their minds. This is an important point in the story. Remind students that earlier they learned that authors add to the important points of their stories key details such as what the character is thinking or saying.

Encourage your writers to end their stories by clearly describing what the main character is doing as the tale ends as well as considering what that main character might say or think.

Try Guide students to quickly rehearse what they need to learn and do in preparation for practice

Transition students to considering their own work by asking them to have available the draft of the fairy tale they are currently working on.

Tell students to discuss their ending with a partner. Together partners should consider if this is indeed a strong ending to the tale. If they decide that it isn't, instruct partners to brainstorm stronger endings that include a clear description of a character's action as well as possible dialogue or internal thought. **ELL** Enable Language Production—Increasing Interaction. Discussing drafts with peers lets ELLs see other examples of endings and gives them a chance to practice the teaching point by orally revising their own and others' stories.

Listen in as partners discuss their work and possible strong endings to their fairy tales. Jot down several key moments from conversations to share with the entire class once you have gathered their attention once again. Consider asking one or two students with particularly interesting ideas for a strong ending to share their thinking with the class. Students should describe how the main character's problem will be solved and what the character will be doing at the very end of the tale.

Ways We End Our Fairy Tales

- A dragon uses his fire breath to keep people warm instead of hurting them.
- A princess trades lives with a farmer because she loves playing outside and hates fancy dresses.
- A king makes it illegal to kill spiders because he spent a day as a spider and made many friends.
- A haunted forest isn't scary any more because people learn to take better care of nature.
- A prince decides not to use his final wish because he is happy with his life.
- A talking bear who loves to dance is finally brave enough to audition for a dance recital.

Clarify Briefly restate today's teaching objective and explain the practice task(s)

As you wrap up your fairy tales and revisit drafts of fairy tales you've already ended, keep in mind the importance of a strong ending. Readers want a satisfying ending that leaves a strong image lingering in their minds. How does your character solve the problem presented to him or her? What is going to be the last thing we read about your main character? **ELL** Identify and Communicate Content and Language Objectives—Repeat. Reiterating the teaching point will help ELLs feel confident that they know what to do as they transition to independent practice.

Practice Students work independently and/or in small groups to apply today's teaching objective

Students work independently on their drafts, focusing on crafting strong endings to their fairy tales.

225

Wrap Up Check understanding as you guide students to briefly share what they have learned and produced today

Gather the class. Ask, *Is anyone hoping to create an even stronger ending to their fairy tale?* If so, invite those students to problem solve their ending with the entire class by reading their draft aloud and brainstorming as a group some possibilities for strong endings. **ELL** Enable Language

Production—Increasing Interaction. Collaborating with peers gives ELLs even more models and chances for practice with this language-heavy objective.

If there are no volunteers, have several students read their endings to the class and share why they believe theirs are strong ones; take suggestions from the class as to how these could be made even stronger.

Writing Lesson 9 ....

▼ Teaching Objective

Writers improve their writing by revising and editing their writing collaboratively.

▼ Standards Alignment

W.2.3, W.2.5, W.2.6, SL.2.1a, SL.2.1b, SL.21.c, SL.2.5, SL.2.6, L.2.1, L.2.2, L.2.3, L.2.6

▼ Materials

- Fairy Tale Checklist (Appendix 2.9)
- Student writing

▼ To the Teacher

This lesson may be best taught over two days—one day for revision and one day for editing of conventions. Revision means to "see again," and you will want your students to focus on how they've created dynamic fairy tales using important writing strategies such as adding internal thought, dialogue, and character emotion. Editing is about conventions. Do all of the sentences end in punctuation? Are the names of characters always capitalized? Because this piece of writing was genre-specific, the Fairy Tale Checklist in Appendix 2.9 will serve as an important tool for students to independently account for the story elements they've included, the addition of the types of details focused on throughout the lesson set, as well as the conventions consistent with the second-grade Common Core State Standards that will be most critical to this piece of writing.

Once students have completed their revisions and editing work, it is time to publish their tales prior to sharing them in Reading Lesson 10. Please see a variety of suggestions for publishing student work in the Wrap Up section of this lesson.

▼ Procedure

Warm Up Gather the class to set the stage for today's learning

Review your work from the past few days and orient your students to their job for today, which is to reread their fairy tales for final revisions and the conventions of standard English.

> You have accomplished a lot as authors during this lesson set. For the past few days, we've focused on making our writing more exciting for our readers by adding important details and strong endings. Now, we're ready to do a final read of our stories and check to make sure we've done our job as writers by writing an original adaptation of a classic fairy tale and by making sure our writing is understandable to readers.

Teach Model what students need to learn and do

Revising	Yes/No
Does my fairy tale have magical character(s)?	
Did I describe character actions?	
Did I include character feelings?	
Did I include character thoughts and/or dialogue?	

Revising	Yes/No
Does my fairy tale have a clear problem and solution?	
Does my fairy tale have a strong ending?	
Editing	
Did I check and correct my capitalization?	
Did I check and correct my sentences?	
Did I check and correct my punctuation?	
Did I check and correct my spelling?	

Describe for students what an editor does and explain that they are going to reread their writing to make sure that it has all the components of an imaginative piece of fiction and edit for conventions. **ELL** Identify and Communicate Content and Language Objectives—Key Content Vocabulary. With this lesson, you are reiterating to your students both the key things that characterize a fairy tale, including the type of language used, and reinforcing the conventions of standard written English. Your ELLs really benefit from this explicitness about written language practices.

> When writers go to publish their pieces, they have an editor read over their work to make sure it's clear for the reader. An editor is someone who rereads with a purpose in mind. Today, we are going to reread our stories and use a Fairy Tale Checklist to make sure we've included all the components of a fairy tale, incorporated strong and interesting details, and followed important rules—such as adding periods to the end of our sentences—that make our writing clear to the reader.

Show students the Fairy Tale Checklist and go over each item included for clarity. As you work your way through each item, locate moments or sentences within the original adaptation of "The Princess and the Pea" included in Appendix 2.8 or a piece of writing you created over the past several days that satisfies each component. **ELL** Provide Comprehensible Input—Models. You are continuing to bring your ELLs into the world of English writers by showing them how revision works and demystifying the linguistic conventions of written stories.

Try Guide students to quickly rehearse what they need to learn and do in preparation for practice

Direct students to take out their own piece of writing. Choose an item on the checklist to examine together. Name the item you are going to focus on, and then prompt partners to identify the exact sentence, phrase, or place within their writing that serves as an example of this item. Below is an example of how your directions might unfold:

> Let's take a look together at these next few items on our checklist. Here it says that writers add dialogue to their writing. Turn and talk with your partner: How did you do? Can you find moments where you added character dialogue?

Allow partners sufficient time to turn and talk with one another. Listen in for moments in conversations that you would like to share with the entire class. Then gather the class's attention and highlight the places where students did indeed include various items from the checklist, modeling the process you would like all students to engage in with a partner during Practice. If students are unable to find an example of an item on the checklist, guide them toward making the necessary changes to the piece of writing together. **ELL** Enable Language Production—Increasing Interaction. Discussing with peers will give your ELLs a chance to make sure they understand what the checklist is about and how to review their own work. **ELL** Enable Language Production—Reading and Writing. Make sure your ELLs understand that revision is a normal part of writing and that it's good to find areas to improve. Then help them to figure out *how* to add what is missing: was it an oversight, or are they not sure how to make their meaning clear in English?

Share one or two examples of students' conversations with the class, particularly moments where partners had to work together to revise their writing to incorporate an item from the checklist.

Clarify Briefly restate today's teaching point and explain the independent task(s)

Remind the class to use the Fairy Tale Checklist (in Appendix 2.9) as a guide for their revising and editing. Ensure that students understand that the items on this checklist are not suggestions; rather, they are expectations for student writing.

When reading your fairy tale today, use your Fairy Tale Checklist to ensure that your tale includes all the components of a fairy tale, your writing has the interesting details we discussed during this lesson set, and you've properly used conventions that help our readers understand the story.

Practice Students work independently and/or in small groups to apply today's teaching objective

Students will reread their stories to a partner using the Fairy Tale Checklist. Partners will work to together to determine if the tale satisfies each item on the checklist. In cases where the tale does not satisfy an item, partners will work together to make the necessary changes. **ELL** Provide Comprehensible Input—Graphic Organizers. The checklist will help your ELLs recognize the most important characteristics of fairy tales and will help them stay anchored and focused as they revise and help partners to revise.

Some partnerships may need extra support with this stage of the writing process in order to know how to revise their piece when they see an element missing. Guide these students to revisit the stories they've read so far and to refer back to charts created that offer specifics on the ideas you've discussed during this lesson set. In addition, other students will need additional support with basic writing conventions such as capitalization and punctuation. The Fairy Tale Checklist is designed to help students revise for content as well as for the conventions of standard English.

Wrap Up Check understanding as you guide students to briefly share what they have learned and produced today

Gather the class. Ask students to share examples of moments when their partner contributed to their story by helping them revise or edit one of the items included on the Fairy Tale Checklist.

Collect and analyze students' revised stories as a performance-based assessment to determine if students need additional instruction or support as a whole class, in small groups, or one on one. **ELL** Assess for Content and Language Understandings—Formative Assessment. This is an opportunity for you to assess your ELLs' language and content needs, especially revising and editing strategies. Notice where their gaps are: Have they misunderstood something about the characteristics of fairy tales? Or do they struggle with the

language they need to express those characteristics? Do they need support on written conventions (spelling, punctuation)? Use this information to inform upcoming lessons.

Milestone Performance Assessment

Revising Stories

 Use this checklist to assess student ability to work collaboratively with a partner to edit a story.

Standards Alignment: W.2.3, W.2.5, L.2.1, L.2.2, L.2.3, L.2.6

Task	Achieved	Notes
Revising		
Compare own story elements with checklist.		
Make necessary changes to own fairy tale.		

Task	Achieved	Notes
Revising		
Work with other students to improve fairy tale.		
Fairy tale has magical character(s).		
Describe character actions.		
Include character feelings.		
Include character thoughts and/or dialogue.		
Fairy tale has a clear problem and solution.		
Fairy tale has a strong ending.		
Editing		
Capitalization.		
Sentences.		
Punctuation.		
Spelling.		

As students conclude their partner revisions and editing, guide them toward publishing their writing to share with others. In advance of moving on to Writing Lesson 10 (in which students share their writing), it is necessary to have all students publish their writing. Publishing student writing includes adding illustrations, a cover, and a title. It also includes students presenting their most revised and readable draft. Keep in mind that at this grade level a published work does not always mean perfect command of all writing conventions. Rather, the published work should reflect grade 2–appropriate expectations for spelling, grammar, and punctuation, while still being an accurate representation of a particular student's independent ability. Publishing student work in a way that honors their process and effort may take several days. Allow ample time for this work, as it is an essential piece in the writing process. This box provides fun and practical ideas for publishing student work.

Publishing Idea	Students will need to . . .
Students create a fairy tale picture book.	• add detailed illustrations to each page of their writing • create a cover for their work that includes title, author name, and illustration
Students publish an iBook.	• work with a digital application such as Story Kit or Scribble Press to publish their work as a digital text
Students narrate an audio book with visual support.	• take still photographs of illustrations to go along with their writing • fluently read their writing aloud to be recorded • work with a digital application such as iMovie to create their own audio book

Writing Lesson 10 . . . .

▼ **Teaching Objective**

Writers share their work with pride.

▼ **Standards Alignment**

W.2.6, SL.2.1a, SL.2.1b, SL.21.c, SL.2.2, SL.2.3, SL.2.4, SL.2.5, SL.2.6, L.2.1, L.2.3, L.2.6

▼ Materials

- Completed pieces of student work

▼ To the Teacher

Prior to teaching this lesson, you will want to redistribute the student work you collected as a Milestone Performance Assessment in Writing Lesson 9. Allow your students ample time to publish their work. Please see the table included in Writing Lesson 9 for a variety of publishing options.

Today is a celebratory day! Your students have written and illustrated their own fairy tales. Today is all about sharing their stories with pride.

▼ Procedure

Warm Up Gather the class to set the stage for today's learning

Explain to your class how you plan to recognize their hard work and share their fairy tales with others. (See the low-tech and high-tech options listed below.)

Goal	Low-Tech	High-Tech
Students share and discuss their writing with an authentic audience.	• Invite other classes, staff, and/or parents to a Fairy Tales Extravaganza. Students will read their work aloud to the audience, taking time to show their illustrations. Once students have read their tale, consider holding a brief discussion about their work. • Students donate their fairy tales to the school library, creating a display for their collected works. • Students visit a lower grade to share their fairy tale with kindergarten students.	• Record students as they read their stories aloud, including up-close shots of their illustrations. Upload these recordings online for a virtual Fractured Fairy Tales Festival, asking viewers to respond to what they like about the stories. • Invite students to interact with the digital texts produced by their classmates.

Teach Model what students need to learn and do

Model for students your chosen method of recognition. For example, if you have chosen to make a recording of students reading their original tales to upload onto a class website, demonstrate what that process will look like using your own original tale or "The Princess and the Pea" (Appendix 2.8). Be sure to address behavioral expectations (such as listening with care) and also outline the process for students. Sharing our work with pride meanings conducting ourselves like true students and respectful authors. **ELL** Frontload the Lesson—Set a Purpose for Reading. By making your expectations for sharing clear, you help your ELLs know where to focus their attention as they read aloud.

Try Guide students to quickly rehearse what they need to learn and do in preparation for practice

Ask students to work with a partner to practice reading their fairy tales aloud. Circulate and listen in to partnerships, offering gentle reminders about several key speaking and listening skills to support them as they tell their stories such as including appropriate descriptive details and speaking audibly in coherent sentences. (SL.2.4) **ELL** Enable Language Production—Increasing Interaction. Practicing with peers is a great way to make sure your ELLs feel ready to share their stories with the world in English. Bear in mind also that if you have invited families to the Fairy Tales Extravaganza, you should encourage students to practicing telling their original stories in their home language as well. That way, their parents can be part of the celebration. This also shows respect for all the linguistic and cultural skills your students bring to the classroom.

Clarify Briefly restate today's teaching objective and explain the practice task(s)

Restate your expectations for student performances and behavior.

Practice Students work independently and/or in small groups to apply today's teaching objective

Students share their fairy tales with pride in the method you have selected from the low-tech and high-tech options listed above.

Wrap Up Check understanding as you guide students to briefly share what they have learned and produced today

Ask students to share their favorite moments from friends' fairy tales. Also, have students share what they learned by listening to each other's stories. This will help them think more deeply and critically about how they will share their own stories.

Language Companion Lesson

Note: This lesson is best taught early in the lesson set. Encourage students to recognize descriptive adjectives while reading and to use them to enhance their stories.

▼ Teaching Objective

We can use adjectives to make our writing stronger.

▼ Standards Alignment

L.2.1e

▼ Materials

- Charting supplies or interactive whiteboard

▼ To the Teacher

This lesson is designed to build student awareness of powerful adjectives commonly used in fairy tales. This will serve to strengthen both their reading and writing during the fairy tale lesson set.

▼ Procedure

Warm Up Gather the class to set the stage for today's learning

Introduce the lesson.

> Today we are going to work on adding meaning to our writing by using interesting and exciting adjectives. Adjectives are words that help us describe things. Let's start today by coming up with a list of words we could use to describe things in our fairy tales.

> I have a list started here to give you an idea of the sort of describing words I would use to write a fairy tale.

Display the list on chart paper. Include adjectives commonly found in fairy tales, such as *magical, evil, scary, beautiful,* and *brave.* Read the list to students.

> Now I want you to try to come up with some more descriptive story words to add to our list. Take a minute and think about the characters and places that are in your fairy tales. What words would you use to describe them? When you think you have a really great describing word for our list, put your thumb up.

Have students share their describing words and add them to the list.

ELL Enable Language Production—Listening and Speaking. Realize that your ELLs might not yet have the English vocabulary to describe the characters in their minds. Make sure to clarify the meanings of the words you and their classmates provide to start building their vocabulary; if they offer basic words (like "pretty"), offer more powerful related words (like "elegant" or "breathtaking"); finally, consider letting them offer adjectives in their home language and then use a bilingual peer or a dictionary to help the class determine an English equivalent.

Teach Model what students need to learn and do

> These are some great words you all have come up with! Now we're going to play a game to help us understand what each of these words mean and how they can describe different items. This game is called "Don't Say It!"

Introduce today's word game. It may be helpful to have the rules written somewhere where the class can see them, so they know when to yell "Don't say it!"

> To play, I am going to try to describe one of the words on our list, and I need you all to guess which word it is. There are a couple of rules, though. I can't give you "rhymes with" clues, I can't act out the word in any way, and I definitely can't say the word or any version of the word. If I break any of the rules, you all can yell out, "Don't say it!"

> If you think you know which word I want you to guess, stick your thumb up really high in the air. If you answer incorrectly when I call on you, we'll keep playing the round until somebody gets the right answer.

Try Guide students to quickly rehearse what they need to learn and do in preparation for practice

Try a practice round with the class using the word *magical* before getting into the game. You can use prompts such as these:

- This word could describe a witch.

- It could also describe a fairy godmother.

- You can use it to refer to an event that would be impossible in real life.

Play the game with the class. Try choosing words that are progressively more difficult as you continue. **ELL** Identify Content and Language Objectives—Key Content Vocabulary. This game is a great way for your ELLs to deepen their understanding of new adjectives in a fun, low-pressure setting.

Clarify Briefly restate today's teaching objective and explain the practice task(s)

Encourage students to add to their writing some of the new descriptive words they've learned.

Practice Students work independently and/or in small groups to apply today's teaching objective

Provide students time and encouragement to add interesting and exciting adjectives into the fairy tales. Leave up for inspiration the list you've created together. **ELL** Enable Language Production—Reading and Writing. Check in with your ELLs to see how they are doing in adding adjectives to their writing. Make sure they are clear about what kinds of words adjectives are (content clarification), and help them extend their thinking by offering more challenging synonyms or referring them to the class list (language support).

Wrap Up Check understanding as you guide students to briefly share what they have learned and produced today

Have students share a few sections or sentences from their writing that they have made stronger using adjectives.

GLOSSARY

characters: people in a story, play, or movie.

dialogue: a talk between two or more people or between characters in a play, film, or book.

emotion: a strong feeling such as love, hatred, or fear.

event: something that happens, especially an important thing that occurs.

evil: the opposite of good, anything wrong or bad, wickedness.

fairy tale: a story that tells of magical events and creatures in a make-believe or imaginary world. The story involves characters such as knights and princesses, and usually take place in an imaginary past time.

good: doing what is right, behaving in a proper way, being kind.

illustration: a picture or drawing usually used to explain or decorate a book or other written material or text.

internal thinking: what we assume the character is thinking through his/her actions.

message/lesson: spoken or written information sent from one person or group to another. A message or lesson is usually something valuable you can gain from the story being read or delivered.

plot: the order of events or storyline in a book, play, or movie.

problem: a question or condition that is difficult to understand or to deal with—often a solution is needed or requested.

setting: the surroundings or environment in which an event takes place.

solution: the act or process of solving a problem or question.

Accompanying *Core Ready for Grades K–2*, there is an online resource site with media tools that, together with the text, provides you with the tools you need to implement the lesson sets.

The PDToolkit for Pam Allyn's *Core Ready* Series is available free for 12 months after you use the password that comes with the box set for each grade band. After that, you can purchase access for an additional 12 months. If you did not purchase the box set, you can purchase a 12-month subscription at **http://pdtoolkit.pearson.com**. Be sure to explore and download the resources available at the website. Currently the following resources are available:

- Pearson Children's and Young Adult Literature Database
- Videos
- PowerPoint Presentations
- Student Artifacts
- Photos and Visual Media
- Handouts, Forms, and Posters to supplement your Core-aligned lesson plans
- Lessons and Homework Assignments
- Close Reading Guides and Samples
- Children's Core Literature Recommendations

In the future, we will continue to add additional resources. To learn more, please visit **http://pdtoolkit.pearson.com**.

APPENDIX K.1 Core Message to Students

Do you have a favorite story book? Maybe you have a favorite author or illustrator? How about a favorite character whose adventures and experiences you love to hear? Do you like a stories that feel real, maybe something similar to what you have experienced? Or do you prefer stories that feature talking animals and people flying in the sky? During this lesson set, we are going to read, reread, retell, and create stories together. All stories, whether new or old, real or imagined, are made up of story elements. Throughout this lesson set, identifying the various story elements will help us make meaning of a story and help us create stories to share with our friends. I look forward to enjoying and sharing stories together.

Instructions to Teacher: Copy and clip apart to distribute to students.

Characters	Characters	Characters	Characters
Setting	Setting	Setting	Setting
Event #1	Event #1	Event #1	Event #1
Event #2	Event #2	Event #2	Event #2
Event #3	Event #3	Event #3	Event #3
Conclusion	Conclusion	Conclusion	Conclusion

Instructions to Teacher: Use the following icons as copymasters to create your own Story Elements Chart.

Animal Friends

ALL: We are the animal friends.

We live here on the farm.

Welcome to our home.

Won't you come meet us?

COW: I am the cow, and I say MOOOOO!

HORSE: I am the horse, and I say NEIGGGGGHHHH!

PIG: I am the pig, and I say OOOOOIINNNKK!

DUCK: I am the duck, and I say QUAAACCCK!

GOOSE: I am the goose, and I say HOOONNKK!

SHEEP: I am the sheep, and I say BAAAAAAAA!

OWL: I am the barn owl, and I say HOOOOOHOOOOO!

DOG: I am the dog, and I say WOOOOOFFFFFF!

CAT: I am the cat, and I say MEEEOOOWWW!

CHICKEN: I am the chicken, and I say CLUCK CLUCK!

ROOSTER: I am the rooster, and I say COCK-A-DOODLE-DOOOOOO!

CHICKS: We are the chicks, and we say PEEP PEEP PEEP!

ALL: We are the animal friends. That's what we say. What do YOU say to US today?

APPENDIX K.5 Story Elements Graphic Organizer

Draw and/or write story elements below.

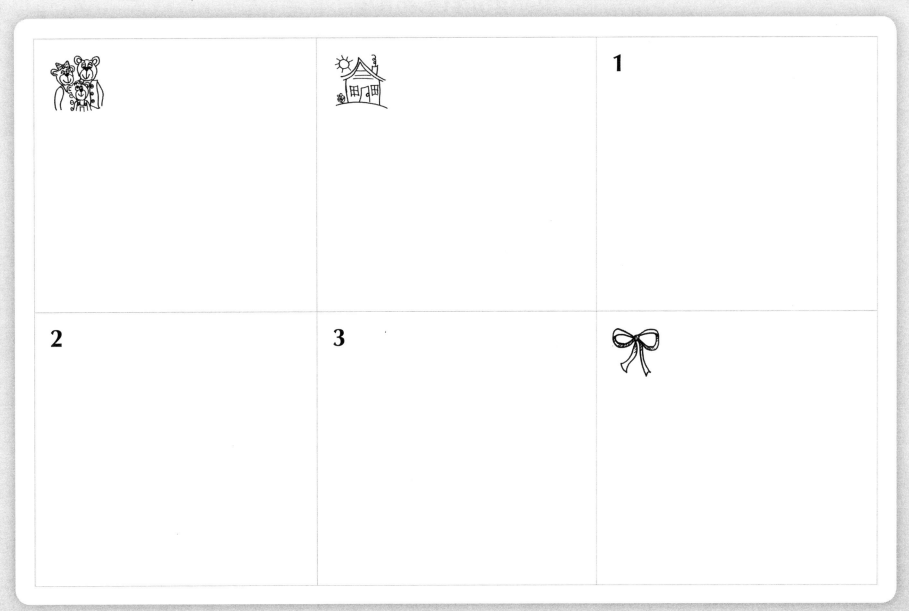

Standards Alignment: RL.K.1, RL.K.3, SL.K.1a, SL.K.1b, SL.K.2, SL.K.6

Reading Lesson 3

Milestone Performance Assessment: Identifying and Using Story Elements

Use this checklist to assess student identification and use of story elements.

Name: _____   Date: _____

Task	Achieved	Notes
Name story elements (character, setting, events, conclusion).		
Refer to illustrations and/or words in book to share thinking about the story elements.		
Speak audibly when sharing ideas.		

Standards Alignment: RL.K.1, RL.K.2, RL.K.3, RL.K.7, SL.K.1a, SL.K.1b, SL.K.2, SL.K.6

Reading Lesson 6

Milestone Performance Assessment: Retelling Stories

Use this checklist to assess the use of story elements to retell stories.

Name: _____   Date: _____

Task	Achieved	Notes
Identify important characters in retelling.		
Identify setting in retelling.		
Retell major events.		
Include conclusion in retelling.		
Speak audibly when retelling.		

Standards Alignment: RL.K.1, RL.8.3, SL.K.1a, SL.K.1b, SL.K.6

Reading Lesson 9
Milestone Performance Assessment: Using Story Elements to Dramatize

Use this checklist to assess student dramatization of their favorite stories.

Name: _____   Date: _____

Task	Achieved	Notes
Speak slowly, clearly, and with expression.		
Include story elements in dramatization of fable.		
Practice good listening by facing the speaker with eyes and ears open and mouth closed when in the audience.		

Standards Alignment: W.K.3, W.K.5, W.K.8, SL.K.1a, SL.K.1b, SL.K.4, SL.K.6, L.K.1, L.K.6

Writing Lesson 4
Milestone Performance Assessment: Sharing I Remember Stories

Use student stories to assess understanding of how to use life experiences and story elements to create stories.

Name: _____   Date: _____

Task	Achieved	Notes
Choose one idea from life experience to share.		
Utilize story elements to share life experience.		
Speak audibly and express thoughts, feelings, and ideas clearly.		

Writing Lesson 6

Standards Alignment: RL.K.1, RL.K.3, W.K.3, W.K.5, SL.K.1a, SL.K.1b, SL.K.2, SL.K.5, SL.K.6

Milestone Performance Assessment: Creating and Retelling Nursery Rhyme

Use the shared writing experience to assess understanding of how to listen and build upon one another's ideas and story elements to create stories.

Name: _____   Date: _____

Task	Achieved	Notes
Participate in group conversation to plan story elements of contemporary nursery rhyme.		
Demonstrate understanding of story element through contribution to the story element drawing.		
Retell contemporary nursery rhyme.		
Speak audibly and express thoughts, feelings, and ideas clearly.		

Writing Lesson 9

Standards Alignment: W.K.3, W.K.5, W.K.6, SL.K.1a, SL.K.1b, SL.K.5, SL.K.6

Milestone Performance Assessment: Publishing Stories

Use student stories to assess understanding of how to use story elements to create real or imagined stories.

Name: _____   Date: _____

Task	Achieved	Notes
Choose one idea, real or imagined, to develop into a story.		
Use story elements to create story.		
Match words and illustrations.		
Include details in drawings and/or words to describe story elements.		
Publish a story with all required components.		
Speak audibly when sharing with partner.		

APPENDIX 1.1 Core Message to Students

What are some of your favorite stories? What do you like about them? Think for a moment of one of them. Could everything in your favorite story really happen? Does it have some things that could be real but also some things that aren't true but make it fun to read and think about? In this lesson set, we're going to read stories full of imagination. We're going to meet talking stuffed bears, a dinosaur who's alive, and mice who want to be artists! Not only are we going to read about these wonderful characters, but we're also going to write our own fantasy stories. What kind of character do you want to create? Where do you want your character to live? For these lessons, you need to have your imagination hats on.

APPENDIX 1.2   The Dinosaur Who Couldn't Come for Tea

The Dinosaur Who Couldn't Come for Tea

One warm and sunny afternoon, Sharptail was walking through the forest looking for food. He found a clump of fresh, sweet smelling ferns, ducked his head, and was just beginning to eat when he heard happy voices.

"I'm having a birthday party tomorrow," said one excited voice.

Sharptail poked his head through the bushes. Rosie the triceratops was talking to Pip the pterodactyl. "It's going to be a tea party. Will you come?" asked Rosie.

"Of course!" said Pip, happily.

"Of course!" said Sharptail. But he spoke too quietly so they didn't hear him through the bushes.

He hurried home to prepare for the party. All that night, Sharptail worked on a present for Rosie: a flowery wreath made out of pinecones and duck lilies. He baked a cake with sweet pink icing.

In the morning, Sharptail put on a yellow polka-dot bowtie and walked to the party with the present and cake strapped to his back. When he arrived at Rosie's house, all of the dinosaurs were already inside. They were singing songs and eating red velvet cupcakes.

"Happy birthday!" said Sharptail when Rosie opened the door.

"Oh, hi," said Rosie with a frown on her face.

Sharptail tried to squeeze past her into the house, but Rosie stopped him.

"Sharptail—you're just too big. You won't fit inside. The spikes on your tail will tear up the walls, and the plates on your back will rip up the roof."

Sharptail was shocked. "But—" he pointed at the present and the cake on his back.

Rosie said, "I'm sorry," and then shut the door with a bang.

Sharptail stayed for a moment, listening to the party inside. Then he walked away. His head hung low. He tore the wreath from his back and threw it to the ground. He began to run; he didn't want anyone to see him crying. Finally he reached his favorite place in the forest, a hollow surrounded by ferns, and fell to the ground.

"Hi," a voice spoke.

Sharptail raised his head. "Who's there?"

"It's me, Pip."

"Go away."

Instead Pip fluttered over. He lifted one clawed foot and put it on Sharptail's back. "I'm sorry about the party."

Sharptail didn't answer.

"Is that cake?" asked Pip.

He nodded. Pip unwrapped the cake and nudged it toward Sharptail.

"I'm not hungry," said Sharptail.

"More for me," said Pip, and he began to eat. After a while, Sharptail said, "Maybe one bite."

They finished the entire cake, sweet pink icing and all.

"Do you want to go on an adventure?" asked Pip.

Sharptail didn't say anything, but his tail swung out, knocking against a tree so pinecones rained down on the hollow. He lumbered to his feet, and Pip climbed onto his back, and they set off through the duck lilies.

Dinosaur Profile: The Stegosaurus

The stegosaurus was a dinosaur that lived in the Late Jurassic Period, about 150 million years ago. It roamed western North America and has been discovered in other parts of the world too. The name stegosaurus means "roofed lizard," since the plates on its back look like tiles for a roof.

A stegosaurus could weigh over 6,000 pounds. It could grow up to 30 feet long and 9 feet tall. Its hind legs were about twice as long as its front legs, which meant it walked with its head low to the ground. It had a long, spiked tail and two rows of bony, triangle-shaped plates on its back. Even though it was huge, the stegosaurus had a very small brain: only 2.8 ounces.

The stegosaurus was an *herbivore*, which means it ate plants. It probably ate bushes and shrubs, mosses, ferns, and fruits. It would have had to defend itself against predators and might have used the spikes on its tail and the plates on its back to protect itself. The stegosaurus probably lived in herds, not alone.

Stegosaurus fossils have been discovered in Colorado, Utah, and Wyoming. They've also been found in Portugal, India, and China. The stegosaurus was named by Othniel Charles Marsh in 1877. Marsh was a scientist who studied dinosaurs and discovered many new species. He fought with another scientist, Edward Drinker Cope, in the Bone Wars, a mad race across America to find fossils. Marsh and Cope hated each other, and they found lots of fossils while trying to beat each other.

Name: _____ Date: _____

Draw and write story elements below.

Character	Setting	Event 1	Event 2	Event 3	Conclusion

Name: _____ **Date:** _____

Use this template to create story cubes.

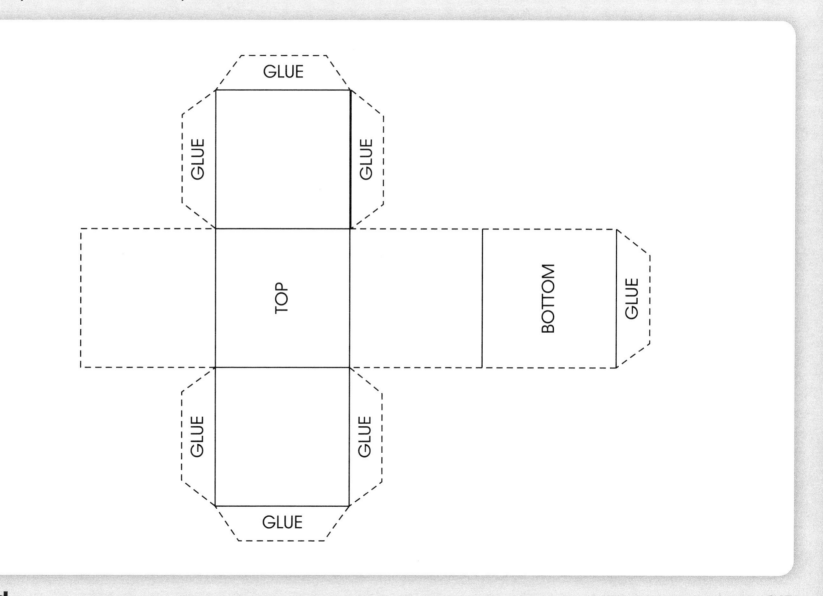

Name: _____ **Date:** _____

Fill in story elements below.

Comparing My Story to _Corduroy_

Title of my story	
Characters	
Setting	
Things that CAN happen	
Things that CAN'T happen	
How my story is the SAME as _Corduroy_	
How my story is DIFFERENT than _Corduroy_	

Sample Story: Maple's Dream

Maple was a tree with a dream. She was tired of sitting in front of her house. She wanted to go to school.

One day she followed the neighborhood kids to school. She was way too big to fit inside the doorway, but that was okay because she could see and hear through a window. During music class, Maple waved her branches. When the kids made crafts in art class, Maple made her own crafts out of leaves and bark. Maple even did a cartwheel during gym class and almost crushed the principal's car!

When the bell rang at the end of the day, Maple let the kids play in her branches. They loved the funny tree in the middle of their school yard. Maple ran home to tell her friend Willow about her day.

Sketch the events of your story below.

Beginning	Middle	End

Name: _____ **Date:** _____

Imaginative Stories Checklist

Revising	Yes/No
Did I compare own story elements with the checklist?	
Did I include strong character(s)?	
Did I include a setting?	
Did I include a sequence of events?	
Did I use temporal words?	
Did I include things that CAN happen?	
Did I include things that CAN'T happen?	
Did I include a good ending?	
Editing	
Did I check and correct my capitalization?	
Did I check and correct my sentences	
Did I check and correct my punctuation?	
Did I check and correct my spelling?	

✂ -

Standards Alignment: RL.1.1, RL.1.2, RL.1.3, W.1.8, SL.1.5

Reading Lesson 3

Milestone Performance Assessment: Identifying the Story Elements

Use this checklist to assess performance on the Story Elements Graphic Organizer.

Name: _____ Date: _____

	Achieved	Notes
Identify character.		
Identify setting.		
Three or more key events in order (including conclusion).		

✂ -

Standards Alignment: RL.1.1, RL.1.2, RL.1.3, RL.1.9, W.1.8

Reading Lesson 8

Milestone Performance Assessment: Comparing and Contrasting Imaginative Stories

Use this checklist to assess students' work on Comparing My Story to *Corduroy* Graphic Organizer .

Name: _____ Date: _____

Task	Achieved	Notes
Accurately identify one or more characters in the story.		
Accurately identify one or more settings in the story.		
Accurately identify one event that could really happen.		
Accurately identify one event that could not happen (if applicable to his or her book).		
Accurately identify one way his or her book is similar to *Corduroy*.		
Accurately identify one way his or her book is different from *Corduroy*.		

Standards Alignment: RL.1.1, W.1.8, SL.1.5, SL.1.6, L.1.1, L.1.6

Reading Lesson 10
Milestone Performance Assessment: Lesson Set Reflection

Use this checklist to assess students' reflections.

Name: _____ Date: _____

Task	Achieved	Notes
Describe a strong memory from the lesson set.		
Describe something he/she learned that will help him/her be a stronger reader.		
Explain a contribution to the mural that makes him/her proud.		

Standards Alignment: W.1.3, SL.1.6, L.1.1, L.1.2, L.1.6

Writing Lesson 1
Milestone Performance Assessment: Asking "What If" Questions to Inspire Writing

Use this checklist to assess student work generating "what if" questions.

Name: _____ Date: _____

Task	Achieved	Notes
Generate three or more "what if" questions.		
Choose one question that inspires him/her to write a story.		

Standards Alignment: W.1.3, W.1.5, SL.1.5, L.1.1, L.1.2, L.1.6

Writing Lesson 7
Milestone Performance Assessment: Revising Writing

Use this checklist to assess student revisions.

Revising	Achieved	Notes
Compare elements of story with checklist.		
Include a main character.		
Include a setting.		
Include a sequence of events.		
Use temporal words to suggest order of events and closure.		
Include things that could happen.		
Include things that couldn't happen.		
Include a good ending.		
Include detailed illustrations that match the words on each page.		
Editing		
Capitalization		
Sentences		
Punctuation		
Spelling		

Standards Alignment: SL.1.1a, SL.1.1b, SL.1.1c, SL.1.3, SL.1.4, SL.1.6

Writing Lesson 9
Milestone Performance Assessment: Sharing Own Stories

Use this checklist to assess student performances of stories.

Task	Achieved	Notes
Speak loudly and clearly.		
Read complete sentences.		
Pause at appropriate moments such as at end punctuation.		
Listen carefully to the stories of others.		

Close your eyes and imagine a magical land. Maybe it's a castle. Maybe it's beside the ocean. Maybe it's on a wintry mountaintop. Now, imagine the characters and other magical creatures who might fill that land. In a fairy tale, all magical things are possible—talking wolves, fire-breathing dragons, and fairy godmothers are just the beginning! What kind of magic do you want to create?

Name: _____ Date: _____

Elements of Fairy Tales

Title:	Author:
Characters:	
Setting:	
Problem:	
Key Event 1:	
Key Event 2:	
Key Event 3:	
Solution:	

APPENDIX 2.3 Tracing Character Change

Name: _____   Date: _____

Tracing Character Change

Title:

Character:

Beginning	Middle	End

HOW did the character change?

_____

_____

WHY did the character change?

_____

_____

Name: _____ **Date:** _____

Use the Venn Diagram to compare and contrast fairy tales.

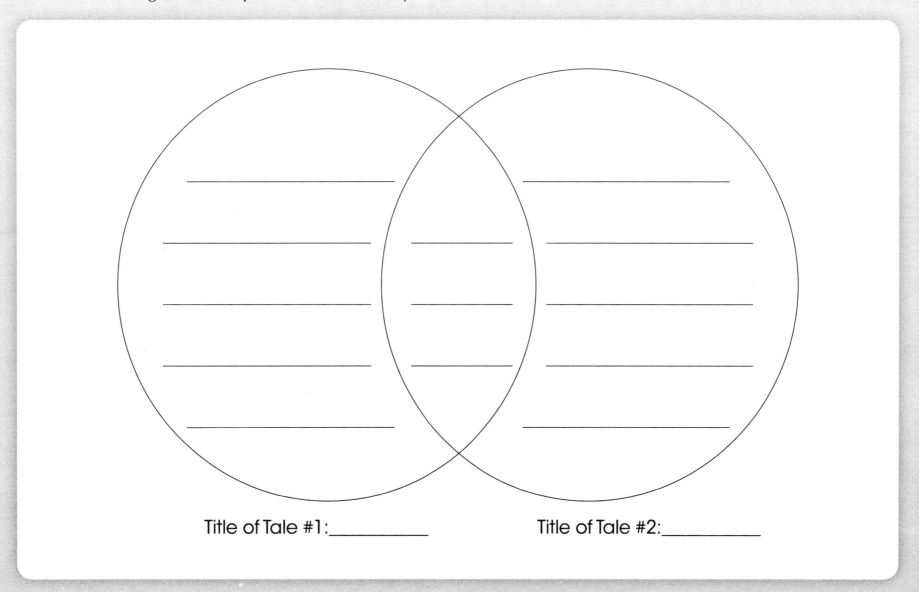

Title of Tale #1:_____   Title of Tale #2:_____

Jack and the Beanstalk

Parts: Jack, Mother, Giant, Giant's Wife, Reader 1, Reader 2

Jack: Mother! Look what I got at the market when I sold our cow! Four magical beans!

Mother: Shame on you, Jack! These are plain old lima beans.

Reader 1: Jack's mother was so angry that she threw the beans out the window. Jack went to bed without any supper. The next morning when he woke up, there was something sticking into his window. It was a giant leaf! Jack ran outside and saw a giant beanstalk growing where the beans had fallen.

Jack: I think I'll just climb it to see where it goes.

Reader 2: Jack climbed the beanstalk all the way to the top and came out into a world of giants. There was a huge castle in front of him, and he saw the giant's wife standing at the door.

Jack: Please, ma'am, could you spare some food for breakfast? I haven't eaten anything since yesterday.

Reader 1: The woman was kind enough to feed him, but as Jack finished his breakfast, a loud knock came on the front door. It shook the whole castle.

Giant's Wife: Oh no! My husband is returning, and he will be very angry. You must hide in the teapot!

Reader 2: The giant's wife quickly popped Jack into the teapot and opened the door.

Giant: Fee fi fo fum! I smell the blood of an Englishman! Eee hi oh ho! I will never let him go!

Giant's Wife: What nonsense! It's just your dinner you smell.

Reader 2: The giant sat down to his dinner of a whole ox and gobbled it all up.

Giant: Wife, bring me the little brown hen!

Reader 1: The giant's wife brought their little brown hen inside and put it on the table.

Giant: Lay! Lay! Lay!

Reader 1: The hen laid three huge golden eggs.

Giant's Wife: That will do for today.

Reader 2: While the giant stretched out in his chair to go to sleep and his wife busied herself with the housekeeping, Jack crept quietly out of the teapot. He grabbed the little brown hen and ran for the door. The hen began to crow just as he escaped, and he climbed as fast as he could down the beanstalk to his mother.

Jack: Mother! I need an axe, quick!

Reader 1: Jack chopped down the beanstalk so the giant would never find them, and he and his mother lived happily ever after with the money from the hen's golden eggs.

The Princess and the Pea

Parts: King, Queen, Prince, Princess, Reader 1, Reader 2

Reader 1: As the storm thundered outside, a knock came on the castle door. A young woman was standing outside in the pouring rain, wet from head to toe.

Princess: Hello, Your Highnesses. I am a princess from a distant land, and I am terribly lost in this storm. Might I stay the night in your warm castle?

King: Of course you may, young lady. Enter.

Reader 2: Although the king trusted her, his wife was suspicious. She wanted to find a wife for her son, the prince. The prince could only marry a real princess, and the queen needed to find out for sure.

Queen: My dear king, I do not believe that this girl dressed in wet rags could be a princess. I am going to find out for myself.

King: How on earth will you do that?

Queen: I will stack twenty mattresses on top of each other, and under the bottom one I will put a little pea. If she can feel the pea through twenty mattresses, she is a real princess.

Reader 1: The queen made the girl a bed exactly as she said, and everyone went to sleep. The next day the storm was gone and it was sunny and warm outside.

Prince: Who is the girl who came here last night?

King: She is a princess who may become your wife.

Queen: We will see about that.

Reader 2: Finally, the princess arrived to eat breakfast.

Queen: Dear girl, did you sleep well?

Princess: Not at all! There was something hard and uncomfortable in my bed. I am black and blue all over from tossing and turning all night!

Queen: How wonderful!

King: You can marry our son!

Prince: Would you like to go for a walk in the beautiful weather?

Reader 1: The prince and princess fell in love and lived happily ever after.

The Little Red Hen

Parts: Hen, Pig, Duck, Cat, Reader 1, Reader 2

Reader 1: The little red hen cut the corn that she had planted all by herself. She took out all the grains of corn from their husks, and soon she had many sacks full.

Hen: Who will help me take this corn to the mill so it can be ground into flour?

Pig: Not I.

Duck: Not I.

Cat: Not I.

Hen: Very well. I will take the corn to the mill all by myself.

Reader 2: So the little red hen took the corn to the mill and asked the miller to grind it into flour. Soon the miller sent the sack of flour to the farm.

Hen: Who will help me make this flour into bread?

Pig: Not I.

Duck: Not I.

Cat: Not I.

Hen: Very well. I will make the flour into bread all by myself.

Reader 1: So the little red hen went into her kitchen to mix the flour into dough. She put it in the oven to bake, and soon there was a lovely smell of fresh, hot bread. The pig, the duck, and the cat all wandered into the house, curious about the delicious smell.

Hen: Who will help me eat the bread?

Pig: I will!

Duck: I will!

Cat: I will!

Hen: Oh no, you won't. I planted the seed, cut the corn, took it to the mill, and made the flour into bread all by myself. Now I will eat the bread all by myself.

Happily Ever After?

Title

How it ends now…

Another ending could be…

1.

2.

3.

Name: _____   Date: _____

Planning a Fairy Tale

Title:		
Setting:	Good Characters:	Evil Characters:

Introduction	Problem	Key Event 1	Key Event 2	Solution

Adaptation of "The Princess and the Pea"

One stormy night, a young woman knocked on the door of a castle. She had gotten lost in the dark, and her horse was tired and hungry. A servant opened the door, but only a crack.

"May I come inside until the storm passes?" asked the young woman.

"No," said the servant, and began to close the door.

"Please," said the young woman. "I am a princess."

The door swung open. Without a word, the servant led the princess through a great stone hall where candlelight flickered on the walls, into a room where the queen and her son sat eating dinner.

The room had thick lion-skin rugs, and a fireplace roared in the corner. The servant whispered into the queen's ear, and her eyes lit up.

"Join us," she said. The princess was suddenly nervous. "Maybe I should leave," she thought, but icy rain drummed on the windows. She began to eat instead and soon relaxed.

She learned that the prince was looking for a woman to marry.

"But he can't find a true princess," said the queen.

After dinner, the princess was shown into a guest chamber. The bed was piled with mattresses and featherbeds nearly to the ceiling. She climbed up the pile and sat on top of it, feeling ridiculous.

She remembered a rumor that one way to test a royal was to hide a pea in the bed. If she could feel it, she was a true princess. "But how silly," she thought. "That wouldn't tell you anything about someone."

She searched under every mattress and finally, near the bottom, found a small green pea.

The next morning at breakfast, the queen asked, "Did you sleep well?"

"Very," said the princess.

The queen smiled. The test had worked again.

"Oh, but I found this," said the princess. She placed the pea on the table.

The queen clapped her hands. The prince dropped to one knee. "Will you marry me?" he asked.

"No, thank you," said the princess. "It was a test. I don't believe either of you passed."

The queen and the prince sat with their jaws open. The princess bridled her horse and rode off into the dewy, shining countryside.

Name: _____ Date: _____

Fairy Tale Checklist

Revising	Yes/No
Does my fairy tale have magical character(s)?	
Did I describe character actions?	
Did I include character feelings?	
Did I include character thoughts and/or dialogue?	
Does my fairy tale have a clear problem and solution?	
Does my fairy tale have a strong ending?	
Editing	
Did I check and correct my capitalization?	
Did I check and correct my sentences?	
Did I check and correct my punctuation?	
Did I check and correct my spelling?	

Standards Alignment: RL.2.1, RL.2.2, RL.2.5, W.2.8

Reading Lesson 3
Milestone Performance Assessment:
Identifying the Key Elements of a Fairy Tale

Use this checklist to assess student work on the Elements of Fairy Tales Graphic Organizer.

Task	Achieved	Notes
Identify character(s).		
Identify setting.		
Identify problem.		
Identify 3 key events.		
Identify solution.		

Standards Alignment: RL.2.1, RL.2.3, W.2.8

Reading Lesson 6
Milestone Performance Assessment: Identifying Change in Character

Use this checklist to assess students work on the Tracing Character Change Graphic Organizer.

Task	Achieved	Notes
Identify character who changes.		
Identify how a main character changes.		
Infer why a main character changes.		

Standards Alignment: RL.2.1, RL.2.2, RL.2.9, W.2.8

Reading Lesson 8

Milestone Performance Assessment: Comparing and Contrasting Fairy Tales

Use this checklist to assess students work on the Comparing and Contrasting Fairy Tales Graphic Organizer.

Task	Achieved	Notes
Identify two versions of the same tale.		
Correctly identify each element of the fairy tale.		
Accurately articulate elements that are similar and different about the two tales.		

Standards Alignment: RL.2.2, RL.2.3, RL.2.5, RL.2.9, W.2.8

Reading Lesson 10

Milestone Performance Assessment: Expressing Yourself Clearly

Use this checklist to assess student work on answering the Core Questions.

Task	Achieved	Notes
Accurately articulate the features or elements of a fairy tale.		
Include as examples complete and accurate details from a story.		

Standards Alignment: RL.2.1, RL.2.2, RL.2.3, W.2.3, W.2.5, W.2.8

Writing Lesson 4
Milestone Performance Assessment: Sequence and Key Elements

Use this checklist to assess student work on the Planning a Fairy Tale Graphic Organizer.

Task	Achieved	Notes
Plan a sequential tale.		
Identify key elements of a classic tale.		
Change one key element of a classic tale.		

Standards Alignment: W.2.3

Writing Lesson 7
Milestone Performance Assessment: Additional Character Information

Use this checklist to assess students' ability to accurately include additional information about characters.

Task	Achieved	Notes
Accurately add descriptive character action.		
Include character dialogue.		
Include character internal thinking.		
Accurately add reference to character emotion.		

Standards Alignment: W.2.3, W.2.5, L.2.1, L.2.2, L.2.3, L.2.6

Writing Lesson 9
Milestone Performance Assessment: Revising Stories

Use this checklist to assess students' ability to work collaboratively with a partner to edit a story.

Name: _____   Date: _____

Task	Achieved	Notes
Revising		
Compare own story elements with checklist.		
Make necessary changes to own fairy tale.		
Work with other students to improve fairy tale.		
Fairy tale has magical character(s).		
Describe character actions.		
Include character feelings.		
Include character thoughts and/or dialogue.		
Fairy tale has a clear problem and solution.		
Fairy tale has a strong ending.		
Editing		
Capitalization.		
Sentences.		
Punctuation.		
Spelling.		

References

Allington, D. (2012). Private experience, textual analysis, and institutional authority: The discursive practice of critical interpretation and its enactment in literary training. *Language and Literature, 21*(2).

Carrier, K. A., & Tatum, A. W. (2006). Creating sentence walls to help English-language learners develop content literacy. *The Reading Teacher, 60*(3), 285–288.

Ehri, L. C., Dreyer, L. G., Flugman, B., & Gross, A. (2007). Reading rescue: An effective tutoring intervention model for language-minority students who are struggling readers in first grade. *American Educational Research Journal, 44*, 414–448.

Goldenberg, C. (2008). Teaching English language learners: What the research does—and does not—say. *American Educator, 32*(2), 8–23, 42–44.

Lewis, M. (1993). *The lexical approach: The state of ELT and the way forward.* Hove, England: Language Teaching Publications.

Nattinger, J. R. (1980). A lexical phrase grammar for ESL. *TESOL Quarterly, 14*(3), 337–334.

PARCC Model. (2012). *PARCC model content frameworks: English language arts/literacy grades 3–11.*

Notes

Notes

Notes

Notes

Notes

Notes

Notes

Notes